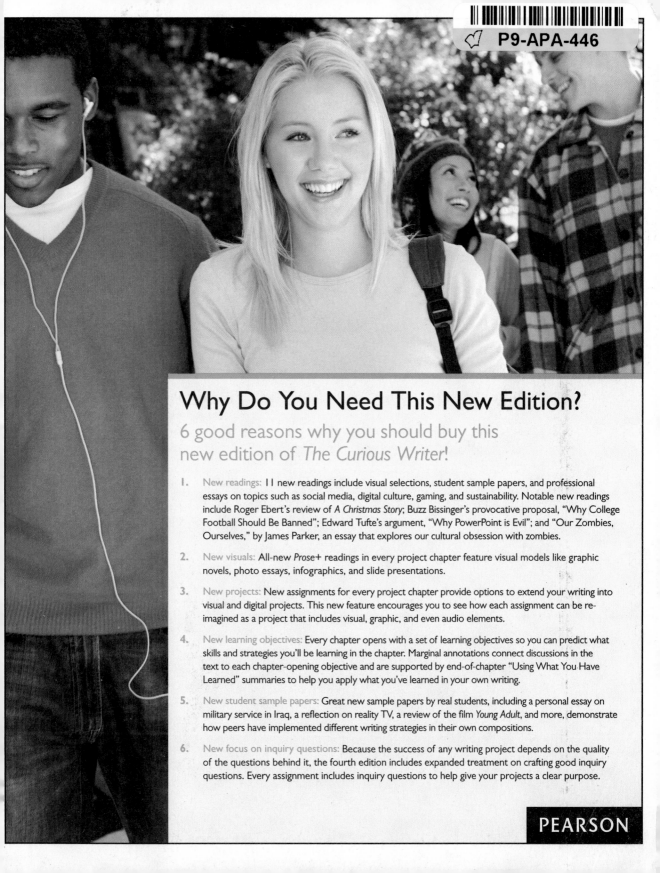

Why Do You Need This New Edition?

6 good reasons why you should buy this
new edition of *The Curious Writer*!

1. New readings: 11 new readings include visual selections, student sample papers, and professional
    essays on topics such as social media, digital culture, gaming, and sustainability. Notable new readings
    include Roger Ebert's review of *A Christmas Story*; Buzz Bissinger's provocative proposal, "Why College
    Football Should Be Banned"; Edward Tufte's argument, "Why PowerPoint is Evil"; and "Our Zombies,
    Ourselves," by James Parker, an essay that explores our cultural obsession with zombies.

2. New visuals: All-new *Prose+* readings in every project chapter feature visual models like graphic
    novels, photo essays, infographics, and slide presentations.

3. New projects: New assignments for every project chapter provide options to extend your writing into
    visual and digital projects. This new feature encourages you to see how each assignment can be re-
    imagined as a project that includes visual, graphic, and even audio elements.

4. New learning objectives: Every chapter opens with a set of learning objectives so you can predict what
    skills and strategies you'll be learning in the chapter. Marginal annotations connect discussions in the
    text to each chapter-opening objective and are supported by end-of-chapter "Using What You Have
    Learned" summaries to help you apply what you've learned in your own writing.

5. New student sample papers: Great new sample papers by real students, including a personal essay on
    military service in Iraq, a reflection on reality TV, a review of the film *Young Adult*, and more, demonstrate
    how peers have implemented different writing strategies in their own compositions.

6. New focus on inquiry questions: Because the success of any writing project depends on the quality
    of the questions behind it, the fourth edition includes expanded treatment on crafting good inquiry
    questions. Every assignment includes inquiry questions to help give your projects a clear purpose.

PEARSON

THE CURIOUS WRITER

THE CURIOUS WRITER

Concise Fourth Edition

Bruce Ballenger

Boise State University

Boston   Columbus   Indianapolis   New York   San Francisco   Upper Saddle River
Amsterdam   Cape Town   Dubai   London   Madrid   Milan   Munich   Paris   Montréal   Toronto
Delhi   Mexico City   São Paulo   Sydney   Hong Kong   Seoul   Singapore   Taipei   Tokyo

Senior Acquisitions Editor: Lauren A. Finn
Senior Development Editor: Michael Greer
Editorial Assistant: Shannon Kobran
Senior Supplements Editor: Donna Campion
Senior Media Producer: Stefanie Snajder
Senior Marketing Manager: Sandra McGuire
Production Manager: Eric Jorgensen
Project Coordination, Text Design, and Composition: Integra
Electronic Page Makeup: Integra
Cover Design: John Callahan
Cover Image: Exactostock/SuperStock
Photo Research: Integra
Image Manager: Jorgensen Fernandez
Senior Manufacturing Buyer: Dennis J. Para
Printer and Binder: RRD-Crawfordsville
Cover Printer: Lehigh/Phoenix Color/Hagerstown

This title is restricted to sales and distribution in North America only.

For permission to use copyrighted material, grateful acknowledgment is made to the copyright
holders on pp. CR-1 to CR-2, which are hereby made part of this copyright page.

Library of Congress Cataloging-in-Publication Data
Ballenger, Bruce P.
   The curious writer/Bruce Ballenger.—4th ed.
      p. cm.
   Includes bibliographical references and index.
   ISBN 978-0-205-23577-3—ISBN 978-0-205-87665-5 (Brief ed.)—ISBN 978-0-205-87664-8
(Concise ed.)
   1. English language—Rhetoric—Handbooks, manuals, etc.   2. Interdisciplinary approach in
education—Handbooks, manuals, etc.   3. Academic writing—Handbooks, manuals, etc.   I. Title.
   PE1408.B37 2012
   808'.042—dc23

                                                                        2012028008

Full (Hardcover) Edition
13-Digit ISBN: 978-0-205-23577-3
10-Digit ISBN: 0-205-23577-8

Brief (Softcover) Edition
13-Digit ISBN: 978-0-205-87665-5
10-Digit ISBN: 0-205-87665-X

2 3 4 5 6 7 8 9 10—DOC—15 14 13

Concise (Softcover) Edition
13-Digit ISBN: 978-0-205-87664-8
10-Digit ISBN: 0-205-87664-1

Contents

Preface   xvii

Acknowledgments   xxiv

Chapter 1 Writing as Inquiry 3

Motives for Writing   4

Beliefs About Writing and Writing Development   5

EXERCISE 1.1 This I Believe (and This I Don't)   5

ONE STUDENT'S RESPONSE Bernice's Journal   6

INQUIRING INTO THE DETAILS Journals   7

Unlearning Unhelpful Beliefs   7

The Beliefs of This Book   8

Allatonceness   8

Believing You Can Learn to Write Well   8

Habits of Mind   8

Starting with Questions, Not Answers   9

Making the Familiar Strange   9

Suspending Judgment   10

Being Willing to Write Badly   10

Searching for Surprise   11

EXERCISE 1.2 A Roomful of Details   11

ONE STUDENT'S RESPONSE Bernice's Journal   12

Writing Situations and Rhetorical Choices   13

A First Reflection on Your Writing Process   16

A Case Study   16

INQUIRING INTO THE DETAILS Organizing Your Computer Files   17

Thinking About Your Process   17

INQUIRING INTO THE DETAILS Portfolios   18

EXERCISE 1.3 Literacy Narrative Collage   18

EXERCISE 1.4 What Is Your Process?   19

Problem Solving in Your Writing Process   22

The Nature of the Writing Process   23

The Writing Process as Recursive and Flexible   24

A System for Using Writing to Think   24

INQUIRING INTO THE DETAILS Invention Strategies   25

EXERCISE 1.5 Two Kinds of Thinking   26

A Writing Process That Harnesses Two Currents of Thought   27

The Sea and the Mountain   28

Answering the So What? Question   29

A Writing Process Driven by Questions   30

Questioning, Generating, and Judging: A Strategy for Inquiry   32

EXERCISE 1.6 A Mini Inquiry Project: Cell Phone Culture   33

EXERCISE 1.7 **Scenes of Writing**   35

Using What You Have Learned   37

Chapter 2 Reading as Inquiry   39

Purposes for Academic Reading   40

EXERCISE 2.1 **Using the Four Purposes for Academic Reading**   41

Beliefs About Reading   43

EXERCISE 2.2 **A Reader's Memoir**   44

One Common Belief That Is an Obstacle   44

Reading Situations and Rhetorical Choices   45

Four Frames for Reading   46

Reading Scenarios   46

Scenario #1   46

Scenario #2   47

INQUIRING INTO THE DETAILS **Reading Perspectives**   48

EXERCISE 2.3 **Reading a Life**   48

A Process for Reading to Write   50

Questions for the Process of Reading to Write   50

What Do I Want to Know?   50

What Should I Read to Find Out?   51

What Do I Do with What I've Read?   51

Having a Dialogue with What You Read   52

INQUIRING INTO THE DETAILS **Reading the Visual**   54

EXERCISE 2.4 **Double-Entry Journaling with a Visual Text**   55

Techniques for Keeping a Double-Entry Journal   57

EXERCISE 2.5 **Reading Creatively, Reading Critically**   57

READING **Bruce Ballenger, "The Importance of Writing Badly"**   58

ONE STUDENT'S RESPONSE **Briana's Journal**   61

Wrestling with Academic Discourse: Reading from the Outside In   62

EXERCISE 2.6 **Reading Reality TV**   63

Features of Academic Discourse   65

Using What You Have Learned   67

Chapter 3 Writing a Personal Essay   69

Writing About Experience and Observations   69

Motives for Writing a Personal Essay   70

The Personal Essay and Academic Writing   71

Features of the Form   73

READINGS   75

PERSONAL ESSAY 1 **Laura Zazulak, "Every Morning for Five Years"**   75

Inquiring into the Essay   76

PERSONAL ESSAY 2 **Judith Ortiz Cofer, "One More Lesson"**   77

Inquiring into the Essay   81

THE WRITING PROCESS   82

Inquiry Project: **Writing a Personal Essay**   82

WRITING BEYOND THE CLASSROOM **Essaying "This I Believe"**   83

What Are You Going to Write About?   84

Opening Up   85
  Listing Prompts   85
  Fastwriting Prompts   86
  Visual Prompts   86
  Research Prompts   88
Narrowing Down   88
  What's Promising Material and What Isn't?   88
  Questions About Purpose and Audience   88
Trying Out   89
  Questions for Reflection   90
Writing the Sketch   91
STUDENT SKETCH Amanda Stewart, "Earning a Sense of Place"   91

Moving from Sketch to Draft   92
  Evaluating Your Own Sketch   93
  Reflecting on What You Learned   93
Developing   94
Drafting   95
  Methods of Development   95
  Using Evidence   96
Workshopping   96
  Questions for Readers   96
  Reflecting on the Workshop   97
Revising   97
  Shaping   97
  Polishing   98
STUDENT ESSAY Seth Marlin, "Smoke of Empire"   98

Evaluating the Essay   100
Using What You Have Learned   101

Chapter 4 Writing a Review   103

Writing That Evaluates   103
Motives for Writing a Review   104
The Review and Academic Writing   106
SEEING THE FORM Choosing the Best Picture   106
Features of the Form   108

READINGS   110
REVIEW 1 Roger Ebert, "A Christmas Story"   110
Inquiring into the Essay   113
REVIEW 2 Seth Schiesel, "Grand Theft Auto Takes on New York"   113
Inquiring into the Essay   117

THE WRITING PROCESS   118
Inquiry Project: **Writing a Review Essay**   118
What Are You Going to Write About?   119
Opening Up   119
  Listing Prompts   119
  Fastwriting Prompts   119
  Visual Prompts   119
  Research Prompts   120
Narrowing Down   120
  What's Promising Material and What Isn't?   120
  Questions About Audience and Purpose   121
Trying Out   121
  Focusing the Category   121
  Fastwriting   122

Web Research   122

Interviews   123

Experiencing Your Subject   123

Thinking About Criteria   123

Refining Criteria for Better Evidence   123

Considering Criteria and Rhetorical Context   124

Writing the Sketch   125

STUDENT SKETCH **Laura Burns, "Recipe for a Great Film: Unlikeable People, Poor Choices, and Little Redemption"   125**

Moving from Sketch to Draft   126

Evaluating Your Sketch   127

Reflecting on What You've Learned   127

Developing   127

Talking It Through   127

Re-Experience   128

Interview   128

Read   128

Drafting   129

Finding an Opening   129

Methods of Development   129

Using Evidence   130

Workshopping   130

Reflecting on the Draft   131

Revising   131

Shaping   131

Polishing   132

STUDENT ESSAY **Laura Burns, "How to Not Feel Good and Feel Good About It"   133**

Evaluating the Essay   135

Using What You Have Learned   135

Chapter 5 Writing a Proposal   137

Writing About Problems and Solutions   137

Problems of Consequence   138

Problems of Manageable Scale   139

Motives for Writing a Proposal   140

The Proposal and Academic Writing   140

INQUIRING INTO THE DETAILS **Writing a Research Proposal   141**

Features of the Form   142

READINGS   144

PROPOSAL 1 **Buzz Bissinger, "Why College Football Should Be Banned"   144**

Inquiring into the Essay   146

PROPOSAL 2 **"Green Dining"   147**

Inquiring into the Essay   149

SEEING THE FORM **A Problem in Pictures   150**

THE WRITING PROCESS   152

Inquiry Project: **Writing a Proposal   152**

What Are You Going to Write About?   153

Opening Up   153

Listing Prompts   153

Fastwriting Prompts   153

Visual Prompts   154

Research Prompts   154

Narrowing Down   155

What's Promising Material and What Isn't?   155

Questions About Audience and Purpose   155

Trying Out   156

Researching to Answer the *So What?* Question   156

Giving Your Answer on a PowerPoint   156

Writing the Sketch   157

STUDENT SKETCH   Jenna Appleman, "Loving and Hating Reality TV"   158

Moving from Sketch to Draft   159

Evaluating Your Own Sketch   159

Reflecting on What You Learned   160

Developing   160

Research   160

Focusing on the Justifications   161

INQUIRING INTO THE DETAILS Design Tips for Basic Web Pages   162

Drafting   162

Methods of Development   162

Using Evidence   163

Workshopping   163

Reflecting on the Draft   164

Revising   164

Shaping   164

Polishing   165

STUDENT ESSAY   Jenna Appleman, "Avoidable Accidents: How to Make Reality TV Safer"   165

Evaluating the Essay   168

Using What You Have Learned   169

Chapter 6 Writing an Argument   171

Writing to Persuade People   171

What Is Argument?   172

Two Sides to Every Argument?   173

The Machinery of Argument: Claims, Reasons, and Evidence   174

Claims: What You Want People to Believe   174

Reasons: The "Because…" Behind the Claim   175

Evidence: Proof of the Point   175

SEEING THE FORM   The "Imagetext" as Argument   176

Credibility, Emotion, and Logic   177

Analyzing Argument   178

EXERCISE 6.1   Argument as Therapy   178

ONE STUDENT'S RESPONSE   Rebecca's Journal   179

INQUIRING INTO THE DETAILS   Common Logical Fallacies   180

Motives for Writing an Argument   182

WRITING BEYOND THE CLASSROOM   Public Argument in a Digital Age   183

The Argument and Academic Writing   183

Features of the Form   184

READINGS   186

ARGUMENT 1   Edward Tufte, "PowerPoint Is Evil"   186

Inquiring into the Essay   190

ARGUMENT 2   Loye Young, "Is Humiliation an Ethically Appropriate Response to Plagiarism?"   191

Inquiring into the Essay   193

THE WRITING PROCESS   194

Inquiry Project: **Writing an Argument**   194

What Are You Going to Write About?   195

Opening Up   195

Listing Prompts   195

ONE STUDENT'S RESPONSE **Rebecca's Journal**   196

Fastwriting Prompts   196

Visual Prompts   197

Research Prompts   197

Narrowing Down   198

What's Promising Material and What Isn't?   198

Questions About Audience and Purpose   199

Trying Out   199

Kitchen Knives of Thought   200

Research Considerations   200

Interviews   201

Writing the Sketch   201

STUDENT SKETCH **Rebecca Thompson, "Twitter a Profound Thought?"**   202

Moving from Sketch to Draft   203

Evaluating Your Own Sketch   203

Reflecting on What You've Learned   204

Developing   204

Writing for Your Readers   204

Researching the Argument   204

Drafting   206

Designing Your Argument Rhetorically   206

Methods of Development   207

INQUIRING INTO THE DETAILS **What Evidence Can Do**   208

Using Evidence   208

Workshopping   208

Reflecting on the Draft   209

Revising   209

Shaping   209

INQUIRING INTO THE DETAILS **Toulmin: A Method for Analyzing an Argument**   210

Polishing   211

STUDENT ESSAY **Rebecca Thompson, "Social Networking Social Good?"**   212

Evaluating the Essay   216

Using What You Have Learned   216

Chapter 7 Writing a Critical Essay   219

Writing About Literature   219

Motives for Writing a Critical Essay   220

The Critical Essay and Academic Writing   221

Features of the Form   222

READINGS   225

SHORT STORY **Leslie Marmon Silko, "Lullaby"**   225

Inquiring into the Story   232

ONE STUDENT'S RESPONSE **Noel's Journal**   232

INQUIRING INTO THE DETAILS **Why Literary Theory Is Not a Sleep Aid**   233

FILM CRITICISM **James Parker, "Our Zombies, Ourselves"**   234

Inquiring into the Essay   238

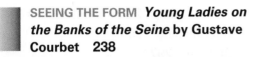

SEEING THE FORM *Young Ladies on the Banks of the Seine* by Gustave Courbet **238**

THE WRITING PROCESS 241

Inquiry Project: **Writing a Critical Essay** 241

What Are You Going to Write About? 242

Opening Up 242

   Listing Prompts 242

   Fastwriting Prompts 242

   Visual Prompts 243

   Research Prompts 243

INQUIRING INTO THE DETAILS

Common Literary Devices 244

Narrowing Down 245

   What's Promising Material and What Isn't? 245

   Questions About Audience and Purpose 246

Writing the Sketch 246

STUDENT SKETCH Julie Bird, "What Is the Role of Nature in 'Lullaby'?" 247

Moving from Sketch to Draft 248

   Evaluating Your Own Sketch 248

   Reflecting on What You've Learned 248

Developing 249

   Analysis 249

   Research 249

Drafting 250

   Methods of Development 250

   Using Evidence 251

Workshopping 251

   Reflecting on the Draft 252

Revising 252

   Shaping 252

Polishing 253

STUDENT ESSAY Julie Bird, "Nature as Being: Landscape in Silko's 'Lullaby'" 254

Evaluating the Essay 256

Using What You Have Learned 257

Chapter 8 Research Techniques 259

Methods of Collecting 259

Research in the Electronic Age 260

   Research Routines 260

   Power Searching Using Google 261

      Google Scholar 262

   Power Searching in the Library 263

      Combing Terms Using Boolean Searching 263

      Using Controlled Language Searches 264

Developing Working Knowledge 265

   A Strategy for Developing Working Knowledge 266

      Refine the Research Question 266

Developing Focused Knowledge 267

   A Strategy for Developing Focused Knowledge 268

      Library Research 268

      Web Research 270

Evaluating Library Sources 271

INQUIRING INTO THE DETAILS **The Working Bibliography** 272

Advanced Internet Research Techniques 273

   Go Beyond Google 273

Evaluating Web Sources   273
An Evaluation Process for Web Sources   275
Research with Living Sources: Interviews, Surveys, and Fieldwork   276
Interviews   276
Arranging Interviews   277
Conducting the Interview   278
Using the Interview in Your Writing   279
Surveys   280
Defining a Survey's Goals and Audience   280
Types of Survey Questions   281
Crafting Survey Questions   281
INQUIRING INTO THE DETAILS **Types of Survey Questions   282**
Conducting a Survey   283
Using Survey Results in Your Writing   284
Fieldwork: Research on What You See and Hear   284
The Ethics of Fieldwork   285
Note-Taking Strategies   285
Using Field Research in Your Writing   286
Writing in the Middle: Note-Taking Techniques   286
Double-Entry Journal   287
Research Log   288
ONE STUDENT'S RESPONSE **Claude's Research Log   289**
Using What You Have Learned   290

Chapter 9 Using and Citing Sources   293

Controlling Information   293
Using Sources   293

Summarizing   295
Paraphrasing   296
Quoting   297
Citing Sources   299
Avoiding Plagiarism   300
EXERCISE 9.1 **The Accidental Plagiarist   301**
MLA Documentation Guidelines   303
INQUIRING INTO THE DETAILS **The Common Knowledge Exception   303**
Citing Sources   304
Where to Put Citations   304
INQUIRING INTO THE DETAILS **Citations That Go with the Flow   305**
When You Mention the Author's Name   306
When There Is No Author   306
Works by the Same Author   307
When One Source Quotes Another   308
Personal Interviews   308
Several Sources in a Single Citation   308
Sample Parenthetical References for Other Sources   309
Format   311
The Layout   311
Preparing the Works Cited Page   314
Format   315
Citing Books   316
Sample Book Citations   317
Citing Periodicals   320
Sample Periodical Citations   322
Citing Online and Other Sources   325
A Sample Paper in MLA Style: Gordon Seirup, "College Dating"   328
Evaluating the Essay   339

APA Documentation
Guidelines 339
How the Essay Should Look 340
Page Format 340
Title Page 340
Abstract 340
Body of the Paper 341
References Page 342
Appendix 342
Notes 342
Tables and Figures 343
Language and Style 344
Citing Sources in Your Essay 344
When the Author Is Mentioned in
the Text 344
When the Author Isn't Mentioned in
the Text 344
When to Cite Page Numbers 344
A Single Work by Two or More
Authors 345
A Work with No Author 345
Two or More Works by the Same
Author 345
An Institutional Author 345
Multiple Works in the Same
Parentheses 346
Interviews, E-Mail,
and Letters 346
New Editions of Old Works 346
A Website 346
Preparing the References
List 347
Order of Sources 347
Order of Information 347
Sample References: Articles 349
Sample References: Books 351
Sample References: Other 354

A Sample Paper in APA Style:
Kersti Harter, "Beyond 'Gaydar':
How Gay Males Identify Other
Gay Males" 357
Evaluating the Essay 368
Using What You Have Learned 368

Chapter 10 Revision
Strategies 371
Why Revise? 371
Divorcing the Draft 373
Strategies for Divorcing the
Draft 374
Five Categories of Revision 375
Problems with Purpose 376
Revision Strategy 10.1: The Motive
Statement 377
Revision Strategy 10.2: What Do
You Want to Know About What You
Learned? 378
ONE STUDENT'S RESPONSE Julia's
Draft 379
Revision Strategy 10.3: Finding the
Focusing Question 379
Revision Strategy 10.4: What's the
Relationship? 381
Problems with Meaning 381
Where Does Meaning Come From? 381
Methods for Discovering Your
Thesis 383
Revision Strategy 10.5: Find the
"Instructive Line" 383
Revision Strategy 10.6: Looping Toward
a Thesis 384
Revision Strategy 10.7: Reclaiming Your
Topic 385
Revision Strategy 10.8: Believing and
Doubting 386

Methods for Refining Your Thesis **387**

Revision Strategy 10.9: Questions as Knives **387**

Revision Strategy 10.10: Qualifying Your Claim **388**

Problems with Information **389**

Revision Strategy 10.11: Explode a Moment **389**

Revision Strategy 10.12: Beyond Examples **390**

Revision Strategy 10.13: Research **391**

Revision Strategy 10.14: Backing Up Your Assumptions **392**

Problems with Structure **393**

Formal Academic Structures **394**

Revision Strategy 10.15: Beginnings, Middles, Ends, and the Work They Do **395**

Revision Strategy 10.16: Reorganizing Around Thesis and Support **395**

Revision Strategy 10.17: Multiple Leads **397**

Revision Strategy 10.18: The Frankenstein Draft **398**

Problems with Clarity and Style **400**

Solving Problems of Clarity **401**

Revision Strategy 10.19: The Three Most Important Sentences **401**

The First Sentence **401**

The Last Line of the First Paragraph **401**

The Last Line of the Essay **401**

Revision Strategy 10.20: Untangling Paragraphs **402**

Revision Strategy 10.21: Cutting Clutter **404**

INQUIRING INTO THE DETAILS **Transition Flags 404**

Revision Strategy 10.22: The Actor and the Action Next Door **406**

Improving Style **406**

Revision Strategy 10.23: Actors and Actions **407**

Revision Strategy 10.24: Smoothing the Choppiness **407**

Revision Strategy 10.25: Fresh Ways to Say Things **408**

Using What You Have Learned **409**

Credits **CR-1**

Index **I-1**

Preface

I have a friend, a painter, who teaches art at my university, and his introductory courses teach the sub-skills of painting, things like how to use a brush, mix paints, and understand color theory. Common sense suggests that such fundamentals are the starting place for any creative activity, including writing. But college writers walk into our classes with a lifetime of language use. They already know a lot about making meaning with words, more than they think they know. Yet there is much to teach, and perhaps the most powerful thing is that writing isn't just for getting down what you know but discovering what you think. I've learned to never underestimate the power of this, and that's why discovery is the beating heart of this book.

What's New in This Edition?

This fourth edition represents a substantial revision. Building on suggestions from teachers using the third edition, I have made revisions throughout with the overall aim of improving the book's teachability and appeal for students, including:

- **NEW multimodal assignment options** for every project chapter provide options to encourage students to see how each assignment can be re-imagined as a project that includes visual, graphic, and even audio elements. The fourth edition provides new support for these multimodal projects by including technical tips on designing web pages, using audio software, and publishing online.

- **NEW *Prose+* readings** in every project chapter feature visual models such as infographics, slide presentations, photo essays, graphic novels, and other visual genres.

- **NEW expanded treatment of how to craft an inquiry question:** Recognizing that the success of any inquiry project depends on the quality of the questions behind it, the fourth edition explains how questions of "fact" can evolve into questions that require judgment. Every assignment is framed by the inquiry questions relevant to the genre, which gives each project a clear purpose.

- **NEW readings selections:** 11 new readings appear in the fourth edition, including visual and multimodal selections, student sample papers, and professional essays on topics including social media, digital culture, gaming, and sustainability. Notable new readings include "A Matter of Perspective," by Josh Neufeld, a personal essay in visual form; Roger Ebert's review of *A Christmas Story*; Buzz Bissinger's provocative proposal, "Why College Football Should Be Banned"; Edward Tufte's famous argument, "Why PowerPoint is Evil"; and "Our Zombies, Ourselves," by James Parker, an analytical essay on film that explores our cultural obsession with zombies.

■ **NEW focus on learning outcomes:** Every chapter in the fourth edition opens with a series of Learning Objectives tied to the inquiry-based approach of the book and grounded in the principles of the WPA outcomes for first-year composition. These learning objectives are highlighted by annotations in the margins that help connect discussions in the text to each objective and are supported by "Using What You Have Learned" summaries at the end of each chapter, helping students to apply strategies in their own writing.

Inquiry in the Writing Classroom

Most of us already teach inquiry, although not all may realize it. For instance, our writing classes invite students to be active participants in making knowledge in the classroom through peer review workshops. When we ask students to fastwrite or brainstorm, we encourage them to suspend judgment and openly explore their feelings or ideas. And when we ask students to see a draft as a first look at a topic, and revision as a means of discovering what they may not have noticed, we teach a process that makes discovery its purpose. Indeed, most composition classrooms create a "culture of inquirers" rather than passive recipients of what their teachers know.

Historically, composition teachers have struggled to decide what besides reading and writing skills students can export to their other classes and, later, into their lives. Often we vaguely refer to "critical-thinking" skills. *The Curious Writer* offers a comprehensive approach for teaching inquiry.

For inquiry-based courses on any subject, there are five key actions I believe instructors should take:

1. Create an atmosphere of mutual inquiry. Students are used to seeing their teachers as experts who know everything that students need to learn. But in an inquiry-based classroom instructors are learners too. They ask questions not because they already know the answers but because there might be answers they haven't considered.

2. Emphasize questions before answers. The idea that student writers begin with an inflexible thesis or a firm position on a topic before they engage in the process of writing and thinking is anathema to inquiry-based learning. Questions, not preconceived answers, lead to new discoveries.

3. Encourage a willingness to suspend judgment. Student culture at most schools works against this. Papers get written at the last minute, multiple deadlines in multiple classes compete for students' time, and multiple-choice

tests or lecture courses imply that there is one true answer and the teacher knows it. To suspend judgment demands that we trust the process that will lead us to new insights. This requires both faith in the process and the time to engage in it. The composition course, with its emphasis on process, is uniquely suited to nurture such faith.

4. Introduce a strategy of inquiry. It's not enough to simply announce that we're teaching an inquiry-based class. We have to introduce students to the strategy of inquiry we'll be using. In the sciences, the experimental method provides a foundation for investigations. What guidance will we give our students in the composition course? *The Curious Writer* features a strategy that is genuinely multidisciplinary, borrowing from science, social science, and the humanities.

5. Present inquiry in a rhetorical context. An essay, a research project, an experiment, any kind of investigation is always pursued with particular purposes and audiences in mind. In an inquiry-based class, the situation in which the inquiry project is taking place is always considered.

You'll find all of these elements of inquiry-based learning integrated in *The Curious Writer*. For example, each project presented in Chapters 3 through 7 leads students toward writing subjects that offer the most potential for learning. Rather than write about what they already know, students are always encouraged to choose a topic that they want to find out more about. In addition, the discussion questions that follow the student and professional essays are crafted to do more than simply test their comprehension of the piece or reduce it to a single theme. In many cases, questions are open ended and can lead students in many directions as they analyze a reading. *The Curious Writer* maintains a voice and persona throughout the book that suggests that I am working along with the students as a writer and a thinker, which is exactly the experience of mutual inquiry I try to create in my classes. Finally, *The Curious Writer* is organized around a strategy of inquiry that is present in every assignment and nearly every exercise. Introduced in Chapters 1 and 2, I call on the model often in every subsequent chapter. The inquiry strategy is the thematic core of the book.

The Inquiry Strategy of *The Curious Writer*

A strategy of inquiry is simply a process of discovery. In the sciences, this process is systematic and often quite formal. The model I use in this book borrows from science in some ways through its insistence on continually looking closely at the "data" (sensory details, facts, evidence, textual passages, and so on) and using it to shape or test the writer's ideas about a subject. But the heart of the model is the alternating movement between two modes of thinking—creative and critical—in a dialectical process. One way of describing this is shifting back and forth between suspending judgment and making judgments (see Figure A).

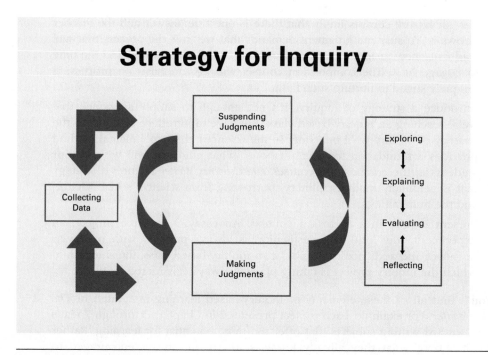

Figure A   In nearly every assignment in *The Curious Writer,* students will use this strategy of inquiry.

This inquiry strategy works with both reading and writing, but in Chapter 2, "Reading as Inquiry," I offer four categories of questions—those that explore, explain, evaluate, and reflect—that I think will help guide students in reading most texts more strategically. These types of questions will be most evident in the follow-up questions to the many readings throughout *The Curious Writer*.

Finally, a strategy of inquiry is useful only if it makes sense to students; I've tried very hard, particularly in the first section of the book, to make the model comprehensible.

Other Features

Because the inquiry-based approach is central to *The Curious Writer*, it's crucial for students to work through Chapter 1, "Writing as Inquiry," and Chapter 2, "Reading as Inquiry." Chapters 3 through 7 focus on "inquiry projects." The range of assignments in these chapters should satisfy the needs of most composition instructors. If your university is lucky enough to have a two-semester sequence, *The Curious Writer* includes assignments suitable for both courses, including personal, argument, and research essays.

The book's focus on genres of writing also makes it appealing for advanced composition courses. For example, assignments such as the personal essay and the review help students see how to apply what they've learned to distinct rhetorical situations and help them to understand how those situations shape the genres.

In recent years, I've become interested in reading strategies, a topic that I never mentioned as a novice teacher. There was simply so much to say about the writing process that I didn't think reading was a topic that should get much airtime. Yet, as in writing, students bring many prior beliefs and assumptions about reading into our classrooms, and because reading is always an important part of teaching writing, I've come around to talking more about it. *The Curious Writer* reflects this. Chapter 2, "Reading as Inquiry," is devoted to the topic. I've also expanded the discussion to reading images. This emphasis on visual rhetoric echoes the latest developments in composition in response to the growth of the Web and the growing visual literacy of our students.

Finally, the approach of *The Curious Writer* grows in part from my own scholarship on research writing, particularly the criticism that research is too often isolated in the writing course. Students understandably get the idea that research is reserved only for the research paper if they're asked to do it only when they're assigned a research project. This book makes research a part of every assignment, from the personal essay to the proposal, emphasizing that it is a useful source of information, not a separate genre.

This is the third textbook I've written with the "curious" moniker. Because all are inquiry-based, the word is a natural choice. And although I'm very interested in encouraging my students to be curious researchers, readers, and writers, I also hope to remind my colleagues who use the books that we should be curious, too. We should model for our students our own passion for inquiring into the world. We should also celebrate what we can learn from our students, and not just about writing, or the many topics they might choose to write about. I'm curious every time I walk into the writing classroom what my students will teach me about myself. That's a lifetime inquiry project for all of us, as teachers and as people.

Approaches to Teaching with the Book

The Instructor's Manual, written by my colleague Michelle Payne, will give you detailed suggestions about ways to teach *The Curious Writer*. Here are a few additional suggestions drawn with a much broader stroke.

I organized the book to span, if necessary, a two-semester composition course, though it can easily be adapted to one semester. Typically, in a two-semester sequence the first course focuses on the writing process, exposition, critical analysis, writing to learn, and so on. The second semester often focuses on argument and research. A single-semester composition course tries to combine them all. Fortunately, *The Curious Writer* is extremely flexible, with ample material to keep students busy for one or two semesters.

Sequence

Whether you use this book for one course or two, it's wise to introduce *The Curious Writer* to students by first working through Chapters 1 and 2, because this section lays the foundation for all that follows. The many exercises in these chapters will help students experience firsthand what we mean by inquiry. The "Inquiry Projects" in Chapters 3 through 7 are the heart of the book. I've organized chapters in an order that roughly follows typical composition courses, beginning with genres that draw heavily on students' personal experiences and observations and then moving them outward toward other sources of information and encounters with other people's experiences and ideas.

The selection of assignments in the concise edition has a strong emphasis on persuasive writing, including the proposal, review, critical, and argument essays. You might wonder how the personal essay and profile fit in. The best answer is that every assignment in the book relies on the same basic inquiry strategy, one that is especially evident in the personal essay. The profile assignment is also an excellent prelude to more argumentative forms because what's at stake in argument is always how something affects people. The profile reminds writers of this. Don't forget as well that there's considerable material on research in the Concise edition, and this is relevant to whatever assignment you teach.

Integrating the Research and Revision Sections

An unusual feature of the book is its treatment of research skills and revision. Research is an element of every assignment, but it receives special attention in Chapters 8 and 9, in which students are introduced not only to the research essay but to research strategies and skills. I hope you will find that this section, particularly Chapter 8, "Research Techniques," is immediately relevant because students will be encouraged to consider research angles in every assignment they tackle. Consider assigning this chapter early in your course, particularly the sections on developing a working and focused knowledge of a subject.

Similarly, revision is an element of every assignment. That's hardly a novel idea, but what is unusual is that *The Curious Writer* devotes an entire chapter to revision. Like the chapter on research, the chapter on revision is relevant to students from their very first assignment.

Using the Exercises

Learning follows experience, and the exercises in *The Curious Writer* are intended to help students make sense of the ideas in the text. I often plan the exercises as an in-class activity, and then assign the relevant reading to follow up that experience. Sometimes the discussion following these in-class exercises is so rich that some of the assigned reading becomes unnecessary. The students get it without having to hear it again from the author. More often, though, the reading helps students deepen their understanding of what they've done and how they can apply it to their own work.

However, assigning all of the exercises isn't necessary. Don't mistake their abundance in the book as an indication that you must march your students in lockstep through every activity, or they won't learn what they need to. *The Curious Writer* is more flexible than that. Use the exercises and activities that seem to emphasize key points that you think are important. Skip those you don't have time for or that don't seem necessary. If you're like me, you also have a few rabbits of your own in your hat—exercises and activities that may work better with the text than the ones I suggest.

For Instructors

The following resources are available to qualified adopters of Pearson English textbooks.

The Instructor's Resource Manual

ISBN 0-205-87740-0/978-0-205-87740-9
This manual includes several sample syllabi, as well as a helpful introduction that will offer general teaching strategies and ideas for teaching writing as a form of inquiry. It also gives a detailed overview of each chapter and its goals, ideas for discussion starters, handouts and overheads, and a large number of additional writing activities that teachers can use in their classrooms to supplement the textbook.

PowerPoint Presentation

A downloadable set of PowerPoint slides can be used by instructors who want to use presentable visuals to accompany chapter readings and discussions. These slides, designed by Michelle Payne (who also developed the *Instructor's Manual*), focus on illustrating each learning objective and key idea in the text in visual form. Each slide includes instructors' notes.

Pearson MyLabs

The Pearson English MyLabs empower students to improve their skills in writing, grammar, research, and documentation with market-leading instruction, multimedia tutorials, exercises, and assessment tools. Students can use the MyLabs on their own, benefiting from self-paced diagnostics and extra practice in content knowledge and writing skills. Instructors can use MyLabs in ways that best complement their courses and teaching styles. They can work more efficiently and more closely with students by creating their own assignments and using time-saving administrative and assessment tools. To learn more, visit www.pearsonhighered.com/englishmylabs or ask your Pearson representative.

Acknowledgments

Making such a large and complex book as this one is a team effort. From the first edition of *The Curious Writer* I've been lucky to have an extraordinarily gifted group of Pearson people working with me. Some of these I'll never know because they work off stage on production and design. But among those with whom I worked directly, there are several collaborators who deserve special thanks. Randee Falk was development editor for much of this edition. She was demanding and brilliant, an editor who made me work harder than any I've ever had. The result is a much, much better book. Toward the end of the project, Randee passed the editorial baton to Michael Greer, a talented and congenial collaborator who is one of the best development editors in the business. On the production side, I got to work with my old friend Sarah Burkhart. Her keen eye for the details, combined with her wit and charm, make Sarah a joy to work with. Lauren Finn, senior acquisitions editor at Pearson, was instrumental in helping me focus on how to improve the new edition. Finally, thanks, as always, to Joe Opiela, Senior Vice President, for the support and encouragement that have made all the *Curious* books possible.

My students are also key collaborators, though they often don't know it. For their assistance in the fourth edition, I'd like to thank the following students: Andrea Oyarzabal, Becca Ballenger, Julia Ballenger, Seth Marlin, Micaela Fisher, Bernice Olivas, Briana Duquette, Julie Bird, Gordon Seirup, Kersti Harter, Margaret Parker, and Amy-Garrett Brown.

Reviewers of books like these can be crucial to their development. I was lucky enough to have some excellent reviewers for each edition, including the following folks who guided me on the first edition:

Jeffrey T. Andelora, Mesa Community College; Ken Autrey, Francis Marion University; Sandra Barnhill, South Plains College; Patrick Bizzaro, East Carolina University; Sara M. Blake, El Camino College; Pamela S. Bledsoe, Surry Community College; Libby Bradford Roeger, Shawnee Community College; Sharon Buzzard, Quincy College; Maria A. Clayton, Middle Tennessee State University; Dr. Keith Coplin, Colby Community College; Rachelle Darabi, Indiana University/Purdue University–Fort Wayne; Virginia B. Earnest, Holmes Community College–Ridgeland; Terry Engebretsen, Idaho State University; Shari Hammond, Southwest Virginia Community College; Anneliese Homan, State Fair Community College; David C. Judkins, University of Houston; Robert Lamm, Arkansas State University; James C. McDonald, University of Louisiana–Lafayette; Rhonda McDonnell, Arizona State University; Bryan Moore, Arkansas State University; John D. Moore, Eastern Illinois University; Margaret P. Morgan, University of North Carolina–Charlotte; Dr. Peter E. Morgan, University of West Georgia; Brigid Murphy, Pima Community College; Robin L. Murray, Eastern Illinois University; Dorothy J. Patterson, Oakwood College; Steven R. Price, Mississippi College; Mark Reynolds, Jefferson Davis Community College; David H. Roberts, Samford University; Elaine J. Roberts, Judson College; Robert A. Schwegler, University of Rhode Island; Dr. Bonita Selting, University of

Central Arkansas; Vicki Stieha, Northern Kentucky University; Elizabeth A. Stolarek, Ferris State University; Lisa Tyler, Sinclair Community College; Marjorie Van Cleef, Housatonic Community College; Worth H. Weller, Indiana University Purdue University–Fort Wayne; Ann R. Wolven, Lincoln Trail College; and Richard T. Young, Blackburn College.

Reviewers for the second edition included Melissa Batai, Triton College; Jennifer Black, McLennan Community College; Mark Browning, Johnson County Community College; Jo Ann Buck, Guilford Technical Community College; Jason DePolo, North Carolina A&T State University; John Christopher Ervin, University of South Dakota; Greg Giberson, Salisbury University; Nels P. Highberg, University of Hartford; William Klein, University of Missouri–St. Louis; Mary C. Leahy, College of DuPage; Lynn Lewis, University of Oklahoma; Steve Luebke, University of Wisconsin–River Falls; Michael Lueker, Our Lady of the Lake University; Jacqueline L. McGrath, College of DuPage; Betty Porter, Indiana Wesleyan University; Kristie Rowe, Wright State University; Kathleen J. Ryan, University of Montana; and Heath Scott, Thomas Nelson Community College.

Reviewers for the third edition included Angela Cardinale Bartlett, Chaffey College; Jennifer Black, McLennan Community College; James C. Bower, Walla Walla Community College; Susan Butterworth, Salem State College; Donna Craine, Front Range Community College; Brock Dethier, Utah State University; Rosemarie Dombrowski, Arizona State University (DPC); Kevin Ferns, Woodland Community College; Michael Hammond, University of San Francisco; Vicki M. Hester, St. Mary's University; Charlotte Hogg, Texas Christian University; Shelly Horvath, University of Indianapolis; Dawn Hubbell-Staeble, Bowling Green State University; Tom Moriarty, Salisbury University; Jason E. Murray, University of South Dakota; Amy Ratto Parks, University of Montana; Susan Pesznecker, Clackamas Community College; Lynn Raymond, UNC Charlotte; Mark A. Smith, Lock Haven University of Pennsylvania; Ruthe Thompson, Southwest Minnesota State University; BJ Zamora, Cleveland Community College.

And for this latest, fourth edition, reviewers include Susan Achziger, Community College of Aurora; Ellen Barker, Nicholls State University; Shanti Bruce, Nova Southeastern University; Carol Burnell, Clackamas Community College; Donna Craine, Front Range Community College; Daniel Gonzalez, University of New Orleans; Gwendolyn N. Hale, Savannah State University; Charlotte Hogg, Texas Christian University; Chad Jorgensen, Metropolitan Community College; Lilia Joy, Henderson Community College; Rosemary Mack, Baton Rouge Community College; Kara M. Manning, The University of Southern Mississippi; Amanda McGuire Rzicznek, Bowling Green State University; James J. McKeown, Jr., McLennan Community College; Eileen Medeiros, Johnson & Wales University; Betty Porter, Indiana Wesleyan University; Amy Ratto Parks, University of Montana; Teryl Sands, Arizona State University; and Marian Thomas, Boise State University.

Finally, I want to thank my daughters, Rebecca and Julia, who allow themselves to be characters in all of my books. They are both actors, and like good theater people, they are more than willing to play their parts in these texts, no matter what role I assign. I'm especially grateful to Karen, my wife, who has endured multiple editions of these books and their hold on my attention, which has often come at her expense. She's the beacon I follow through this blizzard of words, always guiding me home.

BRUCE BALLENGER

THE CURIOUS WRITER

Writing as inquiry is an invitation to wonder and discover again.

Writing as Inquiry

Learning Objectives

In this chapter, you'll learn to

1.1 Reflect on and revise your beliefs about yourself as a writer.

1.2 Understand what kinds of questions will sustain inquiry into any subject.

1.3 Practice a method of writing and thinking that will help you generate ideas.

1.4 Apply rhetorical knowledge to make choices in specific writing situations.

Yesterday in class, Tina wrote an essay about whether adultery is forgivable. She isn't married but has good friends who are, a couple she said everyone thought had the "perfect" marriage. The woman's husband, apparently, had an affair. Tina, who was in a pretty tight relationship with her boyfriend, had strong feelings about cheating on a partner. It ticked her off. "If it happened to me," she wrote, "I would have dumped him." Tina's essay could easily have become a rant about infidelity—a blunt, perhaps shrill argument about adultery's immorality or the depravity of two-timing men. It wasn't. Instead, she wondered about the relationship between friendship and love in marriage. She wondered about what kind of communication between spouses might short-circuit cheating. She wondered how attitudes towards sex differ between men and women. Many of these questions were explored by Michel de Montaigne, a sixteenth-century writer we were studying in that class, and Tina began to wrap his thinking around hers as she struggled to make sense of how she felt about what happened to her friends.

Tina was engaged in an act of inquiry.

Her motive was to *find out* what she thought rather than prove what she already knew. And writing was the way Tina chose to think it through.

Many of us admit that we really don't like to write, particularly when forced to do it. Or we clearly prefer certain kinds of writing and dislike others: "I just like to write funny stories," or "I like writing for myself and not for other people," or "I hate writing research papers." I can understand this, because for years I felt much the same way. I saw virtually no similarities between a note to a friend and the paper I wrote for my philosophy class in college. Words had power in one context but seemed flimsy and vacant in another. One kind of writing was fairly easy; the other was like sweating blood. How could my experiences as a writer be so fundamentally different? In other words, what's the secret of writing well in a range of writing contexts *and* enjoying it more in all contexts? Here's what I had to learn:

1. You don't have to know what you think before you're ready to write. Writing can be a way of *discovering* what you think.
2. A key to writing well is understanding the *process* of doing it.

They're not particularly novel ideas, but both were a revelation to me when I finally figured them out late in my career as a student, and they changed for good the way I wrote. These two insights—that writing is a means of discovery and that reflecting on how we write can help us write—are guiding principles of this book. I won't guarantee that after they read *The Curious Writer* haters of writing will come to love it or that lovers of writing won't find writing to be hard work. But I hope that by the end of the book you'll experience the pleasure of discovery in different writing situations, and that you'll understand your writing process well enough to adapt it to the demands of whatever situation you encounter.

Motives for Writing

Why write? To start, I'd propose two motives, one obvious and the other less so:

1. To share ideas or information—*to communicate*.
2. To think—*to discover*.

These two motives for writing—to *communicate* with others and to *discover* what the writer thinks and feels—are equally important. And both may ultimately relate to what I call our *spirit of inquiry*, which is born of our deeper sense of wonder and curiosity or even confusion and doubt, our desire to touch other people, our urge to solve problems. The spirit of inquiry is a kind of perspective toward the world that invites questions, accepts uncertainty, and makes each of us feel some responsibility for what we say. This inquiring spirit should be familiar to you. It's the feeling you had when you discovered that the sun and a simple magnifying glass could be used to burn a hole in an oak leaf. It's wondering what a teacher meant when he said that World War II was a "good" war and Vietnam was a "bad" war. It's the questions that haunted you yesterday as you listened to a good friend describe her struggles with anorexia. The inquiring spirit even drives your quest to find a smartphone, an effort that inspires you to read about the technology and visit consumerreports.org. Inquiry was Tina's motive when she decided to turn her academic essay on adultery away from a shrill argument based on what she already believed into a more thoughtful exploration of why people cheat.

Beliefs About Writing and Writing Development

Most of us have been taught about writing since the first grade. We usually enter college with beliefs not only about what makes a good paper and what "rules" of writing to follow, but also about how we can develop as writers. As I mentioned earlier, I've learned a lot about writing since my first years in college, and a big part of that learning involved unraveling some of my prior beliefs about writing. In fact, I'd say that my development as a writer initially had more to do with *unlearning* some of what I already knew than it did with discovering new ways to write. But you have to make your beliefs explicit if you're going to make decisions about which are helpful and which aren't. So take a moment to find out what your beliefs are and to think about whether they actually make sense.

1.1

Reflect on and revise your beliefs about yourself as a writer.

Exercise 1.1

This I Believe (and This I Don't)

STEP ONE: From the following list, identify *the one belief* about writing that you agree with most strongly and *one* that you're convinced isn't true.

1. Writing proficiency begins with learning the basics and then building on them, working from words to sentences to paragraphs to compositions.

2. The best way to develop as a writer is to imitate the writing of the people you want to write like.

3. People are born writers like people are born good at math. Either you can do it or you can't.

4. The best way to develop as a writer is to develop good reading skills.

5. Practice is the key to a writer's development. The more a writer writes, the more he or she will improve.

6. Developing writers need to learn the modes of writing (argument, exposition, description, narration) and the genres (essays, research papers, position papers, and so on).

7. Developing writers should start with simple writing tasks, such as telling stories, and move to harder writing tasks, such as writing a research paper.

8. The most important thing that influences a writer's growth is believing that he or she can improve.

9. The key to becoming a better writer is finding your voice.

STEP TWO: Look over the following journal prompts (for more on journals, see the "Inquiring into the Details: Journals" box). Then spend five minutes writing in your journal about *why* you agree with the one belief and disagree with the other. This is an open-ended "fastwrite." You should write fast and without stopping, letting your thoughts flow in whatever direction they go. In your fastwrite, you can respond to any or all of the prompts to whatever extent you want.

Rules for Fastwriting
1. There are no rules.
2. Don't try to write badly, but give yourself permission to do so.
3. To the extent you can, think through writing rather than before it.
4. Keep your pen moving.
5. If you run out of things to say, write about how weird it is to run out of things to say until new thoughts arrive.
6. Silence your internal critic to suspend judgment.
7. Don't censor yourself.

Journal Prompts

- *What* do you mean, exactly, when you say you agree or disagree with the belief? Can you explain more fully why you think the belief is true or false?

- *When* did you start agreeing or disagreeing with the belief? Can you remember a particular moment or experience as a student learning to write that this agreement or disagreement connects to?

- *Who* was most influential in convincing you of the truth or falsity of the belief?

One Student's Response

Bernice's Journal

EXERCISE 1.1
STEP TWO

I used to be a firm believer in the idea of born writers—it was a genetic thing. People were gifted with the gold pen genes, or they weren't. Writing as a process involved a muse, inspiration, and luck. Things uncontrollable by the writer. Then I started writing, mostly for my 101 class, and I started to feel powerful when I put words on paper. In control. The idea of my voice, my words, just being on the page and other people reading it and maybe liking it was a rush. I was always the girl who specialized in the art of being unnoticed, unseen, blending in. My Comp 101 prof. liked my writing and pushed really hard to work on my basics, to think about my process, to prewrite and revise. I started to see a clear distinction between how to write and what to write. How is all mixed up with the process, with discipline, with practice and perseverance....The how isn't something you are born with; its something you develop, something you practice, a skill you hone....Becoming a good writer takes learning how to write, figuring out a process that works for you, and then letting your voice be heard on the page.

Inquiring into the Details

Journals

Here are five things that make a journal especially useful for writers:

- Whether print or digital, the journal must be a place where you're able to largely ignore your internal critic, a place where you feel comfortable *writing badly*.

- Use it *throughout the writing process*. Journals can be indispensible for invention whenever you need more information, not just at the beginning. They can also be a place where you talk to yourself about how to solve a writing problem.

- Write both *specifically and abstractly*. Sometimes you'll be trying to be as concrete as possible, generating details, collecting facts, exploring particular experiences. Other times, use the journal to think in more-abstract language, thinking through ideas, reflecting on process, analyzing claims.

- *Don't make any rules* about your journal. These usually begin with a thought like "I'll only write in my journal when . . . ." Write in your journal whenever you find it useful, and in any way that you find useful, especially if it keeps you writing.

- *Experiment.* Your journal will be different from my journal, which will be different from the journal of the woman sitting next to you in class. The only way to make a journal genuinely useful is to keep trying ways to make it useful.

Unlearning Unhelpful Beliefs

You won't be surprised when I say that I have a lot of theories about writing development; after all, I'm supposedly the expert. But we are *all* writing theorists, with beliefs that grow out of our successes and failures as students who write. Because you don't think much about them, these beliefs often shape your response to writing instruction without your even knowing it. For example, I've had a number of students who believe that people are born writers. This belief, of course, would make any kind of writing class a waste of time, because writing ability would be a matter of genetics.

A much more common belief is that learning to write is a process of building on basics, beginning with words and then working up to sentences, paragraphs, and perhaps whole compositions. This belief was very common when I was taught writing. I remember slogging my way through Warriner's *English Grammar and Composition* in the seventh and eighth grade, dutifully working through chapter after chapter.

Today, along with a lot of experts on writing instruction, I don't think that this foundational approach to writing development is very effective. While I can still diagram a sentence, for example, that's never a skill I call on when I'm composing.

And yet building on the basics seems like common sense, doesn't it? This brings up an important point: Unlearning involves rejecting common sense *if* it conflicts

Unlearning involves rejecting common sense if it conflicts with what actually works.

with what actually works. Throughout this book, I hope you'll constantly test your beliefs about writing against the experiences you're having with it. Pay attention to what seems to work for you and what doesn't. Mostly, I'd like you at least initially to play what one writing instructor calls the *believing game*. Ask yourself, *What do I have to gain as a writer if I try believing this is true?* For example, even if you've believed for much of your life that you should never write anything in school that doesn't follow an outline, you might discover that abandoning this "rule" sometimes helps you to use writing to *discover* what you think.

The Beliefs of This Book

Allatonceness. One of the metaphors I very much like about writing development is offered by writing theorist Ann E. Berthoff. She said learning to write is like learning to ride a bike. You don't start by practicing handlebar skills, move on to pedaling practice, and then finally learn balancing techniques. You get on the bike and fall off, get up, and try again, doing all of those separate things at once. At some point, you don't fall and you pedal off down the street. Berthoff said writing is a process that involves *allatonceness* (all-at-once-ness) and it's simply not helpful to try to practice the subskills separately. This book shares the belief in the allatonceness of writing development.

Believing You Can Learn to Write Well. Various other beliefs about writing development—the importance of critical thinking, the connection between reading and writing, the power of voice and fluency, and the need to listen to voices other than your own—also help to guide this book. One belief, though, undergirds them all: *The most important thing that influences a writer's growth is believing that he or she can learn to write well.* Faith in your ability to become a better writer is key. From it grows the motivation to learn how to write well.

Faith isn't easy to come by. I didn't have it as a writer through most of my school career, because I assumed that being placed in the English class for underachievers meant that writing was simply another thing, like track and math, that I was mediocre at. For a long time, I was a captive to this attitude. But then, in college I wrote a paper I cared about; writing started to matter, because I discovered something I really wanted to say and say well. This was the beginning of my belief in myself—and of my becoming a better writer. Belief requires motivation, and one powerful motivator is to approach a writing assignment as an opportunity to learn something—that is, with what I have called the spirit of inquiry.

Habits of Mind

When I first started teaching writing, I noticed a strange thing in my classes. What students learned about writing through the early assignments in the class didn't seem to transfer to later assignments, particularly research papers. What was I doing wrong? I wondered. Among other things, what I failed to make clear to my students was that certain "habits of mind" (or *dispositions*, as one writer terms them) could be consistently useful to them, in writing papers in my course and in any course involving academic inquiry—habits related to seeing writing as a process of discovery. We'll look at several closely related habits here; later in this chapter, you'll see how they play a role in the writing process.

Starting with Questions, Not Answers

A lot of people think that writing is about recording what you already know, which accounts for those who choose familiar topics to write on when given the choice. "I think I'll write about _____," the thinking goes, "because I know that topic really well and already have an idea what I can say." Writers who write about what they know usually start with answers rather than questions. In some writing situations this makes a lot of sense, because you're being asked specifically to prove that you know something. I'm thinking of an essay exam, for instance. But more often writing in a university is about inquiry, not reporting information. It's about discovery. It's about finding the questions that ultimately lead to interesting answers.

1.2
Understand what kinds of questions will sustain inquiry into any subject.

Making the Familiar Strange. Starting with questions rather than answers changes everything. *It means finding new ways to see what you've seen before.* Take this for example:

What is it? An iPhone, of course. Not much more to say, right? But imagine that your purpose wasn't to simply provide the quickest answer possible to the simple factual question *What is it?* Consider instead starting with questions that might inspire you to think about the iPhone in ways you haven't before; for example,

- *What does it mean* that iPhone owners spend twice as much time playing games as other smartphone users?
- *What should be done* about the environmental impacts of iPhone production in China?

Both these questions lead you to potentially new information and new ways of seeing that familiar phone in your pocket. They promise that you'll discover something you didn't know before.

Questions open up the inquiry process, while quick answers close it down. When you discover what you think, you don't cook up a thesis before you start—you discover the thesis as you explore. But to work, the inquiry process demands something of us that most of us aren't used to: suspending judgment.

Suspending Judgment

We jerk our knee when physicians tap the patellar tendon. If everything is working, we do it reflexively. We're often just as reflexive in our responses to the world:

- "What do you think of American politicians?"
  "They're all corrupt."

- "Is it possible to reconcile economic growth with the preservation of natural resources?"
  "No."

- "Isn't this an interesting stone?"
  "It's just a rock."

> It's okay to write badly. Resist the tendency to judge too soon and too harshly.

We make these judgments out of habit. But this habit is in fact a way of seeing, based on this premise: Some things are really pretty simple, more or less black-and-white, good or bad, boring or interesting. Academic inquiry works from another, very different premise: The world is really a wonderfully complex place, and *if we look closely and long enough*, and ask the right questions, we are likely to be surprised at what we see. A condition of inquiry is that you *don't* rush to judgment; you tolerate uncertainty while you explore your subject. Academic inquiry requires that you see your preconceptions as hypotheses that can be tested, not established truths. It is, in short, associated with a habit of *suspending* judgment.

Being Willing to Write Badly

In a writing course such as this one, the challenge of suspending judgment begins with how you approach your own writing. What's one of the most common problems I see in student writers? Poor grammar? Lack of organization? A missing thesis? Nope. *It's the tendency to judge too soon and too harshly.* A great majority of my students—including really smart, capable writers—have powerful internal critics, or, as the novelist Gail Godwin once called them, "Watchers at the Gates." This is the voice you may hear when you're starting to write a paper, the one that has you crossing out that first sentence or that first paragraph over and over until you "get it perfect."

The only way to overcome this problem is to suspend judgment. In doing so, you essentially tell your Watchers this: *It's okay to write badly.* Godwin once suggested that writers should confront their internal critics by writing them a letter.

Dear Watcher,

Ever since the eighth grade, when I had Mrs. O'Neal for English, I've been seeing red. This is the color of every correction and every comment ("awk") you've made in the margins on my school writing. Now, years later, I just imagine you, ready to pick away at my prose every time I sit down to write. This time will be different...

It might help to write your internal critic a letter like this. Rein in that self-critical part of yourself, and you'll find that writing can be a tool for *invention*—a way to generate material—and that you can *think through writing* rather than waiting around for the thoughts to come. You need your internal critic. But you need it to work with you, not against you. Later in this chapter, I'll show you how to accomplish this.

Searching for Surprise

Starting with questions, making the familiar strange, suspending judgment, and writing badly—all are related to searching for surprise. In fact, one of the key benefits of writing badly is *surprise*. This was a revelation for me. I was convinced that you never pick up the pen unless you know what you want to say. Once I realized I could write badly and use writing not to *record* what I already knew, but to *discover* what I thought, this way of writing promised a feast of surprises that made me hunger to put words on the page. If you're skeptical that your own writing can surprise you, try the following exercise.

1.3 Practice a method of writing and thinking that will help you generate ideas.

> **Conditions That Make "Bad" Writing Possible**
> 1. Willingness to suspend judgment
> 2. Ability to write fast enough to outrun your internal critic
> 3. Belief that confusion, uncertainty, and ambiguity help thought rather than hinder it
> 4. Interest in writing about "risky" subjects, or those about which you don't know what you want to say until you say it

Exercise 1.2

A Roomful of Details

STEP ONE: Spend ten minutes brainstorming a list of details based on the following prompt. Write down whatever comes into your mind, no matter how silly. Be specific and don't censor yourself.

> Try to remember a room you spent a lot of time in as a child. It may be your bedroom in the back of the house at the edge of the field, or the kitchen where your grandmother kneaded bread or made thick, red pasta sauce. Put yourself back in that room. Now look around you. What do you see? What do you hear? What do you smell?

> **Brainstorming**
> - Anything goes.
> - Don't censor yourself.
> - Write everything down.
> - Be playful but stay focused.

STEP TWO: Examine your list. If things went well, you will have a fairly long list of details. As you review the list, identify the one detail that surprises you the most, a detail that seems somehow to carry an unexpected charge. This might be something that seems connected to a feeling or a story. You might be drawn to a detail that confuses you a little. Whatever its particular appeal, circle it.

STEP THREE: Use the circled detail as a prompt for a seven-minute fastwrite. Begin by focusing on the detail: What does it make you think of? And then what? And then? Alternatively, begin by simply describing the detail more fully: What does it look like? Where did it come from? What stories are attached to it? How does it make you feel? Avoid writing in generalities. Write about specifics—that is, particular times, places, moments, and people. Write fast, and chase after the words to see where they want to go. Give yourself permission to write badly.

You may experience at least three kinds of surprise after completing a fastwriting exercise such as the one above:

1. Surprise about *how much* writing you did in such a short time
2. Surprise about discovering a topic you didn't expect to find
3. Surprise about discovering a *new way of understanding or seeing a familiar topic*

One Student's Response

Bernice's Journal

EXERCISE 1.2
STEP THREE

DETAIL: STAINLESS STEEL COUNTERS

When I was five or six my father and I made cookies for the first time. I don't remember what prompted him to bake cookies, he liked to cook but he didn't very well so he didn't like to use cook books. I remember sitting on the cold stainless steel, the big red and white cook book splayed over my lap. I was reading it out loud to my dad. The kitchen was warm but everything gleamed; it was industrial and functional. It was the only room in our house that still looked like it belonged to the "Old Pioneer School." My dad and uncles had renovated every other room into bedrooms, playrooms, family rooms. The place was huge but cozy, it was home. I remember reading off ingredients until I got to the sugar. It called for 3/4 cup and I didn't understand the fraction. I thought it meant three or four cups. We poured so much sugar into the bowl. The cookies were terrible. Hard and glassy, too sweet and brittle. It wasn't until years later that I understood that my dad didn't understand the measurement either. He was persistent though. We pulled down every cook book in the house until we found one that described the measuring cups and what they meant. We started all over and our second batch was perfect. My dad is one of the smartest people I know, inventive, imaginative but he only has a rudimentary education. He can read and write enough to get by, he's gifted with numbers, but I can't help looking back and wondering what he could have been, what he could have done for the world if just one person had taken him by the hand and showed him what he showed me. If just one person had told him not to give up, to keep trying, that in the end it will be worth all the work, I wonder who he could have been if one person had seen his curiosity and imagination and fostered it instead of seeing his muscles and capable hands and putting him to work. If just one person had told him that his mind was the greatest tool he possessed. If just one person baked cookies with him.

The kind of surprises you encounter doing this sort of writing may not always be profound. They may not even provide you with obvious essay topics. With any luck, though, by hunting for surprises in your own work, you will begin to experience the pleasure of writing *to learn*. That's no small thing, particularly if you've always believed that writers should have it all figured out before they pick up the pen.

Writing Situations and Rhetorical Choices

The following isn't good writing, is it?

> im happy to be back w/u guys it was a too long of a weekend- dancing friday then? u hailey and i runnin tomorrow- sounds fun 2 me

1.4

Apply rhetorical knowledge to make choices in specific writing situations.

Actually, the answer is, of course, that it depends.

Writing occurs in a writing situation, and different writing situations are associated with different types of writing and forms of communication—different genres and media. Think of how many writing situations we encounter these days and how many types of writing we do. For example, besides writing part of this textbook chapter, I wrote e-mails to an editor and a student, freewrote in my journal, drafted some text for a web page, sent a text to my daughter, and posted a comment on Facebook.

In each case, the writing situation demanded something different from me. In each, however, I had to make appropriate *rhetorical* choices—choices related to the following four considerations:

- **Purpose for writing:** What is the text trying to do?
- **Audience:** For whom is it intended?
- **Subject:** What is it about?
- **Genre/Medium:** What type of writing—what form of communication—would work best in view of my purpose, audience, and subject? What are its strengths and limitations, and what are its conventions?

That is, to write effectively, I had to think about why I was writing, to whom I was writing, what I was writing about, and what type of text I was writing. The effectiveness of my writing depended on my making appropriate choices in light of these considerations. And the rhetorical choices that we make in a writing situation are wide ranging; they include not only big choices (What's the best genre for accomplishing my purpose with this audience?), but also many smaller choices (Is it okay to say "ur" instead of "you're"?).

Now let's go back to the text message, written by my daughter to a friend.

Rhetorical Consideration	The Text Message
Purpose	Expressive and informational purposes: to reinforce intimacy; to plan
Audience	A close friend, with considerable shared knowledge
Subject	Personal details related to knowledge of a shared experience
Genre/ Medium	Text message; limited to 160 characters, with a shorthand shared by users

Based on this analysis, my daughter's text message is clearly good writing after all. It uses the conventions of the genre/medium to fulfill its purpose—reinforce intimacy and make a Friday-night plan—for the audience the writer had in mind. My daughter used her *rhetorical knowledge* to make choices that resulted in an effective piece of writing. Of course she would think it was weird to call her understanding of how to write a text message "rhetorical knowledge." But that's exactly what it is. She just doesn't think about it that way.

But what happens when you *do* think about it?

1. You become more skillful at composing in writing situations with which you are familiar.

2. You can learn to master unfamiliar writing situations much more quickly.

You have more rhetorical knowledge than you think. After all, you've been writing and speaking all your life. But when you start becoming aware of this knowledge, it becomes more powerful, and you become a better writer. Throughout *The Curious Writer*, I'll encourage you to think rhetorically.

In the next few years of college, you'll be encountering unfamiliar writing situations, so learning to reflect on how each involves *rhetorical choices* will make you a much better communicator. (By the way, we also use this rhetorical knowledge to analyze how well someone else communicates, which is the focus of Chapter 2.) Learning to write well, then, isn't simply learning how to craft transitions, organize information, and follow grammatical rules—it's also learning to recognize that each writing situation asks you for something different. For example, in college writing situations, the basic rhetorical considerations, as in Figure 1.1, "Thinking rhetorically," may be expanded with questions such as these:

- What is the purpose of the assignment? To interpret or analyze? Synthesize or summarize? Argue or explore?

- What is the subject, and what does that imply about my approach? Are there certain ways of writing about topics in history, psychology, or literature that differ from writing about topics in biology, social science, or business?

- Am I writing for an expert audience or a general audience? For my instructor or my peers?

- What is the form or genre for this assignment, and what are its conventions? What kind of evidence should I use? How is it organized?

You won't always have control over all of these choices. In college, you'll get writing assignments that may supply you with a purpose: "Write an essay that compares the energy efficiency of solar panels with that of a conventional coal power plant." Sometimes the form isn't up to you: "Write a five-page argument paper." But even when you have such constraints, you still have a lot of rhetorical choices to make—things like: "Should I use the first person? What evidence do I need, and where should it come from?"

Each genre and medium imposes its own conditions on the writer. For example, my daughter's text message can't be more than 160 characters, and that

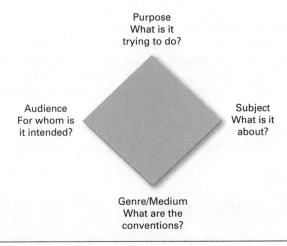

Purpose
What is it
trying to do?

Audience
For whom is
it intended?

Subject
What is it
about?

Genre/Medium
What are the
conventions?

Figure 1.1 Thinking rhetorically. Rhetorical choices involve four considerations: purpose, subject, audience, and genre/medium. Each consideration is associated with questions. For genre/medium, these include conditions and conventions regarding what you can say and especially how you say it. While all considerations have always been important in rhetorical thinking, genre and medium are especially critical to consider now that you may have alternatives to writing traditional term papers, including PowerPoints, podcasts, video, visuals, and a host of other multimodal approaches.

limitation inspired, among other things, a shorthand for composing that uses characters sparingly. Considering genre and medium is especially important now that the forms of communication have expanded radically, even in academia. You may write not just a term paper. You might do a PowerPoint, make a poster, build a web page, collaborate on a wiki, or produce a podcast.

Thinking about rhetorical contexts increases the chance that you'll make good choices when you solve problems as a writer, particularly in revision. Much like riding Berthoff's bike, in composing, writers usually think about purpose, audience, subject, and genre/medium all at once, drawing on their experience with similar writing situations.

A First Reflection on Your Writing Process

There is a process for doing almost anything—fixing a broken washing machine, learning how to play tennis, studying for the SAT, and, of course, writing. Why, then, do some English teachers seem to make such a big deal out of the writing process? Here's why:

- First, the process of writing, like any process that we do frequently, is not something that we think about.

- As a consequence, when we write, we tend to focus just on *what* and not on *how*, just on the product and not on the process. And then, when problems arise, we don't see many options for solving them—we get stuck and we get frustrated.

- If, however, we start to pay attention to how we write in a variety of situations, two things happen: We become aware of our old habits that don't always help and may actually hinder our success with writing. Second— and this is most important—we begin to understand that there are actually *choices* we can make when problems arise, and we become aware of what some of those are.

- In short, *the more we understand the writing process, the more control we get over it*. Getting control of the process means the product gets better.[1]

A Case Study

Here's an example of what I mean. Chauntain summarized her process this way: "Do one and be done." She always wrote her essays at the last minute and only wrote a single draft. She approached nearly every writing assignment the same way: Start with a thesis, and then develop five topic sentences that support the

---

[1]There is considerable research in learning theory that confirms these conclusions; in particular, so-called *metacognitive thinking*—the awareness of how you do things—increases the transfer of relevant knowledge from one situation to another. In other words, what you learn about how to do something in one situation gets more easily activated in another.

Inquiring into the Details

Organizing Your Computer Files

Avoid lots of headaches later on by working out a convention for naming files at the beginning of your course. One method might be the following:

- Genre (i.e., essay, exercise, letter, response, and so on)
- Title of document
- Version number
- Date

Using the underscore key, separate each element when naming your document. For example, *essay_importanceofwritingbadly_v2_2012-December-12*. A file name like this takes a little more time to compose, but it ultimately saves time by helping you locate documents more easily.

thesis, with three supporting details under each. This structure was a container into which she poured all her prose. Chauntain deliberated over every sentence, trying to make each one perfect, and as a result, she spent considerable time staring off into space searching for the right word or phrase. It was agony. The papers were almost always dull—she thought so too—and just as often she struggled to reach the required page length. Chauntain had no idea of any other way to write a school essay. As a matter of fact, she thought it was really the *only* way. So when she got an assignment in her economics class to write an essay in which she was to use economic principles to analyze a question that arose from a personal observation, Chauntain was bewildered. How should she start? Could she rely on her old standby structure—thesis, topic sentences, supporting details? She felt stuck.

Because she failed to see that she had choices related to both process and this particular writing situation, she also had no clue what those choices were. That's why we study process. It helps us solve problems such as these. And it must begin with a self-study of your own habits as a writer, identifying not just how you tend to do things, but the patterns of problems that might arise when you do them.

Thinking About Your Process

You will reflect on your writing and reading processes again and again throughout this book, so that by the end you may be able to tell the story of your processes and how you are changing them to produce better writing more efficiently. The reflective letter in your portfolio might be where you finally share that story in full. Now is a good time to begin telling yourself that story.

Inquiring into the Details

Portfolios

Why are portfolios—end-of-the-semester submissions of student work—so popular?

- They work from the assumption that you should perform better at the end of the semester because that's when you know the most.

- They create a powerful opportunity for student writers to reflect on what they've done and what they've learned.

- They provide students with some control over how to present what they've learned.

- Electronic portfolios, especially, allow students to incorporate multimodal genres— podcasts, PowerPoints, video, and so on.

- They promote revision. Because final evaluation of writing is often tentative until it is submitted in the portfolio at the end of the course, it can be considered work in progress until then.

What do you remember about your own journey as a writer both inside and outside of school? One of my earliest, most pleasant memories of writing is listening to the sound of the clacking of my father's old Royal typewriter in the room down the hall as I was going to sleep. I imagine him there now, in the small study that we called the "blue room," enveloped in a cloud of pipe smoke. It is likely that he was writing advertising copy back then, or perhaps a script for a commercial in which my mother, an actress, would appear. I loved the idea of writing then. The steady hammering of typewriter keys sounded effortless yet at the same time solid, significant. This all changed, I think, in the eighth grade when it seemed that writing was much more about following rules than tapping along to a lively dance of words.

Spend some time telling your own story about how your relationship to writing evolved.

When you get a writing assignment, your habit may be to compose carefully. This assignment, in contrast, is all about invention—about generating ideas.

Exercise 1.3

Literacy Narrative Collage

In your journal, create a collage of moments, memories, and reflections related to your experience with writing. *For each prompt, write fast for about four minutes. Keep your pen or fingers on the keyboard moving, and give yourself permission to write badly*. After you've responded to one prompt, skip a line and move on to the next one. Set aside about twenty minutes for this generating activity.

1. What is your earliest memory of writing? Tell the story.

2. We usually divide our experiences as writers into private writing and school writing, or writing we do by choice and writing we are required to do for a grade. Let's focus on school writing. Tell the story of a teacher, a class, an essay, an exam, or a moment that you consider a *turning point* in your understanding of yourself as a writer or your understanding of school writing.

3. Writing is part of the fabric of everyday life in the United States, and this is truer than ever with Internet communication. Describe the roles that writing plays in a typical day for you. How have these daily roles of writing changed in your lifetime so far?

4. What is the most successful (or least successful) thing you've ever written in or out of school? Tell the story.

Congratulations. You've made a mess. But I hope this collage of your experiences as a writer is an interesting mess, one that brought some little surprises. As you look at these four fragments of fastwriting, you might begin to sense a pattern. Is there a certain idea about yourself as a writer that seems to emerge in these various contexts? It's more likely that one, or perhaps two, of the prompts really took off for you, presenting trails you'd like to continue following. Or maybe nothing happened. For now, set your journal aside. You may return to this material if your instructor invites you to draft a longer narrative about your writing experiences, or you might find a place for some of this writing in your portfolio.

Now that you've spent some time telling a story of your background as a writer, use the following survey to pin down some of your habits and experiences related to school writing. The questions in the survey can help you develop a profile of your writing process and help you identify problems you might want to address by altering your process.

Exercise 1.4

What Is Your Process?

STEP ONE: Complete the Self-Evaluation Survey.

Self-Evaluation Survey

1. When you're given a school writing assignment, do you wait until the last minute to finish it?

    Always———Often———Sometimes———Rarely———Never

2. How often have you had the experience of learning something you didn't expect through writing about it?

      Very often———Fairly often———Sometimes———Rarely———Never

3. Do you generally plan out what you're going to write before you write it?

      Always———Often———Sometimes———Rarely———Never

4. *Prewriting* describes activities that some writers engage in before they begin a first draft. Prewriting might include such invention activities as freewriting or fastwriting, making lists, brainstorming or mapping, collecting information, browsing the web, talking to someone about the essay topic, reading up on it, or jotting down ideas in a notebook or journal. How much prewriting do you tend to do for the following types of assignments? Circle the appropriate answer.

■ A personal narrative:

      A great deal———Some———Very little———None———Haven't written one

■ A critical essay about a short story, novel, or poem:

      A great deal———Some———Very little———None———Haven't written one

■ A research paper:

      A great deal———Some———Very little———None———Haven't written one

■ An essay exam:

      A great deal———Some———Very little———None———Haven't written one

5. At what point(s) in writing an academic paper do you often find yourself getting stuck? Check all that apply.

❑ Getting started

❑ In the middle

❑ Finishing

❑ I never/rarely get stuck (go on to question 9)

❑ Other: _____

6. If you usually have problems getting started on a paper, which of the following do you often find hardest to do? Check all that apply. (If you don't have trouble getting started, go on to question 7.)

❑ Deciding on a topic

❑ Writing an introduction

❑ Finding a good place to write

❑ Figuring out exactly what I'm supposed to do for the assignment

❑ Finding a purpose or focus for the paper

❑ Finding the right tone

❑ Other: _____

7. If you usually get stuck in the middle of a paper, which of the following cause(s) the most problems? Check all that apply. (If writing in the middle of a paper isn't a problem for you, go on to question 8.)

❑ Keeping focused on the topic

❑ Finding enough information to meet page-length requirements

❑ Following my plan for how I want to write the paper

❑ Bringing in other research or points of view

❑ Organizing all my information

❑ Trying to avoid plagiarism

❑ Worrying about whether the paper meets the requirements of the assignment

❑ Worrying that the paper just isn't any good

❑ Messing with citations

❑ Other: _____

8. If you have difficulty finishing a paper, which of the following difficulties are typical for you? Check all that apply. (If finishing isn't a problem for you, go on to question 9.)

❑ Composing a last paragraph or conclusion

❑ Worrying that the paper doesn't meet the requirements of the assignment

❑ Worrying that the paper just isn't any good

❑ Trying to keep focused on the main idea or thesis

❑ Trying to avoid repeating myself

❑ Realizing I don't have enough information

❑ Dealing with the bibliography or citations

❑ Other: _____

9. Rank the following list of approaches to revision so that it reflects the strategies you use *most often to least often* when rewriting academic papers. Rank the items 1–6, with the strategy you use most often as a 1 and least often as a 6.

_____ I just tidy things up—editing sentences, checking spelling, looking for grammatical errors, fixing formatting, and performing other proofreading activities.

_____ I look for ways to reorganize existing information in the draft to make it more effective.

_____ I try to fill holes by adding more information.

_____ I do more research.

_____ I change the focus or even the main idea, rewriting sections, adding or removing information, and changing the order of things.

_____ I rarely do any revision.

10.   Finally, do you tend to impose a lot of conditions on when, where, or how you think you write most effectively? (For example, do you need a certain pen, do you always have to write on a computer, do you need to be in certain kinds of places, must it be quiet or noisy, do you write best under pressure?) Or can you write under a range of circumstances, with few or no conditions? Circle one.

Lots of conditions————Some————A few————No conditions

If you impose conditions on when, where, or how you write, list some of those conditions here:

1.

2.

3.

STEP TWO: In small groups, discuss the results of the survey. Begin by picking someone to tally the answers to each question. Post these on the board, a large sheet of paper, or a spreadsheet, so they can then be added up for the class. Analyze the results for your group. In particular, discuss the following questions:

- Are there patterns in the responses? Do most group members seem to answer certain questions in similar or different ways? Are there interesting contradictions?

- Based on these results, what "typical" habits or challenges do writers in your class seem to share?

- What struck you most?

Problem Solving in Your Writing Process

If you took the survey, you probably uncovered some problems with your writing process. The great news for those of us who struggle with certain aspects of writing—and who doesn't?—is that you can do something about it. As you identify the obstacles to doing better work, you can change the way you approach writing tasks. For instance, consider some of the more common problems students struggle with and some ideas about how *The Curious Writer* can help you with them.

Writing Problem	Possible Cause	A Solution
Consistently writes short. Often can't meet page requirements for assignments.	Writer works from scarcity. Begins the draft with too little information on the topic.	Focus on invention. Generate more material *before* you begin the draft, through research, fastwriting, etc. (see "Inquiring into the Details: Invention Strategies" on p. 25).
Dislikes revision, especially if it involves more than "tidying" things up.	Writer spends a great deal of time writing the first draft and trying to make it "perfect." Gets overcommitted to the initial approach to topic.	Write a fast draft and then do deeper revision. Attack the draft physically (see Revision Strategy 10.18 in Chapter 10).
Writer's block.	Internal critic is too harsh too early in the writing process. Often involves anxiety about audience.	Find a place where you can write badly without it feeling like a performance. A journal or notebook often works (see "Journals" on p. 7).
Dislikes open-ended assignments. Would rather be told what to write about.	Writer may be unused to valuing own thinking. Little experience with assignments in which writer must discover own purpose.	Use your own curiosity and questions to drive the process. Craft questions that are useful guides for exploration and promise discovery and learning (see "Starting with Questions, Not Answers" in this chapter).
Struggles with focus. Able to write a lot but can't seem to stay on topic.	Writer doesn't exploit key opportunities to look at writing critically, to evaluate and judge what she has generated.	Effectively combine invention with evaluation, generating with judging, by using a process that makes room for both as you write (see "The Nature of the Writing Process" below).

The Nature of the Writing Process

Earlier you saw Chauntain's writing process. Here was my writing process when I was in school:

1. Get the assignment. Find out when it is due and how long it is supposed to be.
2. Wait until the night before it is due and get started.
3. Stare off into space.
4. Eat ice cream.
5. Write a sketchy outline.

6. Write a sentence; then cross it out.
7. Stare off into space.
8. Write another sentence, and then squeeze out a few more.
9. Think about Lori Jo Flink, and then stare off into space.
10. Write a paragraph. Feel relief and disgust.

Suspending judgment feels freer, exploratory... Making judgments shifts the writer into an analytical mode.

I would get the work done eventually, but the process was agonizing and the product mediocre. What did I conclude from this back then? That I wasn't good at writing, which was no big surprise because I pretty much hated it. Something happened to me to change that view, of course, because you hold my book in your hands. I came to understand the problems in my writing process: I looked on writing as a straight march forward from beginning to end, one where I had to wait for something to come into my head and then try to get it down. At all costs, I avoided things like new ideas or other ways of seeing a topic—anything that might get in the way of the drive to the conclusion. If I thought about anything, it was trying to find the "perfect" way of saying things or worrying about whether I was faithfully following a certain structure. I rarely learned anything from my writing. I certainly never expected I should.

The Writing Process as Recursive and Flexible

But this straight march isn't the way experienced writers work at all. The writing process isn't a linear trajectory, but a looping, recursive process—one that encourages *thinking*, not simply recording the thoughts that you already have. Writing doesn't involve a series of steps that you must follow in every situation; on the contrary:

- The writing process is *recursive*, a much messier zigzag between collecting information and focusing on it, exploring things and thinking about them, writing and rewriting, reviewing and rearranging, and so on. For example, invention strategies are useful at many points in the writing process.
- The process is *flexible* and always influenced by the writing situation. For instance, experienced writers have a keen sense of audience, and they use this to cue their choices about a change in tone or whether an example might help clarify a point. These are exactly the kinds of adjustments you make in social situations all the time.

A System for Using Writing to Think

What do I mean when I say the writing process encourages thinking? Usually, when we imagine someone who is "deep in thought," we see them staring off into space with a furrowed brow, chin nested in one hand. They are not writing. They may be thinking about what they're *going* to write, but in the meantime the cursor is parked

Inquiring into the Details

Invention Strategies

Invention is a term from rhetoric that means the act of generating ideas. While we typically think of *rhetoric* as something vaguely dishonest and often associated with politics, it's actually a several-thousand-year-old body of knowledge about speaking and writing well. Invention is a key element in rhetoric. It can occur at any time during the writing process, not just at the beginning in the "prewriting" stage. Some useful invention strategies include:

- **Fastwriting:** The emphasis is on speed, not correctness. Don't compose, don't think about what you want to say before you say it. Instead, let the writing lead, helping you discover what you think.

- **Listing:** Fast lists can help you generate lots of information quickly. They are often in code, with words and phrases that have meaning only for you. Let your lists grow in waves—think of two or three items and then pause until the next few items rush in.

- **Clustering:** This nonlinear method of generating information, also called *mapping*, relies on *webs* and often free association of ideas or information. Begin with a core word, phrase, or concept at the center of a page, and build branches off it. Follow each branch until it dies out, return to the core, and build another. (For an example, see p. 86.)

- **Questioning:** Questions are to ideas what knives are to onions. They help you cut through to the less obvious insights and perspectives, revealing layers of possible meanings, interpretations, and ways of understanding. Asking questions complicates things but rewards you with new discoveries.

- **Conversing:** Conversing is fastwriting with the mouth. When we talk, especially to someone we trust, we work out what we think and feel about things. We listen to what we say, but we also invite a response, which leads us to new insights.

- **Researching:** This is a kind of conversation, too. We listen and respond to other voices that have said something, or will say something if asked, about topics that interest us. Reading and interviewing are not simply things you do when you write a research paper, but activities to use whenever you have questions you can't answer on your own.

- **Observing:** When we look closely at anything, we see what we didn't notice at first. Careful observation of people, objects, experiments, images, and so on generates specific information that leads to informed judgments.

on the computer screen or the pen rests on the desk. Thinking like this is good—I do it all the time. But imagine if you also make thought external by following your thinking on paper or screen and not just in your head. Here is some of what happens:

- You have a record of what you've thought that you can return to again and again.
- As you *see* what you've just said, you discover something else to say.
- Because the process of thinking through writing is slower than thinking in your head, you think differently.
- Because externalizing thought takes mental effort, you are more immersed in thought, creating what one theorist called a state of "flow."

As I've already mentioned, thinking through writing is most productive when you suspend judgment, reining in your internal critic. You may actually do some pretty good thinking with some pretty bad writing.

Using writing as a way of thinking is even more powerful if there is a *system* for doing it that reliably produces insight. One method, which we could call a *dialectical system*, exploits two different kinds of thinking—one creative and the other critical, one wide open and the other more closed. So far in this chapter, we've focused on the creative side, the generating activities I've called "writing badly," which restrain your internal critic. But you need that critical side. You need it to make sense of things, to evaluate what's significant and what's not, to help you figure out what you might be trying to say. If you use both kinds of thinking, "dialectically" moving back and forth from one to the other, then you're using a method that is at the heart of the process you'll use throughout *The Curious Writer*.[2] Try the next exercise to see how this might work for you.

Exercise 1.5

Two Kinds of Thinking

Let's return to the subject you began writing about in Exercise 1.3—your experiences as a writer—but focus on something that was probably part of your response to the third prompt in that exercise: your experience with writing technology.

Using Creative Thinking

STEP ONE: What are your earliest memories of using a computer for writing? In your journal or on the computer, begin by telling the story and then let the writing lead from there. Keep your pen or the cursor moving, and allow yourself to write badly.

---

[2]For Greek philosophers such as Plato, *dialectic* was a way of arriving at truth through back-and-forth conversation between two people who were open to changing their minds. Similarly, the process of writing and thinking I propose here is a back and forth between two parts of yourself—each receptive to the other—in an effort to discover your own "truths," ideas, and insights.

STEP TWO: Brainstorm a list of words or phrases that you associate with the word *literate* or *literacy*.

Reread what you just wrote in steps 1 and 2, underlining things that surprise you or that seem significant or interesting to you. Skip a line and move on to step 3.

Using Critical Thinking

STEP THREE: Choose one of the following sentence frames as a starting point. Complete the sentence and then develop it as a paragraph. This time, compose each sentence while thinking about what you want to say before you say it and trying to say it as well as you can.

> *What I understand now about my experiences with writing on computers that I didn't understand when I started out is _____.*
>
> *When they think about writing with computers, most people think _____, but my experience was _____.*
>
> *The most important thing I had to discover before I considered myself "computer literate" was _____.*

Reflecting

If you're like most people, then the parts of this exercise where you creatively generated material felt different than the part where you judged as you wrote. But *how* were they different? How would you distinguish between the experience of generating and judging? Talk about this or write about it in your journal.

A Writing Process That Harnesses Two Currents of Thought

The two parts of Exercise 1.5 involving creative and critical thinking were designed to show you the difference between the two and also to simulate the shift between them, the shift from suspending judgments to making judgments—something I referred to as "dialectical" thinking. In the first two steps, you spent some time fastwriting without much critical interference, trying to generate some information from your own experience. In the third step, which began with "seed" sentences that forced you into a more reflective, analytical mode, you were encouraged to look for patterns of meaning in what you generated.

As you probably noticed, these two distinct ways of thinking each have advantages for the writer:

- *Suspending judgment* feels freer, is exploratory, and may spark emotion.
- *Making judgments* shifts the writer into an analytical mode, one that might lower the temperature, allowing writers to see their initial explorations with less feeling and more understanding.

Thus, creative thinking creates the conditions for discovery—new insights or ways of seeing—while critical thinking helps writers refine their discoveries and focus on the most significant of them.

The Sea and the Mountain. Here's another way to conceptualize creative and critical thinking (see Figure 1.2):

- When you write creatively, you plunge into the sea of information. You don't swim in one direction, but eagerly explore in all directions, including the depths.

- When you write critically, you emerge from the water to find a vantage point—a mountain—from which to see where you've swum. From the mountain, you are able to see patterns that aren't visible from the water. You are able to make judgments about what you encountered there: What's significant? What isn't? Why?

The key is not to stay on the mountain. Instead, you take the patterns you saw and the judgments you made and plunge back into the sea, this time with a stronger

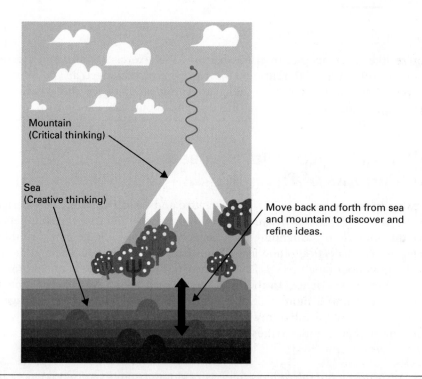

Mountain
(Critical thinking)

Sea
(Creative thinking)

Move back and forth from sea and mountain to discover and refine ideas.

Figure 1.2 Generating insight using critical and creative thinking. Thinking to inquire is like the movement back and forth from the sea of information to the mountain of reflection. In one you explore, and on the other you evaluate. Insight develops when you continually move back and forth; as you refine your ideas, when in the sea, you swim in ever smaller circles with a stronger sense of purpose.

sense of purpose. You're clearer about what you want to know and where you need to swim to find it. This back and forth between mountain and sea continues until you've discovered what you want to say. In fact, you made just this sort of movement in Exercise 1.2 and then in Exercise 1.5 when you moved from generating to judging. It is a process of induction and deduction, working upwards from specifics to infer ideas, and then taking those ideas and testing them against specifics.

Figure 1.3 lists yet other ways in which you can visualize the movement between creative and critical thinking. In narrative writing, for instance, creative thinking helps you generate information about *what happened*, while critical thinking may lead you to insights about *what happens*. Likewise, in research writing, investigators often move back and forth between their *observations of* things and their *ideas about* them.

As you work through the book, you'll find it easier to shift between contrasting modes of thought—from collecting to focusing, from generating to judging, from showing to telling, from exploring to reflecting, from believing to doubting, from playing to evaluating. In short, you'll become better able to balance creative and critical thinking. You'll know when it's useful to open up the process of thinking to explore and when it's necessary to work at making sense of what you've discovered.

Answering the *So What?* Question. An important function on the critical thinking side is to make sure you can answer the one question you must answer when writing for an audience:

So what?

Figure 1.3   Alternating currents of thought. When writers alternate between creative and critical thinking, they move back and forth between two opposing modes of thought—the creative and the critical. One seems playful and the other judgmental; one feels open ended and the other more closed. Activities such as fastwriting and brainstorming promote one mode of thought, and careful composing and reflection promote the other.

So what? can be a pretty harsh question, and I find that some students tend to ask it too soon in the writing process, before they've fully explored their topic. A danger is that this can lead to a feeling of frustration. You may, for example, have found yourself high and dry if you've tried to reflect on possible meanings of a moment you've written about for only eight minutes. Another danger is that the writer is tempted to seize on the first convenient idea or thesis that comes along. This abruptly ends the process of inquiry before the writer has had a chance to explore.

When you can't come up with an answer to *So what?* the solution is usually to generate more information.

A Writing Process Driven by Questions

The inquiry approach is grounded in the idea that the writing process depends, more than anything else, on finding good questions to address.

I recently visited teachers in Laredo, Texas, and I told them that with a good question even the most boring topic can become interesting. I would prove it, I said, and picked up a lemon that was sitting on a table and asked everyone, in turn, to ask a question about the lemon or about lemons. Twenty minutes later, we generated sixty questions. In the process, we began to wonder how the scent of lemons came to be associated with cleanliness. We wondered why lemons appeared so often in wartime British literature. We wondered why the lime and not the lemon is celebrated in local Hispanic culture. We wondered a lot of interesting things that we never expected to wonder about, because a lemon is ordinary. Questions can make the familiar world we inhabit yield to wonder.

The point is this: *There are no boring topics—just wrong questions.*

But what are good inquiry questions? Obviously, for a question to be good, you have to be interested in it. Furthermore, others must also have a stake in the answer, because you'll be sharing what you learn.

Usually, when we investigate something we don't know much about, we start by asking informational questions. Say you're interested in the Disney Corporation's sustainability projects. You first need to know what those are. You might search online and read about Disney's commitment to recycling or to energy efficiency. This is basic background information—facts about what has already been said about a topic. But in college writing, you're usually not writing a report or a summary of what's known about a topic. Just explaining what Disney is doing to reduce emissions isn't enough. You have to *do* something with that information. This involves that critical mind that we talked about earlier, one that asks you to make judgments.

Different types of questions lead to different kinds of judgments. And it's landing on the appropriate type of question for your project that will launch you into meaningful inquiry. These question types include the following:

- *Value questions:* Is it good or bad? Useful or useless?
- *Relationship questions:* Are they similar or dissimilar? Is there a cause and effect? What's the connection?

- *Policy questions:* What should be done?
- *Interpretation questions:* What might it mean?
- *Hypothesis questions:* What is the best explanation?
- *Claim questions:* Are the assertions valid? What is most persuasive?

You can apply these kinds of questions to nearly any topic, depending what interests you about it. For example, in Figure 1.4 I tried to imagine how someone exploring Disney's sustainability programs might use each of these question types. With a little factual background, it isn't hard to start framing possible inquiry questions that can really steer your project in different—and possibly interesting—directions.

A good question not only lights your way into a subject, but may also illuminate what form you could use to share your discoveries. Certain kinds of writing—reviews, critical essays, personal essays, and so on—are often associated with certain types of questions, as you can see in Figure 1.4. In Part 2 of *The Curious Writer*, which features a range of inquiry projects from the personal essay to the research essay, you'll see how certain questions naturally guide you towards certain kinds of writing.

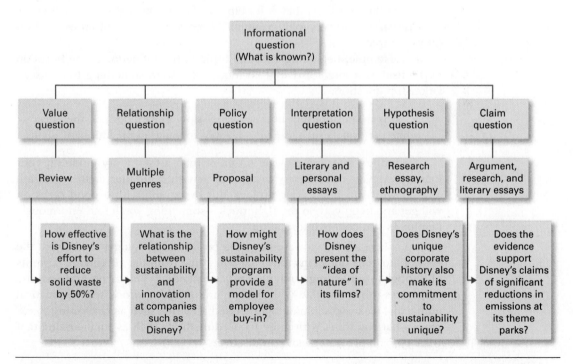

Figure 1.4 Categories of inquiry questions. The inquiry process often begins with informational questions: What is already known about this? As writers learn more about their topics, they refine their questions so that they are more likely to lead to analysis or argument rather than mere report. Some of these questions are associated with certain kinds of writing that are covered in this book.

Questioning, Generating, and Judging: A Strategy for Inquiry

If you combine the power of good questions with the back-and-forth process of writing creatively and critically, you have a strategy of inquiry that you can use for every assignment in this book:

- Typically, you begin exploring a subject, sometimes generating some initial thoughts through fastwriting, listing, or other invention methods.

- Like landscape shots in photography, subjects cover a huge amount of ground. You need to narrow your subject and eventually arrive at a yet narrower topic, or some *part* of the landscape to look at more closely.

   As an example, take popular music. That's a huge subject. But as you write and read about it a little, you may begin to see that you're most interested in the blues, and especially in its influence on American popular music. This last might seem promising as a general topic.

- With a tentative topic in hand, you are searching for a few inquiry questions about your topic that both interest you and will sustain your project. These are the questions that will help you focus your topic, that will guide your research, and that may eventually become the heart of an essay draft on your topic.

   For example, beginning with the topic of the influence of the blues on pop music, you might arrive at an inquiry question something like this relationship question:

   > What is the relationship between Mississippi delta blues and the music of white performers such as Elvis who were popular in the fifties and sixties?

   An inquiry question may be no more than a temporary guide on your journey. As you continue to write, you may find another, better question around which to build your project. But beginning with a good question will get and keep you on the right track—something you'll find enormously helpful as you collect information.

- As you collect information, some of the best insights you get about what the answers to your questions might be will come from the alternating currents of thought—generating and judging, suspending judgment and making judgments—that energize your writing and thinking processes. In practical terms, this means combining open-ended methods such as fastwriting to explore what you think with more focused methods such as summarizing that will help you evaluate what you discover.

Most of all, this inquiry strategy uses questions to direct your attention to what's relevant and what's not. Imagine that an inquiry question is a flint that gives off sparks when it strikes potentially meaningful information, whether that information comes from personal experiences or research. These sparks are the things that will light your way to discoveries about your topic.

The inquiry strategy I'm proposing should work with nearly any topic. Let's try one in Exercise 1.6.

Exercise 1.6

A Mini Inquiry Project: Cell Phone Culture

The alternating currents of thought—generating and judging, exploring and evaluating, opening up and focusing, mountain and sea—can be put to work in any situation where you want to figure out what you think. Writing is a key part of the system. In this exercise, I'll guide you to think one way and then another. Later, you may find you do this on your own without thinking about it. But for now, let me guide you.

More than 90 percent of us now have cell phones, and according to one study, about a third of people aged eighteen to twenty-nine say that they "couldn't live without" them. Cell phones make us feel safer, and of course they're an enormous convenience. But they've also introduced new annoyances into modern life, like the "halfalogue," the distracting experience of being subjected to one half of a stranger's conversation with someone on their cell phone. It's a technology that is fundamentally changing our culture—our sense of community and connection, our identities, the way we spend our time. But how? Try exploring that question for yourself, to see if you can discover what *you* find interesting about the topic.

Invention: Generating

STEP ONE: Let's first take a dip in the sea of information. Recent research on "cell phone addiction" suggests that, as with Internet addiction, "overuse" of the technology can result in anxiety, depression, irritability, and antisocial behavior. This research also suggests that college students are particularly vulnerable to cell phone addiction. One survey to determine whether someone is cell phone addicted asks some of the following questions:

- Do you feel preoccupied about possible calls or messages on your mobile phone, and do you think about it when your cell is off?
- How often do you anticipate your next use of the cell phone?
- How often do you become angry and/or start to shout if someone interrupts you when you're talking on a cell phone?
- Do you use a cell to escape from your problems?

Start by exploring your reaction to this list in a fastwrite in your journal, print or digital. Write for at least three minutes, but write longer if you can. What do you make of the whole idea of "cell phone addiction"? What does this make you think about? And then what? And then?

Judging

STEP TWO: Reread your fastwrite, underlining anything that you find interesting, surprising, or possibly significant. Pay particular attention to anything that might have surprised you. Then thoughtfully finish the following sentence.

> *One interesting question that this raises for me is: _____ ?*

Generating

STEP THREE: Focus on the question you came up with in step 2. Return to the sea and write about specific *observations, stories, people, situations, or scenes* that come to mind when you consider the question you posed. Don't hesitate to explore other questions as they arise as well. Let the writing lead. Write fast for *at least* another three minutes without stopping.

Judging

STEP FOUR: Review what you just wrote, then thoughtfully complete the following sentence, and then follow that first sentence for as long as you can compose here, rather than fastwriting, thinking about what you're going to say before you say it.

> *So far, one thing I seem to be saying is that we . . .*

Finding a Question

STEP FIVE: You haven't generated much writing on cell phone culture yet, but if you've written for ten minutes or so, you should have enough information to take a stab at writing a tentative inquiry question. Using the question categories in Figure 1.4, try to draft a question about cell phones, cell phone culture, cell phone addiction, or any other topic suggested by your writing. Remember, the question should be one of the following:

- A value question: Is it any good?
- A policy question: What should be done?
- A hypothesis question: What is the best explanation?
- A relationship question: What is the relationship between _____ and _____?
- An interpretation question: What might it mean?
- A claim question: What does the evidence seem to support?

Reflecting on the Process

STEP SIX: In your journal, or on an online discussion board, answer the following questions about what you've just done.

1. What, if anything, do I understand now that I didn't before?
2. What most surprised me?
3. What's the most important thing I take from this?

Reflective Inquiry About Your Writing

I should be a really good guitar player. I've played since I was eleven. I'm okay. But among my other problems was a lousy sense of rhythm—at least until recently, when I began playing with my friend Richard, who can play skillfully in all the ways I can't. How did I solve the rhythm problem by playing with Richard? What exactly did I learn to do that helped me adjust my strum so I could provide passably good backup to Richard's leads?

To get better at a process, we need to ask questions about it. And to answer these questions, we have to have three things:

1. Some knowledge of how the process is done or how it might be done
2. The language to define the problem
3. Some ideas about possible solutions

Since the beginning of this chapter, I've argued that taking the time to reflect on your knowledge and think about writing, and paying attention to how you use this knowledge and thinking as you write, is well worth the effort. It will speed up your learning, help you to adapt more easily in a range of writing situations, and make writing less frustrating when things go wrong. Experts call this "reflective inquiry," and they observe that experienced professionals in many fields often do this kind of thinking. In a way, reflective inquiry is thinking *about* thinking. It isn't easy. But it is also one of the most important ways in which we *transfer* what we know from one situation to another. Reflective thinking is key to making the most of your learning in this writing course.

You've tried your hand at reflective inquiry in several exercises so far, including the previous one on "cell phone culture." Let's get a little more practice with it before we move on.

Exercise 1.7

Scenes of Writing

Think about the writing and thinking you've done about yourself as a writer in this chapter. Review your notes from all of the exercises you tried that asked you to reflect on that (Exercise 1.1, your beliefs about writing; Exercise 1.3, your literacy collage; and Exercise 1.4, the survey on your writing process). Now imagine the kind of writer *you would like to be*.

Scene 1

A month ago, you got a writing assignment in your philosophy course: a twelve-page paper that explores some aspect of Plato's dialogues. It's the night before the paper is due. Describe the scene. What are you doing? Where? What's happening? What are you thinking? If you can, make use of the various types of writing that can convey scene: description, narration, dialogue.

Scene 2

Rewrite scene 1. This time, script it as you *wish* it would look.

Finally, imagine that each scene is the opening of a film. What would they be titled?

Reflective Inquiry

Think about the terms we've used in this chapter to talk about the writing process—terms such as these:

- *Prewriting*
- *Revision*
- *Focusing*
- *Critical and creative thinking*
- *Invention*
- *Reflection*
- *Exploration*
- *Inquiry questions*
- *Habits of mind*
- *Suspending judgment*
- *Genre*
- *Alternating currents of thought*
- *Writing situation*
- *Rhetorical choices*

Draft a 200- to 250-word essay or discussion-board post about your own writing process—past, present, or future—that uses as much of the terminology of the writing process as you find relevant and useful to your essay or post.

Using What You Have Learned

Remember the learning goals at the beginning of the chapter?

1. **Reflect on and revise your beliefs about yourself as a writer.** In this chapter, you started to tell yourself the story of yourself as a writer. Like any good story, you tell it for a reason: What does it tell you about the kind of writer you think you've been? Is that the writer who will work for you now as you deal with a wider range of writing situations in college and out of college? The great thing is that if your beliefs about yourself are holding you back, you can change them. And you will as you work your way through this book. Reflect continuously on what you do as a writer that works for you (and on what you do that doesn't). This isn't just an academic exercise; it is knowledge that you can put to work for you to help solve writing problems.

2. **Understand what kinds of questions will sustain inquiry into any subject.** Academic inquiry is driven by questions that will keep you thinking. But what kinds of questions will sustain your investigation of a subject over time? In this chapter, you learned how you can start with an informational question— What is known about a topic?—and refine that into a question that will help you discover what you want to say. You'll see later how these questions often lead to certain kinds of writing. The ability to understand what kinds of questions will guide your writing and thinking is something that you can draw on in nearly every college class.

3. **Practice a method of writing and thinking that will help you generate ideas.** Throughout *The Curious Writer*, you'll use the technique you were introduced to here: using your creative mind to explore and generate material, and your critical mind to narrow down and evaluate what you've generated. As you get more practice with this method, you'll find that you may not even think about it, as you shift naturally from withholding judgment to making judgments. If this works for you, you'll find that it's a powerful way to use writing to discover what you think in nearly any writing situation when you're trying to figure that out.

4. **Apply rhetorical knowledge to make choices in specific writing situations.** In this book, *rhetoric* is never a bad word. You learned here that the term doesn't describe someone who blows smoke in an attempt to deceive, but rather represents a way of thinking about how to communicate effectively. Rhetoric is a system for analyzing writing situations by looking at purpose, audience, and genre, so that you can see more clearly what your choices are when you're composing any kind of text. You already have considerable rhetorical understanding. Anyone with any skill in social situations does. But as you become more conscious of rhetorical analysis, you'll discover how fundamental it is to speaking and writing well.

Reading to inquire opens a conversation with a text in which the words on the page are only part of the dialogue between the author and the reader.

Reading as Inquiry

Learning Objectives

In this chapter, you'll learn to

2.1 Apply reading purposes relevant to reading in college.

2.2 Examine your existing beliefs about reading and how they might be obstacles to reading effectively.

2.3 Recognize reading situations and the choices about approaches to reading they imply.

2.4 Understand the special demands of reading to write and practice doing it.

2.5 Understand some conventions of academic writing and recognize them in texts.

You've been reading all of your life. Why read a chapter on the subject, especially in a book about writing? Well, I'm going to argue that reading in college is different than much of the reading you've done in school up until now. To start with, the *kinds* of reading, or *genres*, you'll encounter will range widely from poems to journal articles with pretty-dense academic prose. You'll also be reading subjects about which you may have very little prior knowledge. It's hard to overstate what a difference this makes in your ability to understand what you read and use it in your writing. The graphic on this page is a sort of symbolic representation of this difference. When readers know a lot about a subject, they have mental categories and hierarchies for that subject—slots into which the new information they read is organized—which makes it easier for them to retrieve and use the information later in their writing. In contrast, when readers don't know much about the subject of their reading—and that's often the case in undergraduate inquiry-based projects—they don't know what to make of what they're reading. We can picture their mental process as a scrambled struggle to simply understand the text. Going on to actually *use* the information in their writing will be an entirely different, and much bigger, problem. You probably know these situations, and they don't feel good. You're bored or frustrated with what you're reading. You can't focus. All you want to do is watch *Jersey Shore* on TV, and you actually hate that program.

An obvious solution to this problem is to develop some knowledge about a topic so you can read with more understanding. But there are other strategies, too, that can help you read—and use—difficult texts in unfamiliar genres, and I'll introduce you to them in this chapter. They include the following:

- *Be clear about your goals in reading a text.*

- *Use questions to drive the process.* In reading to inquire, I think there are four types of questions that can direct your attention as you read: exploring, explaining, evaluating, and reflecting questions.

- *See a text in its rhetorical context.* In other words, you can work more effectively with any kind of reading if you can see the kind of work its author *intended* it to do.

- *Understand that reading is a process.* The more you reflect on how you do it, including in different situations, the more control you get over the process.

- *Write as you read.* You can apply creative and critical thinking to generating insight about texts, too, through something such as a double-entry journal (described further on in this chapter).

- *Understand the features of academic discourse.* Knowing what to look out for will help you understand what you're reading.

Purposes for Academic Reading

2.1

Apply reading purposes relevant to reading in college.

Why read? We pick up a book for pleasure, read a news website for information, and so on. But I'd like to be more specific. What are the purposes for reading in college? First imagine some typical contexts for academic reading. You might, for example,

- Read a textbook to acquire knowledge about a subject. You may be required to demonstrate what you've learned on a test or in a paper.

- Read a textbook (such as this one?) that is a guide to a process. You use it to help you *do* something—write, perform an experiment, design a website.

- Read a journal article or short story closely, to analyze the arguments of the article or interpret the meaning of the story.

- Read material you have found online, to see how you might use information in your own writing or to prepare a presentation.

Each of these reading situations involves multiple purposes, and in each case one or two purposes is especially important. Although reading is a cognitively complex thing, I'd propose that the purposes of academic reading boil down to four—to *explore*, *explain*, *evaluate*, and *reflect*.

Imagine that each purpose involves asking a text different kinds of questions. We don't typically start reading with questions in mind. I know when I was an undergraduate, the question I usually had when I was reading a textbook was (aside from "When will I be done so I can go play the guitar?") "Will this be on the test?" On my really deep thinking days, I might read an assigned article in, say, my environmental studies class and wonder, "Do I agree or disagree with this?" These are reasonable questions. But they aren't very good guides for reading well. The research on reading says that the best readers have conscious goals when they read. These can expressed as questions. Here, then, are some general questions that can express the different purposes. Notice that you can ask these questions about both the text and parts of the text.

> Reading with the spirit of inquiry turns books, essays, and articles into one side of a dialogue that you're having with an author.

Purpose	Some Examples of Readers' Questions
Explore	Why could I learn from this? What does this make me think?
Explain	What do I understand this to be saying?
Evaluate	Is this persuasive? How do I interpret this?
Reflect	How is this put together? What do I notice about how I'm thinking about this?

Each of these questions will lead you to read the same text in a different way. In using the purposes and questions, keep in mind that we often have more than one main purpose for reading a text. For example, when we read a biology textbook to learn things about cell structure for a test in two weeks, we will read it to explore *and* explain. When we have to analyze a website as a source for an academic paper, we have to make a judgment about whether it has persuasive content (evaluate) *and* think about how it's designed to be persuasive (reflect).

But to demonstrate how each of these purposes might change the way you read a text, we'll try to apply each of them separately in the following exercise.

Exercise 2.1

Using the Four Purposes for Academic Reading

Every year, the *Chronicle of Higher Education* publishes data about last year's college undergraduates. Here's a table (Figure 2.1) from that report that describes students' employment levels outside of school. Read the table using the four purposes for reading—exploring, explaining, evaluating, and reflecting—one at a time.

Percentage of college students age 16 to 24 who were employed, by hours worked per week, October 2009				
	Full-time students		Part-time students	
	Worked 20 or more hours	Worked less than 20 hours	Worked 20 or more hours	Worked less than 20 hours
All undergraduates	23%	16%	62%	11%
Female	25%	18%	64%	12%
Male	21%	13%	59%	10%
Hispanic	27%	10%	60%	12%
White	24%	19%	63%	13%
Black	20%	9%	64%	n/a
Asian	12%*	9%	n/a	n/a
By type of Institution attended:				
Public 2-year	28%	16%	59%	11%
Public 4-year	24%	15%	63%	13%
Private 4-year	13%	20%	80%	n/a
* Large margin of error				
Note: The designation "n/a" means no figures were provided because statistical standards were not met. For that reason, no figures were provided for American Indians or Pacific Islanders.				
Source: Census Bureau				

Figure 2.1   Employment patterns for college undergraduates

Explore

STEP ONE: First just figure out what you make of this information. Tables, like fiction, tell a story that is implied. What are some of the stories this table seems to be telling? Make a list of these in your journal. Some inferences are probably obvious. For example, part-time students clearly work more than full-time students. No surprise there. Work towards teasing out some of the less obvious implications, especially those that you find surprising. When you're done, look at your list of inferences. What questions do these raise? For example, private college students who are full-time clearly worked less than full-time students enrolled in public schools. And yet, if they attend part-time, students enrolled at private colleges work *far more than* part-time students at public institutions. Why? What might explain this?

Explain

STEP TWO: Turn your list from step 1 into a fat paragraph that summarizes what you think are the story lines in this table. What are the things it seems to be saying?

Evaluate

STEP THREE: Based on your reading of the data in the table, make a one-sentence assertion about what you think is *the most significant finding*. Write this down in your journal.

Reflect

STEP FOUR: Statistical tables are inevitably selective on what data to include. They also group information into categories that make the data easier to understand but may obscure other important results. In this table, students' employment was categorized by students who work more or less than 20 hours. Does this seem sensible to you? Make a case for or against using that distinction.

In class, or on the online discussion board, talk about your experience with reading for each of these four purposes.

- Which step of the exercise was hardest for you?
- With which of these purposes do you typically read texts in school? Which are new to you?
- How did each reading purpose change the focus of your reading?

We always have a purpose for reading something. We rarely think about this purpose. In this section, I've tried to convince you that you'll read much more skillfully and efficiently—particularly in college—when you do consider *why* you're reading something. The advantages of this awareness are huge: You'll know what to look for in a text that's relevant to the task. You'll know what questions to ask yourself to evaluate what you're reading. And you'll know what you might use from a text in your own writing. There's another thing that will help, too. Reading, like writing, is something you've done much of your life, and you've developed habits and beliefs that govern how you approach reading. These can help you or they can hurt you. But you can't determine that until you know what they are.

Beliefs About Reading

2.2

Examine your existing beliefs about reading and how they might be obstacles to reading effectively.

You have theories about reading much like you have theories about writing—including beliefs about what makes a "good" reader and about yourself as a reader. They're not beliefs you're aware of, probably, but they profoundly affect how you read everything you read. Through an exercise that gets you thinking a little about your own literacy history, let's start to tease some of these beliefs out into the open so you can get a look at them.

Exercise 2.2

A Reader's Memoir

Generating

STEP ONE: There is considerable evidence that attitudes about reading are heavily influenced by how reading is viewed at home. Were there books around when you were growing up? Did you parents encourage you to read? Did they read? Fastwrite for five minutes about your memories of reading as a child in your home. Describe what you remember, and try to be as specific as possible.

Judging

STEP TWO: Speculate about the beliefs these early experiences with reading might have encouraged. In your journal, compose an answer to this inquiry question: *What is the relationship between my early reading experiences at home and my current beliefs about reading?*

Generating

STEP THREE: Now think about your reading experiences in school up until now. Fastwrite for five minutes, telling stories about your experiences with particular books or teachers, especially those that might have influenced the way you think of reading and of yourself as a reader.

Judging

STEP FOUR: As before, try to summarize how these experiences in school might have influenced how you view yourself as a reader now. Answer this question: *What is the relationship between my experiences reading in school and my current beliefs about reading and myself as a reader?*

One Common Belief That Is an Obstacle

I hope that Exercise 2.2 revealed some of the beliefs that shape how you feel about reading. When I wrote about my memories of reading at home, I realized that I had been lucky to grow up in a family that celebrated reading but that I had preferred to "read" television instead of a book. I can see now how this made me a reluctant reader who lacked confidence in his reading ability. When I wrote about my memories of academic reading, I immediately remembered—with revulsion—tanking on the reading portion of the SAT, and I realized that for years I'd thought the only purpose of reading in school was to say back what it said in a test or a paper.

My belief about school reading is a common one, and for good reason. Most reading instruction seems to focus on comprehension—you know, the SAT- or ACT-inspired kind of situation in which you are asked to read something and then explain what it means. This often becomes an exercise in recall and vocabulary, an analytical challenge in only the most general way. Essentially, you train yourself to distinguish between specifics and generalities and to loosely follow the author's reasoning. In English classes, sometimes we are asked to perform a similar exercise with stories or poems—what is the theme, or what does it mean?

> Only by understanding how we read in certain situations can we acquire more control over what we get out of the reading experience.

Instruction and assignments such as these encourage students to see reading as an archaeological expedition where they must dig for hidden meaning. The "right" answers to the questions are in the text, like a buried bone; you just have to find them. The trouble with this approach is the belief that it tends to foster, which is that *all meaning resides in the text and the reader's job is merely to find it*. This belief limits the reader's interaction with the text. If meaning is fixed within the text, embedded like a bone in antediluvian mud, then all the reader has to do is dig. Digging isn't a bad thing, but reading can be so much more than laboring at the shovel and sifting through dirt.

Reading Situations and Rhetorical Choices

This chapter began with a list of typical reading situations you might encounter as an undergraduate. You read a textbook to acquire information for a test. You mine an article for material to put in a paper or analyze a short story to interpret its theme, and so on. In each of these situations, you're going to make choices about *how* you read that text. Usually, these choices are governed by habit. This is the way you *always* read a textbook or a short story.

2.3
Recognize reading situations and the choices about approaches to reading they imply.

I'm going to try to convince you to make these choices differently. First, they should be conscious choices. For example, earlier we talked about purpose-directed reading. To read by asking questions based on your purpose is to make conscious choices.

Recall from Chapter 1 that to write effectively in a writing situation, you need to make appropriate rhetorical choices and that one of the considerations these are based on is your writing purpose. Similarly, in a reading situation, to read effectively you make choices based in part on your reading purpose.

When you're reading for a writing assignment, your purpose for reading basically has already been determined. For example, you might get an assignment like this in an English class:

■ *Closely read and **explicate** the poem by Mary Oliver.*

Or perhaps you get an assignment like this in a marketing class:

■ *Find and read company websites for mission statements and **explain** how companies distinguish between goals and objectives.*

In each of these situations, what you need to do is to start by *reading the assignment rhetorically*, to make sure you understand your purpose for reading. The main clue is usually the verb: *explicate, explain, argue, summarize, interpret, analyze,* and so on. These verbs tell you what you are supposed to do with what you read.

Frequently, however, you will have much less direction than this on what to do with your reading. Sometimes reading is just a part of a larger project, presentation, or paper, and *you* have to figure out what to do with every text you encounter. In these cases, you will need to figure out your purpose along with three other considerations that affect the choices you make about how to read something. These considerations, which I'll call *frames for reading*, are similar to those that come into play in rhetorical choices for writing.

Four Frames for Reading

- **Your purpose:** Why are you reading this text? (To explore, explain, evaluate, and/or reflect?)
- **Your knowledge of the genre/medium:** What do you know about this kind of text, and what do you therefore expect? What is it trying to do, and for whom is it likely written?
- **Your knowledge of the subject:** What do you already know about the subject of the reading? What biases might you have about it?
- **Self-perception:** How good do you think you are at reading a text in this genre and on this subject?

These considerations inevitably affect our reading. For example, a few years ago, when I was a novice at the shorthand of text messaging, I was painfully aware that I lacked genre knowledge. What do those abbreviations mean? When one of my daughters sent me a message, my first concern was decoding some of it. As I gained familiarity with the form, the problem of genre knowledge faded and I could focus more immediately on *why* they were telling me what they were telling me. They were asking for money? They wanted me to back off on the boyfriend? Experienced readers are aware of these frames and deliberately look at a text through them in order to make their reading more efficient.

Reading Scenarios

Consider a couple of scenarios involving academic reading and how an experienced writer might apply the four frames for reading.

Scenario #1. You're assigned two chapters in your college physics textbook for an exam. You don't know physics, much less college physics. Based on your feelings about reading textbooks and your inexperience with the subject, you're not feeling good about the time you'll spend reading for the assignment.

Faced with this situation, an experienced reader might apply the four frames as follows:

1. *Purpose.* I'm reading this to be able to explain what I know for an exam. I better pay attention to key concepts and terms when I read it and make sure I can explain them to myself. I think I'll write a summary in my

notebook of the key ideas—and a running list of terms and definitions—as I read. This is gonna slow me up but in the end will be worth it.

2. *Genre/medium knowledge.* I know that textbooks for intro courses are intended for readers with low subject knowledge, but even so it might be a struggle for me to understand and remember terms. Textbooks usually have cues about what's important—I'll pay particular attention to terms that are emphasized by length of treatment and visual cues such as italics and headings.

3. *Subject knowledge.* I don't know much about physics, so I can't skip around when I read this. I'll need to work through the text from the beginning and not move on to a new section until I think I understand the last one.

4. *Self-perception.* I stink at science and don't much like reading textbooks. Because I know I'm going to get frustrated, I'll allow some time to get through this—maybe reading over a few days rather than in one sitting.

Scenario #2. You're writing a research essay for your composition class on the impact of climate change in Australia, a place that one observer noted was a kind of "miner's canary" on the issue—in other words, likely to be among the first to experience problems and provide a warning sign for what is to come for the rest of the world. The question you're asking is whether chronic water shortages in the Outback are really climate related. Along with other material, you've found a great article in *Rolling Stone Magazine* that seems really on topic.

Here's how an experienced reader might approach reading the article:

1. *Purpose.* No one is telling me why I should read this article. I've got to figure that out. The *Rolling Stone* piece might be the most strongly stated thing I've read so far that argues that climate change is responsible for Australia's environmental problems. I'm going to read it to find some of those passages. Maybe I can use them in my paper. I'm also going to pay particular attention to the evidence provided on water shortages.

2. *Genre/medium knowledge.* This is *Rolling Stone,* not an academic article. It won't provide the quality of evidence that a journal article would. I also know that because of the magazine's youthful audience and its focus on popular music, *Rolling Stone* might be prone to overstating things a bit for dramatic effect. I'm going to read a little more critically.

3. *Subject knowledge.* I know a fair amount about the climate-change issue, and because I feel really strongly about it, I'm going to try to read this article critically, as a doubter more than a believer (see "Inquiring into the Details: Reading Perspectives"). What is the writer ignoring? Does he address counterarguments?

4. *Self-perception.* This article should be easy for me to read and understand.

Inquiring into the Details

Reading Perspectives

One of the best ways to read strategically is to consciously *shift* our perspective while we read. Like changing lenses on a camera or changing the angle, distance, or time of day to photograph something, this shift in reading perspective illuminates different aspects of a text. Here are some of the perspectives you might take:

■ *Believing:* What the author says is probably true. Which ideas can I relate to? What information should I use? What seems especially sound about the argument?

■ *Doubting:* What are the text's weaknesses? What ideas don't jibe with my own experience? What are the gaps in the information or the argument? What isn't believable about this?

■ *Updating:* What does this add to what I already know about the subject?

■ *Hunting and gathering:* What can I collect from the text that I might be able to use?

■ *Interpreting:* What might be the meaning of this?

■ *Pleasure seeking:* I just want to enjoy the text and be entertained by it.

■ *Connecting:* How does this information relate to my own experiences? What is its relationship to other things I've read? Does it verify, extend, or contradict what other authors have said?

■ *Reflecting:* How was this written? What makes it particularly effective or ineffective?

■ *Resisting:* This doesn't interest me. Why do I have to read it? Isn't *Survivor* on television right now?

Exercise 2.3

Reading a Life

Here's a scenario for you to consider, one that involves reading a different kind of text—a photograph. I'd like you to apply the four frames for reading to this photograph, much the way I applied them in the previous two scenarios.

First, some background. One of the many ways we all make inferences about people is by paying attention to the details of their lives. What things do they value? What is their behavior in significant social situations? What groups do they belong to? While we may do this informally all the time, academics and writers do it, too—for example, when they study members of social or cultural groups or when they plan to write a profile of someone. One academic version of this is called *ethnography*. It relies on very close observation of people in the places that their groups typically inhabit. Photographs can be an important source of data for such inquiries.

The photograph above, "Ruth's Vanity (on the day she died)," potentially tells us a lot about who Ruth was, through the things on her vanity and the dresser that is visible in the mirror above the vanity. I'd like you to think about how to read this photograph, by applying the four frames for reading: purpose, genre/ medium knowledge, subject knowledge, and self-perception. Explain, as I did in the previous scenarios, how each frame might influence *how* you might read this photograph: Number each frame, and then write a brief paragraph explaining how the frame influences how you will read the photograph to make inferences about Mrs. Smith. Your instructor may ask you to do this in your journal, submit it as a short response, or post it to the online discussion board.

Reading situations, like writing situations, can really differ, and each asks something different from you. There is no one "right" way to read well, or to write well, in most situations. Instead, there are choices. These choices are rhetorical; in every reading situation, you need to think about your purpose in reading the text, about the text itself—its subject, its genre/medium, and the author's likely purpose and audience—and about your self-perception in relation to the text's subject and genre/medium. You need to think about what these frames together imply about how you *might* approach the text. It's not a science. There's no formula to follow. Mostly, you simply want to be a *flexible* reader and writer, one who can read a situation well enough to make decisions about how to approach it. This becomes possible when you pay attention to your process.

A Process for Reading to Write

2.4

Understand the special demands of reading to write and practice doing it.

The process of reading to write is going to be different than, say, that of reading for pleasure. For example, lately I'm reading books about the Chicago mobster Al Capone. My motives are both learning and pleasure, but I really don't plan on writing anything about Capone, so I'm not as active a reader as I am when I'm reading something for, say, an essay I'm writing or a book I'm researching. I spend considerably less time taking notes, marking passages, mining the bibliography, and doing other things like that. I'm less worried about *what I can do* with what I'm reading.

Not long ago, I was working on an essay in which I was exploring why certain landscapes—usually the ones we know best from our childhoods—often get under our skins even if we no longer live in those places. My reading for this project led me to all kinds of sources—articles in anthropology, history, and literary works. This reading was enjoyable, but it was also work. In the back of my mind, I was always asking, *Does this relate to the questions I'm interested in?* It was a reading process that was much more directed by my purposes—by my desire to use what I was reading in my own writing.

Questions for the Process of Reading to Write

So far we've explored the various ways we might approach academic reading situations in general. We've explored questions like these: What are typical situations? How might frames such as purpose or genre knowledge influence what we do? Now let's look specifically at processes for those reading situations—typical in college—in which you have to write about what you read, especially when this involves inquiry into a topic.

What Do I Want to Know? Inquiry is driven by questions, not answers. What do you want to know? In Chapter 1 (see "A Writing Process Driven by Questions" on pp. 30–31), I explained that inquiry into most topics about which you know little often begins with informational questions: What is known about the impact

Figure 2.2 Reading to write is one of the most goal-oriented types of reading. First, you are guided by your research question: What do you want to know? If you know this, you know what to look for and how to use it in your own work.

of climate change in the Australian Outback? Why are reality shows so popular? In the beginning of an inquiry project, this larger goal—to develop some background knowledge—provides some guidance for how you read, but the reins will be pretty loose. You're likely to wander around a lot. That's okay as a start, but the reading and writing processes need the discipline of good questions that will keep you focused.

Consider some writing I did about theories of dog training. This writing actually originated with the behavior of our golden retriever: Ada was being bad—jumping on people, barking, and generally being a pest. Ada's behavior launched some research on websites, in books, and even in academic articles. At first, I just wanted to know what the schools of thought were on getting Ada in line—a question of fact. Before long, I knew enough to come up with much better questions, more specific and more directive, which changed not only what I was reading, but also how I read it. From the question "What are theories of dog training?" I ended up asking "What is the relationship between the use of shock collars and dog aggression and submission?"

Obviously, the second question is a much better guide to what I should read and what I should ignore. That one step of focusing the reading process on a narrower question, taken at an appropriate point, can then make a huge difference in the efficiency of the process.

What Should I Read to Find Out? Should I buy a new iPhone? Who cares? Well, I care. But because this is a question in which only I have a stake, I'm likely to read all kinds of things to help me answer the question. I won't be picky. But suppose my question were less personal and more academic, or less concerned with just me and instead addressed to a larger audience—for example, "Do people's emotional attachments to their iPhones have any of the qualities of clinical addiction?" With this question, I'll be a lot more picky about what I read. I'll look in the usual places—some quality websites—but I'll also check out some books on addictive behavior and search scholarly articles, probably in psychology, to see if anyone has studied users' emotional bonds to cell phones.

In other words, *what* you read (the kinds of texts you focus on) is determined not just by the question you're asking but the context in which you're asking it—the rhetorical choices related to your writing: Who are you writing for and why? What kinds of information will that audience find most persuasive? Are there certain kinds of evidence they would expect you to offer?

What Do I Do with What I've Read? There are lots of reading situations in which this question is answered by someone else:

> *Based on your reading about painters in the Italian Renaissance, explain in 250 words how an artist such as Caravaggio chose his subject matter.*

In this case, you know why you're reading and what you need to do with what you've read—explain a particular point. But in many reading situations, especially those that are inquiry based, you'll have considerable freedom to determine not only your own purposes for your reading, but also, more specifically, how you might use some of it in your paper or presentation. For example, are you reading a book chapter to find an explanation for a particular idea? Are you analyzing a statistical table to find evidence that supports a point you're trying to make?

In either type of reading situation, to actually do something with what you've read, you first have to know what you think about what you've read. How can you possibly make a decision about whether to quote an author or summarize someone's ideas or select this fact or another if you don't know what *you* make of what the text is saying? If you don't know much about the Italian Renaissance, let alone Caravaggio, then at the very least you'll need to try to *understand* as much as you can from your reading about both.

We've already talked about how reading isn't a monologue. "Blah, blah, blah," says a text, and you mindlessly write, "The text says, 'blah, blah, blah.'" That's a monologue, not a conversation. You're not talking with—or back to—what you're reading; you're parroting what you've read. In the next section, I'll propose a method for encouraging conversations with what you read that will help you to discover what you think.

Having a Dialogue with What You Read

A typical process for reading to write:

1. Google some keywords on a topic.
2. Go to the first link that seems promising and click on it.
3. If the site seems relevant, read it once quickly online. Bookmark or print.
4. Go read something else and repeat the process.
5. Hope that you'll remember what you've read when you have to write on the topic.

Another standard version of the process:

1. Get a reading assignment.
2. Read it once, maybe twice. Highlight a few things.
3. Compose something quickly about what you've read for the assignment, looking for a slot to put what you highlighted.

These are passive readings. While they're fine for some reading tasks, they don't work well when you have to write about what you read in a paper or for a presentation.

Imagine an alternative scenario: An assigned reading, a book, or an article is open in front of you, but so is your notebook. Your pen is poised to mark up the text—underlining, making marginal notes, adding question marks next to confusing passages and checks next to those you think are important (see Figure 2.3). When you're finished with your first reading, you go back and focus on what you marked. On the left-hand page of your notebook, you write down quoted passages that seem

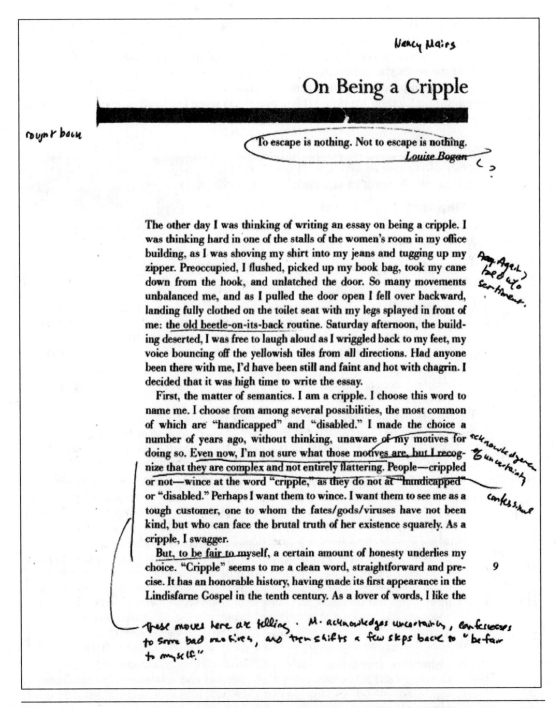

Nancy Mairs

On Being a Cripple

round back

To escape is nothing. Not to escape is nothing.
Louise Bogan

The other day I was thinking of writing an essay on being a cripple. I was thinking hard in one of the stalls of the women's room in my office building, as I was shoving my shirt into my jeans and tugging up my zipper. Preoccupied, I flushed, picked up my book bag, took my cane down from the hook, and unlatched the door. So many movements unbalanced me, and as I pulled the door open I fell over backward, landing fully clothed on the toilet seat with my legs splayed in front of me: the old beetle-on-its-back routine. Saturday afternoon, the building deserted, I was free to laugh aloud as I wriggled back to my feet, my voice bouncing off the yellowish tiles from all directions. Had anyone been there with me, I'd have been still and faint and hot with chagrin. I decided that it was high time to write the essay.

First, the matter of semantics. I am a cripple. I choose this word to name me. I choose from among several possibilities, the most common of which are "handicapped" and "disabled." I made the choice a number of years ago, without thinking, unaware of my motives for doing so. Even now, I'm not sure what those motives are, but I recognize that they are complex and not entirely flattering. People—crippled or not—wince at the word "cripple," as they do not at "handicapped" or "disabled." Perhaps I want them to wince. I want them to see me as a tough customer, one to whom the fates/gods/viruses have not been kind, but who can face the brutal truth of her existence squarely. As a cripple, I swagger.

But, to be fair to myself, a certain amount of honesty underlies my choice. "Cripple" seems to me a clean word, straightforward and precise. It has an honorable history, having made its first appearance in the Lindisfarne Gospel in the tenth century. As a lover of words, I like the

Pmp. Agst. / tied up to sentiment.

acknowledges uncertainty

confessions

9

these moves here are telling. M. acknowledges uncertainty, confesses to some bad motives, and then shifts a few steps back to "be fair to myself."

Figure 2.3   When you read to write, you should leave your tracks everywhere on a text—underlining, asking questions, making comments. This is the beginning of a dialogue between you and an author.

important; you jot down some facts that struck you. You might add a summary of a key idea or paraphrase the author's assertions. Then, on the right-hand page of your notebook, you fastwrite for five minutes, thinking about what you just read, looking left at the notes you collected on the opposing page to spur you along.

What I'm proposing, quite simply, is that you write when you read. But I'm also suggesting a method for doing this writing that some call a "double-entry notebook"

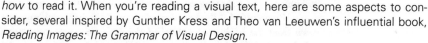

Inquiring into the Details

Reading the Visual

As you know by now, it helps enormously when reading a new text to have some knowledge of *how* to read it. When you're reading a visual text, here are some aspects to consider, several inspired by Gunther Kress and Theo van Leeuwen's influential book, *Reading Images: The Grammar of Visual Design.*

- **Framing:** As in writing, what the photographer, advertiser, painter, or designer chooses to include in an image and what she chooses to leave out profoundly affect the story, idea, or feeling that an image communicates. Framing might also establish a viewer's distance from the action. An up-close-and-personal image suggests intimacy, while a long shot has the opposite effect.

- **Angle:** A front-on view of a subject creates a different effect than looking up, or down, at it.

- **Relationships:** One of the most important of these is the relationship between you and the image itself. Is the subject of an image looking directly at the viewer or looking away? In the first case, the subject seems to make some kind of demand, and in the second, perhaps an invitation to simply be an onlooker.

- **Color:** Designers know that color affects mood. Not surprisingly, for example, red is a color that communicates feelings of passion and energy. White suggests "purity" and innocence. Yellow is sunny and joyous. For further analysis on color and emotion in visuals, search the web on the subject.

- **Arrangement:** In writing, we give certain information emphasis by where we place it in a sentence, in a paragraph, or in the composition as a whole. Visual information also uses the physical arrangement of objects for emphasis, making some things larger or smaller, in the foreground or background, to one side or the other. Kress and Leeuwen, for example, suggest we perceive the left side of an image as information that is a "given," things that viewers readily accept, while the right side is perceived as "new," information that viewers aren't familiar with. Thus, the right side becomes a key feature for communicating a message.

- **Light:** What is most illuminated and what is in shadows—and everything in between—also influences what is emphasized and what is not. But because light is something we strongly associate with time and place, it also has an emotional impact.

or "dialogue journal." If you're using a notebook, you use the left-hand page to collect important ideas, facts, quotations, or arguments from what you've read, and then you use the right-hand page to think about them through writing. You can use this method with any kind of text, including visual texts. See how the double-entry journal technique works for you to analyze an image. (You can find some ideas about analyzing images in "Inquiring into the Details: Reading the Visual.")

Exercise 2.4

Double-Entry Journaling with a Visual Text

Advertisements make arguments. They are carefully designed to combine text and images to persuade a particular audience to *do* something: buy a product, join an organization, vote for a referendum, make a donation. You know this, of course. But most of us are generally unaware of the methods of visual arguments. We don't think much about how they use visual language to direct our gaze and touch our emotions. To read an advertisement with these things in mind involves *rhetorical analysis*. Up until now, we've looked at analyzing the rhetorical situations we find ourselves in as readers. Now we'll turn our attention to analyzing texts. What is the intended audience of an ad? What are the appeals designed specifically for that audience? How does the ad use emotion? How was it composed to emphasize certain ideas or feelings?

In Chapter 6, on writing arguments, we'll look at this kind of rhetorical analysis more closely, but for now, take a close look at the following ad for a male fragrance and practice using the double-entry journal technique to analyze the ad's argument.

STEP ONE: Here are the questions for your reading of the ad:

- What specifically are the appeals in the advertisement, and to whom are they directed?
- What specific evidence in the ad would you point to as examples of those appeals?
- Do you think they are persuasive for the intended audience? Why or why not?

Following the instructions below, use two blank opposing pages in your journal to explore these questions.

STEP TWO: On the left-hand page, collect some information from the ad. Make a list of everything you look at in the ad, *in the order you look at it*. What do you see first? Then what? Then what? Be as specific as you can. When you've got a satisfactory list, circle those items that you think are particularly effective.

STEP THREE: On the right-hand page, explore your thinking about what you've collected. Begin a fastwrite by explaining to yourself why you think the items you circled on the other side of the page were effective. For whom? What kind of audience response might they get? How would these visual arguments convince a man to buy a "fragrance"?

STEP FOUR: Go back to the questions in step 1. How would you answer them?

STEP FIVE: Reflect in writing, in class, or on your class's online discussion board about your experience using the double-entry journal to analyze the ad.

- What worked? What didn't?
- How might you apply the double-entry journal to other reading situations?
- What did the method encourage you to do in the exercise that you don't usually do when you read?

Techniques for Keeping a Double-Entry Journal You're going to discover ways to make a reading journal work best for you. But if the journal is going to help you have *conversations* with what you read, I think there are some essential elements.

1. **You must focus on what the author or text actually says.** That's the beauty of the left-facing page of a double-entry journal. Because it contains passages, facts, ideas, and claims from your reading, you're working with what the text said, not what you vaguely remember that it said.

2. **Try to suspend judgment.** When we feel strongly about what we're reading, it's human to decide right away whether we agree or disagree with an author or come to a quick conclusion about what a text says and what it means. But you can use writing—and especially the open-ended, exploratory process of fastwriting—to really think things through before you come to conclusions.

3. **Use questions.** Sometimes, as in Exercise 2.4, the questions are provided to direct your reading. More often, you read to discover the questions that interest you about a topic. These will fuel bursts of writing that lead you towards having something to say about what you read.

4. **Read to write and write to read.** This is fundamental. No matter what technique you use to help you use what you read in your writing, you should always write *as you read* and, if possible, immediately after.

The double-entry journal method I'm proposing here typically involves a notebook and a pen, but if you prefer to work on a tablet or laptop, you can accomplish much the same thing with a two-column Word or Pages document. If you use a notebook, imagine that the spiral binding that divides opposing pages is a kind of table. On the left sits a text and an author; on the right sits you. You're having a conversation across that imaginary table. What do you talk about?

First, you have to try to understand what a text is saying. That's what the left-hand page is for—to try to collect information and ideas from what you're reading that you think are central to understanding the reading. On the right-hand page of your journal, you respond to, think and ask questions about, and explore what you've collected on the opposite page.

Here's one approach for organizing a conversation with a text using the double-entry approach.

Exercise 2.5

Reading Creatively, Reading Critically

Now that you've seen how the double-entry journal can help analyze an image, let's try it with a more familiar kind of text. I published the essay "The Importance of Writing Badly" some years ago, but I think it still expresses several of the main ideas behind this book. I'd like you to read the piece critically, though, using the double-entry journal method I've described in the previous section.

As before, you'll use opposing pages of your journal.

STEP ONE: Read the essay once through, marking it up. (Make a copy if you don't want to write in your book.) Read it a second time and, on the left-hand page of your notebook, carefully *copy* lines or passages from the essay that

- Connected with your own experience and observations
- Raised questions for you
- Puzzled you
- You thought seemed to be key points
- You disagreed or agreed with or you think about differently
- You found surprising or unexpected

The Importance of Writing Badly
Bruce Ballenger

1   I was grading papers in the waiting room of my doctor's office the other day, and he said, "It must be pretty eye-opening reading that stuff. Can you believe those students had four years of high school and still can't write?"

2   I've heard that before. I hear it almost every time I tell a stranger that I teach writing at a university.

3   I also hear it from colleagues brandishing red pens who hover over their students' papers like Huey helicopters waiting to flush the enemy from the tall grass, waiting for a comma splice or a vague pronoun reference or a misspelled word to break cover.

4   And I heard it this morning from the commentator on my public radio station who publishes snickering books about how students abuse the sacred language.

5   I have another problem: getting my students to write badly.

6   Most of us have lurking in our past some high priest of good grammar whose angry scribbling occupied the margins of our papers. Mine was Mrs. O'Neill, an eighth-grade teacher with a good heart but no patience for the bad sentence. Her favorite comment on my writing was "awk," which now sounds to me like the grunt of a large bird, but back then meant "awkward." She didn't think much of my sentences.

7   I find some people who reminisce fondly about their own Mrs. O'Neill, usually an English teacher who terrorized them into worshipping the error-free sentence. In some cases that terror paid off when it was finally transformed into an appreciation for the music a well-made sentence can make.

8   But it didn't work that way with me. I was driven into silence, losing faith that I could ever pick up the pen without breaking the rules or drawing another "awk" from

a doubting reader. For years I wrote only when forced to, and when I did it was never good enough.

Many of my students come to me similarly voiceless, dreading the first writing assignment because they mistakenly believe that how they say it matters more than discovering what they have to say.   9

The night before the essay is due they pace their rooms like expectant fathers, waiting to deliver the perfect beginning. They wait and they wait and they wait. It's no wonder the waiting often turns to hating what they have written when they finally get it down. Many pledge to steer clear of English classes, or any class that demands much writing.   10

My doctor would say my students' failure to make words march down the page with military precision is another example of a failed education system. The criticism sometimes takes on political overtones. On my campus, for example, the right-wing student newspaper demanded that an entire semester of Freshman English be devoted to teaching students the rules of punctuation.   11

There is, I think, a hint of elitism among those who are so quick to decry the sorry state of the sentence in the hands of student writers. A colleague of mine, an Ivy League graduate, is among the self-appointed grammar police, complaining often about the dumb mistakes his students make in their papers. I don't remember him ever talking about what his students are trying to say in those papers. I have a feeling he's really not that interested.   12

Concise, clear writing matters, of course, and I have a responsibility to demand it from students. But first I am far more interested in encouraging thinking than error-free sentences. That's where bad writing comes in.   13

When I give my students permission to write badly, to suspend their compulsive need to find the "perfect way of saying it," often something miraculous happens: Words that used to trickle forth come gushing to the page. The students quickly find their voices again, and even more important, they are surprised by what they have to say. They can worry later about fixing awkward sentences. First, they need to make a mess.   14

It's harder to write badly than you might think. Haunted by their Mrs. O'Neill, some students can't overlook the sloppiness of their sentences or their lack of eloquence, and quickly stall out and stop writing. When the writing stops, so does the thinking.   15

The greatest reward in allowing students to write badly is that they learn that language can lead them to meaning, that words can be a means for finding out what they didn't know they knew. It usually happens when the words rush to the page, however awkwardly.   16

I don't mean to excuse bad grammar. But I cringe at conservative educational reformers who believe writing instruction should return to primarily teaching how to punctuate a sentence and use *Roget's Thesaurus*. If policing student papers for mistakes means alienating young writers from the language we expect them to master, then the exercise is self-defeating.   17

It is more important to allow students to first experience how language can be a vehicle for discovering how they see the world. And what matters in this journey—at least initially—is not what kind of car you're driving, but where you end up.   18

Page #	Notes from Reading	Exploratory Response
	■ Direct quotations ■ Summaries of key ideas ■ Paraphrases of assertions, claims ■ Facts, specific observations, data ■ Premises and reasons ■ Interesting examples or case studies	Focused fastwrite on material in left-hand column or page. ■ What's relevant to the question? ■ What questions does it raise? ■ What do I think and feel about this? ■ How does it change the way I think about the subject? ■ What surprised me? ■ What's the most important thing I take away from the reading? ■ How does it connect to what I've heard, seen, or read before?

Figure 2.4 An approach to keeping a double-entry journal. Note that you should keep track of page numbers (if any) in the reading from which you collected information and put in the left-hand column or page. Particularly when doing research, you should begin by jotting down key bibliographic information about each source.

STEP TWO: Now use the right-hand page of your notebook to think further about what you wrote down on the left-hand page. Use the questions in Figure 2.4 as prompts for a focused fastwrite. Write for five or six minutes without stopping.

STEP THREE: Reread what you've written. Again, on the right-hand page of your notebook, write your half of the imaginary dialogue below with someone who is asking you about the idea of "bad writing."

> Q: I don't understand how bad writing can help anyone write better. Can you explain it to me?
>
> A:
>
> Q: Okay, but is it an idea that makes sense to you?
>
> A:
>
> Q: What exactly (i.e., quotation) does Ballenger say that makes you feel that way?
>
> A:

STEP FOUR: Finish the exercise by reflecting in your journal for five minutes on what, if anything, you noticed about using the double-entry journal to have a "conversation" with a text. In particular:

- How did it change the way you usually read an article such as this one?
- How might you adapt it for other situations in which you have to read to write?
- What worked well? What didn't?
- Do you think the method encouraged you to think more deeply about what you read?

One Student's Response

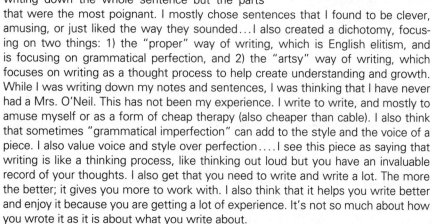

Briana's Journal

EXERCISE 2.5
STEP TWO

I took pieces of the sentences, not necessarily writing down the whole sentence but the parts that were the most poignant. I mostly chose sentences that I found to be clever, amusing, or just liked the way they sounded...I also created a dichotomy, focusing on two things: 1) the "proper" way of writing, which is English elitism, and is focusing on grammatical perfection, and 2) the "artsy" way of writing, which focuses on writing as a thought process to help create understanding and growth. While I was writing down my notes and sentences, I was thinking that I have never had a Mrs. O'Neil. This has not been my experience. I write to write, and mostly to amuse myself or as a form of cheap therapy (also cheaper than cable). I also think that sometimes "grammatical imperfection" can add to the style and the voice of a piece. I also value voice and style over perfection....I see this piece as saying that writing is like a thinking process, like thinking out loud but you have an invaluable record of your thoughts. I also get that you need to write and write a lot. The more the better; it gives you more to work with. I also think that it helps you write better and enjoy it because you are getting a lot of experience. It's not so much about how you wrote it as it is about what you write about.

STEP THREE

Q: I don't understand how bad writing can help anyone write better. Can you explain it to me?
A: What you have to say is just as important as how you write it. Writing is a way of thinking, sort of like thinking out loud—a way of thinking through things and reflecting more deeply on things. It feels awesome to write with reckless abandon and show no concern for punctuation or grammar. It helps you think unhindered, to find out how you truly think and feel. Thoughts and feelings have little concern for these things. Looking back at your thoughts that you have written you can see your thoughts. Then you can look at how you have written. Being observant and introspective of your own writing will help you develop better writing skills.

Q: Okay, but is it an idea that makes sense to you?
A: Definitely, I prefer to write badly. I believe that it's a better expression of my actual thoughts, flaws and all. When I write on my computer my spellcheck goes crazy with "fragment sentences." But who cares? That's what I want to say and that is how it comes out and how it sounds in its natural state. I don't change it. Give me all your green squiggly underlinings, Windows Vista. It has been driven into so many students that we have to write perfectly—use correct punctuation, no vague pronouns, correct verb tense, good sentence syntax, and structure. I think that writing should be more than that. I think that it should be more of a form of expression.

One Student's Response *(continued)*

Q: What exactly (i.e., quotation) does Ballenger say that makes you feel that way?

A: "Many of my students come to me similarly voiceless, . . . because they mistakenly believe that how they say it matters more than discovering what they have to say."

I have never actually used the "double-entry" journal method before. I think it gave me a more articulate and clear idea of what I thought and how I came to think that. It became a map of my thought process. I usually have trouble pulling my thoughts in my writing together, but this gave me my thoughts more concisely. I also liked that I had a record of my thoughts and that regardless of the quality of writing, it was an accurate record because we all know that memory is not all that reliable. I think that method would be good when you have to opine on a subject at length. I liked the explore, explain, evaluate, and reflect structure because when you are writing off the top of your head it is easy to lose focus. So this helps keep you on track.

Wrestling with Academic Discourse: Reading from the Outside In

The one thing that most influences your ability to understand and use what you read is prior knowledge. If you're reading about a topic you know little about—say, the biology of the Palouse worm, a creepy, disturbingly large creature that lives deep underground in northern Idaho—then you will work harder than if you read about a topic you know a lot about. In college, unfortunately, much of what you read will be about subjects that are new to you. This means, quite simply, that you may struggle. You'll get frustrated. In your worst moments, you might want to throw an assigned reading out the window. I did that once.

But here's the good news: The more you learn about a topic, the more competent you'll feel. And it isn't just topic knowledge that will make you feel this way. It's also learning to understand the *discourse* of a particular discipline. You learn how to read, for instance, the discourse of biologists who write about worms, or the discourse social workers use to write to each other about poverty. There are all kinds of *discourse communities*, or groups of people who share certain ways of thinking, asking questions, and communicating—not just scholarly ones. Electricians share certain ways of communicating with each other. So do surfers.

It might seem that reading specialized discourses such as these is just about deciphering jargon. It's actually about much more than that. Academic discourse, for example, includes not just the language insiders use, but also

- The kinds of questions participants typically ask that guide research in the field
- Preferred methods for answering questions

   ▪   The kinds of evidence a discourse community considers persuasive

   ▪   Conventions for reporting discoveries

Maybe the best way to introduce the idea of academic discourse is to show you two excerpts from different publications on the same topic: the appeal and effects of watching reality television. One is from the *Internet Journal of Criminology* and the other from a popular book on the reality television phenomenon.

Exercise 2.6

Reading Reality TV

Reflective, rhetorically aware readers will immediately notice significant differences between the excerpts. Some are obvious. For example, there are citations in excerpt 1 but not in excerpt 2. The first has a more formal style than the second. You probably know that the journal excerpt (excerpt 1) is more *authoritative* than the web excerpt, particularly if you are reading them for a college paper. But do you know why? Read the excerpts closely, thinking about the differences.

EXCERPT 1

There has been a considerable interest in how real reality television shows are as well as how such programming creates and reinforces gender and racial stereotypes (Cavender and Bond-Maupin 1993; Eschhotz et al. 2002; Estep and Macdonald 1983; Oliver 1994; Prosise and Johnson 2004).[1] Many researchers focus on crime-based reality television because this type of television programming blurs the line between entertainment and fact. Televised police offers are theoretically sent on real-life calls to interact with actual criminals. More than two decades ago, Sheley and Ashkins (1981) documented that the officer and perpetuator most likely depicted on police television dramas was far from reality (see too Oliver 1994; Oliver and Armstrong 1998). Oliver (1994), in a content analysis of reality-based police shows, found that white characters on these shows were more likely to be portrayed as police officers than perpetrators of crimes, whereas black and Hispanic characters were more likely to be shown as criminals than police officers. If viewers appreciated that this was Hollywood entertainment albeit docudrama, such images might not be so troublesome. However, as Prosise and Johnson (2004) write, most people report that their knowledge of crime, as well as their understanding of law enforcement generally, comes through the media rather than from direct experience (see too Oliver and Armstrong 1998).

---

[1]Monk-Turner, Elizabeth, Homer Martinez, Jason Holbrook, and Nathan Harvey. 2007. "Are Reality TV Crime Shows Continuing to Perpetuate Crime Myths?" *The Internet Journal of Criminology* (n.d.). Web. Retrieved 1 Sept. 2011.

EXCERPT 2

Reality TV: An Insider's Guide to TV's Hottest Market[2]

For all of Reality's faults, I still liken critics who blanketly bash it while favoring sitcoms and dramas to wine snobs who can't just enjoy an orange soda now and then. Good Reality TV rivals the best traditionally scripted television for entertainment value, and its positive impact on popular culture cab be felt just as deeply, if not more so, than its negative . . . .

Consider the number of people emboldened by shows like *The Biggest Loser* to make positive changes in their lives. The popular Reveille series for NBC started a national movement to get in shape that echoed across America, making heroes (and moguls) of personal trainers Bob Harper and Jillian Michaels. While the show has been taken to task by critics for its wall-to-wall product placement, one can hardly argue that any other show in recent history has done so much measureable good for viewers.

Generating

STEP ONE: Explore your reaction to each excerpt. Which *are you* most inclined to believe? Why? What exactly is it about the less persuasive excerpt that makes it unconvincing? How do your own feelings about beliefs about reality TV figure into your reaction? Fastwrite for three minutes, thinking through writing about your reasons for believing one excerpt more than the other.

Judging

STEP TWO: Focus your analysis on the persuasiveness of each excerpt by summarizing what you discovered in the fastwrite. Make a list of at least three reasons why, if you were writing a college essay on the influence of reality TV on fans, you might prefer one excerpt over another.

STEP THREE: In excerpt 1, what do you notice about the author's relationship with others who have written on the topic of reality TV? How would you contrast that with the same relationship in excerpt 2? Jot down a few ideas.

STEP FOUR: You probably noticed that the second excerpt uses the first person, while the first doesn't. Much, though not all, academic discourse avoids the first person. This isn't a rule. It's a convention, a feature of this kind of writing that people typically use because it serves some rhetorical purpose. What purpose might it serve in excerpt 1? List a few ideas about this.

STEP FIVE: Because the excerpts are so brief, you don't have much to work with. But can you speculate on what kind of evidence might be sufficient to support

---

[2]Devold, Troy. 2011. *Reality TV: An Insider's Guide to TV's Hottest Market*. Studio City, CA: Michael Weise Productions, 22. Print.

an assertion when someone writes an essay on a commercial website and what might be necessary in the field of criminology?

STEP SIX: Try to pull some of this together in a short paper or discussion-board post. Using examples from the excerpt, write about 200 words in response to the following two questions:

What are some characteristics distinguishing between the discourse of criminology and the discourse of popular writing on crime? How might these differences influence how you read and use each as a college writer and a reader writing a paper on reality TV?

Features of Academic Discourse

There isn't a single academic discourse. There are *discourses*. Academic discourse varies from discipline to discipline. Why? Though all academic disciplines—from those in the humanities to those in the natural sciences—are dedicated to creating new knowledge, they each look at different aspects of the world. Some, say, look at language. Others observe natural phenomena. A few, like math, work with often highly abstract concepts or ideas. Because the materials for discovery differ, the methods of discovery do, too. These differences naturally lead to unique ways of describing things and reporting them. Before long, you have different discourse communities.

2.5
Understand some conventions of academic writing and recognize them in texts.

Despite all these differences, it is possible to make some observations about academic discourse that apply across discourse communities. As you become more experienced reading in various fields, you will begin to recognize some of these basic patterns, and this will help immensely with your academic reading.

1. **Billboards.** Academic writers announce, usually somewhere near the beginning of an article, what they are going to do.

2. **Reviews.** Like the first excerpt in the previous exercise, academic texts often include a review of what others have already said on a topic. This is also near the beginning.

3. **Hedges.** Contrary to the popular assumption that academic texts usually deal in certainty, much academic writing qualifies assertions. They signal caution by using words such as *appear to be, tend,* or *suggest.*

4. **Signposts.** Most academic subjects are complicated neighborhoods, and scholarly writing offers plenty of explicit direction about turns in an argument (e.g., *however*), presentation of reasons (e.g., *because*), and evidence (e.g., *for example*).

5. **Questions.** Academic writing is about inquiry and discovery, and these arise from questions to explore or problems to solve. Identifying the question or the problem that an academic article proposes to address is key to understanding what it's about; knowing the question driving the research also makes the path authors took to a study's conclusions much more obvious.

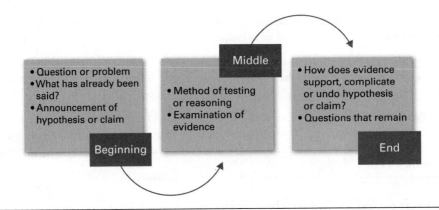

Figure 2.5 How academic articles are organized. Scholarly articles have a beginning, middle, and end, like stories do. Beginnings "billboard" the research question and review the literature. In the middle, writers tell what happened in their own investigation of the question, and in the end, they analyze the significance of what they've found.

These five conventions are some handholds that you can seize as you wrestle your way through much academic discourse. Figure 2.5 may also help you understand how scholarly articles typically organize their content.

I distinctly remember the first time I had to read articles in biology, my undergraduate major. I was lost. I felt stupid. And I vowed to avoid scholarly books and articles if at all possible. In the Internet age, this kind of avoidance can seem even more possible. But the truth is that, even if more possible, it's not a good idea. Popular writing on the web can help you to develop a working knowledge of your topic—and this will help you begin to understand the scholarship—but it is the academic sources that will always lead you in the deepest, richest understandings of the things that interest you. Now is the time to learn how to break through the initial reaction to academic prose—"This is so boring!"—and enter the messy, exciting marketplace where knowledge is made. That, after all, is the business of the university, and, as a curious writer and reader, you're invited to become a part of it.

Using What You Have Learned

Reflect on the learning goals introduced at the beginning of the chapter.

1. **Examine your existing beliefs about reading and how they might be obstacles to reading effectively.** As you become a more experienced reader in college, your beliefs about your own competence should *evolve* along with your understanding of how different kinds of texts work. In the days ahead, think about this. Are you thinking about reading any differently than when you began the course?

2. **Apply reading purposes relevant to reading in college.** You're researching a paper or a presentation, for instance, and you collect all kinds of texts. How do you want to *use* them? To explore, explain, evaluate, or reflect? What "frames" will you use to make that decision?

3. **Recognize reading situations and the choices about approaches to reading that they imply.** Just as there is no "right" way to write in all situations, there is no "right" way to read whenever you have a reading assignment. Hopefully, you will see that each situation implies certain choices. Think about what they are and you'll read much more strategically.

4. **Understand the special demands of reading to write, and practice doing it.** Always have a pen in your hand. We think in dialogue with a text. It is from this conversation that we collaborate with a text to discover our own ideas about something. Throughout *The Curious Writer*, I'll encourage you to keep up this dialogue, using some form of the double-entry journal and through questions.

5. **Understand some conventions of academic writing and recognize them in texts.** In this chapter, you learned about *academic discourse*, a weighty-sounding term that describes the range of conventions that scholarly communities use to ask questions, choose methods, and report on discoveries. Whatever major you end up in, you'll be required to learn some of the conventions of academic discourse in your field. Don't let anyone tell you that academic discourse is just one thing—it varies from scholarly community to scholarly community—but we have explored general features of much academic writing, things such as how many scholarly articles are organized.

Writing a personal essay can be like seeing an old picture of yourself. This publicity photograph of my mother (an actress), my older brother, and me in the 1950s returns me to that world—a time when fathers were often missing from the picture.

Writing a Personal Essay

3

Learning Objectives

In this chapter, you'll learn to

3.1 Use personal experiences and observations to drive inquiry.

3.2 Apply the exploratory thinking of personal essays to academic writing.

3.3 Identify the characteristics of personal essays in different forms.

3.4 Use invention strategies to discover and develop a personal essay topic.

3.5 Apply revision strategies that are effective for shaping narratives.

Writing About Experience and Observations

Most us were taught and still believe that we need to know what we are going to write before we actually pick up the pen or sit in front of the computer. My student Lynn was typical.

"I think I'll write about my experience organizing the street fair," she told me the other day. "That would be a good topic for a personal essay, right?"

"Do you think so?" I said.

"Well, yes, because I already know a lot about it. I'll have a lot to write about."

"Okay, but is there anything about this experience that you want to understand better?" I said. "Anything about it that makes you curious?"

"Curious? It was just a street fair," she said.

"Sure, but is there something about what happened that makes you want to look at the experience again? Is there a chance that you might learn something about yourself, or about street fairs, or about the community, or about people, or...?"

Lynn was clearly sorry she asked. What I should have said was much more to the point: The best personal essay topics are those that are an itch you need to scratch. These tend not to be topics you have already figured out. While the topics can be familiar to you, the results of your inquiry are usually much better if you don't yet know what you think about your topics and you're interested to learn more about them. The best topics ask to be written about because they make you wonder *Why did I do that? What does that mean? Why did that happen? How did I really feel? What do I really think?*

Unlike most other forms of inquiry, the personal essay invites an initial display of confusion or uncertainty from writers regarding their subjects. In other words, the personal essay can be, and often is, a vehicle for writers to work through their thinking and feeling on a subject, directly in front of their readers.

> The personal essay is a vehicle for writers to work through their thinking and feeling on a subject, directly in front of their readers.

As a form, the *personal* essay places the writer at center stage. This doesn't mean that once she's there, her responsibility is to pour out her secrets, share her pain, or confess her sins. Some essays do have these confessional qualities, but more often they do not. Yet a personal essayist, no matter the subject of the essay, is still *exposed.* There is no hiding behind the pronoun *one,* as in "one might think" or "one often feels," no lurking in the shadows of the passive voice: "An argument will be made that…" The personal essay is first-person territory.

In this sense, the personal essay is much like a photographic self-portrait. Like a picture, a good personal essay tells the truth, or it tells *a* truth about the writer/ subject, and it often captures the writer at a particular moment in time. This explains why the experience of taking a self-portrait, or confronting an old picture of oneself taken by someone else, can create the same feeling of exposure that writing a personal essay often does.

But it does more. When we gaze at ourselves in a photograph, we often see it as yanked from a larger story about ourselves, a story that threads its way through our lives and gives us ideas about who we were and who we are. This is what the personal essay demands of us: We must somehow present ourselves truthfully and measure our past against the present. In other words, when we hold a photograph of ourselves, we know more than the person we see there knew, and as writers of the personal essay, we must share that knowledge and understanding with readers.

Though the personal essay may be an exploration of a past experience, it needn't always be about memories. A personal essay can instead focus on some aspect of writers' present lives, just as long as it raises questions that interest them. Why is it so irritating to overhear certain cell phone conversations? Why do I have an obsession with zombie-killing apps? What does it feel like to be an international student in Idaho? All of these kinds of questions might lead to a personal essay, and the challenge of writing about the present is the same as writing about the past: What do I understand about this now that I didn't understand when I started writing about it?

Motives for Writing a Personal Essay

3.1

Use personal experiences and observations to drive inquiry.

Essai was a term coined by the sixteenth-century French nobleman Michel de Montaigne, a man who endured plague epidemics, the bloody civil war between French Catholics and Protestants, and his own bouts of ill health. His tumultuous and uncertain times, when old social orders and intellectual traditions were under assault, proved to be ideal ferment for the essay. The French verb *essaier* means "to attempt" or "to try," and the essay became an opportunity for Montaigne to work out his thoughts about war, the education of children, the evils of doctors, and the importance of pleasure. The personal essay tradition inspired by Montaigne is probably unlike what you are familiar with from school. The school essay is often formulaic—a five-paragraph theme or thesis-example paper—while the personal essay is an open-ended form that allows for uncertainty and inconclusiveness. It is more about the process of coming to know than presenting *what* you know. The personal essay attempts *to find out* rather than *to prove.*

It is an ideal form of inquiry if your purpose is exploratory and if you're particularly interested in working out the possible relationships between your subject and yourself. Because the personal essay is openly subjective, the writer can't hide. The intruding *I* confronts the writer with the same questions over and over again: *Why does this matter to me? What do I make of it? How does this change the way I think of myself and the way I see the world?* Because of this, one of the principal dangers of the personal essay is that it can become narcissistic; it can go on and on about what the writer thinks and feels, and the reader can be left with that nagging question—*So what?* The personal essayist must always find some way to hitch the particulars of his or her experience to something larger—an idea, a theme, or even a feeling that readers might share.

On the other hand, one of the prime rhetorical advantages of the personal essay is its subjectivity. Because it is written with openness and honesty, the essay can be a very intimate form, inviting the reader to share in the writer's often concealed world. The *ethos* of personal essayists, or their credibility (see the rhetorical triangle in Chapter 7, p. 241), revolves around the sense that they are ordinary people writing about ordinary things. In the personal essay, we often get to see the face sweating under the mask. Honesty is one of the essay's primary virtues, and because the form allows for uncertainty and confusion, the writer doesn't need to pretend that he has *the* answer or that he knows more than he lets on about his subject.

The Personal Essay and Academic Writing

In some ways, the personal essay might seem like a dramatic departure from the kind of academic writing you've done in other classes. Openly subjective and sometimes tentative in its conclusions, the personal essay is a relatively open form that is not predictably structured like much academic writing. Additionally, the tone of the personal essay is conversational, even intimate, rather than impersonal and removed. So, if your sociology or economics professor will never ask for a personal essay, why bother to write one in your composition class?

3.2

Apply the exploratory thinking of personal essays to academic writing.

It's a fair question. While the pleasures of personal essay writing can be reason alone to write these essays, there are also other important reasons, related to your academic work:

- Because of your connection to the subject matter, the personal essay, more than any other form, gives you an opportunity to use exploration as a method of inquiry, and to practice those habits of mind that are so important to academic inquiry: suspending judgment, tolerating ambiguity, and using questions to challenge easy assumptions.

- For this same reason, the essay is especially conducive to the kind of thinking typical of academic inquiry: a movement back and forth between critical and creative thinking. In many ways, the personal essay is *inductive* like scientific thinking; it looks closely at the data of experience and attempts to infer from that information theories about the way things are.

- The essay emphasizes the *process* of coming to know about yourself and your subject, exposing your reasoning and the ways you use knowledge to get at the truth of things. Reflecting on these things can tell you a lot about how you think.

Finally, the personal essay and academic writing are actually not that far apart. We often assume that "academic" is supposed to be "objective," that self and subject should never mix. "Never use I" is supposedly the rule, and never, ever talk about yourself in an academic paper. These *are* common conventions, especially in the sciences. One reason for this is that the appearance of objectivity gives research more authority. Another is that in many disciplines attention generally needs to be on the data and not the author.

And yet a surprising number of academic articles make use of the first person, and not just in the humanities, where you might expect a more subjective perspective. The first person—and a more personal approach to scholarship—is evident in many disciplines, including literary criticism, business, anthropology, education, nursing, and even geology. This first-person writing often tells a story, sometimes through a case study, a narrative of the writer's experiences, or an account of his or her intellectual journey.

In any case, don't let the relative rarity of the first person in scholarship fool you into not seeing that there's something personal in even the most formal academic writing. It's *always* personal. What we choose to write about, the questions that interest us, and our particular ways of seeing are always at work, even in academic prose. True, the sciences use methods to minimize the researcher's biases. But it's impossible to eliminate them. Whenever anyone—scientist or humanist—uses language to communicate discoveries, they enter a social marketplace where words have meanings that are negotiated with others. For writers—any kind of writers—language is a social currency.

The essay, more than any other form, gives you an opportunity to use exploration as a method of inquiry.

But most important, much of what you are asked to write in college is about what *you* think. Not what your instructor thinks, or what the textbook author thinks, or what someone said in a journal. All of these things provide you with something to think about. You decide what you want to say. One of the great things about the personal essay is that it insists on flushing writers out into the open. You can't hide in the wings, concealed in the shadow of other people's opinions or someone else's findings. What *you* think is what the essay is all about.

Features of the Form

3.3

Identify the characteristics of personal essays in different forms.

Feature	Conventions of the Personal Essay
Inquiry questions	What does it mean to me? What do I understand about this now that I didn't then?
Motives	Self-discovery is often the motive behind writing a personal essay—the essay is in first person, and the essayist is center stage.
Subject matter	Essayists often write about quite ordinary things; they find drama in everyday life, past or present. Personal essays can be about taking a walk, breaking up on Facebook, the housefly on your beer glass. In some ways, the real subject of a personal essay is the writer herself and how she makes sense of her world.
Structure	Essays often tell stories, but, unlike fiction, they both show *and* tell, using both narrative and exposition, sometimes alternating between the two. When about the past, there are two narrators in the essay—the "then-narrator" and "now-narrator." One describes what happened and the other what the narrator makes *now* of what happened. The thesis may come near the end rather than at the beginning. And the essay isn't necessarily chronological.
Sources of information	Like any essay, the personal essay might use all four sources of information—memory, observation, reading, and interview. But it is likely to lean most heavily on memory and observation.
Language	Personal essays work in two registers—the more general language of reflection and the very specific detail of experience and observation. This specific language is often sensory: What did it look like exactly? What did you hear? How did it feel?

Prose+

Josh Neufeld's "A Matter of Perspective" is a kind of personal essay. The theme—the idea that we have moments in our lives when we feel very, very small—speaks not only to Josh's experience, but our own. A graphic essay such as this one exploits image and text in combination, amplifying the power of each.

READINGS

▶ Personal Essay 1

Try this exercise: Think about things, ordinary objects, that you have held onto all these years because you simply can't throw them away. They *mean* something to you. They are reminders of another time, or a turning point in your life, or a particular moment of joy, or sadness, or perhaps fear. Consider a few of mine: a green plaster Buddha, handmade; a glow-in-the-dark crucifix; an old pair of 7 × 50 Nikon binoculars; a 1969 Martin D 28 guitar; a brown-handled flathead screwdriver with a touch of red nail polish on the handle; a homemade lamp made from a wooden wallpaper roller; a red dog's collar. While they are meaningless to you, naturally, to me each of these objects carry a charge; they remind me of a story, a moment, a feeling. The personal essay makes space for writers to explore the meanings of such ordinary things.

Taking Things Seriously: 75 Objects with Unexpected Meanings, the book from which the following short essay was taken, is a gallery of objects—that are displayed along with the meditations on their significance by the writers who have carefully kept them as reminders on a shelf, in a closet, by their beside. Laura Zazulak's short essay focuses on a doll that she snatched from a neighbor's trash can. Just telling a story about what happened is not enough in an essay. The essay must have something to say to someone else. As you read Zazulak's brief piece, consider what that might be.

Every Morning for Five Years

Laura Zazulak

Every morning for five years, I was not so welcomingly greeted by my middle-aged, developmentally disabled neighbor across the street. Scotty never smiled and seemed to hate everyone. He never left the perimeter of his mother's lawn and apparently didn't know how to do anything but rake, shovel, take out the trash, and yell in a high-pitched voice. I'd pull out of my driveway and see him there, wearing a neon orange hunting cap, raking absolutely nothing at the same spot that he'd raked the day before. I'd think to myself, "Don't make eye contact!" But I always did. He'd stare at me and neither of us would blink.

Near the end of my fifth year on the street, Scotty stopped coming out of his house. At first, I was thankful. But as time passed, I began to worry. Then one Saturday morning in the middle of January I noticed that his window was wide open. Later that day, a police car showed up. Maybe Scotty and his mother got into one of their screaming

(continued)

(continued)

matches again? Then a funeral-home van pulled up and they brought out Scotty's body. Although it came as a surprise to me to discover that he knew how miserable his life was, he had killed himself.

3   The next day Scotty's uncle came over and began furiously carting things off to the dump. He left behind a garbage can in the driveway piled with all of Scotty's earthly possessions. I noticed two little pink feet sticking up into the air.

4   After dark, I crept across the street to the garbage can, armed with a travel-sized bottle of hand sanitizer. I looked left, then right. I dashed forward, tugged at the feet, and then ran as fast as I could back into my own backyard with my prize. Only then did I look at what I'd rescued. I would like you to meet Mabel.

Inquiring into the Essay

Throughout *The Curious Writer*, I'll invite you to respond to readings, using questions related to the four motives for reading discussed in Chapter 2. The following questions, therefore, encourage you to explore (*What do I think about this?*), explain (*What do I understand that this is saying?*), evaluate (*What's my judgment about this?*), and reflect to discover (*How does this work?* or *How am I thinking about it?*) and shape what you think about the reading. In Chapter 2, I encouraged you to write while you read and after. Try that now using the double-entry journal technique (see pp. 55–60). As soon as you finish your first reading of

"Every Morning for Five Years," open up your journal and on the right-hand page fastwrite your response to the explore and explain questions above. Write for at least three minutes. Then go back to Zazulak's essay and on the left-hand page jot down sentences or passages from it that you think are important to your understanding of it. Build your responses to the questions that follow from these first thoughts about what you just read.

1. **Explore.** All of the essays in the book *Taking Things Seriously*, from which the piece you just read was taken, have this to say: It is remarkable how much meaning we can invest in the ordinary when we take the time to notice. Brainstorm a list of objects that might have "unexpected significance" for you. Choose one and fastwrite about it for four minutes. Then skip a line, choose another, and write for another four minutes. Repeat this over a few days and create a collage of brief stories that four or five objects inspired. Are there any themes that seem to run through all of them? Do they speak to each other in any way?

2. **Explain.** Explain how, read together, the photograph and the essay work together to create meanings that might not be apparent if they were read separately.

3. **Evaluate.** Personal essays like "Every Morning for Five Years" *imply* their meaning rather than state it explicitly. Make an argument for your own understanding of the meaning of Zazulak's essay, and use passages from the piece to support your claim.

4. **Reflect.** One of the features of the personal essay is two narrators: the "now-narrator" and the "then-narrator." One looks back on experience from the present, applying knowledge that the "then-narrator" did not have. From this comes fresh insight. But these two narrators aren't always obvious. Can you see them in this essay?

▶ Personal Essay 2

America is a nation of immigrants, whose stories often haunt their children. Judith Ortiz Cofer moved from Puerto Rico as a child with her family in the mid-1950s to a barrio in Paterson, New Jersey. There she became both part of and witness to a familiar narrative, that of the outsider who finds herself wedged between two worlds, two cultures, and two longings: the desire to return "home" and the desire to feel at home in the new place.

In "One More Lesson," Cofer describes both of the places that competed for her sense of self—the Puerto Rico of her childhood, where she spent time as a child while her Navy father was away at sea, and an apartment in New Jersey, where she would go when he returned.

One More Lesson

Judith Ortiz Cofer

1   I remember Christmas on the Island by the way it felt on my skin. The temperature dropped into the ideal seventies and even lower after midnight when some of the more devout Catholics—mostly older women—got up to go to church, *misa del gallo* they called it; mass at the hour when the rooster crowed for Christ. They would drape shawls over their heads and shoulders and move slowly toward town. The birth of Our Savior was a serious affair in our *pueblo*.

2   At Mamá's house, food was the focal point of *Navidad*. There were banana leaves brought in bunches by the boys, spread on the table, where the women would pour coconut candy steaming hot, and the leaves would wilt around the sticky lumps, adding an extra tang of flavor to the already irresistible treat. Someone had to watch the candy while it cooled, or it would begin to disappear as the children risked life and limb for a stolen piece of heaven. The banana leaves were also used to wrap the traditional food of holidays in Puerto Rico: *pasteles*, the meat pies made from grated yucca and plantain and stuffed with spiced meats.

3   Every afternoon during the week before Christmas Day, we would come home from school to find the women sitting around in the parlor with bowls on their laps, grating pieces of coconut, yuccas, plantains, cheeses—all the ingredients that would make up our Christmas Eve feast. The smells that filled Mamá's house at that time have come to mean anticipation and a sensual joy during a time in my life, the last days of my early childhood, when I could still absorb joy through my pores—*when I had not yet learned that light is followed by darkness, that all of creation is based on that simple concept, and maturity is a discovery of that natural law.*

4   It was in those days that the Americans sent baskets of fruit to our barrio—apples, oranges, grapes flown in from the States. And at night, if you dared to walk up to the hill where the mango tree stood in the dark, you could see a wonderful sight: a Christmas tree, a real pine, decorated with lights of many colors. It was the blurry outline of this tree you saw, for it was inside a screened-in-porch, but we had heard a thorough description of it from the boy who delivered the fruit, a nephew of Mamá's, as it had turned out. Only, I was not impressed, since just the previous year we had put up a tree ourselves in our apartment in Paterson.

5   Packages arrived for us in the mail from our father. I got dolls dressed in the national costumes of Spain, Italy, and Greece (at first we could not decide which of the Greek dolls was the male, since they both wore skirts); my brother got picture books; and my mother, jewelry that she would not wear, because it was too much like showing off and might attract the Evil Eye.

6   Evil Eye or not, the three of us were the envy of the pueblo. Everything about us set us apart, and I put away my dolls quickly when I discovered that my playmates would not be getting any gifts until *Los Reyes*—the Day of the Three Kings, when

Christ received His gifts—and that even then it was more likely that the gifts they found under their beds would be practical things like clothes. Still, it was fun to find fresh grass for the camels the night the Kings were expected, tie it in bundles with string, and put it under our beds along with a bowl of fresh water.

The year went by fast after Christmas, and in the spring we received a telegram from Father. His ship had arrived in Brooklyn Yard. He gave us a date for our trip back to the States. I remember Mother's frantic packing, and the trips to Mayagüez for new clothes; the inspections of my brother's and my bodies for cuts, scrapes, mosquito bites, and other "damage" she would have to explain to Father. And I remember begging Mamá to tell me stories in the afternoons, although it was not summer yet and the trips to the mango tree had not begun. In looking back I realize that Mamá's stories were what I packed—my winter store.   7

Father had succeeded in finding an apartment outside Paterson's "vertical barrio," the tenement Puerto Ricans called *El Building*. He had talked a Jewish candy store owner into renting us the apartment above his establishment, which he and his wife had just vacated after buying a house in West Paterson, an affluent suburb. Mr. Schultz was a nice man whose melancholy face I was familiar with from trips I had made often with my father to his store for cigarettes. Apparently, my father had convinced him and his brother, a look-alike of Mr. Schultz who helped in the store, that we were not the usual Puerto Rican family. My father's fair skin, his ultra-correct English, and his Navy uniform were a good argument. Later it occurred to me that my father had been displaying me as a model child when he took me to that store with him. I was always dressed as if for church and held firmly by the hand. I imagine he did the same with my brother. As for my mother, her Latin beauty, her thick black hair that hung to her waist, her voluptuous body which even the winter clothes could not disguise, would have been nothing but a hindrance to my father's plans. But everyone knew that a Puerto Rican woman is her husband's satellite; she reflects both his light and his dark sides. If my father was respectable, then his family would be respectable. We got the apartment on Park Avenue.   8

Unlike El Building, where we had lived on our first trip to Paterson, our new home was truly in exile. There were Puerto Ricans by the hundreds only one block away, but we heard no Spanish, no loud music, no mothers yelling at children, nor the familiar *¡Ay Bendito!*, that catch-all phrase of our people. Mother lapsed into silence herself, suffering from *La Tristeza,* the sadness that only place induces and only place cures. But Father relished silence, and we were taught that silence was something to be cultivated and practiced.   9

Since our apartment was situated directly above where the Schultzes worked all day, our father instructed us to remove our shoes at the door and walk in our socks. We were going to prove how respectable we were by being the opposite of what our ethnic group was known to be—we would be quiet and inconspicuous.   10

(continued)

(continued)

11   I was escorted each day to school by my nervous mother. It was a long walk in the cooling air of fall in Paterson and we had to pass by El Building where the children poured out of the front door of the dilapidated tenement still answering their mothers in a mixture of Spanish and English: "Sí, Mami, I'll come straight home from school." At the corner we were halted by the crossing guard, a strict woman who only gestured her instructions, never spoke directly to the children, and only ordered us to "halt" or "cross" while holding her white-gloved hand up at face level or swinging her arm sharply across her chest if the light was green.

12   The school building was not a welcoming sight for someone used to the bright colors and airiness of tropical architecture. The building looked functional. It could have been a prison, an asylúm, or just what it was: an urban school for the children of immigrants, built to withstand waves of change, generation by generation. Its red brick sides rose to four solid stories. The black steel fire escapes snaked up its back like an exposed vertebra. A chain-link fence surrounded its concrete playground. Members of the elite safety patrol, older kids, sixth graders mainly, stood at each of its entrances, wearing their fluorescent white belts that criss-crossed their chests and their metal badges. No one was allowed in the building until the bell rang, not even on rainy or bitter-cold days. Only the safety-patrol stayed warm.

13   My mother stood in front of the main entrance with me and a growing crowd of noisy children. She looked like one of us, being no taller than the sixth-grade girls. She held my hand so tightly that my fingers cramped. When the bell rang, she walked me into the building and kissed my cheek. Apparently my father had done all the paperwork for my enrollment, because the next thing I remember was being led to my third-grade classroom by a black girl who had emerged from the principal's office.

14   Though I had learned some English at home during my first years in Paterson, I had let it recede deep into my memory while learning Spanish in Puerto Rico. Once again I was the child in the cloud of silence, the one who had to be spoken to in sign language as if she were a deaf-mute. Some of the children even raised their voices when they spoke to me, as if I had trouble hearing. Since it was a large troublesome class composed mainly of black and Puerto Rican children, with a few working-class Italian children interspersed, the teacher paid little attention to me. I re-learned the language quickly by the immersion method. I remember one day, soon after I joined the rowdy class when our regular teacher was absent and Mrs. D., the sixth-grade teacher from across the hall, attempted to monitor both classes. She scribbled something on the chalkboard and went to her own room. I felt a pressing need to use the bathroom and asked Julio, the Puerto Rican boy who sat behind me, what I had to do to be excused. He said that Mrs. D. had written on the board that we could be excused by simply writing our names under the sign. I got up from my desk and started for the front of the room when I was struck on the head hard with a book. Startled and hurt, I turned around expecting to find one of the bad boys in my class, but it was Mrs. D. I

faced. I remember her angry face, her fingers on my arms pulling me back to my desk, and her voice saying incomprehensible things to me in a hissing tone. Someone finally explained to her that I was new, that I did not speak English. I also remember how suddenly her face changed from anger to anxiety. But I did not forgive her for hitting me with that hard-cover spelling book. Yes, I would recognize that book even now. It was not until years later that I stopped hating that teacher for not understanding that I had been betrayed by a classmate, and by my inability to read her warning on the board. *I instinctively understood then that language is the only weapon a child has against the absolute power of adults.*

I quickly built up my arsenal of words by becoming an insatiable reader of books.   15

Inquiring into the Essay

Here's another chance to use writing to think about what you've just read. On a right-hand notebook page (or top of a Word document), finish your first reading of Cofer's essay with a fastwrite that explores and explains your reaction to and understanding of what you just read. Then on the left-hand page (or below your initial fastwrite in a Word document) collect some sentences or passages from the essay that seem relevant to your first thoughts.

1. **Explore.** In the 1950s and 1960s, many saw America as a "melting pot." The idea was that although we may have many different immigrant backgrounds, we should strive toward some common "Americanism." For some this is still a powerful idea, but for others the melting pot metaphor reflects cultural dominance and even prejudice, a demand that differences be ignored and erased rather than celebrated. In your journal, write about your own feelings on this controversy. Tell the story of a friend, a relative, a neighbor who was an outsider. Tell about your own experience. What did it mean to assimilate, and at what cost?

2. **Explain.** Explain what you understand Cofer to mean in the second-to-last sentence of the essay: *I instinctively understood then that language is the only weapon a child has against the absolute power of adults.* To arrive at this explanation, consider exploring your thinking first. Fastwrite for one full minute without stopping.

3. **Evaluate.** What might this essay be asserting about cultural assimilation in America during the 1950s and 1960s? Would such an assertion still be relevant?

4. **Reflect.** One of the most common reasons students cite for liking a story is that "they could relate to it." Can an Anglo reader of Cofer's essay genuinely "relate to" her experience as an American of Puerto Rican descent? Reflect on what it means to "relate to" something you read by talking about your experience reading Cofer's essay.

THE WRITING PROCESS

Inquiry Project **Writing a Personal Essay**

Here are some approaches to writing a personal essay as an inquiry project—a traditional essay and some multimodal methods. Your instructor will give you further guidance on the details of the assignment.

Inquiry questions: What does it mean to me? What do I understand about this now that I didn't understand then?

Write a personal essay on a topic that you find confusing or that raises interesting questions for you. Topics need not be personal, but they should arise from your own experiences and observations. The essay should offer a central insight about what you've come to understand about yourself and/or the topic. In other words, you will "essay" into a part of your life, past or present, exploring the significance of some memories, experiences, or observations. Your motive is personal discovery—reaching that new insight.

Your essay should do all the following (see also p. 75 for typical features of the personal essay):

- Do more than tell a story. There must be a *purpose* behind telling the story that speaks in some way to someone else. It should, ultimately, answer the *So what?* question.
- Include some reflection to explain or speculate about what you understand *now* about something that you didn't understand *then*. Your essay should have both a then-narrator and a now-narrator, one who remembers what happened and the other who sees what happened with the understanding you have now.
- Be richly detailed. Seize opportunities to *show* what you mean rather than simply explain it.

Prose+

Write your essay as a radio essay/podcast, and digitally record yourself reading the piece, using Audacity, GarageBand, or other audio software. (See p. 143 for more information on using Audacity.) This essay should be no longer than 2 to 3 minutes. The incorporation of music is optional. Keep the following in mind:

- This is a conversational medium. Write the piece like you talk.
- Be concise. Don't waste any words.
- The point (S.O.F.T.—say one fricking thing) of your essay should be clearly stated.
- Emphasize story, and avoid long stretches of exposition.

Write your essay to then publish on the web using Blogger, Wordpress, or other blogging software. You can use the site throughout the semester to post personal essays on other topics, and use this experience in a final paper to explore some aspect of the theme "The Public and the Personal." Some tips for writing a personal essay in this form include:

- Craft a good title for your essay so search engines and RSS readers will notice your piece.
- People who read unfamiliar blogs will often merely glance at them first. Write your essay to get your readers' attention and make it easily "scannable." Use subheadings, images, boxes, and so on.
- Write with voice. Your essay should have a strong persona that you can imagine using in almost any blog you write.

Write a personal essay modeled after "Every Morning for Five Years" (p. 77–78). Begin with a digital photograph of an object that is meaningful to you, and then explore its significance.

Writing Beyond the Classroom

Essaying "This I Believe"

The essay genre, which has been around for about five hundred years, is a vibrant and increasingly common form of writing on the radio and online audio. Why? One reason might be that the intimacy of the essay—the sense of a writer speaking directly to a reader without the masks we often wear when we write—seems particularly powerful when we hear

A public dialogue about belief—one essay at a time.

this i believe®

What Are You Going to Write About?

3.4

Use invention strategies to discover and develop a personal essay topic.

With the personal essay, nearly anything goes. Essayists write about everything from their struggles with eating disorders, adjusting to life after military service, or dealing with the loss of a sibling to what we typically consider utterly commonplace things: a walk, negotiating use of an armrest with a fellow airplane passenger, a fondness for weird hats. Whatever you write about, what matters most is that you've chosen the topic because you aren't quite sure what you want to think about it. Write about what confuses you, what puzzles you, or what raises itchy questions.

The process for discovering a topic (see Figure 3.1) begins simply with what I call opening up, or generating lots of material. Open the warehouse of memory and walk around, or open your eyes and look around you *now*. Just collect some things, without judging their value for this project. Next, narrow things down. Make some judgments. Decide on an experience or observation that raises the most interesting questions—about how you feel or what it means. Now try out this topic by generating more material that focuses on it. Finally, make some judgments about what (if anything) all this writing has helped you to understand about yourself or the topic. These insights help you to clarify what your essay might really be about. The essayist Vivian Gornick writes that personal essays have both a *situation* and a *story*. The situation is what happened—the doctor told you when you were twelve that your leg was broken. The story is what you understand *now* about the significance of that situation. Maybe that time of walking on crutches gave you insight into a kind of suffering that you otherwise wouldn't have known, and this inspired the empathy you feel now for a disabled friend.

Opening up (generating): What do I remember or see that I'd like to think about?

Narrowing down (judging): Which of these raise the most interesting questions to explore?

Trying out (generating, then judging): What do I understand now about this topic that I didn't before?

Figure 3.1   A process for discovering a personal essay topic

Generate material about possible situations to write about, narrow them down, and then focus on trying to discover the larger story you might be trying to tell.

Opening Up

Even if you've already got an idea for a personal essay topic, spend some time exploring the possibilities before you make a commitment. It doesn't really take much time, and there's a decent chance that you'll discover a great topic for your essay you never would have thought of otherwise.

The journal prompts that follow will get you going. What you're after is to stumble on an interesting topic. Actually, it's more like stumbling through the *door* to an interesting topic—a door that gives you a look at what you might fruitfully explore with more-focused writing. Try several prompts, looking for a topic that might, after some writing, raise questions such as these:

- *Am I uncertain about what this might mean?*
- *Is this topic more complicated than it seemed at first?*
- *Might I understand these events differently now than I did then?*

Listing Prompts. Lists can be rich sources of topic ideas. Let them grow freely, and when you're ready, use an item as the focus of another list or an episode of fastwriting. The following prompts should get you started thinking about both your experiences and your observations.

1. Make a list of experiences you've had that you can't forget. Reach into all parts and times of your life.
2. Make a list of things that bug you. Think about everyday things like people with Apple computer fetishes or friends who send text messages in the middle of a serious conversation.

Fastwriting Prompts. Early on, fastwriting can help you settle on a narrower topic, *if* you allow yourself to write "badly." Then use a more focused fastwrite, trying to generate information and ideas within the loose boundaries of your chosen topic.

1. Choose an item from a list you've created to use as a prompt. Just start fastwriting about the item; perhaps start with a story, a scene, a situation, a description. Follow the writing to see where it leads.

2. Most of us quietly harbor dreams—we hope to be a professional dancer, a good father, an activist, a marketing executive, an Olympic luger, or a novelist. Begin a fastwrite in which you explore your dreams. When the writing stalls, ask yourself questions: *Where did this dream come from? Do I still believe in it? In what moments did it seem within reach? In what moments did it fade?* Plunge into those moments.

3. What was the most confusing time in your life? Choose a moment or scene that stands out in your memory of that time, and, writing in the present tense, describe what you see, hear, and do. After five minutes, skip a line and choose another moment. Then another. Make a collage.

4. What do you consider "turning points" in your life, times when you could see the end of one thing and the beginning of something else? Fastwrite about one of these for seven minutes.

Visual Prompts. Images trigger ideas, and so can more-visual ways of thinking. Let's try both. Boxes, lines, arrows, charts, and even sketches can help us see more of the landscape of a subject, especially connections between fragments of information that aren't as obvious in prose. The clustering or mapping method is useful to many writers early in the writing process as they try to discover a topic. (See the "Inquiring into the Details" box on p. 92 for more details on how to create a cluster.) Figure 3.2 shows my cluster from the first prompt listed here.

1. What objects would you most regret losing in a house fire? Choose a most-treasured object as the core for a cluster. Build a web of associations from it, returning to the detail in the core whenever a strand dies out.

2. Find a photograph from your past, perhaps like the one from mine that opens this chapter. Fastwrite about what you see in the picture, what you don't see, and a story that it inspires.

3. Draw a long line on a piece of paper in your journal. This is your life. Divide the line into segments that seem to describe what feels like distinct times in your life. These don't have to correspond to familiar age categories such as adolescence or childhood; they could correspond to periods in your life you associate with a place, a relationship, a dilemma, a job, a personal challenge, and so on. In any case, make the segments chronological. Examine your timeline, and, as a fastwrite prompt, put two of these periods in your life together. Explore what they had in common, particularly how the earlier period might have shaped the later one. See Figure 3.3 for a sample timeline.

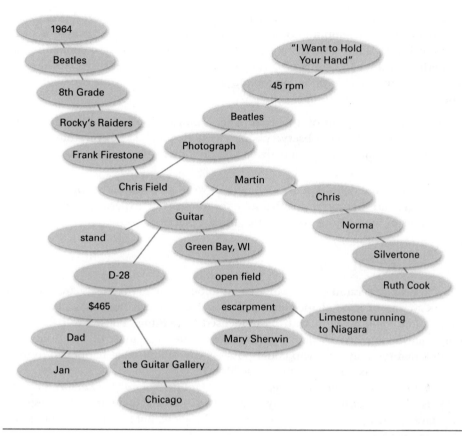

Figure 3.2 A cluster built around the one object I would most regret losing in a house fire: my Martin guitar

4. Get on Google Earth. Find the town or city where you were born or lived as a young child. Zoom in on your neighborhood. Fastwrite about what this makes you remember. Alternatively, find the house you live in now. Using the "street view" feature, "walk" down the street, stopping at the homes of interesting neighbors that you know or have observed. With the image on the screen, fastwrite in your journal, telling yourself stories about the people in your neighborhood.

Figure 3.3 A sample timeline from my own life

Research Prompts. Things we hear, see, or read can be powerful prompts for personal essays. It's tempting to believe that personal essays are always about the past, but just as often essayists are firmly rooted in the present, commenting and pondering on the confusions of contemporary life. In that sense, personal essayists are researchers, always on the lookout for material. Train your eye with one or more of the following prompts.

1. Put this at the top of a journal page: "Things People Do." Now go outside and find a place to observe people. Write down a list of everything you see people doing. Choose one action you find interesting and fastwrite about it. Is it weird? Why?

2. Look up the definition of "infatuation." Write it down on the top of a journal page, and then write for five minutes about your experience and observations of infatuations with people, things, places, ideas.

Narrowing Down

Okay, you've generated some bad writing about your experiences and observations. Can any of it be shaped into a personal essay? Are there any clues about a topic you could develop with more-focused fastwriting? These are particularly tough questions when writing a personal essay, because most of us are inclined to think that the only one who could possibly care about what happened to us or what we observe is ourselves (or maybe Mom).

Don't make the mistake of judging the material too soon or too harshly. Personal essayists write successfully about any topic—often including quite ordinary things—so don't give up on a promising topic this early in the game. But first, how do you decide what's promising?

What's Promising Material and What Isn't? The signs of a promising personal essay topic include the following:

- **Abundance.** What subject generated the most writing? Do you sense that there is much more to write about?
- **Surprise.** Did you see or say something you didn't expect about a topic?
- **Confusion.** What subject raises questions you're not sure you can answer easily?

In the personal essay, this last item—confusion and uncertainty—may yield the most-fertile topics. All of the questions listed at the beginning of "Opening Up," on page 88, are related in some way to a feeling that some experience or observation—even if it's familiar to you—has yet to yield all of its possible meanings.

Questions About Purpose and Audience. Who cares about my middling career as a high school cross-country runner? Who cares that I grew to love that gritty neighborhood in Hartford? Who cares that I find high school reunions weird? When we write about ourselves, we can't help but wonder why anyone, other than ourselves, *would* care. Maybe they won't. But if you discover something about your life that helps you to understand it better—even in a small way—you will begin to find an audience. After all, we are interested in understanding our own, often ordinary lives, and perhaps we can learn something from you.

To find an audience for a personal essay, you have to discover something to say about your experiences and observations that speak to others—a theme that you could express in a "we statement."

Obviously, why you're writing and for whom will profoundly influence your approach. That's a fundamental principle of rhetoric, one that you applied when you jotted that note to your teacher explaining the late assignment or texted your friend about your new bicycle. Although it is useful to consider your purpose and audience early on, make sure you don't let purpose and audience considerations squeeze off your writing. You always want to be open to the unexpected places your writing might lead you, especially in the early stages of the process. Being too vigilant about what readers think can discourage you from welcoming the messy accidents that can make for helpful discoveries.

Trying Out

Recently, I began working on a personal essay about my experiences going to high school reunions. I went to my fortieth last fall. As I generated "bad writing" on the subject of high school reunions, I kept returning to the same question: If I find these reunions generally weird and unsatisfying, why do I keep going? Using this inquiry question, I tried out my topic with the focused fastwrite that follows:

> *Last fall, I went to my 40th high school reunion...I had been to the 10th and the 20th, both of which required travel, once from the East coast and once from the West. I have no idea why I went to the effort...I didn't like high school...and I don't have many friends left in the Chicago suburb where I grew up. Why does anyone go to a high school reunion? I wonder if I've gone because...like it or not...high school is part of the narrative of our growing up that is at once mysterious and utterly familiar. I can remember everything...my failure to make the swim team that my brother was a star on...breaking the mercury barometer in physics class with my elbow while cleaning chalk erasers at the window...the sexual thrill of sitting on a bench next to Suzie Durment at a football game and feeling her thigh press close to mine. And yet I can't explain so much of high school...It just doesn't make sense. Why would I run cross country for four years and absolutely hate every minute of it?...How could I so thoroughly mishandle the kindness and affection of Jan Dawe, my first serious girlfriend?...And why all those years did I still pine for Lori Jo Flink, a girl from the 7th grade?...I guess that's one reason*

I go to my high school reunion...To enjoy the melancholy of seeing Lori Jo again and to relish the bittersweet taste of rejection....She always comes...Yet when I did see her this time it wasn't the same. We had a very brief conversation..."I looked you up on the Internet," she said, and was promptly swept to the dance floor by Larry Piacenza...She looked me up on the Internet...This should have given me a thrill but it didn't...Why not?...These days I've been stripping the siding off so many old narratives about myself, stories that I've mistaken for walls that bear weight...Perhaps I tossed Lori Jo on that pile of discarded lumber...along with the desire to attend another high school reunion. As I'm counting the gifts of middle age, I gladly add this one.

What I hope you notice in my focused writing on reunions is how I keep using questions to tease out meaning, starting with a question I've never really asked myself before: Why do I go to high school reunions? Why would anyone? These inquiry questions pulled me out of the sea of experience and onto the mountain of reflection (highlighted passages), where I begin to see a possible answer: I go to reunions to revive old stories about myself that may no longer matter. In the personal essay, judging involves *reflection*. What do we make of what happened then that we didn't quite see until now? What might our observations of the world around us now *say* about that world and, maybe more important, about ourselves?

Questions for Reflection. In Chapter 1, I talked about thinking with writing as a movement back and forth between the creative and critical minds. In a way, personal essays and other narrative genres make this movement of the mind visible. In the essays you read earlier in the chapter, you may have noticed that some of the pieces seem to subtly shift from situation to story, from narrative to exposition, memory to reflection. This movement often has to do with time. You remember that something happened, recently or long ago. You describe what you remember, traveling back in time. But you aren't really a time traveler. You write from the present, and it is the present that allows you to understand what you couldn't have understood in the past. This is the source of reflection in the personal essay.

One way of thinking about this is in terms of the then-narrator and the now-narrator. The two narrators collaborate to make meaning. But it is the now-narrator who provides the judgment. Now that you've tried out your topic, put yourself in the now-narrator's perspective, answering questions such as these:

- What do you understand now about this topic that you didn't fully understand when you began writing about it? Start some writing with this phrase: "As I look back on this now, I realize that..."

- What seems to be the most important thing you're trying to say so far?

- How has your thinking changed about your topic? Finish this seed sentence as many times as you can in your notebook: *Once I thought _____, and now I think _____.*

Writing the Sketch

Throughout *The Curious Writer*, I'll encourage you to write what I call "sketches." As the name implies, this is a first look at something roughly drawn. It is a pretty rough draft of your piece, perhaps no more than about 300 words, with a tentative title. Though it may be sketchy, your sketch should be reader-based prose. You want someone else to understand what it's about. Don't assume they know what you know. When you need to, explain things.

A sketch is a good starting point for a personal essay in any mode. If you're working on a radio essay, for example, the sketch will be much the same as one that you write for a conventional essay. It's simply a very early script.

Choose your most promising material, and tell the story. If it's drawn from memory, incorporate both what happened then and what you make of it now. If it's built on observations, make sure they are detailed, anchored to particular times and places, and in some way significant.

You may or may not answer the "So what?" question in your sketch, though you should try. Don't muscle the material too much to conform to what you already think; let the writing help you figure out what you think.

To summarize, then, in a sketch try to do the following:

- Have a tentative title.
- Keep it relatively short.
- Write it fast.
- Don't muscle it to conform to a preconceived idea.
- Write to be read, with an audience in mind.
- Make it specific instead of general.

▶ Student Sketch

Amanda Stewart's sketch, "Earning a Sense of Place," faintly bears the outlines of what might be a great personal essay. On the surface, "Earning a Sense of Place" could seem simply a piece about Amanda's passion for skiing. So what? And yet, there are lines here that point to larger ideas and unanswered questions. For example, Amanda writes that the "mental reel" of her swishing down a mountain on skis is "the image that sustains me when things are hard, and when I want to stop doing what is right and start doing what is easy." Why is it that such a mental image can be sustaining in hard times? How well does this work? This really might be a piece about trying to find a "sense of place" that doesn't rely on such images; in a sense, the sketch seems to be trying to say that joy on the mountain isn't enough.

The pleasure of writing and reading a sketch is looking for what it might teach you, learning what you didn't know you knew.

I've highlighted portions of the text to illustrate a revision exercise that follows Amanda's essay.

Earning a Sense of Place

Amanda Stewart

1   The strings to my earflaps stream behind me, mixing with my hair as a rooster-tail flowing behind my neck. Little ice crystals cling to the bottom of my braid and sparkle in the sunlight. The pompom on top of my hat bobs up and down as I arc out, turning cleanly across the snow. I suck in the air, biting with cold as it hits my hot lungs, and breathe deep as I push down the run.

2   This is what I see when I picture who I want to be. It's the image that sustains me when things are hard, and when I want to stop doing what is right and start doing what is easy. I have made so many terrible decisions in the past that I know how far astray they lead me; I don't want that. I want the girl in the mental reel in her quilted magenta jacket and huge smile. She's what I grasp at when I need help getting through the day.

3   She's an amalgam of moments from the past mixed with my hopes for the future. I love to ski, and have since my parents strapped little plastic skis onto my galoshes when I was a year and a half old. From that day I flopped around our snow-covered yard, I've been in love with skiing. It's the only time I feel truly comfortable. Day to day I often feel so awkward. I wonder if my hair is right, or if my clothes fit. Last night, my roommate had a boy over, and as he sat on the couch talking to me, all I felt was discomfort and awkwardness. I didn't know what to say, felt judged, felt out of place. I never feel that way on skis. Even floundering in heavy, deep snow, or after a fall that has packed my goggles with snow and ripped the mittens off my hands I know exactly what to do. I'm a snow mermaid, only comfortable in my medium. I often wish I could trade in my walking legs for something like a tail that is more truly me.

4   My dad's coffee cup at home says, "I only work so I can ski," and for him, it's true. Sometimes I feel like I only push through my daily life so I can get to the next mountain and zip up my pants and go. I don't want to live like that though: it's too much time looking forward to something, and not enough looking at what I'm living in. I need to appreciate my life as it is, snowy cold or sunny warm. That sense of place I have on skis can probably be earned here on the flat expanses of campus just as easily as I got it pushing myself down the bunny slopes so long ago. I just have to earn it.

Moving from Sketch to Draft

Here's the journey with the assignment you've taken so far:

1. You've generated some "bad writing," openly exploring possibilities for personal essay topics while suspending judgment.
2. You landed on a tentative topic.
3. You tried out this topic through more writing, some of it still "bad."
4. Your critical mind took over as you began to judge what you have so far. What questions does this material raise for you? What might it *mean?* With judgment comes a growing concern for audience. Why would they care about this?
5. You tried out the topic in a sketch. It's written with an audience in mind.

At the heart of the process I'm describing is a movement from "writer-based" to "reader-based" prose. This movement occurs with any type of writing, but it's particularly tricky with the personal essay. When you're writing about yourself, there is always this: *Who cares?*

The movement from sketch to draft must address this question. But how?

Evaluating Your Own Sketch. One way to assess whether your sketch might be meaningful to someone other than you is to look for the balance between narrative and reflection, or the then-narrator and the now-narrator. Try this:

- Take two highlighters, each a different color.
- Go through your sketch from beginning to end, using one color to highlight text that's story-telling, what happened or what you saw, and then use the other color to highlight text that is explanatory, more-general commentary about what happened or what you saw. What's the pattern of color?

There are several possibilities here:

1. **One color dominates.** Your sketch is mostly narrative or mostly summary, all then-narrator or all now-narrator. A personal essay that is mostly narrative usually fails to address the "So what?" question. It seems to tell a story without a purpose. On the other hand, a personal essay that is all explanation fails to engage readers in the writer's *experiences*. It's all telling and no showing. Personal essays must both show *and* tell.

2. **One color dominates except at the end.** Typically, there is all narrative until the very end, when the writer briefly reflects, much like the formula for a fable, with its moral at the end. This can seem predictable to readers. But you can work with it in revision by taking the reflection at the end and using it to reconceive the essay *from the very beginning*. Can you take the ending and use the insight to organize your thinking in a revision?

3. **The colors alternate.** Sometimes this is the most interesting type of personal essay, because the two narrators are in genuine collaboration, trying to figure out what happened and what it *means*.

In my markup of Amanda's sketch (pp. 96–97), you can see how there is some shifting in the pattern of color. But exposition dominates. Her revision might need more story, more *showing* readers what happened that has made her think the things she now thinks.

If our personal experiences and observations are to mean anything to someone else, then they must, at the very least, both show and tell. They should, through details, descriptions, and scenes, invite an audience into the sea of our experiences. But they must also be clear about the *reason* behind the invitation—about what we have come to understand and want our audience to understand. In revising your sketch, focus on these two concerns above all.

Reflecting on What You Learned. In Chapter 1, I introduced the dialectical method of thinking through writing that moves back and forth between creative thinking and critical thinking, generating and judging. Highlighting the two narrators in your sketch is a way to actually see yourself thinking that way *in your own writing*—or not, depending on the patterns of color you see. Make a journal entry about this. In your sketch, which of the two narrators is more active, and why do you think that's so? In a revision of this sketch, how might you address any imbalance between the two? Where could the now-narrator tell more, or where could the then-narrator show more?

Developing

In the last section, you focused on using a sketch to identify the *purposes* of telling someone else about your memories, experiences, or observations. For example, in the sample sketch, Amanda seems to be telling us about her love for skiing because it suggests a longing that most of us feel: to transfer the confidence we feel in one part of our lives to every part. The key to developing your draft is to arrive at a fuller understanding of what your purpose is in telling your own stories *and then rebuild your essay around that insight from the beginning.*

In other words, as you begin your revision, focus on exploring the answer to these questions:

- What might this essay be saying, not only about me, but more generally about people who find themselves in similar situations?

- What questions does it raise that might be interesting, not only to me, but also to others who may not know me?

Fastwrite in your journal about these questions for as long as you can. One word of caution, though, and I can't stress it enough: YOU DO NOT NEED TO BE PROFOUND. Most of us aren't philosophers or really deep thinkers. We are ordinary people who are just trying to make sense of our lives and work towards those little insights that make us understand things a little better.

As you get a grip on the purpose behind your essay, you can focus your efforts on developing those parts of the narrative that are relevant. What scenes, anecdotes, details, observations, facts, stories, and so on might focus your attention—and later your readers' attention—on what you're trying to say about the topic?

For this, try some of the following strategies:

- *Explode a moment.* Choose a scene or moment in the story or stories you're telling that seems particularly important to the meaning of the essay. Reenter that moment and fastwrite for a full seven minutes, using all your senses and as much detail as you can muster.

- *Make lists.* Brainstorm a list of details, facts, or specifics about a moment or scene that was part of an experience or about an observation. Then list other experiences or observations that seem connected to this one (see "Cluster" below).

- *Research.* Do some quick-and-dirty research that might bring in other voices or more information that will deepen your consideration of the topic.

- *Cluster (or fastwrite).* Try to move beyond narrating a single experience or observation and discover others that might help you see important patterns. For example, let's say your sketch is about your experience working with the poor in Chile. Have you had other encounters with extreme poverty (or extreme wealth)? Can you describe them? What do they reveal about your feelings or attitudes about poverty or your reactions to what happened in Chile?

Drafting

Some of my students get annoyed at all the "stuff" I encourage them to do before they begin a first draft of a personal essay. In some cases, all the journal work isn't necessary; the writer very quickly gets a strong sense of direction and feels ready to begin composing. But from the beginning, I've encouraged you to gravitate toward topics that you find confusing, and with that kind of material, exploratory writing is time well spent. Remember, too, that journal writing counts as writing. It not only offers the pleasures of surprise, but can ultimately make the drafting process more efficient by generating material that you won't have to conjure up during those long, painful periods of staring at the computer screen, wondering what to say next.

As you begin drafting, keep in mind what you've learned from your writing so far. For example:

- What is the most important question that is behind your exploration of the topic?
- What do you understand now that you didn't understand fully when you started writing about it?
- How can you show *and* explain how you came to this understanding?
- Have you already written a strong first line for the draft? Can you find it somewhere in all your journal writing?

Draft with your reader in mind. As you draft, ask yourself,

What does the reader most need to know to understand my thinking and feelings about this topic? What should I show about what happened, to give the reader a clear sense of what happened?

Methods of Development. Narrative is an especially useful method of development for personal essays. How might you use it to develop your subject?

Narrative. Narrative can work in a personal essay in at least three ways. You can use it to:

1. Tell an extended story of what happened.
2. Tell one or more anecdotes, or brief stories, that somehow address the question behind your interest in the topic.
3. Tell the story of your thinking as you've come to understand something you didn't understand before.

Often, a single essay uses narrative in all three types of ways.

Consider beginning your draft with the anecdote or the part of the story you want to tell that best frames the question, dilemma, or idea that is the focus of your essay (see "Inquiring into the Details: More Than One Way to Tell a Story"). If you're writing about the needless destruction of a childhood haunt by developers, then consider opening with the way the place looked *after* the bulldozers were done with it—description related to the end of your narrative.

Time in writing is nothing like real time. You can ignore chronology, if it serves your purpose. You can write pages about something that happened in seven minutes or cover twenty years in a paragraph. The key is to tell your story or stories in ways that emphasize what's important.

Using Evidence. How do you make your essay convincing, and even moving, to an audience? It's all in the details. Like most stories, the personal essay thrives on particularity: What exactly did it look like? What exactly did she say? What exactly did it sound and smell like at that moment? Evidence that gives a personal essay authority are details that make a reader believe the writer can be trusted to observe keenly and to remember accurately. All of the professional essays in this chapter are rich in detail. The neighbor with the "neon orange hunting cap" who rakes the same spot every day in Laura Zazulak's "Every Morning for Five Years" and the wilting banana leaves that curl around the coconut candy in Judith Ortiz Cofer's "One More Lesson." This focus on the particular—what it *exactly* looked like, smelled like, felt like, sounded like—makes an essay come alive for both writer and reader.

As you draft your essay, remember the subtle power of details. Tell, but always show, too.

Workshopping

At this stage in writing the personal essay—the first full draft—what you may need most are responses that address the things you've worked on most in your sketch: Does the draft clearly answer the "So what?" question (purpose)? Is it clear what the one main thing is that the essay is trying to say (meaning)? All other revision concerns are subordinate to these questions. Why? Because without a clear purpose and clear sense, it's impossible to make any judgments about content.

Annie Dillard, a writer of many nonfiction books and essays, once said that she believed that the biggest challenge in writing comes down to this basic question: *What to put in and what to leave out.* In a narrative essay such as the one you're working on, you might conclude that the answer to the question is equally simple: You tell the "whole" story. Yet the truth is that you never do, even in telling a story to friends. We shape and shade a story depending on our motive for telling it. The same is true in prose. Your purpose and what you are trying to say are the two things that determine what belongs in a story and what doesn't. So this is where you should begin.

Questions for Readers. The following grid, which focuses on these two key concerns, can help you to guide your peers' response to your first draft.

Questions for Peer Reviewers	
1. Purpose	What would you say this essay is about? Do you have a clear sense of *why* I'm writing about this topic?
2. Meaning	Most essays need to say one fricking thing (S.O.F.T.). What would you say is the point of this draft? What is the main thing I seem to be saying about this topic?

Reflecting on the Workshop. After the workshop session, do a follow-up entry in your notebook that summarizes what you heard, what made sense and what didn't, and how you plan to approach the next draft. Your instructor may ask you to share this information in a cover letter submitted with the revision.

Revising

Revision is a continual process—not a last step. You've been revising—"reseeing" your subject—from the first messy fastwriting in your journal. But the things that get your attention vary depending on where you are in the writing process. With your draft in hand, revision becomes your focus through what I'll call "shaping and tightening your draft."

3.5

Apply revision strategies that are effective for shaping narratives.

Shaping. Shaping focuses on larger concerns first: purpose and meaning—the very largest concerns, which you've looked at if you workshopped your draft—and the next-to-largest concerns of information and organization. It starts with knowing what your essay is about—your inquiry question and maybe your theme—and then revising to make every element of the draft focused on that question or idea.

What to Cut and What to Add. A key to revising a personal essay is this:

Given my essay's purpose and meaning, what should I cut and what should I add?

- What information—scenes, descriptions, observations, explanations—is no longer relevant to the purpose and meaning?
- What information is missing that should be added to help readers understand and, in a small way, experience, so that they will appreciate my point?

The Question of Time. Revising a narrative essay also involves the question of time. Consider this in two ways:

1. Where will information come from to develop your story—from the past or from the present? The then-narrator is master of the past. What happened? And then what? The now-narrator is charged with commenting from the present. What do I make of what happened from where I sit now? Personal essays that tell stories need information from both past and present.

2. How does time organize the information in the draft? Do you tell your story chronologically? Is that the best way to structure the essay? What might happen, for example, if you begin in the middle of the story, or even at the end? Will that better dramatize the question or dilemma that you're exploring?

Research. I'm not talking about extensive research, but about quick searches for background information, relevant facts, and maybe even something on what other writers or experts have said. Say you're writing an essay about iPhone infatuation. Why not look up a definition of "infatuation" and then do some quick research on how students use their iPhones in a typical day?

Other Questions for Revision. Make sure you address the following questions as you revise:

- Does the draft begin in a way that gives your readers a sense of where the essay is going? Is your purpose clear? (This is especially important for podcast essays.)

- Is there too much explaining? Narrative essays are usually built on the backbone of story—anecdote, scene, description. This is how we help the audience appreciate, in some small way, the experiences that have inspired the insights we want to share. Personal essays *do* need to tell, but they must also *show*.

- By the end of your essay, does the reader appreciate the significance of the story you're telling? Have you said what you need to say about how, though it's your experience, the meaning you discover might apply to others as well?

Polishing. When you are satisfied with the shape of your draft, focus on paragraphs, sentences, and words. Are your paragraphs coherent? How do you manage transitions? Are your sentences fluent and concise? Are there any errors in spelling or syntax?

Before you finish your draft, work through the following checklist:

✓ Every paragraph is about one thing.

✓ The transitions between paragraphs aren't abrupt.

✓ The length of sentences varies in each paragraph.

✓ Each sentence is concise. There are no unnecessary words or phrases.

✓ You've checked grammar, particularly for verb agreement, run-on sentences, unclear pronouns, and misused words (*there/their*, *where/were*, and so on).

✓ You've run your spellchecker and proofed your paper for misspelled words.

▶ Student Essay

Military veterans often bring their rich, complicated experiences into my writing classes, and because what they've seen and done often raises questions they can't easily answer, they learn to love the personal essay. Seth Marlin served in Iraq. In the essay "Smoke of Empire," he remembers that during his first night in the country, there was a stench he didn't recognize. It turns out this was the smell of things—often perfectly good things—burning. The refuse of war. This memory inspires a meditation on war, waste, and empire.

The piece was written for the radio, and Seth produced an audio essay using Audacity software that blended his voice reading of "Smoke of Empire" with music that gave the essay even more power. As you read Seth's essay, keep in mind that he wrote it with the idea that his audience would hear it a single time. Consider as you read it how that changes his approach to the writing. You can also listen to the essay at bruceballenger.com.

Smoke of Empire

Seth Marlin

When I was in Iraq, we used to have this rotating detail. Call it "*Hajji*-watch." Bring in local guys, pay them ten bucks to move sandbags, haul trash. Post a couple soldiers with rifles in case anyone gets froggy. Locals try to sell you stuff, turn them down. They ask for soap, shampoo, toothpaste, say you don't have any. That's the order they drill into you: *Do Not Buy, Sell, or Give Items to Local Nationals.*   1

Locals were poor. Dirt poor. Steal the gloves out of your pocket if they thought they'd get some use. Who could blame them? One guy I saw stole a bedroll once; another, maybe fifteen, jacked a soccer-ball, said it was for his little brother. Our squad-leader said it was contraband, said the ball would be waiting for him when he came back next week, soon as he got a memorandum from the base-commander.   2

That kid never got his ball, you kidding me? Lot of poor guys with families; that line stretched two miles up the road back into town. He'd have been lucky to get in at all. I doubt he ever got that ball back; most likely, it just went to the burn-pit.   3

* * *

Fun fact: Wars generate waste. The Department of Defense estimates that its wars each generate ten pounds of garbage per service member per day. At over 150,000 service members deployed, that's a lot of trash. Unfortunately, the locals tend not to cotton to your leaving messes all over their soil; thus, in the name of diplomacy, the invaders have to clean up after themselves. On places like Joint Base Balad, all that refuse goes to one place: the burn-pit.   4

Picture a base, fifteen miles across, set in a swath of palm-dotted farmland. Now picture on part of that a landscape of hills, valleys, and craters—all of it garbage, all bigger than a dozen football fields. Now picture that on fire. Through the haze, you might see the figures who manage all that incoming drek—orange-turbaned Sikhs wearing blue jumpsuits, some of them wearing goggles and surgical masks if they're lucky. These pits are typically run by private contractors; OSHA guidelines mean little to nothing here. Your tax dollars at work.   5

My first night in Iraq, I remember looking west from my trailer and being surprised to see a sunset of blazing orange. It was at least two hours after dusk, and the stars were out, at least a couple anyway. Then I realized that *that wasn't sunlight I was seeing*—that it was *flames*. Those weren't clouds I was seeing, but rather smoke. I didn't know what all   6

(continued)

(continued)

that was yet, only that it took up half the northern sky. But oh, I learned. The first thing I learned about was the smell, like burning oak-leaves mixed with scorched plastic and warping aluminum. Wood, fabric, paper, metal—if it burned, they burnt it. If not, they threw something on it until it did. On a clear day it threw smoke a half-mile high; on the cold days during the rainy season, October through March, the flames got tamped down by the constant downpour. Made the world smell like a half-smoked cigarette, all wet soot and chemicals. Made you gag passing through it on your way to the motor pool. During the summer months the ashes blew into the town just north of us, a little two-rut burg called Yethrib. Turned the air gray, sent hot embers raining down on the farmers' fields. Sitting in a tower on a weeklong rotation of guard-duty, I remember watching one day as some hundred-odd acres of sunflower, sorghum, and lentils went up in flames. An entire season's crops destroyed, in a part of the country where the median income was two dollars a day.

* * *

7   I remember convoying home from bridge-sites late at night; I used to peer over the steering-wheel and look for the banded floodlights, the blood-red haze of smoke. Waste never sleeps. On a bulletin-board in my platoon's Ops office, I remember they'd posted a memo signed by two Air-Force lieutenants-colonel. The memo cited the effects of long-term exposure to the smoke, expressed outrage at the lack of incinerators, ordered the memo posted in every company headquarters, every permanent file of every soldier in service on that base. I'm sure that memo's still in my record somewhere; then again, the VA does have a tendency to lose things.

8   I saw a lot of strange, scary, moving things during my time deployed. Sunrises over the Tigris, Sumerian ruins, farmers praying in their fields at dawn. But the image that sticks with me is the burn-pit. Why? Maybe because the sight of all that waste, made tangible, left some mark on me, like tracking mud on floors as a guest, uninvited. War is consumption, I've realized. Conspicuous consumption. It's embarrassing, really: this is the democracy we bring to a foreign nation, consumption and waste. Look at all we've got. Fast-food, electronics, medicine. You can't have any, and we're going to burn it all right in front of you.

9   You know, the last night I was writing this I pulled up Google Earth, pinned down where I was posted. Our old motor-pool was taken down, bulldozed over; our old living-areas and trailers had been carted away. Even the burn-pit was silent, but it still sits there, like a grease-stain you can see from the air. Big sign in English: "NO DUMPING," it says, while behind it sits a mountain of blackened, twisted steel. The Balad pit may sit quiet now, but I'll bet even money those fires are still going elsewhere.

10   All day. Every day. The smoke of consumption, of Empire.

Evaluating the Essay

Discuss or write about your response to Seth Marlin's essay, using some or all of the following questions.

1.   What do you understand this essay to be saying about war, empire, and waste? Where does it say it most clearly or memorably?

2.   Throughout this chapter, I've promoted the idea that personal essays have two narrators—the now-narrator and the then-narrator. Are they both present in "Smoke of Empire"? Where?

3.   What is the main thing you might take away from reading this piece and apply when you write or revise your own personal essay?

4.   Imagine this rhetorical situation: You're in the car listening to the radio driving to campus and you hear Seth reading "Smoke of Empire." Because he's not in the car with you, you don't have to be polite. You don't even know him. You can change the station if what you hear doesn't interest you. What special demands does this situation make on *how* a personal essay is written? How might it affect the writing and organization of a piece?

Using What You Have Learned

Let's revisit the list of things at the beginning of this chapter that I hoped you'd learn.

1.   **Use personal experiences and observations to drive inquiry.** The questions that drive our inquiry into how we understand our lives are no less important than the questions that inspire us to explore other subjects.

2.   **Apply the exploratory thinking of personal essays to academic writing.** Next time you get a writing assignment in another class, start the work by "essaying" the topic—by developing a quick list of questions and responding to them. What you discover might lead to a thesis later.

3.   **Identify the characteristics of personal essays in different forms.** If you know what a personal essay looks like, you can write yours in one of these different forms. Some of the most vibrant examples of the genre are podcasts, radio essays, photographic essays, or blogs. Though these media can work with almost any form of writing, they seem to lend themselves especially to autobiographical work.

4.   **Use invention strategies to discover and develop a personal essay topic.** You can use techniques such as fastwriting and clustering. But perhaps more important, you can use such invention techniques to generate *insight*—not just an idea about something to write about, but discoveries about what you think about that topic.

5.   **Apply revision strategies that are effective for shaping narratives.** Even if you never write another personal essay, you can use narrative to tell the story of what you first thought about a subject and what you came to understand.

Writing a Review

4

Learning Objectives

In this chapter, you'll learn to

4.1 Use reasons and evidence to support a judgment about something's value.

4.2 Identify the criteria behind a judgment and determine their relevance.

4.3 Identify the characteristics of different forms of the review, including academic applications.

4.4 Use invention and focusing strategies to discover and develop a review essay.

4.5 Apply revision strategies that are effective for shaping reviews.

Writing That Evaluates

One of the occasions when I feel fairly stupid is after watching a movie with my wife, Karen. She always wants to know what I think. I don't have much of a problem arriving at a gut reaction—I loved the movie *Amelie*, for example, but I have a hard time saying why.

Essentially, Karen is asking me to evaluate a film, to make a judgment about its quality. This is something we do all the time. Buying a pair of jeans involves evaluating the reputation of the manufacturer, the quality of the denim, the particular design, and especially the way the jeans look on us when we wear them. I think most of us like to think these decisions are quite rational. But, in fact, many of our evaluations have a lot more to do with emotion than logic. We *really do* buy that pair of jeans because an ad suggests that we'll look sexy or attractive in them.

One challenge of evaluating something is keeping an open mind, sometimes *despite* our initial feelings about it. Because evaluation often begins in emotion and in what are essentially subjective value judgments, a tension always exists between our *desire* to prove our point and our *willingness* to consider other points of view. That emotion figures into our judgments of things isn't a bad thing. It's a human thing. And emotion can lead us to insight and understanding. We just need to be aware of the role of emotion, so we can suspend judgment long enough to get a more balanced look.

103

Evaluation involves four things:

1. *Judgment(s)*. Something is good or bad, useful or not useful, relevant or not relevant, convincing or not convincing, worth doing or not worth doing—or perhaps somewhere in between.

2. *Reasons*. We have reasons for deciding that something is good or bad or somewhere in between and for all our other judgments. Our reasons usually are based on our criteria and evidence.

3. *Criteria*. These form the basis for deciding that something is good or bad, useful or not useful, and so on. The more we know about something—cars, movies, or whatever—the more elaborate and sophisticated our criteria become.

4. *Evidence*. The evidence (specific details, observations, or facts about the thing itself) in support of our reasons is what makes our judgment—and evaluation—persuasive.

When we evaluate something, most of us have no problem expressing a judgment—"Amazon's new Kindle Fire is disappointing"—or offering up some reason—"Its web browser is too slow"—and evidence for it. We may have a tougher time expressing the criteria behind our judgment (see Figure 4.1). Our criteria often involve our implicit beliefs—beliefs we are not even aware of—about what makes a thing "good" and about the standard against which something is being judged.

When you write a review, your evaluation of something, you may not always state these criteria, but you should always be aware of them. As part of suspending judgment and taking a balanced look, you should examine the beliefs on which your criteria are based and think about whether these are sound. A review is an evaluation for an audience. So you will also want to ask yourself: Are my criteria based on widely held beliefs? If not, do I need to defend my criteria?

Motives for Writing a Review

4.1

Use reasons and evidence to support a judgment about something's value.

Once you start thinking about evaluative writing, you'll find it everywhere—the book reviews in the Sunday *Times*, the music reviews in *Spin*, the analysis of websites on Web Sites That Suck. It's probably the most common form of workplace writing, too, for everything from assessing the performance of an employee to evaluating a plan to preserve historic buildings. One motive for reviews is to help people make informed decisions.

In inquiry-based projects, especially, you may be reviewing something about which you simply haven't made a judgment yet. You may not even have a gut reaction. Reviews usually begin from a question that we often ask about things: How good is it? They are an attempt to answer that question by basing whatever judgment

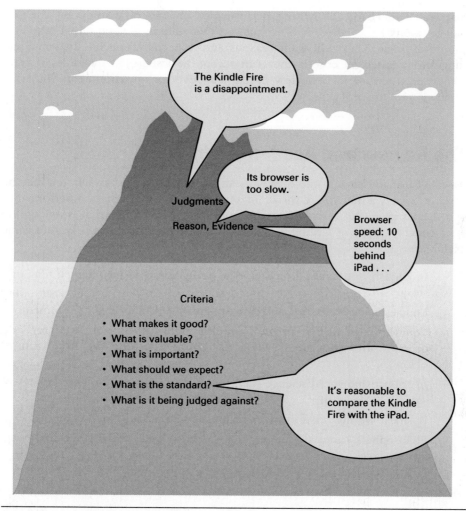

Figure 4.1 Evaluation. Like an iceberg, much of what goes into our evaluation of something may be submerged. We make judgments and might even give some reasons and evidence. But we're often not aware of the criteria behind our judgments, let alone of the beliefs on which these criteria are based—beliefs about what is good, valuable, important, or the standard. So we also need to look at our criteria and the beliefs they rest on to see if they're sound.

4.2

Identify the criteria behind a judgment and determine their relevance.

you come to on criteria you've thought about and on evidence you've found. You don't simply say, "That smartphone isn't any good." Instead, you say "that smartphone is disappointing… and here's why." Like any inquiry-based project, a review gives you a chance to explore.

Your gut reaction to something's value might satisfy a friend, but it won't satisfy an audience that needs to be *persuaded* that your judgment is sensible. Imagine, for instance,

Evaluative writing is an enormously practical form, relevant in all sorts of situations in and out of school.

that you're in charge of writing performance reviews of employees. The employees won't be satisfied with evaluations that state in general terms how they should improve. They will want reasons and, especially, specific evidence and suggestions based on criteria they can accept. In a sense, a review is an argument, and a motive for a review is like a motive for any argument: You want someone else to see it your way.

The Review and Academic Writing

We don't usually think of the review as an academic form, although you may be asked to review a film you're shown in an English class or perhaps a performance in a theater class. But reviews are a form of evaluative writing that is among the most common types of writing in all kinds of college classrooms. Here are some examples:

- In English, you might do a rhetorical evaluation of a document, a film, or a story.
- Courses in music, theater, and dance might include a review of performances.
- Courses in art history or photography might call for you to review one or more artworks (see "Seeing the Form: Choosing the Best Picture" below).
- In science and social science classes, you may evaluate the methodology of studies.
- Business writing often involves reviewing proposals or marketing plans.
- Philosophers make arguments, but they also evaluate whether arguments are effective.
- In composition, you'll review the writing of your peers.

Seeing the Form

Choosing the Best Picture

When documentary photographer Dorothea Lange encountered Florence Thompson and her family camped by a frozen pea field, she took multiple pictures. One—and only one—of them became famous. Titled "Migrant Mother," it is considered an indelible image of the Depression. If you were charged with evaluating the six shots that Lange took of Thompson and her family, seen here, which would you choose as the best shot? What reasons would you have for making this judgment?

Seeing the Form (*continued*)

Five photographs Dorothea Lange took of Florence Thompson.

4.3
Identify the
characteristics
of different
forms of the
review, includ-
ing academic
applications.

Features of the Form

Feature	Conventions of the Review Essay
Inquiry questions	How good is it? What is its value?
Motives	Your basic motive is to make a judgment about something that you may or may not be familiar with, and then, using reasonable criteria and evidence, convince others that your judgment is sensible.
Subject matter	Reviews aren't just about books, films, and performances. Nearly anything is fair game: consumer products, web pages, cars, apps, policies, restaurants, ski areas, college dorms, vacation destinations, and so on. The key is that you evaluate something that interests you but also might matter to someone else.
Structure	Many reviews have the following elements: • *Description.* What does it look like? What are some other key characteristics? • *Back story.* What is the background? What do readers need to know about if they don't know as much as you do? • *Judgments.* What do you think? These don't have to lead to some grand thesis—it was good or bad—but can be a series of assessments given over the course of the review. • *Reasons, evidence.* What are the reasons behind your judgments? And what evidence do you have to support these reasons? • *Criteria.* What is the basis for your reasons? Criteria may be stated explicitly or implied. • *Relevant comparisons.* What category does it belong to? What else is it like, and why is it better or worse?
Sources of information	The raw material of any review is specific evidence drawn from your experience and research on the subject. What specifically influenced your judgment? What did you see? What did you hear? How did it work? What did they say? What were the results? What are the facts? How does it compare? Many review topics (e.g., film, plays, cars, clothes, books) will be most informed by your direct experience with your subject. But research can help any review. You can read about it or ask people what they think of it.

Feature	Conventions of the Review Essay
Language	The review can be tricky, especially if you're an expert on the thing you're reviewing. Be careful of "insider" language—terms, definitions, and so on that people unfamiliar with your topic may not know.

Frequently, the "voice" of the reviewer, especially a particular way of saying things, is especially strong. For example, think about successful music or movie reviewers. Often, the persona they project through their writing voice is part of their appeal: sometimes cranky or even snarky, sometimes humorous, frequently clever. |

Prose+: Beyond Words

An online review such as this on the Kindle Fire, an excerpt from the full site, is a powerful combination of text, links, images, and video. The reviewer exploits video to demonstrate some of the features of the device. The text of the review, along with comparison charts, images, and links, is largely supportive of the video content. Notice that criteria for this evaluation of the Kindle are based in part on the idea of Apple's iPad as a standard for comparison.

The Kindle Fire (left) uses a 7-inch screen that is roughly half the area of the Apple iPad 2. I prefer the iPad's larger screen for Web browsing, reading magazines, and watching videos, but I also like the idea of saving $300.

READINGS

▶ Review 1

One test of a great film is one's willingness to see it again and again, with each viewing yielding some new pleasure. However, holiday films seem like a special category. We see them every year at least in part because of ritual; we watch a movie at Christmastime because we always watch that movie at Christmastime. For a lot of people, *A Christmas Story* (1983) is one of those cinematic rituals. The film tells the story of Ralphie, who more than anything wants a Daisy Red Ryder BB gun for Christmas. Unfortunately, everyone in Ralphie's universe is convinced that if he possesses such a weapon, he will surely "shoot his eye out."

What distinguishes *A Christmas Story* from other popular holiday films, according to the critic Roger Ebert, is that the film possesses "many small but perfect moments" that remind us of "a world that no longer exists in America." In other words, this isn't simply a Christmas film. It's a great film by any measure.

Roger Ebert is perhaps the dean of American movie critics. He is a longtime columnist for the *Chicago Sun Times*, and his website is a popular resource for all things related to film.

A Christmas Story
Roger Ebert

1   One of the details that "A Christmas Story" gets right is the threat of having your mouth washed out with Lifebouy soap. Not any soap. Lifebouy. Never Ivory or Palmolive. Lifebouy, which apparently contained an ingredient able to nullify bad language. The only other soap ever mentioned for this task was Lava, but that was the nuclear weapon of mouth-washing soaps, so powerful it was used for words we still didn't even know.

2   There are many small but perfect moments in "A Christmas Story," and one of the best comes after the Lifebouy is finally removed from Ralphie's mouth and he is sent off to bed. His mother studies the bar, thinks for a moment, and then sticks it in her own mouth, just to see what it tastes like. Moments like that are why some people watch "A Christmas Story" every holiday season. There is a real knowledge of human nature beneath the comedy.

3   The movie is based on the memoirs of Jean Shepherd, the humorist whose radio programs and books remembered growing up in Indiana in the 1940s. It is Shepherd's voice on the soundtrack, remembering one Christmas season in particular, and the young hero's passionate desire to get a Daisy Red Ryder 200-shot Carbine Action BB Gun for Christmas—the one with the compass in the stock, "as cool and deadly a piece of weaponry as I had ever laid eyes on."

In a memorable scene from *A Christmas Story*, Ralphie observes firsthand what happens when a warm tongue meets cold metal.

I owned such a weapon. I recall everything about it at this moment with a tactile memory so vivid I could have just put it down to write these words. How you stuffed newspapers into the carton it came in to use it for target practice. How the BBs came in a cardboard tube with a slide-off top. How they rattled when you poured them into the gun. And of course how everybody warned that you would shoot your eye out.

4

Ralphie's life is made a misery by that danger. He finds that nobody in northern Indiana (not his mother, not his teacher, not even Santa Claus) is able to even *think* about a BB gun without using the words "shoot your eye out." At one point in the movie, in a revenge daydream, he knocks on his parents' door with dark glasses, a blind man's cane and a beggar's tin cup. They are shocked, and ask him tearfully what caused his blindness, and he replies coolly, "Soap poisoning."

5

The movie is not only about Christmas and BB guns, but also about childhood, and one detail after another rings true. The school bully, who, when he runs out of victims, beats up on his own loyal sidekick. The little brother who has outgrown his snowsuit, which is so tight that he walks around looking like the Michelin man; when he falls down he can't get up. The aunt who always thinks Ralphie is a 4-year-old girl, and sends him a pink bunny suit. Other problems of life belong to that long-ago age

6

(continued)

(continued)

and not this one: clinkers in the basement coal furnace, for example, or the blowout of a tire. Everybody knows what a flat tire is, but many now alive have never experienced a genuine, terrifying loud instantaneous *blowout*.

7   "A Christmas Story" was released in the Christmas season of 1983, and did modest business at first (people don't often go to movies with specific holiday themes). It got warm reviews and two Genie Awards (the Canadian Oscars) for Bob Clark's direction and for the screenplay. And then it moved onto home video and has been a stealth hit season after season, finding a loyal audience. "Bams," for example, one of the critics at the hip Three Black Chicks movie review Web site, confesses she loves it: "How does one describe, in short form, the smiles and shrieks of laughter one has experienced over more than 15 years of seeing the same great movie over and over, without sounding like a babbling, fanboyish fool who talks too much?"

8   The movie is set in Indiana but was filmed mostly around Toronto, with some downtown shots from Cleveland, by Clark, whose other big hits were "Porky's" and "Baby Geniuses." It is pitch-perfect, telling the story through the enthusiastic and single-minded vision of its hero Ralphie, and finding in young Peter Billingsley a sly combination of innocence and calculation.

9   Ralphie's parents, Mr. and Mrs. Parker, are played by Darren McGavin and Melinda Dillon, and they exude warmth, zest and love: They are about the nicest parents I can remember in a non-smarmy movie. Notice the scene where Mrs. Parker gets her younger son, Randy, to eat his food by pretending he is "mommy's little piggie." Watch the delight in their laughter together. And the enthusiasm with which the Old Man (as he is always called) attacks the (unseen) basement furnace, battles with the evil neighbor dogs and promises to change a tire in "four minutes flat—time me!" And the lovely closing moment as the parents tenderly put their arms around each other on Christmas night.

10   Some of the movie's sequences stand as classic. The whole business, for example, of the Old Man winning the "major award" of a garish lamp in the shape of a woman's leg (watch Mrs. Parker hiding her giggles in the background as he tries to glue it together after it is "accidentally" broken). Or the visit by Ralphie and Randy to a department store Santa Claus, whose helpers spin the terrified kids around to bang them down on Santa's lap, and afterward kick them down a slide to floor level. Or the sequence where a kid is not merely dared but Triple-Dog-Dared to stick his tongue onto a frozen lamp post, and the fire department has to be called. And the deep disillusionment with which Ralphie finally gets his Little Orphan Annie Secret Decoder Ring in the mail, and Annie's secret message turns out to be nothing but a crummy commercial.

11   There is also the matter of Scut Farcas (Zack Ward), the bully, who Ralphie assures us has yellow eyes. Every school has a kid like this, who picks on smaller kids but is a coward at heart. He makes Ralphie's life a misery. How Farcus gets his comeuppance makes for a deeply satisfying scene, and notice the perfect tact with which Ralphie's mom handles the situation. (Do you agree with me that Dad already knows the whole story when he sits down at the kitchen table?)

In a poignant way, "A Christmas Story" records a world that no longer quite exists   12
in America. Kids are no longer left unattended in the line for Santa. The innocence
of kids' radio programs has been replaced by slick, ironic children's programming on
TV. The new Daisy BB guns have a muzzle velocity higher than that of some police
revolvers, and are not to be sold to anyone under 16. Nobody knows who Red Ryder
was, let alone that his sidekick was Little Beaver.

So much has been forgotten. There is a moment when the Old Man needs an   13
answer for the contest he is entering. The theme of the contest is "Characters in
American Literature," and the question is: "What was the name of the Lone Ranger's
nephew's horse?"

Victor, of course. Everybody knows that.   14

Inquiring into the Essay

1. **Explore.** Think about the holiday film that you'd like to see every year.
   Fastwrite for five minutes about the film and your memories of watching
   it. After the fastwrite, answer this question: What makes this a "good" film?
   Or think about some other film that you'd like to see every year and do the
   fastwrite and answer the question.

2. **Explain.** Underline or highlight sentences or passages in which Ebert is
   telling readers how and why *A Christmas Story* is a great movie. Then
   summarize in your own words what Ebert is saying about the film, incorporating several words or phrases from the material you underlined or
   highlighted.

3. **Evaluate.** Ebert uses various kinds of evidence to support his judgment
   that this is a great movie because of its "small but perfect moments"
   that get all the details of childhood in America right. He uses personal
   evidence, evidence from others, and of course lots of evidence from the
   movie. Find examples of these different kinds of evidence, and assess how
   effective they are in supporting the reasons Ebert gives for his judgment of
   the movie.

4. **Reflect.** In evaluative writing, judgments can be as small as brief comments
   or as big as thesis statements. Is there a thesis statement somewhere in
   Ebert's review of *A Christmas Story*? If so, where is it? If not, is this a problem? Does every piece of persuasive writing need a thesis?

▶ Review 2

The video gaming industry hauls in something like $10 billion a year, so it's no
surprise that more writers than ever are penning reviews of the latest releases.
These reviews, if they're any good, balance technical information about the game

Niko Bellic (top center) is the main character of the video game "Grand Theft Auto IV," a game that Seth Schiesel calls "violent, intelligent, profane, endearing, obnoxious, sly, richly textured and thoroughly compelling."

with attention to the experience of playing it. It is a well-described gaming experience, not arcane detail, that will appeal to most readers. That's why Seth Schiesel's review of "Grand Theft Auto IV," a hugely popular video game released in 2008, is such a great example of how to write a review that might make even non–video game players interested in giving it a try.

Even when he doesn't make them explicit, the criteria Schiesel uses to determine the qualities of a good game aren't hard to find. One criterion he clearly uses is what we often look for in film and literature: "fully realized characters." When you think about it, this is a pretty extraordinary accomplishment in a video game. After all, characters in a game such as "Grand Theft Auto IV" must consistently service the action, making things (usually violent things) happen, and this wouldn't seem to provide the time or the situations to develop character. But according to Schiesel, protagonist Niko Bellic is "one of the most fully realized characters video games have yet produced."

Seth Schiesel sidesteps the ethics of producing games such as "Grand Theft Auto IV," which makes efficient killing a key to advancement. But this is a review, not a public argument on the virtues of gaming, and his readers likely aren't interested in such ethical questions. They just want to know whether the game is any good. As you read "Grand Theft Auto Takes on New York," consider what exactly Schiesel sees as being a good video game. On what other criteria does he base his judgment?

Grand Theft Auto Takes on New York
Seth Schiesel

I was rolling through the neon deluge of a place very like Times Square the other night in my Landstalker sport utility vehicle, listening to David Bowie's "Fascination" on the radio. The glittery urban landscape was almost enough to make me forget about the warehouse of cocaine dealers I was headed uptown to rip off.

Soon I would get bored, though, and carjack a luxury sedan. I'd meet my Rasta buddy Little Jacob, then check out a late show by Ricky Gervais at a comedy club around the corner. Afterward I'd head north to confront the dealers, at least if I could elude the cops. I heard their sirens before I saw them and peeled out, tires squealing.

It was just another night on the streets of Liberty City, the exhilarating, lusciously dystopian rendition of New York City in 2008 that propels Grand Theft Auto IV, the ambitious new video game to be released on Tuesday for the Xbox 360 and PlayStation 3 systems.

Published by Rockstar Games, Grand Theft Auto IV is a violent, intelligent, profane, endearing, obnoxious, sly, richly textured and thoroughly compelling work of cultural satire disguised as fun. It calls to mind a rollicking R-rated version of Mad magazine featuring Dave Chappelle and Quentin Tarantino, and sets a new standard for what is possible in interactive arts. It is by far the best game of the series, which made its debut in 1997 and has since sold more than 70 million copies. Grand Theft Auto IV will retail for $60.

Niko Bellic is the player-controlled protagonist this time, and he is one of the most fully realized characters video games have yet produced. A veteran of the Balkan wars and a former human trafficker in the Adriatic, he arrives in Liberty City's rendition of Brighton Beach at the start of the game to move in with his affable if naïve cousin Roman. Niko expects to find fortune and, just maybe, track down someone who betrayed him long ago. Over the course of the story line he discovers that revenge is not always what one expects.

Besides the nuanced Niko the game is populated by a winsome procession of grifters, hustlers, drug peddlers and other gloriously unrepentant lowlifes, each a caricature less politically correct than the last.

Hardly a demographic escapes skewering. In addition to various Italian and Irish crime families, there are venal Russian gangsters, black crack slingers, argyle-sporting Jamaican potheads, Puerto Rican hoodlums, a corrupt police commissioner, a steroid-addled Brooklyn knucklehead named Brucie Kibbutz and a former Eastern European soldier who has become a twee Upper West Side metrosexual.

(continued)

(continued)

8   Breathing life into Niko and the other characters is a pungent script by Dan Houser and Rupert Humphries that reveals a mastery of street patois to rival Elmore Leonard's. The point of the main plot is to guide Niko through the city's criminal underworld. Gang leaders and thugs set missions for him to complete, and his success moves the story along toward a conclusion that seems as dark as its beginning. But the real star of the game is the city itself. It looks like New York. It sounds like New York. It feels like New York. Liberty City has been so meticulously created it almost even smells like New York. From Brooklyn (called Broker), through Queens (Dukes), the Bronx (Bohan), Manhattan (Algonquin) and an urban slice of New Jersey (Alderney), the game's streets and alleys ooze a stylized yet unmistakable authenticity. (Staten Island is left out however.)

9   The game does not try to represent anything close to every street in the city, but the overall proportions, textures, geography, sights and sounds are spot-on. The major landmarks are present, often rendered in surprising detail, from the Cyclone at Coney Island to the Domino Sugar factory and Grand Army Plaza in Brooklyn and on up through the detritus of the 1964–65 World's Fair in Queens. Central Park, the Empire State Building, various museums, the Statue of Liberty and Times Square are all present and accounted for. There is no Yankee Stadium, but there is a professional baseball team known, with the deliciousness typical of the game's winks and nods, as the Swingers.

10   At least as impressive as the city's virtual topography is the range of the game's audio and music production, delivered through an entire dial's worth of radio stations available in almost any of the dozens of different cars, trucks and motorcycles a player can steal. From the jazz channel (billed as "music from when America was cool") through the salsa, alt-rock, jazz, metal and multiple reggae and hip-hop stations, Lazlow Jones, Ivan Pavlovich and the rest of Rockstar's audio team demonstrate a musical erudition beyond anything heard before in a video game. The biggest problem with the game's extensive subway system is that there's no music underground. (Too bad there are no iPods to nab.)

11   The game's roster of radio hosts runs from Karl Lagerfeld to Iggy Pop and DJ Green Lantern. It is not faint praise to point out that at times, simply driving around the city listening to the radio—seguing from "Moanin'" by Art Blakey and the Jazz Messengers to the Isley Brothers' "Footsteps in the Dark" to "The Crack House" by Fat Joe featuring Lil Wayne—can be as enjoyable as anything the game has to offer.

12   Grand Theft Auto IV is such a simultaneously adoring and insightful take on modern America that it almost had to come from somewhere else. The game's main production studio is in Edinburgh, and Rockstar's leaders, the brothers Dan and Sam Houser, are British expatriates who moved to New York to indulge their fascination with urban American culture. Their success places them firmly among the distinguished cast of Britons from Mick Jagger and Keith Richards through Tina Brown who

have flourished by identifying key elements of American culture, repackaging them for mass consumption and selling them back at a markup.

It all adds up to a new level of depth for an interactive entertainment experience. I've spent almost 60 hours practically sequestered in a (real world) Manhattan hotel room in recent weeks playing through Grand Theft Auto IV's main story line and the game still says I have found only 64 percent of its content. I won't ever reach 100 percent, not least because I won't hunt down all 200 of the target pigeons (known as flying rats here) that the designers have hidden around the city.   13

But like millions of other players I will happily spend untold hours cruising Liberty City's bridges and byways, hitting the clubs, grooving to the radio and running from the cops. Even when the real New York City is right outside.   14

Inquiring into the Essay

1. **Explore.** This review doesn't address the ethical questions raised by a game that celebrates "gloriously unrepentant lowlifes" including pot-heads, gangsters, and "crack slingers." "Grand Theft Auto IV" may be no worse than other violent video games, and unless you've played it, criticism or praise of this particular game is unfair. But in a four-minute fastwrite, explore your own feelings about violent video games. In his review, Schiesel argues that "Grand Theft Auto IV" is cultural satire. Would that make a difference? Can games such as this one serve a larger, even useful purpose?

2. **Explain.** In your own words, state what Seth Schiesel seems to see as the qualities of a good video game.

3. **Evaluate.** How rhetorically effective is this review for different readers? Assess what parts would work—or wouldn't—for the following categories of readers:

   a. People who have never played a video game in their lives but might consider it.

   b. People who are avid and experienced gamers.

   c. People who, when asked, usually consider playing video games "a waste of time."

4. **Reflect.** Video game reviews are but one of a growing number of review subgenres, which include reviews of movies, books, blogs, websites, best and worst dressed, and so on. Consider the subgenres of reviews you read or might read. What exactly would you be looking for in a "good" review?

THE WRITING PROCESS

Inquiry Project **Writing a Review Essay**

Inquiry questions: How good is it? What is its value?

Write a review essay on any subject—a performance, a book, a website, a consumer product, a film, whatever. Just make sure your review has the following qualities (see also pages 108–109 for typical features of the review essay):

- The essay is focused on an specific example of a larger category. (For instance, the film *Maltese Falcon* is an example of forties film noir, *The Curious Writer* is an example of a composition textbook, and Lady Gaga's song "Born This Way" is an example of politically themed contemporary rock music.)
- The writer's judgments are clearly stated and are supported with reasons and evidence.
- The evaluation seems balanced and fair. The criteria for judging the value of the subject seem sound.

Prose+

Write and publish your review for an online audience. There are review sites for nearly anything, from the very focused (e.g., birding binoculars) to the quite broad (music, film, TV, *and* video games). For example,

- For a book review, consider publishing on the Amazon or Barnes & Noble site, or on a site such as Goodreads or LibraryThing.
- For music, check out the website Music-Critic.
- For music, movies, TV, apps, or video games, look to sites such as Metacritic.
- For consumer products, there is Eopinions.

Turn your review into a video project. If you're writing about a consumer product, for example, demonstrate in a short film how it works and how it should work better. (There are a gazillion examples of this on YouTube.) If you're reviewing a movie or television show, put together a short film that incorporates clips, if available online, with your voiceover commentary. Make sure you allow time to learn how to use the basics of your video editing software.

Add images to your essay. You might, for example, take a series of photographs to demonstrate how something works or to highlight key features.

What Are You Going to Write About?

Imagine all the things about which you might ask, "How good is it?" From smart- **4.4**
phones to theater performances, movies to college websites, books to dog-training Use invention
programs—the possibilities are endless. You don't have to start with an opinion and focusing
about your review subject—and it's better if you don't—but it should be something strategies to
that interests you. discover and

Get started thinking about what you're going to write about by opening up the develop a review
possibilities with the following prompts, most of which involve generating ideas. essay.
Later, you'll narrow things down to a promising topic and try it out.

Opening Up

Suspend judgment to explore a range of possible review essay topics.

Listing Prompts. Lists can be rich sources of triggering topics. Let them grow
freely, and when you're ready, use an item as the focus of another list or an episode
of fastwriting. The following prompts should get you started.

1. Fold a piece a paper into four equal columns. You'll be making four different brainstormed lists. In the first column, write "Things I Want." Spend two
   minutes making a quick list of everything you wish you had but don't: a new
   computer, a classical guitar, a decent boyfriend, and so on.

2. In the next column, write "The Jury Is Still Out." In this column, make a fast
   list of things in your life that so far are hard to judge: the quality of the school
   you attend, this textbook, your opinion about the films you saw last month,
   how well Susie cuts your hair, and so on.

3. In the third column, write "My Media." Devote a fast list to particular films, TV
   shows, books, websites, or musicians you like or dislike; jot down whatever
   you watch, listen to, or read regularly.

4. Finally, make a list of "Things of Questionable Quality." Try to be specific.

Fastwriting Prompts. Remember, fastwriting is a great way to stimulate creative
thinking. Turn off your critical side and let yourself write "badly."

1. Choose an item from any of the four preceding lists as a prompt for a
   seven-minute fastwrite. Explore your experience with the subject, or how
   your opinions about it have evolved.

2. Begin with the following prompt, and follow it for five minutes in a fastwrite:
   Among the things I have a hard time judging is _____. If the writing stalls,
   shift subjects by writing, *And another thing I can't judge is* _____.

Visual Prompts. Sometimes the best way to generate material is to see what we
think represented in something other than sentences. Boxes, lines, webs, clusters,

arrows, charts, and even sketches can help us see more of the landscape of a subject, especially connections that aren't as obvious in prose.

1. On a blank page in your journal, cluster the name of an artist, musician, film, book, author, performance, band, building, academic course or major, restaurant, university bookstore, tablet, computer, food store, or pizza joint. Cluster the name of anything about which you have some sort of feeling, positive or negative. Build a web of associations: feelings, details, observations, names, moments, facts, opinions, and so on. Look for a single strand in your essay that might be the beginning of a review.

2. Draw a sketch of what you think is an *ideal version* of something you need or use often: a computer, a classroom, a telephone, a wallet or handbag, and so on. If you could design such a thing, what would it look like? Use this as a way of evaluating what is currently available and how it might be improved.

Research Prompts. Explore what other critics are saying, look around, or collaborate.

1. Do an Internet or library search for reviews on one of your favorite films, books, sports teams, artists, and so on. Do you agree with the evaluations? If not, consider writing a review of your own that challenges the critics.

2. Take a walk. Look for things to evaluate that you see as you wander on and off campus—downtown architecture, the quality of local parks, paintings in the art museum, neighborhoods, coffee shops. You'll be amazed at how much is begging for a thoughtful judgment.

3. Here's an entertaining generating activity: Plan a weekend of movie watching with a few friends. Ask each of them to suggest two or three favorite films, then obtain a slew of them, and when you're thoroughly spent watching the films, discuss which might be most interesting to review.

Narrowing Down

Now that you've opened up possibilities for review topics, there are choices to make. Which do you want to write about?

What's Promising Material and What Isn't? My favorite coffee shop in my hometown of Boise, Idaho, is a place called the Flying M. It's a funky place with an odd assortment of furniture, overstuffed couches, worn armchairs, and wobbly tables. On the walls, there's work from local artists, mostly unknowns with talent and unusual taste. There are other coffee places in town, including the ubiquitous Starbucks and another more local chain called Moxie Java. I don't find much difference in the coffee at any of these places, and they're all rather pleasant. What makes me prefer the Flying M?

I've never really thought about it. That's one of the reasons I liked the idea of reviewing my favorite local coffeehouse when the Flying M appeared on one of my lists. The best inquiry-based projects begin when you're not quite sure what you think and want to explore a topic to find out.

- *Is there anything in your lists and fastwrites that you might have an initial judgment about but really haven't considered fully?*

- *As you consider potential subjects for your review, do some clearly offer the possibility of comparison with other similar things in that category?*

- *Do any of your potential subjects offer the possibility of primary research, or research that might involve direct observation?* Can you listen to the music, attend the performance, read the novel, examine the building, visit the website, look at the painting?

- *Does a topic lend itself to demonstration through visuals or video?* Can you download clips, film a demonstration, take pictures, create an infographic?

Questions About Audience and Purpose. When people read reviews, they either are actively *seeking information* (they are considering buying the tablet or attending the dance performance) or are *looking for reinforcement* (reasons why what they've already decided to do makes sense). I bought a Ford Escape recently, and now I read every review I see on the car, hoping to feel good about my decision. These two audiences have very different dispositions. The information-seekers are more critical readers than those who seek reinforcement. But what they both share is a stake in the topic under review. They're *interested*. As you consider a review topic, ask yourself whether it's easy to imagine an audience who would care, one way or another, about a judgment about the usefulness or value of the thing.

Trying Out

Let's work with your tentative topic, doing some more-focused work, culminating in a sketch, or a first try at writing it up for an audience.

Focusing the Category. First, let's try focusing your topic in the context of a category. Can you see how your topic fits into broader and narrower categories? An inverted pyramid is a nice model for this:

Movies

Hollywood films

Hollywood crime films

Hollywood crime films of the 1940s

1940s film noir

Suppose you love the 1940s film classic *The Maltese Falcon*, and you'd like to explore why it's so good. You can evaluate the film as an example of movies generally, but that makes little sense because the category's too broad. However, suppose you list progressively narrower subcategories of film to which *The Maltese Falcon* might belong. You might end up evaluating the film as an example of 1940s film noir. Why is this useful?

1. *It gives you a way of seeing appropriate comparisons.* You're comparing *The Maltese Falcon* not to all Hollywood movies—there are, after all, so many different kinds—but to other 1940s Hollywood crime films that belong to the film noir genre.

2. *It helps you focus on appropriate criteria.* Just as it would be weird to compare *The Maltese Falcon* with *A Christmas Story* because they are such different types of films, it would be hard to arrive at criteria for such an evaluation. What makes a 1940s crime film "good" will be very different than what makes a family comedy "good."

Try creating an inverted pyramid on your subject, looking for a category that is narrow enough to make comparisons and criteria more appropriate.

Fastwriting. Through a focused fastwrite, explore your initial feelings and experiences, if any, about your subject. Use one of the following prompts to launch this exploration. If the writing stalls, try another prompt to keep you going for five to seven minutes.

- *Write about your first experience with your subject.* This might be, for example, the first time you remember visiting the restaurant, or hearing the performer, or seeing the photographs. Focus on scenes, moments, situations, and people.
- *Write about what you think might be important qualities of your subject.* Ideally, this would be what the thing should be able to do well or what effects it should have on people who use it or see it.
- *Write about how the thing makes you feel.* Explore not just your initial good, bad, or mixed feelings about your subject, but also the place from where those feelings arise. Why do you feel anything at all about this thing?
- *Compare the thing you're evaluating with something else that's similar.*

Web Research. Try some web searches, gathering as much relevant background information as you can.

- *Search for information on product websites or web pages devoted specifically to your subject.* If your review is on Ford's new electric car, visit the company's website to find out what you can about the vehicle. Find Green Day's home page or fan site for your review of the band's new CD.
- *Search for existing reviews or other evaluations on your subject.* One way to do this is to google using the keyword "review" or "reviews" (or "how to

evaluate") along with your subject. For example, "laptop reviews" will produce dozens of sites that rank and evaluate the machines. Similarly, there are countless reviews on the web of specific performers, performances, CDs, consumer products, and so on.

Interviews. If possible, interview people about what they think. You may do this formally by developing a survey, or informally by simply asking people what they like or dislike about the thing you're evaluating. Also consider whether you might interview someone who's an expert on your subject. For example, if you're evaluating a website, ask people in the technical communications program what they think about it, or what criteria they might use if they were reviewing something similar.

Experiencing Your Subject. This may be the most useful activity of all. Visit the coffeehouses, examine the website, listen to the music, attend the performance, read the book, view the painting, visit the building, look at the architecture, watch the movie. As you do this, gather your impressions and collect information. Take notes. Take pictures. Shoot video.

Thinking About Criteria

You hate something. You love something. You have mixed feelings about it. All of these judgments arise from your criteria, your assumptions about the qualities that make such a thing good. And thinking about your criteria can help you know what to look for.

Refining Criteria for Better Evidence. Consider a process of evaluation something like the one in Figure 4.2.

You see a website and think, "This is really ugly." You look more closely and conclude, "I think there's too much text." You could stop there, of course, but you want to provide a more thorough evaluation. A natural next step, then, would be to consider the criterion behind your reason and judgment. You could simply say, "Good websites don't use too much text," but that doesn't advance your evaluation any further because the criterion is too general and vague. After a little research into what this criterion's really about, you arrive at this: "Good sites break text into readable chunks." Sites that don't have readable chunks give the visual appearance of too much text. What's a "readable chunk"? Turns out it is around 80 characters per line. Now you can take another look at your ugly website with a criterion that really helps you support your judgment with better evidence.

This implies a couple things about good criteria in evaluation:

1. The more specific your criterion for evaluation, the better.
2. Identifying criteria is a powerful tool for finding better evidence to support your judgment.

The more you know about something, the more specific your criteria are likely to be. For example, I asked my daughter Becca, a dancer, what criteria she

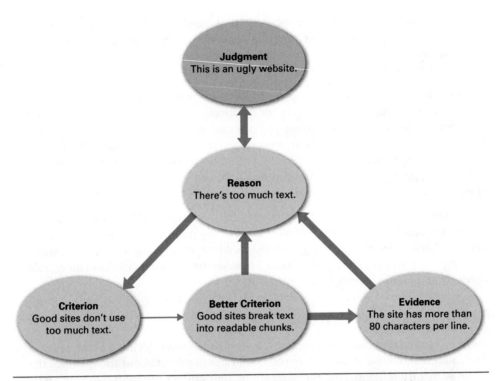

Figure 4.2 A process for refining criteria and using criteria to generate better evidence

would use to judge a modern performance (see box). I'm unschooled in dance, so I don't understand all of her criteria, but I'm certain I could use some of them next time I see a modern performance, to evaluate what I see.

> **Becca's Criteria**
>
> A good modern dance performance has . . .
>
> 1. Interesting features—props, comedy, or music
> 2. Something improvised
> 3. Visible expressions of the dancers' enjoyment
> 4. Interesting variation
> 5. Good balance in choreography between repetition and randomness
> 6. Beginning, middle, and end seamlessly joined

Considering Criteria and Rhetorical Context. We often don't think about our criteria and whether they're valid; we treat them as self-evident and may assume that our audience would agree with them. But careful reviewers at the very least *consider* the criteria that shape their reactions and decide whether they're fair and sensible.

In thinking about criteria, you need to think about rhetorical context: audience and purpose. As you saw in Chapter 1, the qualities of "good" writing really depend on the situation: purpose, audience, genre. A main purpose of a review is to give readers potentially useful information. So, if you're evaluating a new type of downhill skis, you'd need to think about skis for whom. An advanced skier fond of deep powder will have different expectations of her skis' performance than will an intermediate skier like me, who falls on his face off groomed runs. For this reason, in thinking about criteria that might guide your evaluation of the thing you're reviewing, you'll find it useful to

First, identify your audience:

- *Who will be using the thing (going to the performance, etc.)?*

Then, take another look at your criteria:

- *Are the criteria that you are thinking in terms of appropriate for your audience?*

Writing the Sketch

A sketch, as the name implies, is a kind of verbal drawing of your topic—an early draft—to see if you should develop it further. While you write a sketch with readers in mind, it is hardly polished. You are "essaying" the topic to try it out, and you may not know yet what you think or what you want to say. Your review sketch, however, should include the following:

- A tentative title.
- An effort to help readers understand why they might have a stake in the thing you're evaluating. What's significant about this particular CD, book, performance, place, or product?
- A tentative answer to the inquiry question "How good is it?"
- A few clear reasons for your judgment that are tied to specific evidence from the thing itself.

▶ Student Sketch

Here are some common criteria for a good film:

1. There is someone in the film who we come to like, despite their flaws.
2. Characters change. They learn from mistakes.
3. The story ends with some resolution of the conflict.

According to Laura Burns, whose sketch of the Charlize Theron film *Young Adult* follows, that movie doesn't meet any of the three criteria. And yet, she argues, *Young Adult* is a great film. Obviously, Laura is saying that criteria most of us assume must be met for a film to be good in fact don't have to be met. Because she challenges our assumptions, Laura needs to be particularly persuasive in her review. How does she do in this first attempt?

Recipe for a Great Film: Unlikeable People, Poor Choices, and Little Redemption

Laura Burns

1   Charlize Theron is arguably the most traditionally beautiful woman in film. High, smooth cheekbones, long, thin legs, a delicate nose set at the center of a perfectly proportioned face. This considered, it's remarkable how ugly she can get.

2   *Young Adult* is a movie about unlikeable people making poor life choices which they don't learn from. Theron plays Mavis Gary, an ex-prom queen from Mercury, Minnesota, making her living as a ghostwriter of a teen series in what the Mercurians call the "Mine-apple." From the first sequence of the film, we can tell that Mavis is a mess. She gets wasted, slumps around her apartment in sweats, and guzzles Diet Coke in a way that almost gave me heartburn. Upon receiving a birth announcement email from her now-married ex-prom king, the aptly named Buddy (Patrick Wilson), Mavis decides to pop an old mixtape into her dirty Mini Cooper and win him back.

3   This is, essentially, the entire plot of *Young Adult*. Mavis' trip back to Mercury is a kind of *anti*-hero's journey. On her first night in town, getting wasted in a local dive, she meets her "guide," Matt (the wonderful Patton Oswalt), a former classmate who remains crippled from an assault during high school. Through the course of the film, as she reunites with her parents (Jill Eikenberry & Richard Bekins), insinuates herself into Buddy and his wife Beth's (Elizabeth Reaser) lives, and gets plastered on Matt's home-brewed bourbon, rather than moving towards revelation, Mavis seems to retreat further and further into her past.

4   Unlike *Juno*, writer Diablo Cody's most well-known film, *Young Adult* rejects preciousness in favor of obscenity. It's difficult to make a film about terrible people enjoyable, but Cody injects just enough silliness to keep us from feeling too badly. Director Jason Reitman rightly focuses on Mavis, and both Theron and Oswalt are brave enough to let us into their characters' grossness and un-likeability. Smartly, Cody refuses to manufacture empathy for her characters, leaving us to boldly accept the ugliness of these people fully.

5   I don't doubt that *Young Adult* will displease many movie-goers who are used to redemptive stories and characters who are "good at heart." Cody refuses to indulge that expectation. When Mavis dresses to go out (which is often), Theron's extraordinary beauty is obvious. Yet we're never allowed to shake that Mavis is truly ugly at her core—an effective subversion of expectation that is the exemplar of this memorable performance. This isn't a feel-good film, and thank goodness. If Cody and Reitman had tried, I think we might leave the theater feeling worse.

Moving from Sketch to Draft

A sketch is an audition. It's a brief performance for an audience that may or may not work out well. In a review, what do you look for in your own performance? To start with, you've got to still care, of course. This should be a topic you still want to write about. But what else?

Evaluating Your Sketch. Start with a summary of what you think the sketch is saying by finishing the following sentence.

Because of ___(reason 1)___ and ___(reason 2)___, I think that ___(thing you're evaluating)___ is ___(judgment of value)___, and the strongest evidence for this is _____ and _____.

Example: Because of its unusually hefty neck and its thick solid rosewood body, the Martin 0-28VS acoustic guitar has a bright sound that belies its small size, and the strongest evidence for this is how great it sounds with light fingerpicking and its long sustains.

If you can finish the sentence to your satisfaction, your audition was successful. You know, more or less, where you might be going. (Don't be surprised if you change your mind as you revise.) However, you might have encountered some problems. Maybe you haven't yet arrived at a judgment. Or perhaps you can't come up with two compelling reasons for the judgment you do have. In any case, these are the things you should focus on as you develop your review:

- *Clarify your judgment.* What is the one thing you're trying to say (S.O.F.T.) about the thing you're reviewing?

- *Explain your reasons.* What is behind your evaluation? And are the criteria that these reasons are based on sensible?

- *Provide the back story.* What is it, where did it come from, how does it compare, why is it important, what is the history?

- *Gather evidence.* How will you prove that your reasons are persuasive? What specifically can you point to?

Reflecting on What You've Learned. To get some perspective on what you've learned so far about the thing you're reviewing, fastwrite in your journal or on the computer using the following prompt:

When I first started exploring this, I thought _____, and now I'm beginning to think _____.

Developing

Before you revise your sketch into a draft, generate more material through writing and research. This is almost always necessary.

Talking It Through. Generate more material by having a conversation with me about your topic. Imagine I'm sitting across the table from you, asking you the following questions about the thing you're reviewing. Respond in your journal to each question, in order, fastwriting a response for at least a few minutes. If the writing takes off in response to any one question, run with it. The order of the questions may prove to be a useful organizing principle for your draft, so write as much as you can in the exercise.

Bruce	You
To start with, why are you reviewing this? To whom might it matter and under what circumstances?	
Can you describe it? What does it look like? What is the story behind it? Would you compare it to anything else I might know about?	
Okay, so what do you most want me to know about it? What is it you're saying, exactly?	
Interesting. Why do you say this?	
Surely, not everyone thinks this. What do people who disagree with you say? How would you respond to that?	

Consider the following research strategies for developing your draft.

Re-Experience. Probably the single most useful thing you can do to prepare for the next draft is to collect more observations of your subject. Why? You're much more focused now on what you think, what criteria most influence that judgment, and what particular evidence you were lacking in the sketch that will make your review more convincing. You might also consider documenting your research not only with notes but multimedia as well. Could you take pictures to demonstrate a feature or show how the thing you're reviewing is used? Might you include screenshots of the relevant websites? Download images of the thing being used?

Interview. If you haven't already done so, collect the comments, opinions, and observations of others about the subject of your review. If you reviewed a concert or other event, find others to interview who also attended. If you reviewed a film, get some friends to watch the movie with you and jot down their reactions afterward. If it would be helpful to collect data on how people feel, consider designing a brief survey.

Also consider interviewing someone who is an expert on the thing you're reviewing.

Read. Go to the library and go online and search for information about your subject. Try finding:

- *Information about how it's made or designed.*
- *Other reviews on your topic.*

- *Information on relevant people, companies, traditions, local developments—any background that will help readers see the thing you're reviewing in a larger context.*

Drafting

When you've got enough information, start your draft, beginning at the beginning.

Finding an Opening. Seth Schiesel's review of the fourth version of the video game "Grand Theft Auto" (see p. 115–117) begins this way:

> I was rolling through the neon deluge of a place very like Times Square the other night in my Landstalker sport utility vehicle, listening to David Bowie's "Fascination" on the radio. The glittery urban landscape was almost enough to make me forget the warehouse of cocaine dealers I was headed uptown to rip off.

It isn't simply the punchy language (e.g., "neon deluge," "rip off") that makes this lead paragraph compelling. The paragraph does three things that good beginnings should do:

1. Raises questions the reader might want to learn the answers to.
2. Creates a relationship between reader and writer.
3. Gets right to the subject without unnecessary scaffolding.

While we know from the title of the piece that this is about a video game, Schiesel's opening makes us wonder about what exactly is going on here, who this guy is, and what he is talking about. It immediately immerses us in the *experience* of playing the game.

Here are some other approaches to a strong lead for a review:

- Begin with a common misconception about your subject and promise to challenge it.
- Begin with an anecdote that reveals what you like or dislike.
- Help readers realize the relevance of your subject by showing how it's used, what it says, or why it's needed in a familiar situation.
- Provide interesting background that your readers may not know.

Methods of Development. What are some ways to organize your review?

Narrative. If you're reviewing a performance or any other kind of experience that has a discrete beginning and end, then telling a story about what you saw, felt, and thought is a natural move. Another way to use narrative is to tell the story of your thinking about your subject—an approach that lends itself to a delayed thesis essay, where your judgment comes late in the review.

Comparison/Contrast. Comparison with other items in the same category—say, other science fiction films, electric cars, or laptops—is a common and useful element in reviews. If comparison is especially important to your review, you might structure your essay around it.

Question to Answer. One of the most straightforward methods of structuring a review is to simply begin by raising the question *What makes _____ good?* This way, you make your criteria for evaluation explicit. From there, the next move is obvious: How well does the thing you're evaluating measure up?

Using Evidence. As you compose your draft, keep in mind that the most important evidence in a review is probably your own observations of the thing. These should be specific, and most likely they will draw on *primary research* you conducted by attending the concert, listening to the CD, or visiting the coffeehouse. As illustrated in Figure 4.2, thinking about your criteria can be a tool for finding strong evidence. You may also use evidence from secondary sources: For example, what did another critic say or observe?

Workshopping

When you workshop a review, you're sharing your evaluation of something your peers may have no experience with. Maybe they've never seen the movie, tried the coffee, visited the restaurant, or listened to the music. This has rhetorical implications you should consider as you prepare to discuss your draft:

1. *Context.* Do you provide enough background on the thing you're evaluating: who they are, how it works, why it's significant, what it does, etc.?

2. *Comparisons.* Even if none of your readers have, say, ridden the road bike you're reviewing, most have ridden a bicycle of some kind. Did you establish common ground with readers by exploiting any overlaps between their experience and your review topic?

3. *Definitions.* You can't assume that your peers are familiar with insider jargon. Did you define terms and explain features and so on that readers may not know?

In workshopping the first draft of your review, your initial focus should be on what peers make of the purpose and meaning of your essay. Above all else, knowing what you're trying to do and say in an essay will help you decide what to cut and what to add in revision. It's the most powerful knowledge you can have for rewriting. This grid can help you frame the questions for your workshop group.

Questions for Peer Reviewers	
1. Purpose	Why is this being reviewed? Who has a stake in whether it's good or not?
2. Meaning	In your own words, what exactly is my judgment? In your words, what are my main reasons for this judgment? Are they persuasive? Why or why not?

If you're reviewing something that your peers may be familiar with—and perhaps have strong feelings about—you might consider a workshop for your draft that encourages participants to debate your conclusions, both supporting your judgments and challenging them (see box).

Option for Review Essay Workshop

1. Divide each workshop group into two teams—believers and doubters.
2. Believers are responsible for presenting to doubters why the writer's review is convincing and fair.
3. Doubters challenge the writer's judgments and respond to the believers' claims.
4. The writer observes this conversation without participating.
5. After five minutes, believers and doubters drop their roles and discuss suggestions for revision with the writer.

Reflecting on the Draft. Immediately after your workshop session, fastwrite in your journal (paper or computer) on what you learned about writing an effective review *from reading your peers' drafts.* How might you apply these things to your revision?

Revising

Revision is a continual process—not a last step. You've been revising—"reseeing" your subject—from the first messy fastwriting in your journal. But the things that get your attention vary depending on where you are in the writing process. With your draft in hand, revision becomes your focus through what I'll call "shaping and tightening your draft."

4.5

Apply revision strategies that are effective for shaping reviews.

Shaping. You've clarified the purpose and meaning of the piece. Now you want to redesign it around both.

Analyzing the Information. Shaping involves, among other things, arranging and rearranging information so that it is more effectively organized around your main idea. One way to think about the structure of your review is to look at its information in terms of the elements that reviews typically include:

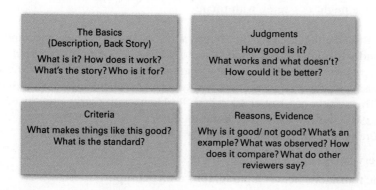

The Basics
(Description, Back Story)

What is it? How does it work?
What's the story? Who is it for?

Judgments

How good is it?
What works and what doesn't?
How could it be better?

Criteria

What makes things like this good?
What is the standard?

Reasons, Evidence

Why is it good/ not good? What's an
example? What was observed? How
does it compare? What do other
reviewers say?

By analyzing your draft in this way, you can look at whether you've included enough information for each element. While there's no formula for ordering this information, consider the structure of your draft rhetorically. If your audience is familiar with the thing you're reviewing, then "the basics" need less emphasis; obviously, the opposite is true if your audience has little knowledge. In either case, the basics are usually early in the draft. Similarly, audiences who are familiar with your topic (e.g., they've seen the movie or used the device) may share your assumptions about criteria already. You can spend less time explaining them. Others who are unfamiliar with your topic need to learn the criteria you're using, so give these more emphasis. Judgments can appear anywhere in the draft, not just as a thesis in your first paragraph.

To imagine organizing strategies, you can try the "Frankenstein Draft" (Revision Strategy 10.18 in Chapter 10): Cut up your draft with scissors into the different elements mentioned here, and then play with the order. What seems to be most effective? Worry about transitions later.

Other Questions for Revision. Because a review's a form of argument, start by asking yourself, "Is my evaluation clear, and will it be persuasive to readers?" For example, here's a paragraph from Jesse's review of the film *Crank*:

> *Crank* (2006), written and directed by Mark Neveldin and Brian Taylor, is a fast-paced, dark, action comedy. This is not your typical "good guy saves the day" action film though. With a lot of profanity, wild antics and defiance of the law, it is very edgy. It really reminds me of a Grand Theft Auto Vice City. The star of the show even steals a cop's motorcycle and rides it around the city recklessly. But don't be quick to judge this film only by its novel gamer appeal. This movie also had good theatrical performances.

Jesse's evaluation is clear: The film *Crank* is good. And he explains why: strong performances and an "edgy" feel similar to that of the video game "Grand Theft Auto." One way to "re-see" an evaluation is to plunge under its surface to see the criteria and assumptions underneath. Jesse works from an assumption that a film that has the feel and look of a familiar video game is a good thing. But why? To make his evaluation more compelling to readers, when Jesse revises, he should probably explain that assumption.

Consider starting your rewrite by thinking about the criteria and assumptions behind the judgments you make. Which need to be explicitly addressed because an audience might not agree with them?

Polishing. Shaping focuses on things such as purpose, meaning, and overall design and structure. No less important is polishing—looking more closely at paragraphs, sentences, and words. Are your paragraphs coherent? How do you manage transitions? Are your sentences fluent and concise? Are there any errors in spelling or syntax? The section of Chapter 10 called "Problems with Clarity and Style," starting on page 398, can help you focus on these issues.

Before you finish your draft, work through the following checklist:

✓ Every paragraph is about one thing.

✓ The transitions between paragraphs aren't abrupt.

✓ The length of sentences varies in each paragraph.

✓ Each sentence is concise. There are no unnecessary words and phrases.

✓ You've checked grammar, particularly verb agreement, run-on sentences, unclear pronouns, and misused words (*there/their, where/were*, and so on).

✓ You've run your spellchecker and proofed your paper for misspelled words.

Chapter 10 has strategies to help you solve all kinds of revision problems, large and small.

▶ Student Essay

Earlier in the chapter, you saw Laura Burns's sketch, a review of the Charlize Theron film *Young Adult*. Here you can see Laura's next draft, in which she's revised her essay into a web page. This is the first web page she's created, and she did it with Microsoft Word; the program has more than enough tools for the novice designer. Laura followed much of the advice in "Inquiring into the Details: Design Tips for Basic Web Pages" (Chapter 5, p. 162), including limiting the character length of each line, working with standard fonts, and keeping things simple. The result is pleasing. It's also more information rich, with links to another review, the film's trailer, and information about the screenwriter. Most important, though, is that it's Laura's writing here that makes the review successful, not the design tricks. Her positive evaluation of the film is nicely captured by the title she chose and the punchy prose that follows it. Like a lot of reviews, "How Not to Feel Good and Feel Good About It" depends on a strong writing voice, and Laura's celebration of "unlikeable people making poor life choices from which they don't learn a thing" is easy to listen to, even if you don't agree with it.

How to Not Feel Good and Feel Good About It

A Review of *Young Adult*

Laura Burns

Charlize Theron is certainly one of the most beautiful women in film. High, smooth cheekbones, long, thin legs, and a delicate nose set at the center of a perfectly proportioned face. This considered, it's remarkable how ugly she can get.   1

Young Adult is a movie about unlikeable people making poor life choices from which they don't learn a thing. Theron plays Mavis Gary, an ex-prom queen from Mercury, Minnesota, making her living in the "Mini-apple" (as the Mercurians call Minneapolis) as the ghostwriter of a formerly popular teen book series. From the first sequence of the film,   2

(continued)

(continued)

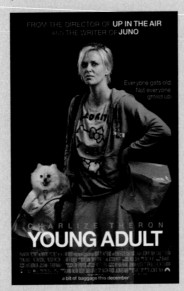

3

we can tell that Mavis is a mess. She gets wasted, slumps around her apartment in sweats, and guzzles Diet Coke in a way that almost gave me heartburn. Upon receiving a birth announcement email from her now-married ex-prom king beau, the aptly named Buddy (the similarly beautiful Patrick Wilson), Mavis decides to pop an old mix tape into her dirty Mini Cooper and go home to Mercury to win him back.

This is, essentially, the entire plot of *Young Adult*. Mavis' trip back to Mercury is a kind of *anti-hero's* journey. On her first night in town, getting wasted in a local dive, she meets her guide, Matt (the wonderful Patton Oswalt), a former classmate who remains crippled from a high school assault by jocks who mistakenly thought he was gay. Through the course of the film, as she reunites with her parents (Jill Eikenberry & Richard Bekins), insinuates herself into the lives of Buddy and his wife Beth (Elizabeth Reaser), and gets plastered on Matt's home-brewed bourbon, rather than moving towards revelation, Mavis seems to retreat further and further into her past.

4

Unlike writer Diablo Cody's most well-known and Oscar-winning screenplay *Juno*, *Young Adult* rejects preciousness in favor of obscenity. It's difficult to make a film about terrible people enjoyable, but Cody injects just enough silliness to keep us from feeling too badly. Director Jason Reitman (who also paired with Cody on *Juno*) wisely keeps us focused on Mavis through every moment, from the night out to the morning after, and both Theron and Oswalt are brave enough to let us into their characters' grimy inner selves. Smartly, Cody refuses to manufacture empathy for her characters, leaving us to boldly accept the ugliness of these people fully.

5

I don't doubt that *Young Adult* will displease many movie-goers who are used to redemptive stories and characters who, as *Salon* put it are "good at heart." Cody refuses to indulge that expectation. When Mavis dresses to go out and drink (which is often), Theron's extraordinary physical beauty is obvious. Yet we're never allowed to shake that Mavis is truly ugly at her core—an effective subversion of expectation that is the reason this memorable performance works. This isn't a feel-good film, and thank goodness. If Cody and Reitman had tried, I think we might leave the theater feeling worse.

Young Adult is writer Diablo Cody's most mature work yet.

Evaluating the Essay

1. Laura "re-mixes" her sketch into a web page. What's your evaluation of that move? Do you find it an effective revision of her review, and what criteria are you using to make that judgment?

2. As I've already mentioned, reviews often thrive on the persona—and the voice—of the reviewer. I think Laura has a strong persona in this review. The question is, how is persona communicated in a piece such as this one? What exactly would you point to in her review that reflects an individual voice and character?

3. Describe the structure of Laura's review. Diagram it using the elements of a review: description, back story, judgment, reasons, evidence, and criteria.

Using What You Have Learned

Let's revisit the list from the beginning of this chapter of things I hoped you'd learn about this form of writing.

1. **Use reasons and evidence to support a judgment about something's value.** Of course, it's not news that judgments are supported by reasons and evidence, but now you can think about these things more systematically and, as a result, have tools to analyze not only your own arguments but the arguments of others.

2. **Identify the criteria behind a judgment and determine their relevance.** Knowing to look for assumptions will give you a strong footing when analyzing any argument.

3. **Identify the characteristics of different forms of the review, including academic applications.** Reviews are a method of evaluating virtually anything. Whenever you are asked to evaluate something you can apply the skills you practiced here.

4. **Use invention and focusing strategies to discover and develop a review essay.** In this chapter, you practiced a skill you can apply in nearly any paper you write: how to see your topic *in context*, recognizing its place in an ever-larger scheme of things.

5. **Apply revision strategies that are effective for shaping reviews.** Using a wide range of evidence requires you to cast a wider net for information as you revise. This is a skill that you'll build on in the next assignments, as you write more and more with outside sources.

Researching and thinking about solutions can be a bit like following a horse race: You might favor one solution until another one suddenly races up from behind as you learn more.

Writing a Proposal

5

Learning Objectives

In this chapter, you'll learn to

5.1 Describe a problem of consequence, framing it narrowly enough to explore convincing solutions.

5.2 Identify the wide range of rhetorical situations that might call for a proposal argument.

5.3 Argue effectively for both the seriousness of the problem and the proposed solutions, using strong evidence.

5.4 Use appropriate invention strategies to discover and develop a proposal topic.

5.5 Apply revision strategies that are effective for a proposal.

Writing About Problems and Solutions

Several students sit around the table in my office. We're talking about problems each of us would love to solve. "I've got a short story due at three this afternoon and I've only written three pages," says Lana. Everyone nods sympathetically. "I'd really like to feel better about work," confides Amy, who works as a chef at a local restaurant. "Most days I just don't want to go." Margaret is a history major, familiar with the making and unmaking of nations and other grand narratives of colonialism, war, and social change. Her problem, however, is a bit more local. "I can't get my boyfriend to clean up the apartment," she says.

"What about you?" they ask me.

"The problem I most want to solve today is how to avoid getting scalded in the shower when someone in my house flushes the toilet," I say, getting into the spirit of things.

This conversation had not gone quite the way I expected. I know these students are socially engaged, politically aware, and academically gifted people. When I asked about problems that need solutions, I expected that they might mention local issues such as housing developments that threaten the foothills, the difficulty that nontraditional students have adjusting to the university, or budget cuts that threaten the availability of courses next semester. If they had been thinking on a larger scale—say, nationally or even internationally—perhaps the conversation would have turned to the federal

137

deficit or the conflict in Darfur. Of course, I hadn't asked them to suggest social or economic problems. I had simply asked them what problems most vexed them at the moment.

I should not have been surprised that these would be boredom with work, too little time, and a messy boyfriend. These problems are quite real, and they demand attention, *now*. One was easy to solve. Lana would carve out extra time in the afternoon to finish her story—"I already know what I need to do," she said. But the other two problems—disenchantment with work and a boyfriend who's a slob—Amy and Margaret actually saw not so much as problems to solve as realities they had to live with. In fact, all the students admitted that they rarely look at the world from the perspective of problem solving—the perspective that's at the heart of a proposal.

"What if you did?" I asked.

"Then I guess I'd ask myself if there was an opportunity to learn something," said Amy.

Problems of Consequence

5.1

Describe a problem of consequence, framing it narrowly enough to explore convincing solutions.

While not all problems are equally solvable, the process of seeking and proposing solutions can be rewarding if you see, as Amy did, the opportunity to learn. There's another motivation, too: If the problem is shared by others, whatever you discover may interest them. Part of the challenge is recognizing problems *of consequence*. What makes a problem consequential?

1. It potentially affects a number of people.

2. The solution may not be simple.

3. There may be multiple solutions and people disagree about which is best.

My problem with getting scalded in the shower if somebody flushes a toilet is clearly not consequential; all I need to do is go to Ace Hardware and buy a device for the showerhead. But what about Margaret's problem with her boyfriend? Is that a problem of consequence? Undoubtedly there are lots of people with messy mates, the solution is not at all obvious (just ask Margaret), and there are likely multiple ways of dealing with the problem.

If a problem is consequential, it's more likely that someone else will have said something about it. Like many other forms of inquiry, problem solving usually requires some research. After all, if we already knew the solution, we wouldn't have the problem. An important consideration, then, is whether others have said something about the problem that might help you think about the best ways to solve it. On a quick search of the web and several library databases, Margaret found some material that she thought could serve as background for an essay that looks at the problem of a messy mate and proposes some solutions. While Margaret may not succeed in getting her boyfriend to pick up his socks, she will probably learn a few things about how to deal with the problem.

> While not all problems are equally solvable, the process of seeking and proposing solutions can be rewarding if you see the opportunity to learn.

Problems of Manageable Scale

What about the sorts of larger-scale problems my students didn't mention that day? Here we're obviously talking about problems of consequence. The problems of world hunger, war, environmental destruction, poverty and lack of economic development, and human rights violations are problems that matter to us all. These are also among the most complex problems to solve. I'm always delighted when writers in my classes are passionate about these issues, and they certainly can be great topics for writing. But narrowing the topic to something manageable is a crucial first step.

Obviously, you're not going to have anything meaningful to say about solving world hunger in a five-page essay (see Figure 5.1). But it might be possible to write a focused essay about the troubles over food production in Zimbabwe, once one of Africa's top agricultural producers. Even better, narrow the topic further and investigate U.S. aid policies that are failing to help feed hungry Zimbabwean children. Your interest in hunger can also easily lead to topics with a local angle—say, the reluctance of some hungry families in your community to use food stamps because of a local supermarket's policies. By focusing on the narrower problem, you can often reveal aspects of the larger problem much more powerfully while developing a solution that's more implementable.

In other words, when you are choosing a problem to explore for a proposal, the *manageable scale* of a problem is as important as its consequentiality.

The problem of world hunger

The problem of food production in Africa

The problem of food production in Zimbabwe

The problem of U.S. food aid programs to Zimbabwe

Figure 5.1 Narrowing the focus of the problem. Most of us want to find solutions to the big problems of the world, but big problems such as world hunger are complicated and do not readily yield to simple solutions. Unless you are writing a book-length proposal, it is better to narrow the focus of the problem to which you will propose solutions.

Motives for Writing a Proposal

Quite simply, people write proposals to try to argue convincingly to others that a problem is worth tackling and a proposed solution is a good way to tackle it. Your motives for writing a proposal will probably include the following:

- *You* care *about the problem*. Whether it's something in your personal life (avoiding procrastination, having a more obedient dog, or finding a way to use less water in the garden) or a public issue (protecting bicyclists from traffic, increasing neighborhood police protection, or battling adolescent obesity) you should feel that the problem deserves your attention.

- *You hope to change something*. Writing a proposal is a way of overcoming powerlessness. Maybe you feel helpless about the daily deluge of scammers and junk messages in your e-mail. You can just complain about it. I do. But you can also research a proposal that might help you—and the many others affected by the problem—to avoid the Nigerian scammers who want to "give" you $8.5 million if you just send them a copy of your passport and $1,750.

- *You hope to learn something*. A proposal is like all other inquiry projects: You choose a topic because you're motivated to discover things you don't know. This motive alone isn't sufficient, of course. Others must be affected by the problem and have a stake in considering your solution. But if the problem is sufficiently complex and the solutions varied, then you stand to learn a lot.

> Writing a proposal is a way of overcoming powerlessness.

The Proposal and Academic Writing

5.2

Identify the wide range of rhetorical situations that might call for a proposal argument.

Numerous academic situations call for proposal writing and, more generally, writing to solve problems. Here are some you might come across in classes you take:

- The case-study approach, popular in business, medicine, and some social sciences, is essentially the presentation of a real-world problem for you to solve.

- Problem-based learning is an approach to inquiry common in the sciences that begins with a messy problem and involves learners in coming up with tentative solutions.

- In some classes, you'll be asked to write proposals. For example, political science courses may include an assignment to write a policy proposal or an essay that looks at a specific public policy problem—say, the organization of the city government or the state's role in wolf management (a big issue here in Idaho)—and suggests some possible solutions. In a marketing class, you might be asked to draft a proposal for dealing with a particular management problem.

Academics in many disciplines write research proposals. These identify a question and then propose a plan for studying it (see "Inquiring into the Details: Writing a Research Proposal"). The research question may relate to a problem—air pollution inversions in the valley, energy inefficiencies in buildings, and so on—or simply to a topic that could be useful to study—use of iPads in the classroom or the effects of birth order. To get grants for their research, academics usually need to submit proposals.

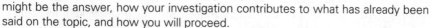

Inquiring into the Details

Writing a Research Proposal

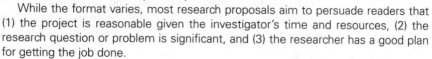

A research proposal is a kind of action plan that explains your research question, what you expect might be the answer, how your investigation contributes to what has already been said on the topic, and how you will proceed.

While the format varies, most research proposals aim to persuade readers that (1) the project is reasonable given the investigator's time and resources, (2) the research question or problem is significant, and (3) the researcher has a good plan for getting the job done.

The following elements are typically included in a research proposal:

- **Title:** Short and descriptive.
- **Abstract:** A brief statement of what you intend to do, including your research question and hypothesis, if you've got one.
- **Background or context:** Why is the project worth doing? What problem does it solve, or how does it advance our understanding of the subject? This key section establishes where your question fits into the ongoing conversation about your topic, in your class, in the academic literature, or both. You also want to demonstrate that you've done your homework—you've got a handle on the relevant literature on your topic and understand how you might build on it.
- **Methodology or research design:** How will you try to answer your research question? How will you limit your focus? What information will you need to gather, and how will you do it?
- **Results:** This isn't a common section for proposals in the humanities, but it certainly is in the sciences. How will you analyze the data you collect?
- **References or works cited:** Almost all research proposals, because they review relevant literature, include a bibliography. Sometimes you may be asked to annotate it.

Because the research proposal is a persuasive document, craft it to keep your reader engaged; find a good balance between generalities and detail, avoid jargon, and demonstrate your curiosity and eagerness to pursue your question.

Features of the Form

Feature	Conventions of the Proposal
Inquiry questions	What is the problem? What should be done?
Motives	You hope to change a problem related to something that matters to you and others, and there is the promise that you will learn something about the problem and possible solutions.
Subject matter	Proposals suggest a best plan of action on any problem of consequence. Proposals could address large problems (the homeless problem in town) or small ones (a boyfriend who doesn't take dirty dishes seriously), as long as others have a stake in solving the problem. Research proposals suggest a plan for studying a problem or other question.
Structure	Proposals typically address both the problem and the solution, in that order, but may emphasize one or the other. When an audience largely agrees that the problem is significant, a proposal might focus on the solution. When there is disagreement about the significance of the problem, a proposal might focus on why the problem needs attention. Other elements of a proposal include: • *Causes and effects.* These can help establish why the problem needs attention and why the proposed solution will deal with the problem. • *Justifications.* Typically proposals that argue for certain solutions over others offer clear reasons why the proposed solutions are the best ones. • *Evidence.* Evidence from research and experience makes a case for the problem and for the solutions. • *Other perspectives.* If you're writing about a problem of consequence, then other people have said something about it and probably have proposed various solutions. • *Visual rhetoric.* Often, problems and/or solutions can be illustrated with pictures, tables, and graphs; headings and bulleted lists can also be useful.
Sources of information	Writers who have experience with a problem should tap that experience in a proposal. However, if they're not experts, then personal experience alone may not be persuasive evidence. Proposals usually depend on information from research—reading or interviews—on what people who *are* experts on the problem say about it.

Feature	Conventions of the Proposal
Language	Proposals are a form of argument. As with other arguments, the language you use depends largely on the rhetorical situation. Formal proposals intended for an expert audience, such as research or marketing proposals, take a formal tone. Others—for example, a proposal that's a letter to the editor or a blog entry—are much more casual and even personal.

Prose+

Alexandra Muresan's infographic "CO$_2$ Paper Pie Chart" highlights the sources of the world's carbon dioxide emissions related to individuals and the ways to reduce these emissions. Notice that both the problems and solutions are integrated into a single paper pie chart. When unfolded as a *C*, the chart shows the sources of emissions in each paper fold. When unfolded as an *O*, it gives suggestions for reducing emissions. Muresan's paper pie chart is an elegant visual proposal. It not only beautifully presents the problem of CO$_2$ emissions, but also literally puts the solution to the problem into a user's hand.

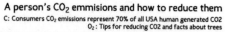

A person's CO$_2$ emmisions and how to reduce them
C: Consumers CO$_2$ emissions represent 70% of all USA human generated CO2
O$_2$: Tips for reducing CO2 and facts about trees

the pollution

the solution

Data Sources: http://www.cutco2.org/ http://www.erasecarbonfootprint.com/ http://www.eoearth.org/   Designed by Alexandra Muresan www.ixycreativity.ro

READINGS

▶ Proposal 1

I teach at a university with a football team that is frequently ranked in the top ten nationally. Our stadium's blue turf is more famous than any one of our academic programs, prompting the university's marketing folks to coin the slogan "Beyond the Blue." In other words, we just want you to know that there is actually teaching and research going on here, not just football. And yet, the games are fun, and the athletic program is the strongest link the university has to the community. The sale of sports paraphernalia—hats, t-shirts, bobble-heads, and dog collars emblazoned with the school colors—funds student scholarships. Is college football really a problem? Buzz Bissinger thinks so. He notes that these are often hugely expensive programs that hemorrhage money in a time of endless tuition hikes. The solution: Ban college football.

Why College Football Should Be Banned
Buzz Bissinger

1   In more than 20 years I've spent studying the issue, I have yet to hear a convincing argument that college football has anything do with what is presumably the primary purpose of higher education: academics.

2   That's because college football has no academic purpose. Which is why it needs to be banned. A radical solution, yes. But necessary in today's times.

3   Football only provides the thickest layer of distraction in an atmosphere in which colleges and universities these days are all about distraction, nursing an obsession with the social well-being of students as opposed to the obsession that they are there for the vital and single purpose of learning as much as they can to compete in the brutal realities of the global economy.

4   Who truly benefits from college football? Alumni who absurdly judge the quality of their alma mater based on the quality of the football team. Coaches such as Nick Saban of the University of Alabama and Bob Stoops of the University of Oklahoma who make obscene millions. The players themselves don't benefit, exploited by a system in which they don't receive a dime of compensation. The average student doesn't benefit, particularly when football programs remain sacrosanct while tuition costs show no signs of abating as many governors are slashing budgets to the bone.

If the vast majority of major college football programs made money, the argument to ban football might be a more precarious one. But too many of them don't—to the detriment of academic budgets at all too many schools. According to the NCAA, 43 percent of the 120 schools in the Football Bowl Subdivision lost money on their programs. This is the tier of schools that includes such examples as that great titan of football excellence, the University of Alabama at Birmingham Blazers, who went 3-and-9 last season. The athletic department in 2008–2009 took in over $13 million in university funds and student fees, largely because the football program cost so much, *The Wall Street Journal* reported. New Mexico State University's athletic department needed a 70% subsidy in 2009–2010, largely because Aggie football hasn't gotten to a bowl game in 51 years. Outside of Las Cruces, where New Mexico State is located, how many people even know that the school has a football program? None, except maybe for some savvy contestants on "Jeopardy." What purpose does it serve on a university campus? None.

The most recent example is the University of Maryland. The president there, Wallace D. Loh, late last year announced that eight varsity programs would be cut in order to produce a leaner athletic budget, a kindly way of saying that the school would rather save struggling football and basketball programs than keep varsity sports such as track and swimming, in which the vast majority of participants graduate.

Part of the Maryland football problem: a $50.8 million modernization of its stadium in which too many luxury suites remain unsold. Another problem: The school reportedly paid $2 million to buy out head coach Ralph Friedgen at the end of the 2010 season, even though he led his team to a 9-and-4 season and was named Atlantic Coast Conference Coach of the Year. Then, the school reportedly spent another $2 million to hire Randy Edsall from the University of Connecticut, who promptly produced a record of 2-and-10 last season.

In an interview with the *Baltimore Sun* in March, Mr. Loh said that the athletic department was covering deficits, in large part caused by attendance drops in football and basketball, by drawing upon reserves that eventually dwindled to zero. Hence cutting the eight sports.

This is just the tip of the iceberg. There are the medical dangers of football in general caused by head trauma over repetitive hits. There is the false concept of the football student-athlete that the NCAA endlessly tries to sell, when any major college player will tell you that the demands of the game, a year-round commitment, makes the student half of the equation secondary and superfluous. There are the scandals that have beset programs in the desperate pursuit of winning—the University of Southern California, Ohio State University, University of Miami, and Penn State University among others.

(continued)

(continued)

10   I can't help but wonder how a student at the University of Oregon will cope when in-state tuition has recently gone up by 9% and the state legislature passed an 11% decrease in funding to the Oregon system overall for 2011 and 2012. Yet thanks to the largess of Nike founder Phil Knight, an academic center costing $41.7 million, twice as expensive in square footage as the toniest condos in Portland, has been built for the University of Oregon football team.

11   Always important to feed those Ducks.

12   I actually like football a great deal. I am not some anti-sports prude. It has a place in our society, but not on college campuses. If you want to establish a minor league system that the National Football League pays for—which they should, given that they are the greatest beneficiaries of college football—that is fine.

13   Call me the Grinch. But I would much prefer students going to college to learn and be prepared for the rigors of the new economic order, rather than dumping fees on them to subsidize football programs that, far from enhancing the academic mission instead make a mockery of it.

Inquiring into the Essay

1. **Explore.** Here's a sampling of assertions from Bizzinger's essay:

    ▪ "College football has no academic purpose."

    ▪ The beneficiaries of college football aren't the students, the athletes, or the school but coaches who pull in salaries in the millions.

    ▪ The vast sums invested in coaches, stadiums, and training facilities often end up being a drain on universities' budgets. This is especially objectionable in an age of tuition increases.

    Choose one of these assertions (or another from the essay you'd like to write about) and fastwrite for five minutes, exploring your own thinking about the claim. If you can, write about what you observe on your own campus.

2. **Explain.** Follow up on your fastwrite in the last step by composing a summary of your own thinking about Bissinger's proposal to ban college football.

3. **Evaluate.** One of Bissinger's key claims is that college football programs often lose big money, and as evidence he cites the NCAA, which reported that 43 percent of the schools in the Football Bowl Subdivision were in the red. Using your own research, evaluate that claim.

4. **Reflect.** A proposal is an argument: There is a problem, here are some solutions, and this is evidence that makes them credible. It's never that simple, of course. For one thing, you have to secure audience agreement

that there is a problem in the first place, and if your audience agrees, then there are many possible solutions. Why yours? Finally, some evidence is better than other evidence, and there is the issue of what you *don't* say. Is there a counter-argument? Is there inconvenient evidence you ignore? With all this in mind, how would you evaluate Bissinger's proposal that college football should be banned?

▶ Proposal 2

A lot of people can't imagine a proposal without PowerPoint (or Keynote for Mac users). It's a remarkably versatile program that exploits the potential of visual rhetoric. You can combine images with text, animation, and even audio. Presentation slides challenge the user to think about what ideas to emphasize and which visual arrangements might dramatize them to an audience. Depending on how you order the slides, you can tell a different story. Maybe because of all these possibilities, PowerPoint presentations can be boring. There may be too much text, the animation can be obnoxious, or the images might be distracting. Worse still, the presenter uses presentation slides like a script rather than a technique for focusing emphasis on key points. Watching someone's back while he or she reads PowerPoint text is an invitation to nod off.

The following PowerPoint proposal, "Green Dining," describes how the dining services at University of California–Santa Cruz are trying to solve the problem of energy inefficiency in the kitchen. This proposal doesn't dramatize the problem. It doesn't really need to, because most everyone agrees that wasting energy in dining halls (or any other campus building, for that matter) is a problem. This slide presentation focuses on some solutions, and it works well because the proposal has modest ambitions. It addresses one very specific aspect of the campus dining operation: dishwashing. Even better, there is concrete evidence that one solution is already making a difference in energy use. After documenting this success, "Green Dining" goes on to present other measures that should have a similar impact.

Notice how much can be accomplished with simple images, minimal text, and logical arrangement.

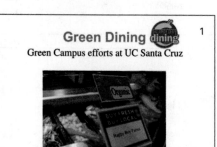

Green Campus dining objectives

- Achieve Monterey Bay Green Business Certification
- Acquire new efficient technology
- Educate students about sustainable dining practices
- Adjust policies and procedures to conserve energy

Monterey Bay Green Business Certification

3

- An official recognition awarded by the *Monterey Bay Area Green Business Program*
- Businesses must take extensive measures to conserve resources prevent pollution, and minimize waste.

MONTEREY BAY AREA

GREEN BUSINESS PROGRAM

Savings Opportunities

4

- A typical dishwashing operation can use **over 2/3** of all water consumed at an establishment

- Often **1/2** of that water use is consumed by **pre-rinse spray nozzles**

- And that water is heated with energy

Smart Rinse Spray Nozzles

5

Low-flow "Smart-rinse" nozzles are one upgrade that can save hot water when rinsing and help businesses achieve Green Business Certification.

Spray Nozzle Specs

6

- Fisher "Ultra Spray"
- 1.15 GPM @ 60 PSI
- 1-hole clearance
- Easy-use, "knife spray" action that allows food to be easily removed
- Cost: roughly $50/unit

Benefits

7

- Saves water
- Saves energy
- Saves money
- Cleans faster
- Less splash back
- Covers larger surface area

Success at UC Santa Cruz

8

5 "low-flow" nozzles were installed in various locations:
- Crown/Merrill Dining
- College 8/9 Dining
- Owl's Nest Café
- Terra Fresca Cafe

Nozzles were supplied and installed FOR FREE through the "Smart Rinse Program," a program of Ecology Action, a local Santa Cruz non-profit

---

Quantifiable Savings

9

Energy Saving Estimates

Total # of Nozzles	Hours used per day	Gallons saved per day	Therms saved per day	Annual Dollar Savings
5	65	3229	16.23	$8,175

Current Dining Projects

10

T8 Lighting retrofit

- 5 major dining halls
- Upgrade 32 watts → 28 Watts
- 1248 Lamps counted
- Roughly 5 KW saved

11

Future Dining Project

Variable control exhaust hoods

- Controls for commercial kitchen ventilation exhaust hoods
- Reduce energy costs by up to 70% during slow cooking periods

---

12

Project Benefits

- Massive energy savings
- Improved indoor air quality
- Optimum kitchen comfort
- Improved fire safety
- 1–4 year payback
- $1,500–$10,00 in annual savings

13

Questions?

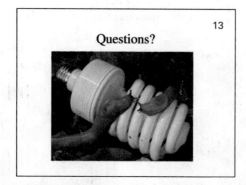

Inquiring into the Essay

1. **Explore.** Finish the following sentences in your journal, and follow each for a minute if you can. Write quickly.

   a. As far as I'm concerned, PowerPoint is _____.

   b. The best slide presentations _____.

   c. The worst slide presentations _____.

   d. When I do PowerPoint (or Keynote), the main thing I think about is _____.

   e. A lot of times, people do PowerPoint when they should _____.

2. **Explain.** Using some of the ideas you generated in the first question, craft a definition of an effective PowerPoint proposal, identifying specifically what qualities it should have.

3. **Evaluate.** Use your definition in the previous question to evaluate "Green Dining." Is it persuasive?

4. **Reflect.** The preceding series of questions, if used consecutively, constitutes a method for thinking through writing about what you've read, working toward a more thoughtful evaluation. Reflect on how that process worked for you. Did you end up getting better ideas about what you think because you took time to do the prewriting?

Seeing the Form

A Problem in Pictures

When members of the San Francisco Bicycle Coalition (SFBC) wanted to dramatize the problem of insufficient space for bikes on a city commuter train, they did it with pictures. It was a powerfully simple idea. They took shots of three morning trains, each overloaded with bicycles and nearly empty of passengers. The contrast is obvious. And so is the solution to the problem: Add more space for bicycles on trains. A few months later, transit authorities did just that.

No Space for Bikes:
A photo study of trains bumping cyclists out of SF.

1: Train 134: Sept 22 9:07 AM   2: Train 134: Sept 22 9:07 AM

Seeing the Form (*continued*)

3: Train 230: Sept 24 8:53 AM

4: Train 230: Sept 24 8:53 AM

5: Train 332: Sept 30 8:56 AM

6: Train 332: Sept 30 8:56 AM

Submitted to JBP Oct 2
by Benjamin Damm

5.3

Argue effectively for both the seriousness of the problem and the proposed solutions, using strong evidence.

THE WRITING PROCESS

Inquiry Project **Writing a Proposal**

Inquiry questions: What is the problem? What should be done?

Write a proposal to help resolve a problem that you care about. Make sure your proposal does the following (see also pp. 142–143 for typical features of proposals):

- Addresses a problem that is of consequence and of a manageable scale, including the problem's causes and effects.
- Provides evidence for the seriousness of the problem and for ways to solve it, justifying these solutions over alternatives. You can draw on your experience but should also use outside sources.
- Is appropriate in both form and content to your purpose and audience.
- Includes graphics if relevant.

Prose+

Design a web page for your proposal that has the following features:

- Links to relevant sites that provide additional evidence or information on the problem and/or solution.
- At least one image or graphic.
- A boxed feature with additional information, suggestions, helpful summaries, key ideas, etc.

(For more information on how to mock up a web page, see "Inquiring into the Details: Design Tips for Basic Web Pages" on p. 162.)

Turn your proposal into a radio documentary. Rewrite the proposal around interview clips with people who are affected by the problem or who are trying to solve it. Tell a story.

Using "Green Dining" (p. 147) as inspiration, develop a PowerPoint presentation on your proposal, combining images and text. It's also easy to embed video and audio files in a PowerPoint if relevant.

Alternatively, use the San Francisco Bicycle Coalition's visual proposal (p. 150) as inspiration and present your "problem in pictures."

What Are You Going to Write About?

Perhaps you already have a topic in mind for your proposal. But if you don't, or you want to explore some other possibilities, begin by generating a list of problems you'd like to solve. Don't worry too much about whether they're problems of consequence or about whether you have solutions to the problems. Try some of the generating exercises that follow.

The explosion of "how-to" and "self-help" books and articles is evidence of the popularity of writing that attempts to solve problems.

Opening Up

Play with some ideas about subjects for the proposal assignment. Remember not to judge the material at this stage.

5.4

Use appropriate invention strategies to discover and develop a proposal topic.

Listing Prompts. Lists can be rich sources of triggering topics. Let them grow freely, and when you're ready, use an item as the focus of another list or an episode of fastwriting. The following prompts should get you started.

1. Title a list "Things That Bug Me" and brainstorm as many things as you can think of for two minutes. Let the ideas come in waves.

2. Spend three minutes brainstorming a list of problems *on your campus, at your workplace,* or *in the local community* that affect you in some way or that you feel something about. Don't worry about repeating items from the list you made in Listing Prompt 1.

3. Explore some possible causes of a problem you listed, by finishing the following sentence as many times as you can: One of the things causing this problem is _____.

Fastwriting Prompts. In the early stages of generating possible topics for an essay, fastwriting can be invaluable, *if* you allow yourself to write badly. Initially, don't worry about staying focused; sometimes you find the best triggering topics by ranging freely. Once you've tentatively settled on something, use a more focused fastwrite to try to generate information and ideas within the loose boundaries of your chosen topic.

1. Pick any of the items from the preceding lists as a launching place for a five-minute fastwrite. Explore some of the following questions:

   - When did I first notice this was a problem?
   - What's the worst part about it?
   - What might be some of its causes?
   - What moment, situation, or scene is most typical of this problem? Describe it as if you're experiencing it by writing in the present tense.

■ How does this problem make me feel?

■ What people do I associate with it?

2. Depending on how familiar you are with a problem that interests you, do a five-minute focused fastwrite that explores solutions, beginning with the sentence I think one of the ways to deal with _____ is _____. Follow that sentence as long as you can. When the writing stalls, use the following prompt: Another possible solution to the problem of _____ might be _____.

Visual Prompts. Only a few problems have a single root cause. Use the following template to begin thinking about some of the possible causes of a problem. Describe the problem in the middle circle and then build arrows to as many explanations of possible causes as come to mind.

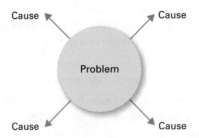

Research Prompts. Reading, observing, and talking to people can be great ways to discover a proposal topic. The following research prompts can help you along.

1. Interview your classmates about what they think are the biggest problems facing them as students. Interview student or faculty leaders or administrators about what they think are the biggest problems facing the university community. Do the same with community leaders.

2. Design an informal survey targeted to a particular group that you're interested in—students, student-athletes, local businesspeople, sports fans, migrant workers, and so on. This group may or may not be one to which you belong. Discover what they believe are the most serious problems they face.

3. Become a student of a local newspaper. In particular, pay attention to the letters to the editor and the local community pages. What seems to be a recurrent problem that gets people's attention? Clip articles, letters, or editorials that address the problem.

4. Google the following phrase: "solution to the problem of." Scan the results for topic ideas.

Narrowing Down

Feeling a little overwhelmed? See problems everywhere? It can be wearing to focus on what's wrong with your life, your university, and your community. But remember that your ultimate goal is to write a proposal that suggests ways these problems might be resolved. You may have already explored some of these solutions, but if you haven't, don't worry—you'll get the chance later. Begin by scrutinizing the material you generated for possible topics.

What's Promising Material and What Isn't? We've talked about some initial judgments you can make. Now look at the material you generated in the fastwrites, lists, research, or clusters, and ask yourself which of the problems listed *do you care about the most*, or which *are you most interested in*? Once you've selected some tentative topics for your proposal, narrow them down using the following questions:

- *Does someone aside from you have a stake in finding a solution? Is there an identifiable audience for proposals about solutions?*
- *Is the problem a manageable one?*
- *Have other people said something about the problem and possible solutions?*
- *Which subject offers you the most opportunity for learning?*

Questions About Audience and Purpose. This assignment asks you to craft a proposal appropriate to your audience and purpose. When you have identified an audience for your proposal, consider what exactly might be your purpose with respect to that audience. Do you want to:

- *Inform* them about the problem and explore possible solutions?
- *Advocate* certain solutions as the best ways to solve the problem?
- *Inform and advocate,* dramatizing the problem because your audience may not fully appreciate and understand it, and then persuading them to support the solutions you favor?

These purposes will shape your approach. And which you choose will depend partly on how your audience might already think and feel about the problem you're tackling and the solutions you offer. Use the chart in Figure 5.2.

Although it might be premature to decide the *form* your proposal will take, sometimes an awareness of purpose and audience will suggest an approach. Ask yourself this question: Given the problem I'm writing about, which audiences are (1) most affected by it and (2) most likely to contribute to the solution? Next, think about how to best reach one or both of those audiences. For example, suppose that Cheryl's purpose is to advocate for a new nontraditional student center on campus and her audience is school administrators. Her best approach for getting her message across might be to write her proposal in the form of a letter to the university's president.

Awareness of the problem	If low, increase emphasis on dramatizing the problem.	If high, emphasize proposed solutions.
Initial disposition toward proposed solution	If favorably disposed, emphasize action that needs to be taken to implement solution. Emphasize pathos over logos.	If unfavorably disposed, offer balanced treatment of possible solutions before stating yours. Emphasize logos over pathos.
Attitude toward speaker	If positive, emphasize stronger action to solve the problem.	If negative, emphasize the views or experience speaker *does* share with audience.

Figure 5.2   Audience analysis chart. As with other forms of argument, the persuasiveness of a proposal depends on a rhetorical understanding of your audience. This is discussed in more detail in Chapter 6, where I introduce the rhetorical triangle, as well as *ethos, pathos*, and *logos* (see p. 177 for a discussion of those terms). See if you can do a rhetorical analysis on your proposal, and use what you discover to revise your essay.

Trying Out

Got a topic you want to try? Good. Let's do some focused work on that topic to generate some more material on it. Unless you've got a lot of personal experience with the problem you're thinking about writing about (and probably even if you do), you need to develop a working knowledge of the topic through some quick research.

Researching to Answer the *So What*? Question. To start with, you need to be able to establish that the problem you're interested in is significant. To do that, you'll need to answer a skeptic's question: *Okay, so what's the big deal about this?* That will be the focus of your initial research.

Using Google, Google Scholar, or library databases, find at least three sources online that show the significance of the problem you're interested in writing about. These sources may

a. Provide statistics or facts that suggest the seriousness of the problem.
b. Tell a story, case study, or anecdote about people who are affected by it.
c. Visually illustrate the effects of the problem.
d. Offer assertions by experts who are concerned with the problem.

Giving Your Answer on a PowerPoint. Using what you've learned, prepare a single PowerPoint slide that you would use to answer the question "So what's the big deal about this?" Here's a slide that one of my students, Andrea, developed to dramatize the problem of disappearing honeybees. While it isn't a

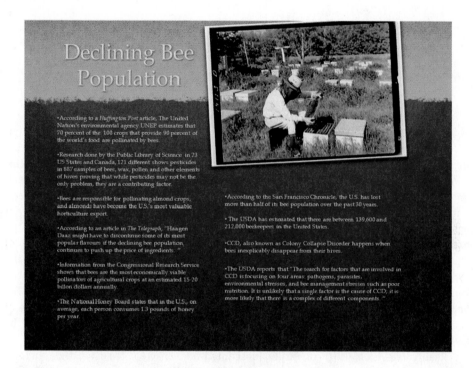

very effective PowerPoint slide—there's too much text, for one thing—it's a really useful summary of the problem. Use the material you generate from this exercise to help establish the significance of the problem in your sketch.

Writing the Sketch

Try out a tentative proposal topic by writing a sketch, a relatively brief early draft written with an audience in mind. Your sketch should:

- Have a tentative title.
- Use appropriate evidence (personal experience, facts, statistics, etc.) to dramatize the problem.
- Identify one or more causes of the problem and offer some tentative solutions for addressing those causes.
- Be written with an appropriate audience and purpose in mind.

You might also develop this sketch in a form that you think might be particularly effective given your purpose and audience. Your sketch might be an essay or a letter, a PowerPoint, a podcast, a web page, or the text of a brochure or ad.

▶ **Student Sketch**

Loving and Hating Reality TV
Jenna Appleman

1   When I moved into my own apartment without TV or cable, I assumed I'd be watching much less television. My TV consumption had never been a problem—I'd watch *Law & Order* and HBO when I was home, but didn't follow very much else. I prided myself on watching intelligent television, avoiding the low-culture reality series with a sneer. But in the silence of a studio apartment in the busiest semester of my college career, I needed a way to fill the space and blow off some steam. That's when I started watching reality TV.

2   There are TV channels dedicated exclusively to reality programming. Bravo houses the various *Real Housewives* series (my gateway), as well as their many spinoffs, E! plays the various Kardashian series, and reality competition shows like *The Biggest Loser* and *The Bachelor* rake in thousands of viewers on primetime. Certainly such success is indicative of something, and there are those who would disagree with my assumptions, but I stand by my initial negative cast on the cultural saturation of reality TV.

3   Reality television is (theoretically) unscripted and unacted, removing thousands of paying jobs for writers and actors from the market. I also sense that such excessive exposure can be exploitative. One show I have guiltily watched on Lifetime called *Dance Moms* follows a team of very young competitive dancers, between the ages of 7 and 14. Surely having their emotional breakdowns and embarrassing parents on camera at that young age isn't helping their development.

4   And yet, I watch it. Frequently. But in public, I pretend I don't know the names of the Kardashians and roll my eyes wildly at front page news about the Housewives. For better or worse, I have grown accustomed to the comfort of curling up in bed with my cat and watching a marathon of *Millionaire Matchmaker* after an exhausting day. I watched an episode of *The Bachelor* while I was drafting this proposal, just to have some noise in the background to help me think. I want to hate it, but there's a lot about it I love.

5   I don't propose that we change the burgeoning culture of reality television entirely. That's far from realistic, and I have a feeling eventually this too will cycle out of popularity. But I do feel that I need to find a way to reconcile how I feel about reality TV with my penchant for it. The first step, I recognize, is admitting that I have a problem.

6   I don't propose that I stop watching reality television. But I do think it's important to clarify *why* I do—if it's to help me focus on schoolwork, that's a benefit. If I find it calming after a long day, that's okay too. But if I start watching because I simply *must* find out what's happening in these people's lives, if I begin to really stake weight in it, that's when I need a reality check. If I can accept the reasons why, then I can start feeling less guilty about it. I also think I should make a point to also watch other television; the normal kind that employs

actors and writers. It would also be good to try to utilize my gym membership and watch these "guilty pleasures" on the cardio machines' TVs while I'm actually doing something physical. I should also recognize the shows that I find particularly exploitative, and avoid them, or at least view them with an intelligent, critical eye in order to form an opinion.

Moving from Sketch to Draft

Return to the inquiry questions behind a proposal: *What is the problem? What should be done?* How well does your sketch answer those questions? Is the problem clear, and would a skeptical reader be convinced that it is serious enough to address? Based on what you know now, do the solutions make sense? Explore these considerations in the next section.

Evaluating Your Own Sketch. Proposal sketches, no matter what the form, usually need work in the following areas:

- **Refining the problem.** It's too big and needs to be more focused.
- **Insufficient evidence.** More research is required to establish the seriousness of the problem, identify key causes, and/or support proposed solutions.

For example, Jason's sketch argued that people watch too much TV. Okay, but might that assertion be easier to write about if it were less general? Which people, exactly, watch too much TV? What do they watch too much? Violent programs? Advertising? Reality TV? What is "too much"? And finally, what are the consequences of watching that much? All of these questions require research. Jason might discover that the effects of TV watching are especially problematic for a certain age group, or that certain kinds of advertising—say, snack food commercials aimed at children—are particularly

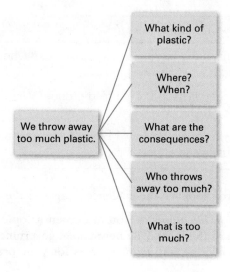

troubling. So Jason can refine his problem from "People watch too much TV" to something more focused like "Television commercials for high-calorie snack foods contribute to childhood obesity." Now that's much easier to work with! Jason's much clearer about the problem and its consequences, and can now focus his research.

See if you can refine the problem statement in your sketch in similar ways. "Wh" questions (who, which, what, where, when, why) can help you pare down a big problem to something more manageable. Use the previous example as a guide, applying the "Wh" questions to the problem you discussed in your sketch. Then restate the problem as Jason did, so that it's more specific.

Reflecting on What You Learned. The thing I like about sketches is that they are very early drafts—attempts, really—at trying out a topic, without a huge investment of time. At least they're not supposed to be huge investments of time. But pretty often I have students who approach nearly every writing assignment as if it required "perfection" or who have such harsh internal critics that writing is always kind of painful and slow. For these students, sketches are no cure. What about you? Do a journal entry in which you fastwrite for a few minutes about your experience writing this sketch. In particular, was it hard for you to accept that your sketch didn't meet your usual standards for writing something to hand in? What are your "usual standards," and do they get in the way of drafting and revising?

Developing

If you refined the problem you're exploring, stating it more clearly and concretely, then you've made it much easier to develop your draft. Developing your draft is a process that will require research.

Research. But what kind will you need to do? What are you looking for? The table below shows some key elements of proposals, and questions to think about for each. Consider these questions as guides for your research.

Element	Questions for Research
Problem	What's the evidence that it's serious? Who does it affect and under what circumstances?
Effects and causes	What will happen if nothing is done? Why is it happening? Why does this matter?
Solutions	What should be done? How do these proposals address key causes and effects?

Where should you look for the evidence to answer these questions?

- *Exploit local publications.* If you've chosen a topic of local interest, then sources such as the local daily newspaper, government reports, and university policies may be important sources for your proposal. Some of these, such as local newspapers and government documents, may be available in online databases at your library.

- *Interview experts*. Here's a chance to use your interview skills. One of the most efficient ways to collect information for your revision is to talk to people who have knowledge about the problem. These may be experts who have researched the problem or people affected by it.

- *Search for experience with similar solutions elsewhere*. If your proposal calls for an education program on binge drinking, what other universities might have tried it? What was their experience? Search for information using keywords that describe the problem you're writing about ("binge drinking"), and try adding a phrase that describes the solution ("binge drinking education programs"). Also check library databases that might lead you to articles in newspapers, magazines, and journals on the problem and its solutions.

A word of advice about solutions: Researching and thinking about solutions can be a bit like following a horse race: You might favor one solution until another one suddenly races up from behind as you learn more. In an inquiry project, that's normal. Make sure that the solutions you end up with are consistent with your own experience and with your values about the best ways to solve problems.

Focusing on the Justifications. In my part of the country, everyone has an opinion about wolves. Many people hate them. Wolf packs were reestablished in the West under the Endangered Species Act, and in recent decades wolves have extended their range well beyond the national parks and into ranching and agricultural areas. The problem is that some wolves kill livestock. What does one do with a wolf pack that won't stop killing sheep? Some popular solutions include: (1) Nothing—they were here first; (2) Capture them and relocate them away from populated areas; (3) Kill them.

Each of these solutions has problems of its own—and advocates and critics who will energetically argue over them. If you're working on an essay that focuses on a problem that affects people (and isn't that the definition of a problem?), then you will discover controversies over what to do about it. One thing your draft should not do is pretend that these controversies don't exist. On the contrary, your draft should not only justify the solutions you prefer, but also identify the solutions you've rejected and show why your solutions are better.

You've done some research on the problem and solutions. Develop your draft by focusing on the justifications for your solutions:

- Why are they the best solutions?
- How do they effectively address the causes and effects of the problem?
- What is evidence that they will work?
- What might critics say? Why are they wrong?

These *justifications* for your solutions will be a key part of your draft.

Inquiring into the Details

Design Tips for Basic Web Pages

You don't have to be an expert to build a web page. In addition to free sites such as Wix, Weebly, and Webs, which provide design templates and even hosting options, you can use a word processing program such as Word to create basic web pages.

When building a web page, consider these design tips:

- Maximize contrast.
- For readability go with 40–80 characters per line (65 is optimal).
- Avoid going over 200–400 words per page.
- Don't be afraid of blank space. Blank space makes it easier for your audience to focus on the content.
- Use titles that make sense and are relevant to your content.
- To offset text, make use of images that are relevant and can give a good visual representation of what your essay is saying.
- Use menus for content that is longer than three pages.
- Avoid fonts other than the standards such as Verdana, Arial, Courier, or Times. Font size should run 12–15 points. Use sans-serif type for body text, and serif for titles.
- Decide on a color scheme and stick with it.

Drafting

As you think about how to organize your draft, consider some of the following suggestions.

Methods of Development. As mentioned earlier in the chapter, a proposal often moves from problem to solution, and some proposals, like the research proposal, need to follow a specific form. But if the form of your proposal has not been specified, you can organize it in a number of ways. One way to think about how to organize your draft is to imagine the questions a typical reader of a proposal, or a problem-solution paper, might ask and the order in which they might ask them:

- What's the big deal?
- Who says it's a big deal besides you?
- What's at stake?
- What causes the problem? What are its effects?
- What solutions have people proposed? Are they justified?
- Which do you prefer? How do you justify it?

- What are the potential problems with the solution you like?
- Why do you still like it?
- If we do this, is everything going to be okay? Is there anything you're asking me to do?

You might play with the order in which you deal with these questions in your draft, but you will likely have to address all of them somewhere.

Using Evidence. You will answer the preceding questions with evidence that you've gathered from research (reading, interview, observation) and experience. Like much else, the evidence you use depends on your intended audience. In other words, choosing the strongest evidence in a proposal is an exercise in audience analysis:

- How much does your audience know about the problem?
- Is your audience likely to favor your idea, oppose it, or have no opinion?
- What kind of evidence is most likely to convince your audience?

The *amount* of evidence you need to provide depends on whether your audience is likely to be predisposed to agree or disagree with the solutions you propose. Obviously, if readers need convincing, you need to offer more justification. The *types* of evidence you provide depend on your assessment of what your audience will be most likely to believe. As you compose your draft, consider who your readers will be and the kinds of evidence they will find most persuasive.

Workshopping

Because a proposal is a form of argument, your workshop is a chance to test its persuasiveness with readers. One key thing to consider before the session is how much your peers already know about the problem you're writing about. The less they know, the more work your draft needs to do in these areas:

1. Convince readers of the seriousness of the problem.
2. Provide a context for the problem: who's involved, who's affected, what's been tried, how long it's been going on, what will happen if nothing is done.

Questions for Peer Reviewers	
1. Purpose	After reading the draft, what do you think is at stake? If nothing is done to solve the problem, what might be the consequences?
2. Meaning	In your own words, how does the essay answer the inquiry question *What should be done?* Play the doubting game for a moment: What potential problems do you see with the solution I'm proposing?

3. Persuade peers that your proposal is fair and reasonable. That not only means providing convincing evidence to support your solution, but also means considering the arguments of critics of your approach.

In addition to these concerns, when you workshop the first draft of your proposal, you should focus on what peers make of the purpose and meaning of your essay, using their responses to guide your revision. The following grid can help you frame these questions for your workshop group.

Reflecting on the Draft. Following your workshop, make an entry in your journal that follows these prompts:

- If I were going to write this over again, the one thing I think I'd do would be . . .
- The most important thing I learned about writing a proposal so far is . . .
- The most difficult part of the process for me was . . .
- The biggest question I have about the draft is . . .

Revising

5.5

Apply revision strategies that are effective for a proposal.

Revision is a continual process—not a last step. You've been revising—"reseeing" your subject—from the first messy fastwriting in your journal. But the things that get your attention vary depending on where you are in the writing process. With your draft in hand, revision becomes your focus through what I'll call "shaping and tightening your draft."

Chapter 10 contains strategies that can help you revise any inquiry project. There are also certain things to think about that are especially useful for shaping a proposal.

Shaping. Shaping involves, among other things, arranging and rearranging information so that it is organized around the main idea.

Analyzing the Information. One way to think about the structure of your review is to see the information you've collected in categories. In a proposal, remember that these typically include the following:

Problem
What is it? Why is it important? What is at stake? Who's involved?

Causes and Effects
What causes it? What's the impact? What will happen? Why does it happen?

Solutions and Justifications
What should be done? Why is this the best solution?

Evidence
What are the facts? What do experts say? What are your experiences and observations?

Other Perspectives
What is the controversy? What do others propose? Who has a different perspective?

This isn't a recipe for organizing your draft, but a way to look at whether you've included enough information in each category. One way to play around with the structure of your proposal is to use the "Frankenstein Draft" (Revision Strategy 10.18 in Chapter 10). Cut up your draft with scissors into pieces that fall into the categories mentioned here—problem, solution, evidence, and so on—and then play with the order. Worry about transitions later.

Other Questions for Revision. Proposals also have some fairly typical problems at this stage in the process, most of which can be addressed by repeating some of the steps in this chapter or selecting appropriate revision strategies in Chapter 10. Here are some questions to consider as you decide which of these strategies might be most helpful.

- ✓ Have you done enough to dramatize the problem if you're writing for an audience that may not be aware of it? Should you do more to establish how your readers have a stake in solving the problem?

- ✓ How well have you justified your solutions? Is there enough evidence? Is it appropriate evidence for your audience?

- ✓ Have you overemphasized one solution at the expense of others? Would your proposal be more balanced and persuasive if you considered alternatives, even if you ultimately reject them?

Polishing. Shaping focuses on things such as purpose, meaning, and design. No less important is looking more closely at paragraphs, sentences, and words. Are your paragraphs coherent? How do you manage transitions? Are your sentences fluent and concise? Are there any errors in spelling or syntax? The section of Chapter 10 called "Problems with Clarity and Style," starting on page 398, can help you focus on these issues.

Before you finish your draft, work through the following checklist:

- ✓ Every paragraph is about one thing.
- ✓ The transitions between paragraphs aren't abrupt.
- ✓ The length of sentences varies in each paragraph.
- ✓ Each sentence is concise. There are no unnecessary words or phrases.
- ✓ You've checked grammar, particularly verb agreement, run-on sentences, unclear pronouns, and misused words (*there/their, where/were,* and so on).
- ✓ You've run your spellchecker and proofed your paper for misspelled words.

Chapter 10 has strategies to help you solve all kinds of revision problems, large and small.

▶ Student Essay

Jenna watches reality TV and feels guilty about it. But that's not the problem that interests her. She can see the appeal of programs such as *American Idol,* and she'd like to continue to watch them from time to time, but she would really like to watch reality shows that follow an ethical code of conduct. Jenna proposes that reality TV producers agree to a code that would minimize the emotional and physical injuries inflicted on participants, which she thinks is a problem on many of the shows.

Avoidable Accidents: How to Make Reality TV Safer

Jenna Appleman

1   When I moved into my own apartment without TV or cable, I assumed I'd be watching much less television. My TV consumption had never been a problem—I'd watch *Law & Order* and HBO when I was home, but didn't follow very much else. I prided myself on watching intelligent television, avoiding the low-culture reality series with a sneer. But in the silence of a studio apartment in the busiest semester of my college career, I needed a way to fill the space and blow off some steam. That's when I started watching reality TV.

2   There are TV channels dedicated exclusively to reality programming. Bravo houses the various *Real Housewives* series (my gateway), as well as their many spinoffs; E! plays the various Kardashian series; there are kid-centered shows like *Toddlers and Tiaras* on TLC and *Dance Moms* on Lifetime; and reality competition shows like *The Biggest Loser* and *The Bachelor* rake in thousands of viewers on prime time. Reality TV dominates American programming.

3   How dominant is it? According to the Nielson ratings for the week I'm writing this, seven of the top ten shows on cable were reality programs. *Jersey Shore* and *Pawn Stars* were one and two ("Top Tens"). On TV, *American Idol* is a perennial viewer favorite, often the most-watched program.

4   Yet my instinctive guilt about watching these shows is indicative of a pressing problem. "People are attracted to reality television because they know it has real consequences," said reality blurred editor Andy Dehnart. "You get the sense this is a real human being who could be hurt or injured" (Dehnart). And in August 2011, Russell Armstrong, the husband of Beverly Hills *Real Housewives'* Taylor Armstrong, committed suicide. While Amstrong's suicide is an extreme example, injuries on reality TV programs are rampant. A brawl on *Survivor* in 2010 resulted in a dislocated shoulder and broken toe. In 2011, an athlete on the reality show *Jump City* fell doing a stunt and shattered his wrist. Injuries on shows like *So You Think You Can Dance* are common.

5   Not only are contestants injured but viewers "inspired" by the programs are also at risk. Recently, for example, the American Medical Association warned that viewers of the TV show *Extreme Makeover*, now off the air, might have had a distorted understanding of the risk of plastic surgery: "Heavily edited and selected scenes from reality TV have lulled the public into thinking there are no real risks or complications in these procedures. It's

easy for viewers to forget that these are real people, who face the real risks—not just the benefits—of surgery" (216). All of this is a brash reminder that reality television is just that—*real*.

"These shows are Roman coliseums that we visit virtually," writes Matt Seitz of Salon. "Participants in contact sports have corner men and doctors on hand to nurse their wounds, and determine if they are fit enough to step in the ring in the first place." So, too, then, should the participants of reality television shows.   6

To lower the risks to participants and viewers of watching reality TV, I propose the following: 7

1. Possible candidates for a reality television show should be pre-screened, to ensure that they are fit emotionally and physically to withstand the rigors of a reality set.

2. Candidates with substance abuse, physical abuse, self-destructive behaviors, among others, would not be permitted to participate on the show *unless* they are provided with the following:

   a. Active counseling throughout the filming process

   b. Guaranteed after-care once filming ceases

   For example, *Hoarders* on A&E provides healthcare services during and after filming to the subjects it follows.

3. *All* participants should be provided with free after-care and counseling once filming wraps, for at least three months.

4. All participants should have immediate and total access to medical care, with the show absorbing all medical costs incurred during filming.

5. No footage of participants under the influence of alcohol should be used *if* the alcohol had been provided by producers.

6. Only non-incidental footage of minors should be used.

7. If a show focuses on minors (such as *Toddlers and Tiaras* and *Dance Moms*), counselors with training in adolescent and child psychology should be present during *all filming* and available to children before and after the conclusion of filming.

8. All participant contracts should be public.

An ethical code like this would admittedly be hard to implement and impossible to require. Further, as NPR's Linda Holmes writes, "there is . . . no solution for people who want to watch *The Real Housewives Of Beverly Hills* without guilt . . . you have to live with the fact that it exploits emotionally charged situations" (Holmes). Nonetheless, having an adoptable ethical code for reality television producers, and public knowledge of which shows abide by the code, would at least put a modicum of power back in the hands of the viewer. We would be given the ability to make informed choices about which programs we choose to watch— "to shop for ethical television the same way [we] might shop for ethically produced goods of any other kind, and to provide the financial incentives [for producers]," as Holmes says.   8

(continued)

(continued)

9   I will probably never stop feeling guilty for watching reality television, particularly the more exploitative shows. However, if I were given the option to watch reality programs that I could feel comfortable indulging in, knowing that there were an ethical code in place, I would like to think I'd choose those shows. Such a code wouldn't cure the problem, but at least it would empower viewers and encourage them to support less destructive programming.

Works Cited

D'Amico, Richard. "Plastic Surgery Is Real, Not Reality TV." *Virtual Mentor: American Medical Association Journal of Ethics* 9.3 (March 2007): 2150-218. Print.

Dehnart, Ann. "Real Housewives Cast Member Russell Killed Himself." *Realityblurred*. 16 Aug. 2011. Web. 20 Feb. 2012.

Holmes, Linda. "'Ethical Reality': A Proposed Code for Producers to Live By." *NPR*. 31 August 2011. Web. 11 Nov. 2011.

Seitz, Matt Zoller. "Reality TV: A Blood Sport That Must Change." *Salon*. 18 August 2011. Web. 20 Jan. 2012.

"Top Tens and Trends." *The Nielson Co.* 20 Feb. 2012. Web. 20 Feb. 2012.

Evaluating the Essay

1. A key part of a persuasive proposal is establishing the seriousness of the problem. Are you convinced that reality stars are at risk on these programs? If not, what would you suggest about strengthening that part of the essay?

2. Suppose Jenna were considering incorporating visuals—images, video, graphics, and tables—into the essay. What would you suggest?

3. What's your evaluation of the solution that she proposes? Is it convincing? Why or why not?

Using What You Have Learned

Let's revisit the list from the beginning of this chapter of things I hoped you'd learn about this form of writing.

1. **Describe a problem of consequence, framing it narrowly enough to explore convincing solutions.** It's hard to overstate the importance of this skill, not just for proposal writing, but also for most writing tasks. A fundamental problem with early drafts in any genre is that they're not focused enough; the writer takes a landscape shot when she needs to take a close-up. This is especially true with research-based writing such as proposals, when you're dealing with a lot of information. See if you can apply some of the things you learned here to, for example, a research essay.

2. **Identify the wide range of rhetorical situations that might call for a proposal argument.** There are all kinds of proposals—marketing proposals, business plans, grant proposals, policy proposals, and so on—but they are all in the service of the same question: What should be done? As you write for other college classes, you will probably have assignments that aren't called proposals but essentially ask you to answer this question.

3. **Argue effectively for both the seriousness of the problem and the proposed solutions, using strong evidence.** If you wrote a review for the previous chapter, then you already have some practice with making arguments, because evaluation is a form of argument. In this chapter, you built on those skills. Among other things, the proposal relies more heavily on research than does the review, and in subsequent assignments you'll be drawing on what you learned here, especially your understanding of what is appropriate evidence to support a claim.

4. **Use appropriate invention strategies to discover and develop a proposal topic.** The invention techniques themselves don't vary much from assignment to assignment. You've gotten considerable practice with fastwriting, clustering, listing, and so on. But with each assignment, you've cast a wider net for information. The proposal, for example, asked you to generate considerably more information from outside sources than, say, the profile or personal essay. Invention isn't just trying to get what's already in your head out on paper or screen. Invention is also techniques for *finding* information and thinking about what you make of it. This will become increasingly important with later assignments.

5. **Apply revision strategies that are effective for a proposal.** As we move towards more-argumentative forms of writing, revision is increasingly focused on considering how a skeptical audience might respond to what you say. In this chapter, you've spent time considering not only how to convince someone that a problem you care about is something he or she should care about, too, but also crafting proposals that are persuasive. Reviews, proposals, public arguments, and research essays are among the most reader-based forms, and it becomes even more important in revising these to imagine readers who may not think much like you.

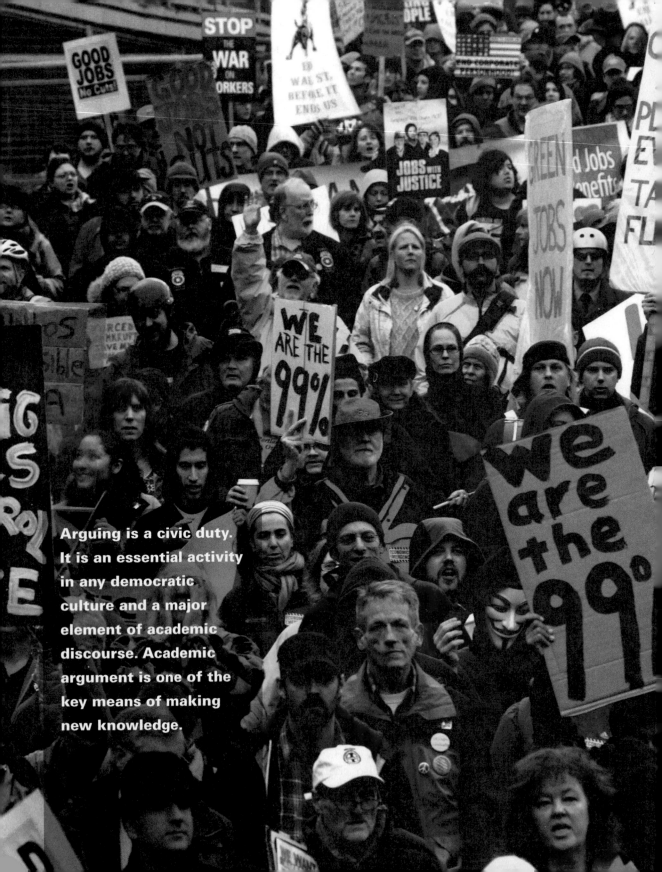

Arguing is a civic duty. It is an essential activity in any democratic culture and a major element of academic discourse. Academic argument is one of the key means of making new knowledge.

Writing an Argument **6**

Learning Objectives

In this chapter, you'll learn to

6.1 Identify the key elements of argument—reasons, claims, and evidence—and apply them in both reading and writing.

6.2 Understand how ethos, pathos, and logos combine in persuasion.

6.3 Use invention strategies appropriate to argument to discover and develop a topic.

6.4 Develop a question that is focused enough to lead to a strong claim and convincing evidence.

6.5 Use audience analysis and logical methods to help guide revision of an argument.

Writing to Persuade People

Where I live, public arguments about wolf reintroduction, saving salmon, property tax rates, and the need for a local community college are waged on the editorial pages of the local newspaper, *The Idaho Statesman*. The paper's editorials and op-ed articles (short persuasive essays that are literally on the opposite page from editorials) present usually well-reasoned arguments of 250 to 600 words, but the real slugfest takes place in the letters to the editor. Reading letters to the editor is a form of recreation here. One correspondent complained a few years ago that the song "Rain, Rain, Go Away" was objectionable because it made her children dislike precipitation. Another letter writer, an animal rights activist, is a regular who always generates heated rebuttals here in cattle country. Last week, she railed about the evils of "Rocky Mountain oysters" (fried cattle testicles), which were served up at the Eagle Fire Department fundraiser. I can't wait to see the responses to that one.

We resort to argument when we have strong feelings about something. We write a letter to the editor, or blog, or compose a paper in a college course, supporting our opinions with research. But in a way, all writing has elements of argument. As the writer Joan Didion once said, writing is, in a sense, a "hostile act." We want people to see the world the way we see it.

In arguments, however, this is more explicit, and sometimes the motive isn't just to convince an audience to see the world the way we see it, but also to convince them to actually *do something about it.* Support a certain candidate, join an organization, contact a legislator, give money.

We've already covered a couple of kinds of arguments, arising from different inquiry questions:

- **Review:** What is the value?
- **Proposal:** What should be done?

In this chapter, we'll work with another kind of argument essay, which answers this question: *What do I believe is true and why do I believe it?* An essay that addresses this inquiry question might be called a lot of things—a position paper, an opinion piece, or a claim–proof essay. Whatever it's called, an argument that states what a writer believes and why might be distinguished by its strong emphasis on factual *claims* and its attention to logic.

Here's the thing, though: While most of us think that argument involves starting with some strong opinion we have and then cherry-picking the evidence to build support for it, academic inquiry initially emphasizes exploration of the question *What is true?* Maybe you have strong feelings about privacy on the Internet. You think, for example, that while Google Street View is pretty cool, it violates privacy because someone might be accidentally photographed while walking down a street in their neighborhood. However, before you make that claim in an argument, it's important to spend considerable time listening in to the debate. What do experts say? What are counterclaims? Are there other, more troubling issues you hadn't considered?

> Persuasive essays such as the op-ed are a great way to participate in public debates that affect your campus and community, and even your nation.

My point is this: *Inquiry always precedes argument.*

But what do we mean by argument?

What Is Argument?

Argument is not war.

When I was growing up, argument meant only one thing: indigestion. My father loved to argue at the dinner table, hotly pursuing any stray comment that would give him the chance to demonstrate his superior knowledge and logic. What I remember about these "arguments" was the hot-faced humiliation and anger I felt back then, and later, the feeling that I would prefer to avoid an argument at any cost. When I mention argumentative writing to my students, I think I recognize in the slumped shoulders and distant looks of some of them that they might have similar feelings.

Some of us think argument is impolite. It means uncomfortable conflict. It is the verbal equivalent of war.

And yet, we engage in argument every day, when we attempt to persuade an instructor to extend the deadline on a paper, try to convince our spouse to help more around the apartment, or seek a loan from a bank.

Arguments *can* involve conflict, but they are rarely combat—despite the war metaphors such as "finding ammunition" or "attacking a position." Far more often, the motives for arguing are more benign. We want others to consider seeing the world the way we see it. Or we want to encourage them to *do* something we believe is in their interests as well as ours. These motives were behind the attempts at persuasion in the review and proposal assignments you may have completed earlier in *The Curious Writer.*

In a sense, all writing is persuasive. *See the world my way,* we ask of readers, *at least for a moment.*

Two Sides to Every Argument?

TV talk shows stage "discussions" between proponents of diametrically opposed positions. Academic debating teams pit those for and those against. We are nurtured on language such as *win* or *lose, right* and *wrong,* and *either…or.* It's tempting to see the world this way, as neatly divided into truth and falsehood, light and dark. Reducing issues to two sides simplifies the choices. But one of the things that literature—and all art—teaches us is the delightful and nagging complexity of things. Huck Finn is a racist, and in *Huckleberry Finn* there's plenty of evidence in his treatment of Jim that confirms this. Yet there are moments in the novel when we see a transcendent humanity in Huck, and we can see that he may be a racist, *but…* It is this qualification—this modest word *but*—that trips us up in our apparent certainty. Rather than *either…or,* can it be *both…and*? Instead of two sides to every issue, might there be thirteen?

Here's an example:

One side: General education requirements are a waste of time because they are often irrelevant to the students' major goal in getting a college education—getting a good job.

The other side: General education requirements are invaluable because they prepare students to be enlightened citizens, more fully prepared to participate in democratic culture.

It's easy to imagine a debate between people who hold these positions, and it wouldn't be uninteresting. But it *would* be misleading to think that these are the only two possible positions on general education requirements in American universities.

One of the reasons why people are drawn to arguing is that it can be a method of discovery, and one of the most useful discoveries is some side to the story that doesn't fall neatly into the usual opposed positions. The route to these discoveries is twofold: *initially withholding judgment* and *asking questions.*

For instance,

What might be goals of a university education other than helping students get a good job and making them enlightened citizens?

Is it possible that a university can do both?

Are general education courses the only route to enlightenment?

Are there certain situations in which the vocational motives of students are inappropriate?

Are there certain contexts—say, certain students at particular schools at a particular point in their education—when general education requirements might be waived or modified?

As often happens with two-sided arguments, all of these questions, and others, tend to unravel the two sides of the argument and expose them for what they are: *starting points* for an inquiry, in this case, into the question *What good are general education requirements?*

The Machinery of Argument: Claims, Reasons, and Evidence

Claims: What You Want People to Believe

6.1

Identify the key elements of argument—reasons, claims, and evidence—and apply them in both reading and writing.

"I have a headache" is simply a statement, and not a claim, because no one is likely to disagree with it. "Headaches can be caused by secondhand smoke" is a statement that is also a claim because reasonable people might agree or disagree with it.

Claims are at the heart of argument, and if you think about it, you already know this. Every time you make a judgment, interpretation, or evaluation, you make a claim. We do this daily: "Macs are better than PCs." "The food in this place sucks." "This town needs more buses." Because reviews and proposals, the forms in Chapters 4 and 5, are arguments, they involved claims. If you write a review, you make and support a *value claim*; if you write a proposal, you make and support a *policy claim*. In this chapter, we'll work with what's often called a *factual claim*.[1] Take this claim, for instance:

> The rise of "Super PACs" in presidential politics is corrupting the electoral process.

You probably can't definitively *prove* that claim is true, but you might find some good factual evidence to support it. Maybe you dig up some research on "attack ads" that are funded by these political action committees, demonstrating that they are often criticized for their inaccuracy. And perhaps you find some expert evidence that supports the claim: You interview a professor at your school, and she notes that most Super PACs are largely funded by huge contributions from a few wealthy individuals. Factual claims can be assertions about something in the present (e.g., "The electric car is unfairly subsidized," "Teaching to the test in high school English undermines the transition to college writing"). Supported by evidence, they can also make a prediction about what will happen; the Super PACs claim above, for example, concerns the future as well as the present. And finally, factual claims

---

[1]Philosophers distinguish between factual claims and conceptual claims. The former is something that can be proved with evidence; the latter a claim that is arrived at through careful reasoning but may never be proven.

can be about the past (e.g., "President Lincoln's abuse of the habeas corpus (laws protecting people from illegal imprisonment) was necessary to save the Union").

Reasons: The "Because..." Behind the Claim

I asked my first-year students what they thought of general education, or "core," classes at our university. It provoked a lively debate. Here's what one of them said:

> "I am all for the rant about higher education costing a fortune. The core classes are a joke, to be quite honest. Who hasn't had math, science, and history in high school?"

This student makes the claim that "core classes are a joke." She gives a reason: Students have already studied math, science, and history in high school. This is the "because" behind her claim. But notice that behind this reason there's an unstated assumption: Math, science, and history classes in high school are equivalent to university core classes in these subjects. Is this true? It may be. But it's certainly debatable, and because this assumption is never addressed, the claim that core classes are a joke is built on a pretty weak foundation.

Reasons—either stated or implied—hold up your claim. Your claim is what you believe is true, and your reasons are why you believe it is true. A claim and a reason can be linked with the word "because." So, stating its assumption explicitly as part of the reason, we could restate the claim and reason above as "Core classes are a joke *because* their content is similar to what most students learn in high school."

Evidence: Proof of the Point

When you're making a factual claim, you need evidence. The motive for making a claim is to persuade an audience to agree with it, and this depends on the quality of the evidence you offer. But what kind of evidence will be most persuasive?

The kind of evidence you need depends partly on the rhetorical situation, of course, but if you're making an argument to a general audience, then evidence for a factual claim might come from the following sources:

- Expert testimony (statements by authorities on the topic)
- Reliable data (facts from credible sources)
- Observation and personal experience (what you see and what has happened to you)
- Stories, case studies, anecdotes (the narratives of others that help you dramatize an issue or support a point)

Keep in mind that the kind of evidence that is persuasive will depend on the disposition of your audience—readers who are skeptical about your claim are harder to convince—and also on the discourse community you're writing in. Obviously, appropriate evidence for a biology article will be different from appropriate evidence for a philosophy article. For the purposes of this assignment, you're probably writing for peers (or a general audience) and, generally speaking, as you move from an expert audience to one that is less so, the rules of evidence get looser.

As important as using evidence persuasively is using it ethically. For example, you need to address—not omit—evidence that does not support your claim. Similarly, you need to avoid putting the evidence into a context that would distort its meaning (see "Seeing the Form: The 'Imagetext' as Argument"). Arguing ethically will contribute to your ethos, one of the elements of persuasion discussed next.

Seeing the Form

The "Imagetext" as Argument

While model Kate Moss is likely disturbed by the appropriation of her image by advocates in the pro-anorexia ("pro-ana") movement, Moss's picture—along with those of other celebrities such as Calista Flockhart, Mary-Kate Olsen, and Keira Knightley—appear as "thinspiration" on websites that argue that eating disorders are a "lifestyle choice," not a disease. Some of these images (though not this one) are digitally altered to make the models seem even thinner than they really are. In an article on the "imagetexts" used by these controversial websites, Robin Jensen notes that in their new context, pictures like this one of Kate Moss are in effect given a "frame" quite different from the one originally intended. In this way, the meaning of the picture is manipulated to make an argument that serves the purpose of the pro-ana movement. In a sense, this is like quoting someone out of context, and raises a similar ethical question: Is it fair?

Kate Moss in ultra-thin pose.

Credibility, Emotion, and Logic

Persuasion, as Aristotle reminded us a few thousand years ago, depends not just on good reasoning (*logos*), but also on moving an audience (*pathos*) and making it believe the speaker is someone worth listening to on the subject (*ethos*). Figure 6.1 shows Aristotle's rhetorical triangle, a visual presentation of this idea. The triangle nicely illustrates that persuasion always incorporates all three appeals and that all three are always in relation to each other.

6.2
Understand how ethos, pathos, and logos combine in persuasion.

What may be a little misleading about the graphic is that it seems to suggest that the recipe for good argument is equal measures of ethos, pathos, and logos. Not at all. These are blended in varying amounts depending on the situation. One factor, for example, is the disposition of an audience toward your claim.

Figure 6.2 broadly indicates the balance between Aristotle's three categories of appeals in the three most common rhetorical situations: when an audience is resistant to what you're trying to say, neutral about it, or receptive. Consider each of these audiences:

- Direct-mail marketers trying to raise money for nonprofit groups and political causes cultivate lists of people who might be receptive to their messages. Direct-mail letters, therefore, are strong on emotional appeals (pathos): The humane society will include photographs of a sad-looking abandoned puppy, a conservative political action group will raise fears about threats to "family values," and so on. There's no need to spend a great deal reasoning (logos) with an audience that already agrees with your message. And because they agree with your message, they're already favorably disposed to the messenger (ethos). Move them with emotion!

- In contrast, resistant audiences will need to be convinced that you know what you're talking about (ethos), so your challenge here is to establish some common ground with the audience. But that's not enough. While a speaker or writer might earn a resistant audience's approval, gaining its assent to a claim depends on the quality of the reasoning (logos). Emotional appeals will be unlikely to move this audience, at least initially.

- Neutral audiences may be difficult to gauge. Sometimes an emotional appeal will spark its members' interest. Sometimes a well-reasoned argument will move them, and sometimes a neutral audience will be persuaded by the credibility of the speaker. Frequently, a careful combination of all three of Aristotle's appeals transforms a neutral audience into one that is receptive to what you have to say.

Figure 6.1   Aristotle's rhetorical triangle

Disposition of Audience	*Ethos*	*Pathos*	*Logos*
Resistant	Most important	Less important	Most important
Neutral	Important	Important	Important
Receptive	Less important	Most important	Less important

Figure 6.2   Audience and the balance of ethos, logos, and pathos

Analyzing Argument

How might you analyze this letter writer's argument?

Dear Editor,

As part of my required humanities class, I was forced to see the art exhibit "Home of the Brave" at the university gallery. As a combat veteran, what I saw there deeply offended me. I saw so-called "art" that showed great American military leaders such as General Petraeus with skulls superimposed on their faces, and a photo of a man with an American flag wrapped around his head and lashed with a plastic tie at his neck. It's popular to say these days that we should support the troops. Apparently, a group of artists who haven't defended our freedom feel free to use that freedom to be unpatriotic. I wonder if they would feel differently if they had to pay the real cost for freedom of speech.

Most arguments like this don't provoke an analytical response at first. We react emotionally: "This guy is so full of it!" or perhaps, "It's about time someone spoke up about the cost of freedom!" This letter, like many that raise controversial issues, triggers a whole set of deeply held beliefs about things such as patriotism, freedom of speech, and the purpose of art. These are things that *should* provoke discussion—and that inevitably trigger feelings. But without involving the head as well as the heart, it's impossible to have a civil discussion—one that will lead to new understanding. We need to understand not only what we ourselves believe, but also what the other guy believes. To see how this might work, try Exercise 6.1, based on some ideas about argument from American psychologist Carl Rogers.

Exercise 6.1

Argument as Therapy

Carl Rogers was a therapist and one of the most famous experts on argument theory. Not surprisingly, he thought that when people feel really, really strongly about something, reason just doesn't work well. Instead, he believed, a prerequisite to entering into an argument with someone else about a value-laden topic is to first listen and "say back" what you understand him or her to be saying. Let's do that here.

STEP ONE: Summarize what you understand to be the letter writer's basic argument. What claim is he making, and what seem to be the (implied) reasons behind it? You might use this as a template for your summary:

Because of _____ and _____, the letter writer argues that _____.

STEP TWO: Now fastwrite for a few minutes in your notebook, exploring your own take on the validity of the claim and the reasons.

STEP THREE: Finally, write a brief analysis of the argument that includes the following:

1. Begin with your understanding of the letter writer's argument and something about the circumstances that might lead someone to make such claims.

2. Analyze the soundness of the reasons behind the argument. Do you agree or disagree with them? Is there a different way of thinking about them?

3. State your own position (e.g., What would you say about the relationship between art and politics?), including the reasons behind it.

One Student's Response

Rebecca's Journal

EXERCISE 6.1

The letter writer, a combat veteran, found himself "deeply offended" by a collection of artwork in his university's gallery called "Home of the Brave." The writer is incensed that the artists are using their freedom of speech—a freedom which the letter writer feels he has defended in war—to present "unpatriotic" images. Had these artists experienced combat firsthand, the writer claims, they might be less inclined to create these images.

In fact, it is partly the letter writer's experience of combat himself that has led to this intense reaction. The process of going to war is traumatic and singular—one a person can't understand unless they've experienced it first-hand. However, the artwork in the exhibition is not claiming to understand war from the perspective of a soldier, but rather to explore the issues from the artists' unique viewpoint in a creative way. The letter writer's argument that the artists might feel differently if they had been in combat is accurate—surely they would. However, such an argument doesn't invalidate the right of American citizens to express themselves and their diverse opinions through words and images.

I think this discussion is an important one, although I wish the letter writer had used it to spark debate. The vast disparity of experience in artist and audience is

---

One Student's Response (*continued*)

what makes art so valuable, encouraging reactions, discussions, and perhaps new understanding. I disagree with the letter writer that the artwork is unpatriotic—in fact, I think the artistic expression of a unique viewpoint is one of the greatest uses of freedom of speech. I also think that the artists could have something valuable to learn from the letter writer as a combat veteran, and I think such a meeting of opposing minds is one of the greatest reactions to art there is.

You can analyze an argument all kinds of ways, including by looking for logical fallacies (see "Inquiring into the Details: Common Logical Fallacies") or by using a method called Toulmin logic (see "Inquiring into the Details: Toulmin: A Method for Analyzing an Argument" on p. 210). But the Rogerian approach provides a wonderful introduction to argument analysis because it forces you to do something we don't typically do, particularly in the current climate of political division in the United States: *Understand and even empathize with the other guy.* That doesn't mean that you will agree. But it does make it more likely that you won't speak past each other. Later, you'll also see how essential it is to not only demonstrate understanding of others' arguments, but also to include some of them to make your own case more effectively.

Inquiring into the Details

Common Logical Fallacies

An important way to evaluate the soundness of an argument is to examine its logic and, in particular, look for so-called logical fallacies that may lead writers' reasoning astray. Aristotle was one of the first to point out many of these, and a quick search on the web using the term "logical fallacies" will reveal dozens and dozens of them that plague public argument. Many have indecipherable Latin names, testifying to their ancient origins.

Here are ten of the most common logical fallacies. I think they cover about 90 percent of the ways in which writers stumble when making an argument.

1. ***Hasty generalization:*** We're naturally judgmental creatures. For example, we frequently make a judgment about someone after just meeting him or her. Or we conclude that a class is useless after attending a single session. These are generalizations based on insufficient evidence. Hasty generalizations *might* be true—the class might turn out to be useless—but you should always be wary of them.

Inquiring into the Details (*continued*)

2. *Ad hominem:*   When arguments turn into shouting matches, they almost inevitably get personal. Shifting away from the substance of an argument to attack the person making it, either subtly or explicitly, is another common logical fallacy. It's also, at times, hard to resist.

3. *Appeal to authority:*   We all know that finding support for a claim from an expert is a smart move in many arguments. But sometimes it's a faulty move because the authority we cite isn't really an expert on the subject. A more common fallacy, however, is when we cite an expert to support a claim without acknowledging that many experts disagree on the point.

4. *Straw man:*   One of the sneakiest ways to sidetrack reason in an argument is to misrepresent or ignore the actual position of an opponent. Unfortunately, the "straw man" fallacy thrives in many political debates: "I can't support this proposal for universal health care," says politician A. "It's clear that politician A doesn't really take the problem of American health care seriously," says politician B. Huh?

5. *False analogy:*   Analogies can be powerful comparisons in argument. But they can also lead us astray when the analogy simply doesn't hold. Are A and B *really* similar situations? For example, when a critic of higher education argues that a public university is like a business and should be run like one, are the two really analogous? Fundamentally, one is nonprofit and the other is designed to make money. Is this really a useful comparison?

6. *Post hoc or false cause:*   Just because one thing follows another doesn't necessarily mean one *causes* the other. It might be coincidence, or the cause might be something else entirely. For example, if you're really keen on arguing that losing the football coach was the cause of the team's losing record, you might link the two. And it's possible that you're right, but it's also just as possible that the injury to the quarterback was one of the real reasons.

7. *Appeal to popularity:*   In a country obsessed by polls and rankings, it's not hard to understand the appeal of reasoning that argues that because it's popular, it must be good or true. Advertisers are particularly fond of this fallacy, arguing that because their brand is most popular, it must be the best. In fact, this might not be the case at all. The majority can be wrong.

8. *Slippery slope:*   I love the name of this one because it so aptly describes what can happen when reasoning loses its footing. You might start out reasonably enough, arguing, for example, that a gun control law restricts the rights of some citizens to have access to certain weapons, but pretty soon you start sliding toward conclusions that simply don't follow, such as that a gun control law is the beginning of the end of gun ownership in the country. Now you might really believe this, but logic isn't the route to get there.

9. *Either/or fallacy:*   In a black-and-white world, something is right or wrong, true or false, good or bad. But ours is a colorful world with many shades. For instance, while it might be emotionally satisfying to say that opponents of the war in Afghanistan must not support the troops there, it is also possible that the

Inquiring into the Details (*continued*)

war's opponents are against the war *because* they're concerned about the lives of American service people. Rather than *either/or*, it might be *both/and*. We see this fallacy often in arguments that suggest that there are only two choices and each is opposite to the other.

10. ***Begging the question:*** This one is also called *circular reasoning*, because it assumes the truth of the arguer's conclusion without bothering to prove it. An obvious example of this would be to say that a law protecting people from Internet spam is good because it's a law, and laws should be obeyed. But why is it a good law?

Motives for Writing an Argument

Argument, obviously, is a part of everyday life. I'm constantly trying to persuade my wife, Karen, that it would be a good thing if I added another guitar to my acoustic collection. I was thinking a new Martin with mahogany back and sides and onboard Fishman electronics would be good.

"You've already got seven guitars," she says. "How many more do you need?"

We argue to get something we want—although these are often our less interesting arguments. More generally, developing arguments is the stuff of everyday life.

Classical rhetoricians such as Plato, Aristotle, and Cicero had a great deal to say about how to argue well. Their focus was largely on public speaking, although their ideas are foundational for a modern understanding of argument. For Aristotle, there were three arenas for persuasion—before the courts, before legislators and others who make public policy, and at social occasions.

Of course, there are plenty of other reasons to argue. As we have seen, common forms such as reviews and proposals are types of arguments. In academic and indeed much other writing, the writer sets out to assert and support a factual claim—whether about the past and what it tells us about the present, the current state of things, or what might happen.

Argument is also a civic duty, an essential activity in any democratic culture (for some examples of forums for argument today, see "Writing Beyond the Classroom: Public Argument in a Digital Age"). To participate fully in civic life, you need to know not only how to make a sound argument, but also how to analyze the arguments of others so you can decide what you believe. Classical rhetoric saw public engagement as a duty of people who speak well.

Finally, the most important motive behind writing and studying argument is that you care about something. Throughout this book, I've argued that the personal motive for writing is the most powerful one of all; in this case, you're passionate about a question or an issue, and building an argument channels that passion into prose that can make a difference.

Public Argument in a Digital Age

An argument with Northwest Airlines over whether they owe you a lunch voucher after your flight was cancelled is typical of everyday uses of persuasion. But, more important, arguing well—and ethically— is a civic duty in a democratic society. A few thousand years ago, the Greeks and Romans created schools of rhetoric where people could learn the art of speaking persuasively in public settings.

These days, probably more than ever, argument is a vibrant part of civic life in the United States, particularly on the Internet. Here are a few of the many genres of public argument available to you for moving people to think or do something you consider important:

- *Op-ed essays:* These essays, ubiquitous in newspapers, remain among the most common brief argumentative essays for a general audience.

- *Letters to the editor:* Like op-ed essays, these appear in print or online publications; they're often a response to a previous contribution.

- *Blogs:* One of the newest forms of public argument is the blog. Hosted by such online sites as Google's "Blogger," the so-called blogosphere has grown so explosively that no one really knows how big it is anymore.

- *Photo essay:* Over one hundred years ago, Jacob Riis used photographs of immigrants' squalid conditions in New York City tenements to incite a public outcry—and policy change—on how we treat the poor.

- *YouTube:* It's not just a forum for published videos on weird cat tricks.

- *PowerPoint:* Former vice president Al Gore's slide presentation "An Inconvenient Truth" made the point that there really can be power in PowerPoint.

The Argument and Academic Writing

While proposals, reviews, and critical essays (discussed in the next chapter) are types of arguments you might write in college, you are most likely to write the type of argument we discuss here: arguments that address claims of fact. Whenever you're asked to write a position paper, an opinion piece, a cause-effect essay, and in some cases a reading response, you're asked to explore the topic, discover a claim that expresses what you think, and then assemble evidence that makes it convincing. In other words, you need to answer the question *What do you believe is true and why?*

Argument is one of the key means of making new knowledge.

Academics value argument not because they're argumentative (though some are), but because it's the way that they "make knowledge," which is the central business of the university. Scholarly communities make discoveries through contesting what was once assumed to be true. Reasoned argument supported by research is the engine behind academic inquiry.

Fundamental to academic argument is an idea that isn't always obvious to newcomers at college: "Facts" can be contested. While it often seems that the facts we take for granted are immutable truths—as enduring as the granite peaks I can see through my office window—things often aren't that way at all. Our knowledge of things—how the planet was formed, the best ways to save endangered species, the meaning of a classic novel, how to avoid athletic injuries—is entirely made up of ideas that are *contested*. And the primary tool for shaping and even changing what we know is argument.

Features of the Form

Feature	Conventions of the Argument Essay
Inquiry question	What do I believe is true and why?
Motives	We hope to convince others to think as we do. Sometimes, however, we first need to convince ourselves, and argument is an invitation to *explore* as well as to persuade. A fundamental motive is discovery.
Subject matter	Any topic is fair game, but one thing is essential: Others must have a stake in the issue. An audience should be persuaded that whatever claim you're making might matter.
Structure	Like any form of writing, the design of arguments depends on the situation. However, outlines for arguments developed by rhetoricians share some of these features: • Background on the issue, especially what people seem to *agree* on. What's the controversy as most people understand it? • The inquiry question. • Claims and supporting reasons and evidence. • Acknowledgement of counterarguments and analysis of their significance. • Closing that refines the claim, summarizes it, or returns to the beginning to affirm how the argument addresses the issue.
Sources of information	Experts on your topic, sources of reliable data on your topic, your experiences and observations, and the stories of others can all potentially provide evidence for your argument.
Language	Who is the audience? Arguments for expert audiences are often formal. Arguments for the general public are much less formal, with relatively relaxed rules of evidence and casual language. The balance of appeals should be appropriate to the audience.

Prose+

Editorial cartoons such as this one are a popular form of argument, and one reason they're effective is a quality that comics share: By simplifying things, they amplify them. Cartoonist Scott McCloud notes that when we render something more abstractly—in this case, taking a coal mine and superimposing a graveyard and smoke—the details that were eliminated make the details that remain more obvious. Cartoons that make an argument, however, also have features typical of any argument: a claim (often implied) and reasons. The cartoon strip here, for example, combines drawings with very few words to make a pretty unambiguous claim: Wind power is preferable to nuclear, oil, and coal energy. The reason offered? The problems associated with wind power are relatively benign.

READINGS

▶ Argument 1

Bad?

Ways to Narrow the Question

❖ **Time.** Limit the time frame of your project. Instead of researching the entire Civil War, limit your search to the month or year when the most decisive battles occurred.

❖ **Place.** Anchor a larger subject to a particular location. Instead of exploring "senioritis" at American high schools, research the phenomenon at the local high school.

❖ **Person.** Use the particulars of a person to reveal generalities about the group. Instead of writing about the homeless problem, write about a homeless man.

❖ **Story.** Ground a larger story in the specifics of "smaller" one. Don't write about dream interpretation, write about a dream *you* had and use the theories to analyze it.

❖ **Relationship.** Find an interesting and relevant relationship between your topic and something else. Pose the question: **What is the relationship between ____ and ____?**

I've used PowerPoint for years. And I've misused it. I've loaded up PowerPoints with text and long lists of bullet points (see above). I've made presentations and read the text aloud directly from the slides. I've cluttered slides up with charts that are hard to read. Then I read a book called *Presentation Zen: Simple Ideas on Presentation Design and Delivery* and started to understand what I was doing wrong. What I needed, among other things, was handouts. Slides are not very good containers for information. I think my PowerPoint is better now, but you'd have to ask my students.

Edward Tufte, whose work in visual storytelling is legendary, hates PowerPoint, and the brief essay below elaborates on that sentiment. He argues that when meetings and classrooms turn to slideware to communicate information, bad things happen. You've undoubtedly used PowerPoint or other presentation software as a student, and you've certainly been an audience for plenty of slide presentations. What does your own experience tell you about the claims Tufte makes here?

PowerPoint Is Evil

Edward Tufte

1   Imagine a widely used and expensive prescription drug that promised to make us beautiful but didn't. Instead the drug had frequent, serious side effects: It induced stupidity, turned everyone into bores, wasted time, and degraded the quality and

credibility of communication. These side effects would rightly lead to a worldwide product recall.

Yet slideware—computer programs for presentations—is everywhere: in corporate America, in government bureaucracies, even in our schools. Several hundred million copies of Microsoft PowerPoint are churning out trillions of slides each year. Slideware may help speakers outline their talks, but convenience for the speaker can be punishing to both content and audience. The standard PowerPoint presentation elevates format over content, betraying an attitude of commercialism that turns everything into a sales pitch.

Of course, data-driven meetings are nothing new. Years before today's slideware, presentations at companies such as IBM and in the military used bullet lists shown by overhead projectors. But the format has become ubiquitous under PowerPoint, which was created in 1984 and later acquired by Microsoft. PowerPoint's pushy style seeks to set up a speaker's dominance over the audience. The speaker, after all, is making power points with bullets to followers. Could any metaphor be worse? Voicemail menu systems? Billboards? Television? Stalin?

Particularly disturbing is the adoption of the PowerPoint cognitive style in our schools. Rather than learning to write a report using sentences, children are being taught how to formulate client pitches and infomercials. Elementary school PowerPoint exercises (as seen in teacher guides and in student work posted on the Internet) typically consist of 10 to 20 words and a piece of clip art on each slide in a presentation of three to six slides—a total of perhaps 80 words (15 seconds of silent

(continued)

(continued)

Estimates of relative survival rates, by cancer site[19]

	% survival rates and their standard errors			
	5 year	10 year	15 year	20 year
Prostate	98.8 0.4	95.2 0.9	87.1 1.7	81.1 3.0
Thyroid	96.0 0.8	95.8 1.2	94.0 1.6	95.4 2.1
Testis	94.7 1.1	94.0 1.3	91.1 1.8	88.2 2.3
Melanomas	89.0 0.8	86.7 1.1	83.5 1.5	82.8 1.9
Breast	86.4 0.4	78.3 0.6	71.3 0.7	65.0 1.0
Hodgkin's disease	85.1 1.7	79.8 2.0	73.8 2.4	67.1 2.8
Corpus uteri, uterus	84.3 1.0	83.2 1.3	80.8 1.7	79.2 2.0
Urinary, bladder	82.1 1.0	76.2 1.4	70.3 1.9	67.9 2.4
Cervix, uteri	70.5 1.6	64.1 1.8	62.8 2.1	60.0 2.4
Larynx	68.8 2.1	56.7 2.5	45.8 2.8	37.8 3.1
Rectum	62.6 1.2	55.2 1.4	51.8 1.8	49.2 2.3
Kidney, renal pelvis	61.8 1.3	54.4 1.6	49.8 2.0	47.3 2.6
Colon	61.7 0.8	55.4 1.0	53.9 1.2	52.3 1.6
Non-Hodgkin's	57.8 1.0	46.3 1.2	38.3 1.4	34.3 1.7
Oral cavity, pharynx	56.7 1.3	44.2 1.4	37.5 1.6	33.0 1.8
Ovary	55.0 1.3	49.3 1.6	49.9 1.9	49.6 2.4
Leukemia	42.5 1.2	32.4 1.3	29.7 1.5	26.2 1.7
Brain, nervous system	32.0 1.4	29.2 1.5	27.6 1.6	26.1 1.9
Multiple myeloma	29.5 1.6	12.7 1.5	7.0 1.3	4.8 1.5
Stomach	23.8 1.3	19.4 1.4	19.0 1.7	14.9 1.9
Lung and bronchus	15.0 0.4	10.6 0.4	8.1 0.4	6.5 0.4
Esophagus	14.2 1.4	7.9 1.3	7.7 1.6	5.4 2.0
Liver, bile duct	7.5 1.1	5.8 1.2	6.3 1.5	7.6 2.0
Pancreas	4.0 0.5	3.0 1.5	2.7 0.6	2.7 0.8

A traditional table: rich, informative, clear

reading) for a week of work. Students would be better off if the schools simply closed down on those days and everyone went to the Exploratorium or wrote an illustrated essay explaining something.

In a business setting, a PowerPoint slide typically shows 40 words, which is about eight seconds' worth of silent reading material. With so little information per slide, many, many slides are needed. Audiences consequently endure a relentless sequentiality, one damn slide after another. When information is stacked in time, it is difficult to understand context and evaluate relationships. Visual reasoning usually works more effectively when relevant information is shown side by side. Often, the more intense the detail, the greater the clarity and understanding. This is especially so for statistical data, where the fundamental analytical act is to make comparisons.

Consider an important and intriguing table of survival rates for those with cancer relative to those without cancer for the same time period. Some 196 numbers and 57 words describe survival rates and their standard errors for 24 cancers.

Applying the PowerPoint templates to this nice, straightforward table yields an analytical disaster. The data explodes into six separate chaotic slides, consuming

6

7

(continued)

(continued)

2.9 times the area of the table. Everything is wrong with these smarmy, incoherent graphs: the encoded legends, the meaningless color, the logo-type branding. They are uncomparative, indifferent to content and evidence, and so data-starved as to be almost pointless. Chartjunk is a clear sign of statistical stupidity. Poking a finger into the eye of thought, these data graphics would turn into a nasty travesty if used for a serious purpose, such as helping cancer patients assess their survival chances. To sell a product that messes up data with such systematic intensity, Microsoft abandons any pretense of statistical integrity and reasoning.

8   Presentations largely stand or fall on the quality, relevance, and integrity of the content. If your numbers are boring, then you've got the wrong numbers. If your words or images are not on point, making them dance in color won't make them relevant. Audience boredom is usually a content failure, not a decoration failure.

9   At a minimum, a presentation format should do no harm. Yet the PowerPoint style routinely disrupts, dominates, and trivializes content. Thus PowerPoint presentations too often resemble a school play—very loud, very slow, and very simple.

10   The practical conclusions are clear. PowerPoint is a competent slide manager and projector. But rather than supplementing a presentation, it has become a substitute for it. Such misuse ignores the most important rule of speaking: Respect your audience.

Inquiring into the Essay

1. **Explore.** Think back to the last time you created a slide presentation using PowerPoint or a similar software program. If it's still lurking there on your hard drive—take a look at it. Fastwrite for a few minutes about how you feel about the effectiveness of the presentation. Do you agree with Tufte that too often slide presentations "trivialize content"?

2. **Explain.** Identify some of the basic machinery of argument in "PowerPoint Is Evil." Identify what you think is Tufte's main claim, a reason supporting that claim, and several examples of evidence.

3. **Evaluate.** Look at "Inquiring into the Details: Common Logical Fallacies" on page 180, and use the list as a way of evaluating Tufte's argument. Do you think the argument commits any of these logical fallacies?

4. **Reflect.** It's fair to say that there is a fairly combative tone in "PowerPoint Is Evil," starting with the title. The speaker's tone is an element of ethos, of course; it influences how we *feel* about Tufte and, ultimately, how we feel about his argument. How did you feel about him? Are there any generalizations you might draw from your response to this essay about how speakers and writers might manage ethos?

▶ Argument 2

Laredo businessman Loye Young agreed for the fall 2008 semester to teach a business management class at nearby Texas A&M International University (TAMIU). Like many instructors, he toiled over his syllabus, trying to make sure his course policies were clear, especially a section on the consequences of plagiarism in his class. Young warned that plagiarists would not only flunk the course but would also be reported to university officials. That's fairly standard punishment at most universities. What got critics' attention was Young's warning that he would publicly humiliate any student caught plagiarizing.

True to his word, when he caught six students plagiarizing a paper, Young published their names on his blog; and soon after, TAMIU officials fired him, arguing that he violated the Family Educational and Privacy Act, a policy designed to protect the confidentiality of certain student information. Young, a former attorney, strongly disagreed.

The firing ignited a national controversy and a wild debate in the blogosphere over whether Loye Young's decision to out students he suspected of academic dishonesty was effective, ethical, and fair. In response to one of his critics, Loye posted the following defense of his approach on his blog.

Is Humiliation an Ethically Appropriate Response to Plagiarism?

Loye Young

I'm a business owner in Laredo, Texas. I had never taught a college course before, and I never asked to teach. The department asked me to teach this course. I accepted because of my commitment to Laredo's future.   1

I worked hard on the syllabus, and everything in the syllabus was deliberate. Specifically, the language about dishonesty was based on moral and pedagogical principles. The department chairman, Dr. Balaji Janamanchi, reviewed the syllabus with me line-by-line, and I made a few changes in response to his comments.   2

I was surprised by how common and blatant plagiarism turned out to be. Six students in one class is an extraordinarily high number. I thought and prayed about what to do for about a week before following through on my promise. I decided I had only one moral choice. I am certain it was right.   3

My decision was guided by two factors: What is good for the students themselves? and What is good for other students?   4

(continued)

(continued)

5   What is good for the students themselves?

6   I am cognizant of the extraordinary moral difficulty involved when deciding what is in another's best interests. Nonetheless, I am convinced that public disclosure, including the concomitant humiliation, is in the interests of the student because it is the best way to teach the student about the consequences of dishonesty and discourage the student from plagiarizing again. Humiliation is inextricably part of a well-formed conscience.

7   The Vice President-elect, Senator Joseph Biden, is perhaps the most well-known plagiarizer in recent history. Biden was caught plagiarizing while at Syracuse Law School. The school gave him an F, required him to retake the course, and subsequently treated the incident as confidential.

8   Unfortunately, Biden didn't learn his lesson at law school. He continued to plagiarize for another 20 years. During the 1988 presidential campaign, Senator Biden's career of plagiarizing came to light, and he was forced to end his presidential bid.

9   It is my belief that the Syracuse incident left a subtle and subliminal message in Biden's mind: plagiarism is not a deal breaker. Consequently, he continued to plagiarize. Unfortunately for the Senator, the facts came to public light at the worst possible time: when he was running for President.

10   I believe that had the Syracuse incident been available publicly, Mr. Biden would have actually learned his lesson and would not have plagiarized later. Twenty years later, if the incident had come up at all, the Senator would have plausibly and convincingly maintained that the incident was a youthful mistake.

11   There is yet another reason for publicity in such cases: unjustly accused students are protected, for two reasons. One, a professor will be more careful before blowing the whistle. I myself knew that posting the students' names would be appropriately subject to intense public scrutiny. Therefore, I construed every ambiguity in the students' favor. Two, public disclosure ensures that subsequent determinations by the university are founded on evidence and dispensed fairly.

12   What is good for other students?

13   On the second question, four reasons convince me: deterrents, fairness, predictability, and preparedness for life.

14   Deterrents—Only if everyone knows that violations of plagiarism will be exposed and punished will the penalties for plagiarism be an effective deterrent. (As a lawyer once told me after hearing of another lawyer's disbarment, "I'm damn sure not going to do THAT again!") In fact, one of the six students had not plagiarized (to my knowledge) until the week before I announced my findings. Had I announced the plagiarism earlier, it is possible that student would not have plagiarized at all.

15   Fairness—Honest students should have, in fairness, the knowledge that their legitimate work is valued more than a plagiarizer's illegitimate work. In my course, the students were required to post their essays on a public website for all to see. Thus,

anyone in the world could have detected the plagiarism. Had another student noticed the plagiarism but saw no action, the honest student would reasonably believe that the process is unfair.

Predictability—By failing publicly to follow through on ubiquitous warnings about plagiarism, universities have convinced students that the purported indignation against deceit is itself deceitful and that the entire process is capricious. TAMIU's actions in this case have confirmed my suspicions that such a perception is entirely justified. 16

Preparedness for life—In the real world, deceitful actions have consequences, and those consequences are often public. Borrowers lose credit ratings, employees get fired, spouses divorce, businesses fail, political careers end, and professionals go to jail. Acts of moral turpitude rightly carry public and humiliating consequences in real life, and students need to be prepared. 17

In closing, I submit that education died when educators came to believe that greater self-esteem leads to greater learning. In fact, the causality is backwards: self-esteem is the result of learning, not the cause. 18

Inquiring into the Essay

1. **Explore.** If you accept that plagiarism is a problem, then what should an instructor do about it? What's a policy that you consider to be both ethical and potentially an effective deterrent? Fastwrite about this question in your journal for four minutes, exploring what you think.

2. **Explain.** Using the Rogerian approach discussed earlier (p. 180), "say back" what you understand to be Young's argument. Can you imagine how his situation leads him to feel the way he does about punishing plagiarism?

3. **Evaluate.** Young writes, "Humiliation is inextricably part of a well-formed conscience." How would you evaluate that claim? Can you imagine the *reasons* why Young believes it's true? (Try filling in the blank in this sentence: *Because _____, humiliation is inextricably part of a well-formed conscience.*) Do you agree with those reasons?

4. **Reflect.** Young published this argument as a blog post. Reflect on the blog as a genre of argument. How would you distinguish it from, say, an op-ed essay or a letter to the editor?

THE WRITING PROCESS

Inquiry Project **Writing an Argument**

Inquiry question: What do I believe is true and why?

Write an essay in which you make a factual claim about an issue or controversy that interests you. You are writing for an audience of nonexperts. Make sure your essay includes the following (see also p. 184 for typical features of arguments):

- Claims that are supported by clear reasons.
- Relevant evidence from your research, observations, and personal experience to support your claims and reasons.
- A strong sense of what is at stake for your readers. Why should they care as much as you do about the issue?
- At least some attention to counterarguments. What are other ways of looking at the issue, and why did you reject them?

Prose +

Make a visual argument. Consider the many ways you might do this:

- A photographic essay
- A PowerPoint
- An advertisement or poster
- A video
- A cartoon
- A t-shirt design

These will likely combine carefully crafted and purposefully selected text to go along with the images. There are *many* examples of visual arguments on the web.

If your argument topic affects people you can interview, develop a documentary podcast that uses interview clips as evidence. Record people who are affected by the issue and, if possible, experts who have interesting things to say about it. Documentary projects such as this one depend heavily on what people say, so consider collecting a lot of audio before you sketch out your argument. Then write your narration around the clips. Add music if you like.

What Are You Going to Write About?

Gun control, abortion rights, and other hot-button public controversies often make the list of banned topics for student essays. This is not because they aren't important public debates. Instead, the problem is much more that the writer has likely already made up his or her mind and sees the chance to ascend a soapbox.

Now, I have my own favorite soapboxes; people with strong convictions do. But as you think about subjects for your essay, consider that the soapbox may not be the best vantage point for practicing inquiry. If you've already made up your mind, will you be open to discovery? If you just want to line up ducks—assembling evidence to support an unwavering belief—will you be encouraged to think deeply or differently? Will you be inclined to filter the voices you hear rather than consider a range of points of view?

> The best argument essays make a clear claim, but they do it by bowing respectfully to the complexity of the subject, examining it from a variety of perspectives, not just two opposing poles.

The best persuasive essays often emerge from the kind of open-ended inquiry that you might have used writing the personal essay. What do you want to understand better? What issue or question makes you wonder? What controversies are you and your friends talking about? Be alert to possible subjects that you might write about *not* because you already know what you think, but because you want to find out. Or consider a subject that you might have feelings about but feel uninformed on, lacking the knowledge to know exactly what you think.

Opening Up

Play around with some ideas first by using some of the following triggers for thinking-through-writing in your journal. Suspend judgment. Don't reject anything. Explore.

6.3
Use invention strategies appropriate to argument to discover and develop a topic.

Listing Prompts. Lists can be rich sources of triggering topics. Let them grow freely, and when you're ready, use an item as the focus of another list or an episode of fastwriting. The following prompts should get you started.

1. In your journal, make a quick list of issues that have provoked disagreements between groups of people in your hometown or local community. What about on campus?

2. Think about these important areas of your life: school, family, work, hobbies, relationships. Title columns with each of these words in your journal or on your computer, and then make a fast list of whatever comes to mind when you think of *issues that threaten* each area.

3. Make a fast list of cultural trends. What's popular? What are the fads? What are people doing these days? Think about whether any of these trends raise interesting questions that might lead to an argument about their origins, meaning, or value.

One Student's Response

Rebecca's Journal

LISTS OF POSSIBLE ARGUMENT TOPICS

1. *Issues:* Gay marriage, rent control, cat calling on the street (or in restaurant jobs!), cleanliness, encouraging diversity vs. affirmative action, underage drinking, abortion rights

2. *School:* funding for the arts

3. *Family:* retirement/money issues, distance between family members, aging

4. *Work:* survival job vs. dream job, bad economy

5. *Hobbies:* too much work, NYC too expensive

6. *Relationships:* too much work, how to meet people?

7. *Cultural trends:* Twitter/Facebook/Tumblr/other social media, going to movies, drinking/clubbing, gossip

4. Jot down a list of the classes you're taking this semester. Then make a quick list of topics that prompt disagreements among people in the fields that you're studying. For example, in your political science class, did you learn that there are debates about the usefulness of the Electoral College? In your biology class, have you discussed global warming? In your women's studies class, did you read about Title IX and how it affects female athletes?

Fastwriting Prompts. Remember, fastwriting is a great way to stimulate creative thinking. Turn off your critical side and let yourself write "badly." Don't worry too much about what you're going to say before you say it. Write fast, letting language lead for a change.

1. Start with a fact that you find interesting, surprising, or disturbing. For example, here's some 2008 data on high school graduation rates in the United States from *Education Week*:

> Nationally, about 71 percent of all students graduate from high school on time with a regular diploma, but barely half of African American and Hispanic students earn diplomas with their peers. In many states the difference between white and minority graduation rates is stunning; in several cases there is a gap of as many as 40 or 50 percentage points.

Here are a few items from Harper's Index, a monthly feature in the magazine:

> Percentage of all Americans who consider themselves part of the top 1 percent of U.S. earners: 13
> Percentage of Hispanic Americans who do: 28

Percentage of 27- to 45-year-old women who have at least four sexual fantasies per week: 35
Percentage of 18- to 26-year-old women who do: 27

Fastwrite about one of these facts or one you chose, perhaps searching online. In your fastwrite, explore the following questions:

- Is this surprising?

- Does this fact seem true? If so, what would explain it? If not, what makes me skeptical?

- What is my personal experience with this? Does it remind me of any stories, people, situations?

- What can be done about it?

2. Use something from your lists in the preceding section for a focused fastwrite.

3. In a seven-minute fastwrite, explore the differences between your beliefs and the beliefs of your parents. Tell yourself the story of how your own beliefs about some question evolved, perhaps moving away from your parents' positions. Can you imagine the argument you might make to help them understand your point of view?

Visual Prompts. In your journal, cluster one or more of the following phrases:

"Things that seem unfair"

"Things that bug me the most"

"The worst thing about living here"

Let your cluster grow as many branches as possible; when one dies out, start another. Focus on ideas, people, places, facts, observations, questions, experiences, and details that pop into your mind when you focus on the words at the center of your cluster. Look for interesting argument topics when you're done. See Figure 6.3 for an example.

Research Prompts. By definition, argument essays deal with subjects in which people beyond the writer have a stake. And one of the best ways to collect ideas about such issues is to do a little quick and dirty research. Try some of the following research prompts:

1. Read the letters to the editor in your local paper a few days in a row. What issues have people riled up locally? Is there one that you find particularly interesting?

2. Do a Google search for terms or phrases on an issue that interests you, such as "global warming Greenland glaciers" or "pro-anorexia websites." Did you produce any results that make you curious or make you feel something about the issue, one way or another?

3. Your Facebook friends may list groups that support or oppose social causes. Browse some of them to see if one inspires an argument topic.

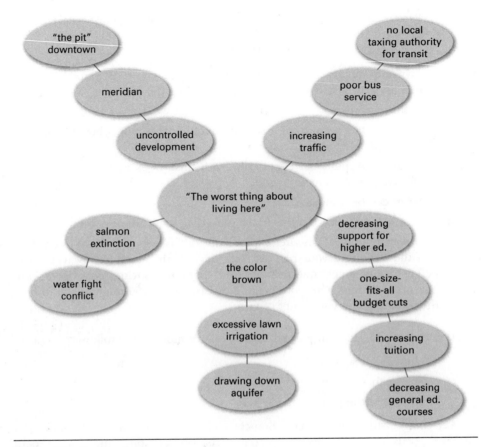

Figure 6.3 Sample cluster

Narrowing Down

Shift back to your more critical mind and sift through the material you generated. Did you discover a topic that might be interesting for your argument essay? Did you stumble over some interesting questions you'd like to explore further? Did anything you wrote or read make you *feel* something? Evaluate the raw material in your journal and keep the following things in mind as you zero in on a topic for your argument essay.

What's Promising Material and What Isn't? Let's take a critical look at the subjects you've generated so far. What promising topics might be lurking there for an argumentative essay? First, you simply must be interested in the topic, even if you know little about it. Also consider some of the following as you make your choice:

- *Evidence.* Do you think you'll be able to find facts, statistics, comments from experts, or stories about people affected by the issue?

- *Disagreement.* A topic lends itself to argumentative writing if it leads to disagreement among reasonable people. *Is smoking bad for your health?* was once a question that was debatable, but now pretty much everyone concedes that this question has been answered. *Is your state's public anti-smoking initiative effective?*, however, is certainly a debatable question and therefore a potential topic.

- *Inquiry.* Do you already have strong feelings about what you think about a topic? If so, consider another that provides more opportunities for learning and discovery.

Questions About Audience and Purpose. Persuasive writing is a very audience-oriented form. *To whom* you make your case in an argument matters a lot in *how* you make it, but audience also matters in *whether* one topic is a better choice for an essay than another topic. In choosing a subject, ask yourself:

- *Do your readers have a stake in the question you're answering?* Readers may or may not realize that they have a *stake* in the question. Say you're writing for fellow students on your campus and your topic addresses whether a 12 percent hike in tuition is justified. In this case, your readers will know they have a stake in the question. Sometimes, however, you choose a topic because readers *need to know* that they have a stake in how a question is answered. For instance, the argument that new antiterrorist rules threaten online privacy may be something you believe your readers, most of whom surf the web, should consider.

- *Can you identify what your readers might already believe?* One of the key strategies of persuasion is to find ways to link the values and attitudes of your audience with the position you're encouraging them to believe. Does your potential topic lend itself to this kind of analysis?

- *Is your potential topic appropriate for encouraging readers to believe or do something?* As you know by now, one of the things that distinguishes argument essays such as the op-ed piece from other forms of writing is the writer's intention to change his or her audience.

Trying Out

Okay, you've got a tentative topic and inquiry question for your argument essay: *Do social media have an effect on society?* At this point, you're thinking that your claim might be that, yes, social media have an effect on society. This isn't a bad start. But your opening question is *huge*. Which social media? What kinds of effects? Which society? Like a lot of research-based projects, the argument essay should pose a question that will help you make the decision about what information to look for and what to ignore. It should be focused enough so that you can wade into a creek rather than a raging river of information. If you think your question might be too general, try the following activity to cut it down to size.

Kitchen Knives of Thought. Try the following steps in your journal:

STEP ONE: Write your tentative research question at the top of a page of your notebook, and circle or underline every general or vague term.

What is the (impact) of (social media) on (society?)

STEP TWO: "Wh" questions (who, what, which, when, where, why) are the kitchen knives of thought. They can help you cut abstractions and generalities down to size. For each circled word in your inquiry question, find an appropriate "Wh" question that might help you make your research question more specific. Then jot down a quick list of ideas to answer the question you pose. For example,

1. *What* **impacts** of social media exactly?
   - Friendship, relationships
   - "Arab spring"
   - Writing
2. *Which* **social media**?
   - Facebook
   - Twitter
   - Blogs
3. *What* **societies**?
   - High school kids
   - Middle East
   - Online dating

STEP THREE: Restate your inquiry question, making it more specific and focused.

How has Twitter proven a challenge to authoritarian regimes in the Middle East?

Research Considerations. While writing this argument essay does involve some research, it isn't exactly a research paper. A research paper is a much more extended treatment of a topic that relies on more-detailed and scholarly information than is usually needed for an argument essay. In addition to the research strategies in this section, in Chapter 8 you'll find more information that might be helpful, including on conducting effective Internet searches and evaluating the sources you find and on library resources.

To develop a working knowledge of the topic for your argument essay, focus your research on the following:

1. *The back story:* What is the history of the controversy? (When did it begin, who was involved, how was the issue addressed, and what were the problems?)
2. *Popular assumptions:* What do most people currently believe is true about the issue?

3. *The evidence:* Who has said what that seems to support your claim or provide backing for your assumptions?

4. *Opposing arguments:* Who offers a counterargument that you might need to consider?

Consider working through some of the following research strategies to find this information.

Researching on the Web

- Google (for relevant websites, online periodicals, and some newspapers)
- Google Scholar (if your topic is discussed by scholars)
- Google Blog Search (to get the gist of the public discussion of your topic)
- GPO Access (go to http://www.gpoaccess.gov/ to search for relevant federal documents)
- Online version of local newspaper (if your topic has a local angle)
- State and Local Government on the Net (go to http://www.statelocalgov .net/ if your topic is an issue of policy)

Researching in the Library

- General subject databases (these cover a wide range of subjects, and many include nonacademic publications as well)
- Newspaper databases (for example, National Newspaper Index or Newspaper Source)
- Newspapers on microfilm (your university library might archive copies of the local paper on microfilm, going back for many years)

Interviews. While both the web and the university library are great sources of information on your topic, often the best way to learn about it—and get some good quotes for your essay—is to find someone to talk to. Your reading will probably give you the best clues about who to contact. Who is often quoted in news stories? Who has been writing or blogging about the issue? You might also be able to find someone on your own campus. If you're writing, say, about measures that attempt to protect students from date rape on your campus, someone in the criminal justice department or in Student Affairs can tell you more about the issue in a few minutes than you might learn in a couple hours online.

Writing the Sketch

Now draft a sketch with the following elements:

- It has a tentative title.
- It makes at least one claim and offers several reasons that support the claim.
- It presents and analyzes at least one contrasting point of view.

- It includes specific evidence to support (or possibly complicate) the reasons offered in support of the claim, including *at least* several of the following: an anecdote or story, a personal observation, data, an analogy, a case study, expert testimony, other relevant quotations from people involved, a precedent.

- It includes a Work Cited or References page listing sources used.

▶ Student Sketch

Rebecca Thompson is a fan of social media, and in doing some quick research for the sketch that follows, she discovers that the Pope is too. At the same time, she concedes that there are many critics who believe that sites such as Facebook do harm by undermining our social relationships rather than enhancing them, as Rebecca starts to argue here. Her sketch is the seed of an argument: There's a claim, reasons that support it, evidence, and consideration of another point of view. We'll see how the argument develops from here later in the chapter.

Twitter a Profound Thought?

Rebecca Thompson

1   Facebook Chat. iPhone texting. Checking in on FourSquare. Twitter hashtags. Tumblr blogging. These days, there's no limit to the ways we can talk to each other. Suddenly, talking and listening is much more complicated. But is this a good thing?

2   I use social media regularly. I use my email, Facebook, Twitter, and iPhone in all areas of my life, from connecting with high school friends now scattered across the country, to networking and advertising projects I'm involved in, to keeping updated on news stories. When Hurricane Irene struck the East Coast, I was out of town. I kept tabs on my friends via Facebook, and followed the news stories by following the hashtag #HurricaneIrene on Twitter. It was a relief to be connected, even from far away. "At its core, it is about connections and community," said Mailet Lopez, the founder of the networking site I Had Cancer, to *Forbes* magazine. "Social networking provides an opportunity beyond physical support networks and online forums...because with a social network, people can connect based on whatever criteria they want, regardless of location."

3   Yet detractors argue that social media does the opposite of what Lopez claims—it encourages *disconnectivity*. By focusing more on the kind of communication based around gadgets and the internet, critics argue that social media deconstructs traditional methods of conversation and undermines interpersonal relationships. "Technology is threatening to dominate our lives and make us less human," writes Paul Harris, referencing Sherry Tunkle's book *Alone Together*. "Under the illusion of allowing us to communicate better, it is actually isolating us from real human interactions in a cyber-reality that is a poor imitation of the real world."

4   While there is certainly truth to this claim, I argue that social media sites have the potential, if used to their best advantage, to facilitate communication and networking.

Because I can respond to emails and texts on the go, I can plan ahead. I can keep in touch with my friends studying abroad when phones aren't an option. I get lost a *lot* less. Even the Pope has spoken of the benefits of the internet, social networking, and media. "Search engines and social networks have become the starting point of communication for many people who are seeking advice, ideas, information and answers," he said. "In our time, the internet is becoming ever more a forum for questions and answers...In concise phrases, often no longer than a verse from the Bible, profound thoughts can be communicated."

Works Cited

Harris, Paul. "Social networking under fresh attack as tide of cyber-skepticism sweeps US." *The Guardian*. 22 January 2011. Web. 10 February 2012.

John, Tracey. "New social network connects cancer survivors, patients, and supporters." *Forbes*. 25 August 2011. Web. 12 February 2012.

Shariatmadari, David. "Pope Benedict praises Twitter-like forms of communication." *The Guardian*. 24 January 2012. Web. 12 February 2012.

Moving from Sketch to Draft

A sketch is a useful starting point for an argument essay in any form because it helps you to focus your thinking on what you discovered. A successful sketch points the way to the next draft. But how can you get your sketch to point the way, particularly for an essay that makes an argument? One of the most useful things you can ask yourself about your sketch is this: *What is the balance between explaining what I think and presenting evidence to support it?* If your sketch is mostly what writing expert Ken Macrorie once called "explainery," then the most important thing you might do is refocus on research. Gather more information on your topic. Test your ideas against your current opinions.

Evaluating Your Own Sketch. There are some other, more specific ways of evaluating your sketch. For example, answering these questions should give you some guidance:

- **Is the question you started with narrow enough?** Does it use specific terms rather than general terms ("society," "people," etc.)? When you did some research, were you either overwhelmed with information or unsure of where to look? If you conclude that your question still isn't focused enough, try "Kitchen Knives of Thought," earlier in this chapter.

- **Does the sketch point to a S.O.F.T.?** What seems to be the main claim you're making based on the evidence you've gathered so far?

- **Is that claim linked to one or more reasons?** Remember that claims are built on reasons (e.g., Twitter played a key factor in the success of Egypt's "Arab spring" *because* the regime couldn't control it.).

Reflecting on What You've Learned. Based on your experience so far with developing an argument essay, make an entry in your journal that explores the following questions:

- What's the difference between a fact and an opinion? Between a claim and an opinion?

- Consider what you've always thought about making arguments. How has that changed since you started working on this project?

Developing

Writing for Your Readers. You've read and written about an issue you care about. Now for the really hard part: getting out of your own head and into the heads of your potential readers, who may not care as much as you do. At least not yet. Successful persuasion fundamentally depends on giving an audience the right reasons to agree with you, and these are likely both logical and emotional, involving both logos and pathos, as you learned earlier in this chapter.

Another element of argument is the way the writer comes across to readers—his or her ethos. In the writing you've done so far on your topic, how do you think you might come off to an audience? Is your tone appealing, or might it be slightly off-putting? Do you successfully establish your authority to speak on this issue, or is the persona you project in the sketch somehow unconvincing, perhaps too emotional or not fair enough?

As we develop convictions about an issue, one of the hardest things to manage in early argument drafts is creating a persuasive persona (ethos). Another is finding ways to establish connections with our audience; this does not merely involve connecting writer and readers, but also includes creating some common ground between readers and *the topic*. There are many ways to do this, including the following:

1. Connecting your readers' prior beliefs or values with your position on the topic.

2. Establishing that readers have a *stake*, perhaps even a personal one, in how the question you've raised is answered; this may be self-interest, but it may also be emotional (remember the advertiser's strategy).

3. Highlighting the common experiences readers may have had with the topic and offering your claim as a useful way of understanding that experience.

4. Being reasonable. Do you devote time to looking at other points of views that you may not share?

Researching the Argument. The key to developing your draft is research. Though you might be able to use some of the information you gathered for your sketch, chances are that your focus or claims are shifting as you learn more. That means going back to the research well. In particular, you need enough information on the following:

- Evidence that supports your claims. Not just anything will do. Which evidence is most *persuasive*? You may have to look hard for this.

- Counterarguments from sources that take a view different from yours.
- Background information that establishes the *context* of the issue you're writing about. What's the debate? Who's involved? How long has this been going on? Why does it matter?

More Looking in the Library. One of the most useful things you can do to prepare for the draft is to spend forty-five minutes at the campus library searching for new information on your topic. Consider expanding your search from current newspapers and periodicals to books or government publications (see Chapter 8 for more information about searching for all kinds of sources, including government documents). In addition, you can refer to online almanacs such as Infoplease and the CIA's online World Factbook (http://www.odci.gov/cia/publications/factbook/), as well as statistical information available from sources such as the U.S. Census Bureau's American Fact Finder (http://factfinder.census.gov/home/saff/main.html?_lang=en), which is a wonderful resource that draws on the Bureau's massive database of information on U.S. trends.

Face-to-Face Interviewing. Try some interviews if you haven't already. People who are somehow involved in your topic are among the best sources of new information and lively material. An interview can provide ideas about what else you should read or who else you might talk to, as well as the quotations, anecdotes, and case studies that can make the next draft of your argument essay much more interesting. After all, what makes an issue matter is how it affects people. Have you sufficiently dramatized those effects? For more information on face-to-face interviewing, see Chapter 8, "Research Techniques."

Using the Web to Obtain Interviews and Quotes. The Internet can also be a source for interview material. Look for e-mail links to the authors of useful documents you find on the web and write to them with a few questions. Interest groups, newsgroups, or electronic mailing lists on the web can also provide the voices and perspectives of people with something to say on your topic. Remember to ask permission to quote them if you decide to use something of theirs in your draft. For leads on finding web discussion groups on your topic, visit the following sites:

- **Google Groups**, allows you to search for online discussion groups on virtually any topic.
- **Yahoo Groups** offers a similar service, allowing you to search for groups by keyword.
- **Catalist**, the official catalog of electronic mailing lists, has a database of about 15,000 discussion groups.

Finding Images. When appropriate, look for images to dramatize your claims or your evidence. Images are easy to find using search engines such as Google Image Search. But any images you use must be specifically relevant to your argument. If you do use online images in your essay make sure to give the source credit in the text and the bibliography.

Drafting

Designing Your Argument Rhetorically. The argument essay is one of those forms of writing that is plagued by organizing formulas. The claim must go in the first paragraph. The reasons behind the claims should be topic sentences, followed by evidence. The conclusion should restate the claim. Take a look at any published arguments and you'll see how far these formulas are from the way they're actually written. For example, take a look again at Edward Tufte's "PowerPoint Is Evil" on page 186. The claim happens to be in the first paragraph, but it's pretty indirect:

> *Imagine a widely used and expensive prescription drug that promised to make us beautiful but didn't. Instead the drug had frequent, serious side effects: It induced stupidity, turned everyone into bores, wasted time, and degraded the quality and credibility of communication. These side effects would rightly lead to a worldwide product recall.*

Tufte's lead paragraph doesn't say, "This essay will argue that PowerPoint is evil." It doesn't need to.

On the other hand, arguments do typically have the features that we've discussed: a question, a claim that addresses it, reasons, evidence, counterclaims. Just don't ever imagine that you march through these things in some strict order. You need to decide the design of your argument. And what will help you most in doing this is thinking about audience, especially:

This rhetorical awareness of your audience has implications for what information you include—and especially what you emphasize—in your draft:

- **Prior knowledge.** If your audience knows little about your topic, then you'll spend more time with background and context than you might if they largely understand the issue.

- **Receptivity.** Audiences that are already inclined to strongly agree are less critical. They probably need less evidence to be convinced of your position than neutral readers do. A resistant audience is the toughest sell: Strong evidence, and lots of it, is key.

- **Stake.** Neutral audiences—the kind you're most likely to encounter—have little awareness that your topic matters to them. You have to make it matter, and make it matter quickly.

Methods of Development. While there is no formula for organizing an argument, there are some ways of developing parts—and sometimes all—of your essay.

Narrative. Telling a story is an underrated way of developing an argument. Can you imagine a way to present your topic in an extended story, perhaps by focusing on the experience of a particular person or group of people, in a particular place, at a particular time? Obviously, the story must somehow be logically linked to your claim.

There are other ways to use narrative, too. Anecdotes, or brief stories that illustrate an idea or a problem, are frequently used in argument essays. One effective way to begin your essay might be to tell a story that highlights the problem you're writing about or the question you're posing.

Question to Answer. Almost all writing is an attempt to answer a question. In the personal essay and other open forms of inquiry, the writer may never arrive at a definite answer, but an argument essay usually offers an answer. An obvious method of development, therefore, is to begin your essay by raising the question and end it by offering your answer.

Are there several key questions around which you might organize your draft, leading to your central claim at the end?

Problem to Solution. This variation on the question-to-answer structure can be particularly useful if you're writing on a topic readers may know very little about. In such cases, you might need to spend as much time establishing what exactly the problem is—explaining what makes it a problem and why the reader should care about it—as you do offering your particular solution.

Effect to Cause or Cause to Effect. At the heart of some arguments is the *relationship* between causes and effects; often what is at issue is pinpointing such a relationship. Once a relationship is pinpointed, solutions can be offered. Sadly, we know the effects of terrorism, but what are its causes? If you were to argue, as some do, that Islamic radicalism arose in response to U.S. policies in the Middle East, including its policies toward Israel and the Palestinians, then you would be arguing from effect to cause. As the solution, you might go on to propose a shift in foreign policy. Some arguments can be organized simply around an examination of causes and effects.

Combining Approaches. As you think about how you might organize your first draft, you don't necessarily have to choose between these various methods of development. In fact, most often they work well together.

What Evidence Can Do

Usually we think of using evidence only to support
an idea or claim we're making. But evidence can
be used in other ways, too. For example, it can do the following:

- *support* an idea, observation, or assertion
- *refute* or challenge a claim with which you disagree
- *show* that a seemingly simple assertion, problem, or idea is really more complex
- *complicate* or even contradict an earlier point you've made
- *contrast* two or more ways of seeing the same thing
- *test* an idea, hypothesis, or theory

Using Evidence. All writing relies on evidence—that is, on specific information that has some relationship to general ideas expressed. For some of these relationships, see "Inquiring into the Details: What Evidence Can Do." Although all these relationships are possible in an argumentative essay, especially common is the use of evidence to support ideas the writer wants the reader to believe. What *kind* of evidence to include is a rhetorical issue. To whom are you writing, and what kind of evidence will they be more likely to believe?

Generally speaking, the narrower and more specialized the audience, the more particular they will be about the types of evidence they'll find convincing. As you continue on in your chosen major, you'll find that the types of evidence that help you make a persuasive argument will be more and more prescribed by the field. In the natural sciences, the results of quantitative studies count more than case studies; in the humanities, primary texts count more than secondary ones.

The important thing for this argument essay, which you're writing for a more general audience, is that you attempt to *vary* your evidence. For example, rather than relying exclusively on anecdotes, include some quotes from an expert as well.

Workshopping

Workshops on argument drafts can be lively affairs. People have opinions, and other people may disagree with them. Facts can be contested with counterfacts. As you prepare to share your draft, I'd encourage you to ask peers to speak to two separate issues:

1. Do you agree with my argument? What are your feelings about it?
2. No matter what your disposition is toward the argument in my draft, can you help me make it better?

Both discussions are important. But it may be hard to get to the second discussion if your workshop group is consumed by a debate over the issue itself.

As always, focus your peer review on the central concerns of a first draft: purpose and meaning. You can use the following grid.

Questions for Peer Reviewers	
Purpose	What is the question driving my argument? At what point in the draft do you first understand the question? Is that early enough?
Meaning	Do you understand the claim I'm making? Are the reasons I'm taking this position clear? Which do you find most convincing? Least convincing?

Reflecting on the Draft. After having spent time choosing an argument topic and developing and drafting your argument, what do you now understand about making effective arguments that you didn't when you started? If you were to make a single PowerPoint slide explaining that, what would it say?

Revising

Revision is a continual process—not a last step. You've been revising—"reseeing" your subject—from the first messy fastwriting in your journal. But the things that get your attention vary depending on where you are in the writing process. With your draft in hand, revision becomes your focus through what I'll call "shaping and tightening your draft."

Chapter 10 contains strategies that can help you revise any inquiry project. There are also certain things to think about that are especially useful for shaping an argument.

6.5
Use audience analysis and logical methods to help guide revision of an argument.

Shaping. In your draft, you made a tentative commitment to your topic, hoping that you could shape it into something that might have meaning for someone other than you. Fundamentally, you've been trying to figure out *what you're trying to say* and then rebuild your essay so that this is both clear and convincing. In an argument essay, you also want it to be convincing.

Shaping focuses first on the largest concerns of purpose and meaning—which you've already looked at if you workshopped your draft—and on the next-to-largest concerns of information and organization. It starts with knowing what your essay is about—your inquiry question and maybe your claim—and then revising to make every element of the draft focused on that question or assertion.

This chapter includes some useful tools that should help you shape the next draft, and in particular examine your reasoning strategies.

1. **Toulmin.** A helpful technique for revising the first draft of your argument essay is to use a method of analyzing argumentative reasoning, such as Toulminian or Rogerian logic. In an earlier exercise in this chapter, you may have experimented with a small element of Rogers' approach. Toulmin might be especially helpful for analyzing your draft. See "Inquiring into the Details: Toulmin: A Method for Analyzing an Argument," to see how you might apply his method.

2. **Logical fallacies.** Did you get yourself on any slippery slopes or beg a question? Find out by looking at the list in "Inquiring into the Details: Common Logical Fallacies," page 180.

3. **Rhetorical triangle.** We've talked about Aristotle's elements of persuasion: ethos, pathos, and logos (see Figures 6.1 and 6.2). Is there an effective emphasis on each of these in your draft, and have you used them in proportions appropriate to your topic and audience?

Inquiring into the Details

Toulmin: A Method for Analyzing an Argument

Stephen Toulmin, an English philosopher, argued that arguments about any subject have features that include:

- claims
- evidence
- warrants
- backing

In an argument, the *claims* are supported by *evidence* (examples, observations, statistics, etc.). The most penetrating aspect of Toulmin's approach is the idea that claims and evidence are linked together by *warrants*—or assumptions about the way things are. Suppose someone concludes that Michelle must be well off because she has six credit cards in her purse. To believe that claim, you also have to believe the warrant behind it: that there is a correlation between wealth and how many credit cards you own. Essentially, then, a warrant is the answer to the question *What do you need to believe is true in order to accept the validity of a claim based on evidence?*

To see how this might work, consider how it applies to the letter to the editor on page 178. Let's find the implicit claim, the evidence, and then the warrants linking the two.

Inquiring into the Details (*continued*)

Claim: In times of war, artists, especially those who have never served, should not create art that is unpatriotic.

Evidence: Art pieces at an exhibition that showed General Petraeus with a skull superimposed on his face, a photograph of a man with a noose made from an American flag. These images, made by artists who had never been to war, were exhibited when servicepeople were deployed in battle overseas. The writer of the letter, a veteran, was deeply offended.

Warrant 1: During wartime, Americans should temper their criticism of the military.

Warrant 2: Those who haven't seen military service don't fully appreciate the costs associated with protecting freedom.

Warrant 3: Art can have the quality of being unpatriotic.

The strongest arguments provide "backing"—or factual support for some or all of the warrants in an argument. The first challenge, of course, is identifying the warrants in an argument. Then you can look for evidence to substantiate them if you believe they make sense.

Toulmin's approach might be visualized this way:

To analyze an argument using Toulmin's method, search for the often implied warrants in the text, beginning with this question: *What are the assumptions about what is true that I must agree with to buy the argument?*

Polishing. When you are satisfied with the shape of your draft, focus on paragraphs, sentences, and words. Are your paragraphs coherent? How do you manage transitions? Are your sentences fluent and concise? Are there any errors in spelling or syntax? The section of Chapter 10 called "Problems with Clarity and Style" can help you focus on these issues.

Before you finish your draft, work through the following checklist:

✓ Every paragraph is about one thing.

✓ The transitions between paragraphs aren't abrupt.

✓ The length of sentences varies in each paragraph.

✓ Each sentence is concise. There are no unnecessary words or phrases.

✓ You've checked grammar, particularly verb agreement, run-on sentences, unclear pronouns, and misused words (*there/their, where/were,* and so on).

✓ You've run your spellchecker and proofed your paper for misspelled words.

▶ Student Essay

One of the things I really like about Rebecca Thompson's essay, "SocialNetworking SocialGood?" is that she readily concedes that there are downsides to social networking even though she's a fan of it. Rebecca could have quickly nodded to critics of her position in a sentence or two. But instead she explores the case against social media in some detail, quoting extensively from people who worry that they undermine conversations and personal relationships. Rebecca agrees with some of this. But she argues that, overall, media such as Facebook and Twitter have made her life better. Acknowledging opposing viewpoints is an important move in argumentative essay. But taking them seriously is rare. Because Rebecca recognizes the complexity of her topic, and tries to deal with it in her essay, the claim she does make seems more persuasive.

Social Networking Social Good?

Rebecca Thompson

1   Facebook Chat. iPhone texting. Checking in on FourSquare. Twitter hashtags. Tumblr blogging. OkCupid matchmaking. These days, there's no limit to the ways we can talk to each other. Suddenly, the basic human foundation of communication—talking and listening—has become much more complicated. It's incontrovertible that our society has changed in response to technological and media advancements. The day-to-day functions of our lives are different than they were even five years ago. We read differently (on Kindle or Nook), we watch differently (on Netflix, Hulu, or OnDemand), we hear differently (earbuds and surround sound), we even learn differently (smart boards, smart phones, Google). Despite the major advancements in rapid response, worldwide networking, as well as major shifts in the arts and sciences, many are concerned that there are major downfalls to the way that we, as a society, have begun to use social networking and media devices. Yet overall the explosion of social networking has provided unforeseen benefits, too. We can now find comfort in the company

of strangers, erase the distance between far-flung friends, and most important, participate in conversations that spread new knowledge.

I use social media, like e-mail, Facebook, Twitter, and Wordpress, in all areas of my life, from connecting with high school friends now scattered across the country, to networking and advertising projects I'm involved in, to keeping updated on news stories. When Hurricane Irene struck the East Coast, I was out of town. I kept tabs on my friends via Facebook, and followed the news stories by following the hashtag #HurricaneIrene on Twitter. It was a relief to be connected, even from far away. Similarly, following the devastating tornado in Missouri in May 2011, so-called "small-media efforts" (such as Facebook, local radio, and Twitter) were the ones that led most mainstream media to the scene. Facebook groups formed instantaneously and expanded exponentially, featuring posts from families searching for survivors as well as complete strangers offering prayers and support. As one poster wrote, "On one hand, my heart is just aching for your loss and devastation...[O]n the other hand, seeing everyone pulling together reminds me how resilient the human spirit is." (Mustich)

In instances of catastrophe like Hurricane Irene and the tornados in the Midwest, social networking is put to effective use in networking relief efforts, gathering and spreading crucial information, and sharing messages of support. Few would argue the positive effects of these technological advances. However, social media also functions on a more personal level, connecting people on a one-on-one basis, often inviting them into the most clandestine parts of their lives. "At its core, it is about connections and community," said Mailet Lopez, the founder of the networking site I Had Cancer, to *Forbes* magazine. "Social networking provides an opportunity beyond physical support networks and online forums...because with a social network, people can connect based on whatever criteria they want, regardless of location" (Tracey).

Thousands of anonymous viewers can read about the inner workings of thousands of other social media users, following their Twitter, subscribing to their blogs, mapping their location on FourSquare. This is a new phenomenon, thanks to the rapid developments in speed and accessibility in the technology, and is often cited as a cause of heightened disconnectivity and impersonality in human relationships. For some, though, social networking's seemingly impersonal associations actually provide great personal comfort. During the time her husband suffered from debilitating cancer and treatment, writer Lee Ann Cox chronicled her struggles on Twitter, her own "defiant cry to be seen, to testify, bearing witness to suffering in 140 characters or less." Cox tweeted about the mundane, the terror, and the absurdities of handling her husband's condition, and though she had followers, the simple act of tweeting in and of itself was her therapy. "Maybe I did get something I needed from Twitter," she writes. "With no one's permission, I gave myself a voice...I needed to say these things and imagine some heart in the Twittersphere absorbing my crazed reality " (Cox).

Social media critics see the downside of Cox's experience, arguing that rather than encouraging communication and interpersonal relationships, it diminishes them. These critics worry that social media deconstructs traditional methods of conversation and undermines interpersonal relationships. I have certainly sat in a room with four of my friends, all of us checking our iPhones and laptops, barely speaking. I've had more communication with some people on Facebook than I have with them in real life. I'm sure that the authors

(continued)

(continued)

of certain blogs I follow have more "blog friends" than real friends. Certainly, this kind of distance makes communication easier. If there's an awkward pause in a conversation, pull out your phone. If you're too shy to actually talk to a boy you're interested in, poke him on Facebook. The risk that online conversations might impoverish actual conversations is real. However, as Susan Greenfield, director of the Royal Institution of Great Britain, put it

> Real conversation in real time may eventually give way to these sanitized and easier screen dialogues, in much the same way as killing, skinning and butchering an animal to eat has been replaced by the convenience of packages of meat on the supermarket shelf. Perhaps future generations will recoil with similar horror at the messiness, unpredictability and immediate personal involvement of a three-dimensional, real-time interaction. (qtd. in Mackey)

6   Greenfield's gruesome image exemplifies the lowered stakes of communication, and therefore, repercussions, online. In 2011, the *Oxford English Dictionary* put the term "cyberbullying" into its lexicons. With increasing anonymity, access to personal information, and expanded public forums, social media has opened the door to new forms of cruelty—and not just for kids. Take the Dharun Ravi case. He used his webcam to tape his college roommate Tyler Clementi in a homosexual encounter with another student, and then shared it online with his friends. Clementi subsequently committed suicide. The case is unusual because it was based primarily on records of online interaction. Both the prosecution and defense used mountains of electronic evidence, including numerous tweets (some of which were tampered with), Facebook posts (including Clementi's final status update), text messages, screenshots, e-mails, and web chats. The sheer volume of evidence on social networking tools is beyond the scope of any other major bullying case in recent history. In many ways, this is a boon to the judicial process, as records of the students' online interactions are prime evidence for both the prosecution and defense. On the other hand, it is disturbing to note how the deteriorated relationship between these two boys "played out on social media with curiously few face-to-face exchanges" (Clayton).

7   Ravi's ability to quickly disperse the contraband video highlights is another inherent problem in social media. In mere seconds, an online post can be captured, saved, reposted, and shared. While a great boon for marketing and the quick dissemination of crucial information (such as in the case of a major natural disaster or a political event), there exists no system to judge the veracity and reliability of viral posts. The most viral video of all time is a 30-minute documentary made by the organization Invisible Children about Ugandan leader Joseph Kony, which received over 100 million hits in under a week when it was first posted in March 2012. However, after that first week had passed and certain critics began to look deeper, deep flaws in the message of the video emerged. "To call [Kony2012's] campaign a misrepresentation is an understatement," writes Angelo Izama, quoted in Time's "Global Spin" blog (Ishaan). The organization itself, Invisible Children, is under fire for its practices as an NGO. Most concerning to critics, though, is the extreme simplification and digestibility of the message itself. In this telling, to simply "know" about Kony...would be enough to bring him down," writes Ishaan Tharoor in "Global Spin."

"That quest takes place in a world of moral simplicity, of good and evil, of innocence and horror…justice is about much more than manhunts and viral video crusades" (Ishaan).

I recall seeing the Kony post on Facebook, and watched a few minutes before closing it down. I almost reposted, but then figured I should perhaps watch the whole 30 minutes before showing my support to my friends and followers. Upon reading the criticism of the documentary, now nearly as viral as the video itself, it seems to me that knowledge has been disseminated, albeit in a non-traditional way. Social networking allows for great diversity of opinion, and also opens the door to conversation. "Knowledge consists of a network of people and ideas that are not totally in sync, that are diverse, that disagree," states David Weinberger in an interview with Salon's Thomas Rogers. "Books generally have value because they encapsulate some topic and provide you with everything you know, because when you're reading it you cannot easily leap out of the book to get to the next book. The Web only has value because it contains difference" (Rogers). 8

Weinberger elucidates precisely the problems with, and the importance of, social media and the way knowledge is shared. It has inherently changed our tools of communication and of functioning in modern society—we can't go back now. "Ask anybody who is in any of the traditional knowledge fields," states Weinberger. 9

> She or he will very likely tell you that the Internet has made them smarter. They couldn't do their work without it; they're doing it better than ever before, they know more; they can find more; they can run down dead ends faster than ever before…Now we have a medium that is as broad as our curiosity. (qtd. in Rogers)

I agree that social networking tools have the potential, if used to their best advantage, to facilitate communication, networking, and the spread of knowledge. It's made functioning on a day-to-day basis much easier. Because I can respond to emails and texts on the go, I can plan ahead. I can keep in touch with my friends studying abroad when phones aren't an option. I get lost a lot less. Even the Pope has spoken of the benefits of the Internet, social networking, and media. "Search engines and social networks have become the starting point of communication for many people who are seeking advice, ideas, information and answers," he said. "In our time, the Internet is becoming ever more a forum for questions and answers…In concise phrases, often no longer than a verse from the Bible, profound thoughts can be communicated" (Shariatmadari). 10

Works Cited

Clayton, Mark. "Rutgers Spycam Case: Why It's Not Open and Shut." *Christian Science Monitor*. 22 February 2012. Web. 15 March 2012.

Cox, Lee Ann. "Losing My Husband, 140 Characters at a Time." *Salon*. 24 January 2012. Web. 12 March 2012.

Harris, Paul. "Social Networking Under Fresh Attack as Tide of Cyber-skepticism Sweeps US." *The Guardian*. 22 January 2011. Web. 12 March 2012.

John, Tracey. "New Social Network Connects Cancer Survivors, Patients, and Supporters." *Forbes*. 25 August 2011. Web. 15 March 2012.

(continued)

(continued)

Mackey, Robert. "Is Social Networking Killing You?" The Lede Blog: *New York Times*. 24 February 2009. Web. 12 March 2012.

Mustich, Emma. "Joplin rescue efforts HQ: Facebook." *Salon*. 23 May 2011. Web. 18 March 2012.

Rogers, Thomas. "Are We on Information Overload?" *Salon*. 1 January 2012. Web. 14 March 2012.

Shariatmadari, David. "Pope Benedict Praises Twitter-like Forms of Communication." *The Guardian*. 24 January 2012. Web. 14 March 2012.

Tharoor, Ishaan. "Why You Should Feel Awkward About the 'Kony2012' Video." *Time*. 8 March 2012. Web. 14 March 2012.

Evaluating the Essay

1. Rebecca claims that, overall, social media offers "comfort," eliminates "the distance between far-flung friends," and contributes to the creation of "new knowledge." Do you agree?

2. Use the rhetorical concepts of ethos, pathos, and logos to analyze the effectiveness of the essay. If the claim is that social networking, despite its potential shortcomings, is beneficial, then what are the reasons Rebecca uses to support the claim? Which do you find most convincing? Least convincing?

Using What You Have Learned

Let's return to the learning objectives I outlined in the beginning of the chapter.

1. **Identify the key elements of argument—reasons, claims, and evidence— and apply them in both reading and writing.** The next time you listen to a friend argue that Boise State's football team isn't a BCS-worthy team, or that general education classes are a waste of time, or that the foreign aid budget is bankrupting the country, you'll have some tools with which to respond. Making and recognizing a claim in an argument isn't hard. But most of us aren't so good at crafting reasons for what we believe and using evidence to make them persuasive. You will find this understanding powerful, not just in school where you make arguments all the time, but in life, too, where we also make arguments all the time.

2. **Understand how ethos, pathos, and logos combine in persuasion.** These three concepts, borrowed from Aristotle, are fundamental to rhetorical analysis and can help you to not only evaluate your own arguments, but also analyze the arguments of others in all kinds of situations. Whenever you're assigned

an argument in a college class, or express your opinion in a blog or other public form of argument, always ask yourself: How do I make myself credible to speak on this topic (ethos), do I use emotional appeals effectively (pathos), and is my reasoning sound (logos)? Remember that the answer to each of these questions depends on the situation and especially your audience.

3. **Use invention strategies appropriate to argument to discover and develop a topic.** As the writing assignments have moved from forms such as the personal essay that rely heavily on memory, experience, and observation to forms such as argument that rely especially on research, I hope that you see how invention strategies such as fastwriting can help you explore topics outside yourself. In this chapter, for example, you generated ideas from some random facts. These were starting points for generating ideas, not simply fodder for supporting an opinion. Approached openly, information is a source of discovery.

4. **Develop a question that is focused enough to lead to a strong claim and convincing evidence.** This is a consistent theme in *The Curious Writer.* Inquiry begins with questions. But not just any questions. You've learned that different kinds of questions spark different kinds of arguments. For instance, *What should be done?* might lead to a proposal. In this chapter, you've worked to narrow a question that would lead to claims of fact. The skills that you developed here of narrowing that question are essential in any research-based project, as you'll see if you tackle the ethnography and research essay later in the book.

5. **Use audience analysis and logical methods to help guide revision of an argument.** Argument is among the most audience-focused forms, and the kind of rhetorical analysis you did here as you revised your draft should prove invaluable whenever persuasion is a motive. If you found Toulmin's methods of analyzing your argument helpful, then you should look more closely at the abundant examples of applying Toulmin scattered across the web, because my treatment of his approach here was necessarily limited.

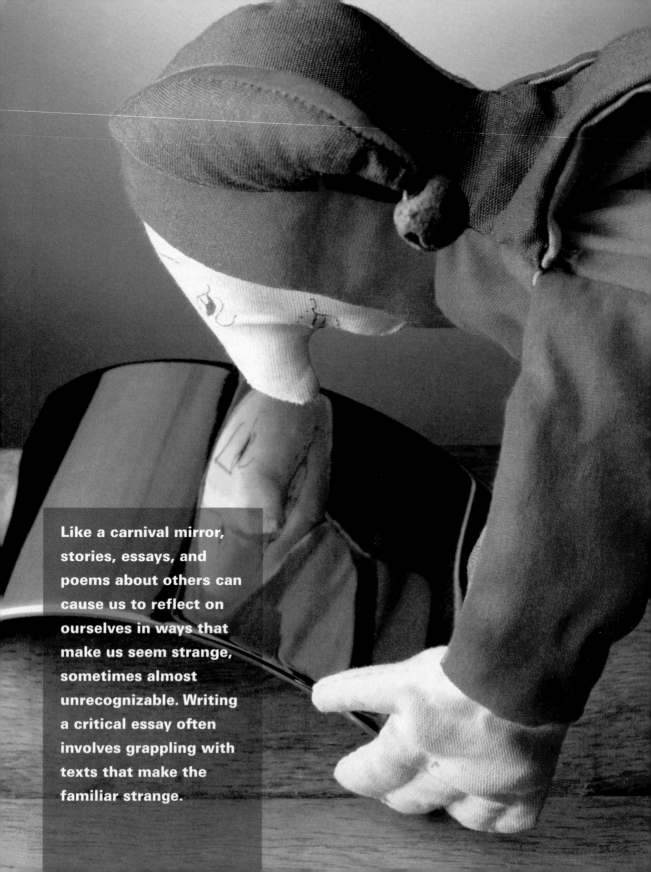

Like a carnival mirror, stories, essays, and poems about others can cause us to reflect on ourselves in ways that make us seem strange, sometimes almost unrecognizable. Writing a critical essay often involves grappling with texts that make the familiar strange.

7

Writing a Critical Essay

Learning Objectives

In this chapter, you'll learn to

7.1 Apply the methods of critical analysis not only to literature but anything whose meanings aren't apparent.

7.2 Use evidence from primary sources to argue effectively for a convincing interpretation.

7.3 Use appropriate invention strategies to discover a topic for a critical essay.

7.4 Apply revision strategies that are effective for the critical essay.

Writing About Literature

One of the world's shortest short stories was reputedly written by Ernest Hemingway in a wager: "For Sale: Baby Shoes. Never worn." While the origin of this six-word short story is disputed, it does point to a quality that much literature shares: It says more than it says. Taken literally, this is simply a classified ad for some never-used baby shoes. Yet it implies so much more. Beneath the fairly mundane facts is the echo of sudden loss. A baby has died before he or she had the chance to wear new shoes, and the parents, somewhat curiously, choose to sell them for what will likely be a pittance. Why would they do that? Who is this baby? Who are these parents? What happened?

Six words trigger a cascade of questions about what might be *inferred* from the literal facts, all seeding the larger inquiry question that is behind any act of interpretation: *What might it mean?*

What might it mean? is the kind of question we ask about things with ambiguous meanings—a painting, a film, a short story, a sculpture—but we might also ask it about a social interaction ("Why did he make that face when I said that?") or a cultural ritual. When we attempt to interpret something, we sense that there is more going on than meets the eye. An explanation of the literal facts—there are never-used baby shoes for sale—doesn't do justice to the thing we're looking at. What else is going on here? What is being implied, intentionally or unintentionally?

219

Here's something I hear nearly every semester: "Why do we have to analyze literature to death? Isn't it enough that it's just a good story?" I actually sympathize with this frustration. It *is* enough sometimes to simply indulge in the pleasure of a well-told story or a beautifully written essay. But reading a good story or essay and refusing the invitation to look underneath is like someone fond of fast cars failing to pop the hood. You can admire the beauty of a Porsche or Alpha from afar, but to really appreciate it fully you should look at what powers the thing.

We interpret literature, film, or art not because we're supposed to, but because it makes our encounter with those things richer and more pleasurable. Yet even if you never take another English course or read a short story, it's impossible to live life without asking, "What might it mean?" We interpret things all the time, and in this chapter, you'll learn some methods for doing it.

Motives for Writing a Critical Essay

7.1

Apply the methods of critical analysis not only to literature but anything whose meanings aren't apparent.

A critical essay makes an argument for a certain interpretation of something. Typically, we think of critical essays as a genre of the literature class, but it just as easily could be used in any writing situation that asks you to look closely at something—a photograph, a political strategy, or even animal behavior—and draw some conclusions about what it means. As I mentioned before, we do this informally all the time. A few days ago, my dog Ada, who is laying under my desk as I write this, suddenly refused to come back in the dog door. Going out was no problem. I watched her wrestle with the door, tentatively approaching and poking the plastic curtain, backing off and then trying again. It made no sense. What does this mean? She's suddenly neurotic? Something scared her? I can't ask the dog, so I may never know the real answer. But the situation called for interpretation: observing her behavior and speculating on its meaning. This is what humans do as we try to make sense of the things around us. The critical essay is a form for reporting such speculations.

The process of critical analysis looks something like Figure 7.1. We direct our gaze to a subject—say, a short story or film—and pay close attention to the particulars as we wonder *What might it mean?* Then, drawing on the evidence, we speculate, working towards an argument that our interpretation is a convincing one. This process, at least initially, is largely *inductive*. We work from the specifics to the general. In writing about literature, this means that we first look very closely at specifics in the work: certain words, lines, passages, scenes, characters, conflicts, and so on. Then we do what we always do in inquiry-based investigations: look for patterns.

To fully appreciate what authors are saying or what effects they're trying to create in an essay, poem, or story, you often need to look closely, and in doing so, you see beyond the obvious.

Recognizing patterns in literary texts (or anything we're not familiar with) is hard. But one of the things that helps enormously are theories about what to look for. Some of these that you're probably most familiar with from English classes suggest categories of things you might analyze: characters, theme, motifs, conflict, structure, language, etc. (See "Inquiring into the Details: Common Literary Devices" on p. 244). Other theories work from

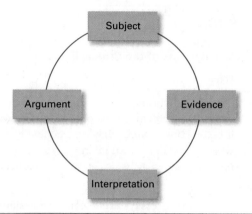

Figure 7.1 Critical analysis involves making inferences about the significance of something by examining it closely—a text, a painting, experimental data—and then enlisting the evidence to argue for a particular interpretation.

premises that might change your gaze altogether. For example, so-called feminist criticism encourages readers to see how gender operates in a story. What are the relations between men and women? How does each exercise authority? Later in this chapter, we'll look at a few of these (see "Inquiring into the Details: Why Literary Theory Is Not a Sleep Aid" on p. 233).

The Critical Essay and Academic Writing

Virtually all academic work—and much of daily life, for that matter—involves looking for patterns in an effort to make sense of things. One way to look for some of these patterns is to ask the interpretation question behind the critical essay: *What might it mean?* In virtually every class you take in college, interpreting from data is central. What differs from course to course is the source of this data. In English, for example, you'll often be drawing evidence from texts. In anthropology, you might observe social behavior and rituals in the field. In physics, you analyze experimental data.

Critical essays are built around a main idea, claim, or interpretation you are making about a text.

While the term "critical essay" is most often used in literary studies, whenever you're asked to interpret or speculate from evidence, you are doing critical analysis. For example, if you write about an experiment you've conducted in biology, a section called "Discussion of Results" is critical analysis. What differs between the disciplines, obviously, are the theories that help you do this interpreting. A scientist might use statistical theories to interpret data. An anthropologist might use theories related to cultural ecology. For many of these disciplines, no matter what the theories that inform it, critical analysis is in the service of an argument that answers the question *What does this mean?*

7.2
Use evidence from primary sources to argue effectively for a convincing interpretation.

Features of the Form

Feature	Conventions of the Critical Essay
Inquiry question	What might it mean?
Motives	We turn to forms such as the critical essay whenever the meaning of something isn't obvious and we want to understand it better. This requires that we examine it more closely, using what we see to form an interpretation. Ultimately, the purpose in a critical essay is to make our particular interpretation convincing.
Subject matter	While critical essays are a common assignment in English, focusing on literary texts, they also might explore film, art, popular culture, or any subject matter whose meanings are uncertain.
Structure	There are three elements in most critical essays: 1. Review of what others have said about the thing being analyzed. What is the current conversation about it among other critics? 2. References to *specific* features of the object being analyzed (e.g. passages, language, images, etc.) that informed the interpretation. 3. Background summary for an audience not familiar with the story, poem, painting, etc., that is being analyzed.
Sources of information	This depends on what's being analyzed. An interpretation of a story, for example, would draw evidence from the story itself: lines, passages, scenes, characters. Critical essays, at least initially, are written *inductively*, through close analysis and observation of the object of study. This yields specific information that influences any interpretation. In addition, critical essays might include information from other critics or analysts who have contributed to the conversation about possible interpretations.
Language	The tone of a critical essay, as for most forms, depends on the audience. Formal essays, the kind assigned in literature classes, rarely use the first person, focusing readers' attention on the argument, not the writer. Less-formal response essays might use much more casual language.

Prose+

Charles Bukowski's touching poem "The Bluebird"—a meditation on how terrifying it can be to drop our masks and expose the face sweating beneath it—inspired a visual interpretation by the artist Monika Umba. This is one of four images that she created in response to the poem.

there's a bluebird in my heart that
wants to get out
but I'm too tough for him,
I say, stay in there, I'm not going
to let anybody see
you.
there's a bluebird in my heart that
wants to get out
but I pour whiskey on him and inhale
cigarette smoke
and the whores and the bartenders
and the grocery clerks
never know that
he's
in there.

there's a bluebird in my heart that
wants to get out
but I'm too tough for him,
I say,
stay down, do you want to mess
me up?
you want to screw up the
works?
you want to blow my book sales in
Europe?
there's a bluebird in my heart that
wants to get out
but I'm too clever, I only let him out
at night sometimes
when everybody's asleep.
I say, I know that you're there,
so don't be
sad.

then I put him back,
but he's singing a little
in there, I haven't quite let him
die
and we sleep together like
that
with our
secret pact
and it's nice enough to
make a man
weep, but I don't
weep, do
you?

READINGS

▶ Short Story

People love stories, and I think they always will. The oral tradition—someone tells a story to one or more listeners—was once a fundamental way to transfer knowledge about the world and how it worked. Then came writing. Now we compose stories in written prose, fixed on paper or a computer screen. There is no visible speaker, or particular occasion for the telling, and the story is static. It never changes. For Native American writers, such as Leslie Silko, who grew up in tribal communities where stories are still told orally, the two narrative traditions might seem to conflict. Instead, much contemporary Native American literature, while written, still preserves qualities and motives of speech.

Silko is widely recognized as one of the finest living Native American writers, and her novel *Ceremony*, published in 1977, received critical acclaim. She's also a talented poet and essayist. Above all, Leslie Marmon Silko is a storyteller in the Laguna tradition, using a kind of narrative that in many ways will be familiar to nonnative readers. There are characters and scenes and a significant event, but also notice how landscape figures into the telling of this story, and in particular what the narrator's relationship is with the natural world. One of the motives for telling a story like this is to deal with loss by seeking recovery through balance or harmony.

Lullaby

Leslie Marmon Silko

The sun had gone down but the snow in the wind gave off its own light. It came in thick tufts like new wool—washed before the weaver spins it. Ayah reached out for it like her own babies had, and she smiled when she remembered how she had laughed at them. She was an old woman now, and her life had become memories. She sat down with her back against the wide cottonwood tree, feeling the rough bark on her back bones; she faced east and listened to the wind and snow sing a high-pitched Yeibechei song. Out of the wind she felt warmer, and she could watch the wide fluffy snow fill in her tracks, steadily, until the direction she had come from was gone. By the light of the snow she could see the dark outline of the big arroyo a few feet away. She was sitting on the edge of Cebolleta Creek, where in the springtime the thin cows would graze on a grass already chewed flat to the ground. In the wide deep creek bed where only a trickle of water flowed in the summer, the skinny cows would wander, looking for new grass along winding paths splashed with manure.

Ayah pulled the old Army blanket over her head like a shawl. Jimmie's blanket— the one he had sent to her. That was a long time ago and the green wool was faded,

(continued)

1

2

(continued)

and it was unraveling on the edges. She did not want to think about Jimmie. So she thought about the weaving and the way her mother had done it. On the tall wooden loom set into the sand under a tamarack tree for shade. She could see it clearly. She had been only a little girl when her grandma gave her the wooden combs to pull the twigs and burrs from the raw, freshly washed wool. And while she combed the wool, her grandma sat beside her, spinning a silvery strand of yarn around the smooth cedar spindle. Her mother worked at the loom with yarns dyed bright yellow and red and gold. She watched them dye the yarn in boiling black pots full of beeweed petals, juniper berries, and sage. The blankets her mother made were soft and woven so tight that rain rolled off them like birds' feathers. Ayah remembered sleeping warm on cold windy nights, wrapped in her mother's blankets on the hogan's sandy floor.

3   The snow drifted now, with the northwest wind hurling it in gusts. It drifted up around her black overshoes—old ones with little metal buckles. She smiled at the snow which was trying to cover her little by little. She could remember when they had no black rubber overshoes; only the high buckskin leggings that they wrapped over their elkhide moccasins. If the snow was dry or frozen, a person could walk all day and not get wet; and in the evenings the beams of the ceiling would hang with lengths of pale buckskin leggings, drying out slowly.

4   She felt peaceful remembering. She didn't feel cold any more. Jimmie's blanket seemed warmer than it had ever been. And she could remember the morning he was born. She could remember whispering to her mother, who was sleeping on the other side of the hogan, to tell her it was time now. She did not want to wake the others. The second time she called to her, her mother stood up and pulled on her shoes; she knew. They walked to the old stone hogan together, Ayah walking a step behind her mother. She waited alone, learning the rhythms of the pains while her mother went to call the old woman to help them. The morning was already warm even before dawn and Ayah smelled the bee flowers blooming and the young willow growing at the springs. She could remember that so clearly, but his birth merged into the births of the other children and to her it became all the same birth. They named him for the summer morning and in English they called him Jimmie.

5   It wasn't like Jimmie died. He just never came back, and one day a dark blue sedan with white writing on its doors pulled up in front of the boxcar shack where the rancher let the Indians live. A man in a khaki uniform trimmed in gold gave them a yellow piece of paper and told them that Jimmie was dead. He said the Army would try to get the body back and then it would be shipped to them; but it wasn't likely because the helicopter had burned after it crashed. All of this was told to Chato because he could understand English. She stood inside the doorway holding the baby while Chato listened. Chato spoke English like a white man and he spoke Spanish too. He was taller than the white man and he stood straighter too. Chato didn't explain why; he just told the military man they could keep the body if they found it. The white man looked bewildered; he nodded his head and he left. Then Chato looked at her and shook his head, and then he told her, "Jimmie isn't coming home anymore," and

when he spoke, he used the words to speak of the dead. She didn't cry then, but she hurt inside with anger. And she mourned him as the years passed, when a horse fell with Chato and broke his leg, and the white rancher told them he wouldn't pay Chato until he could work again. She mourned Jimmie because he would have worked for his father then; he would have saddled the big bay horse and ridden the fence lines each day, with wire cutters and heavy gloves, fixing the breaks in the barbed wire and putting the stray cattle back inside again.

She mourned him after the white doctors came to take Danny and Ella away. She was at the shack alone that day they came. It was back in the days before they hired Navajo women to go with them as interpreters. She recognized one of the doctors. She had seen him at the children's clinic at Cañoncito about a month ago. They were wearing khaki uniforms and they waved papers at her and a black ball-point pen, trying to make her understand their English words. She was frightened by the way they looked at the children, like the lizard watches the fly. Danny was swinging on the tire swing on the elm tree behind the rancher's house, and Ella was toddling around the front door, dragging the broomstick horse Chato made for her. Ayah could see they wanted her to sign the papers, and Chato had taught her to sign her name. It was something she was proud of. She only wanted them to go, and to take their eyes away from her children.

6

She took the pen from the man without looking at his face and she signed the papers in three different places he pointed to. She stared at the ground by their feet and waited for them to leave. But they stood there and began to point and gesture at the children. Danny stopped swinging. Ayah could see his fear. She moved suddenly and grabbed Ella into her arms; the child squirmed, trying to get back to her toys. Ayah ran with the baby toward Danny; she screamed for him to run and then she grabbed him around his chest and carried him too. She ran south into the foothills of juniper trees and black lava rock. Behind her she heard the doctors running, but they had been taken by surprise, and as the hills became steeper and the cholla cactus were thicker, they stopped. When she reached the top of the hill, she stopped to listen in case they were circling around her. But in a few minutes she heard a car engine start and they drove away. The children had been too surprised to cry while she ran with them. Danny was shaking and Ella's little fingers were gripping Ayah's blouse.

7

She stayed up in the hills for the rest of the day, sitting on a black lava boulder in the sunshine where she could see for miles all around her. The sky was light blue and cloudless, and it was warm for late April. The sun warmth relaxed her and took the fear and anger away. She lay back on the rock and watched the sky. It seemed to her that she could walk into the sky, stepping through clouds endlessly. Danny played with little pebbles and stones, pretending they were birds eggs and then little rabbits. Ella sat at her feet and dropped fistfuls of dirt into the breeze, watching the dust and particles of sand intently. Ayah watched a hawk soar high above them, dark wings gliding; hunting or only watching, she did not know. The hawk was patient and he circled all afternoon before he disappeared around the high volcanic peak the Mexicans called Guadalupe.

8

(continued)

(continued)

9   Late in the afternoon, Ayah looked down at the gray boxcar shack with the paint all peeled from the wood; the stove pipe on the roof was rusted and crooked. The fire she had built that morning in the oil drum stove had burned out. Ella was asleep in her lap now and Danny sat close to her, complaining that he was hungry; he asked when they would go to the house. "We will stay up here until your father comes," she told him, "because those white men were chasing us." The boy remembered then and he nodded at her silently.

10   If Jimmie had been there he could have read those papers and explained to her what they said. Ayah would have known then, never to sign them. The doctors came back the next day and they brought a BIA policeman with them. They told Chato they had her signature and that was all they needed. Except for the kids. She listened to Chato sullenly; she hated him when he told her it was the old woman who died in the winter, spitting blood; it was her old grandma who had given the children this disease. "They don't spit blood," she said coldly. "The whites lie." She held Ella and Danny close to her, ready to run to the hills again. "I want a medicine man first," she said to Chato, not looking at him. He shook his head. "It's too late now. The policeman is with them. You signed the paper." His voice was gentle.

11   It was worse than if they had died: to lose the children and to know that somewhere, in a place called Colorado, in a place full of sick and dying strangers, her children were without her. There had been babies that died soon after they were born, and one that died before he could walk. She had carried them herself, up to the boulders and great pieces of the cliff that long ago crashed down from Long Mesa; she laid them in the crevices of sandstone and buried them in fine brown sand with round quartz pebbles that washed down the hills in the rain. She had endured it because they had been with her. But she could not bear this pain. She did not sleep for a long time after they took her children. She stayed on the hill where they had fled the first time, and she slept rolled up in the blanket Jimmie had sent her. She carried the pain in her belly and it was fed by everything she saw: the blue sky of their last day together and the dust and pebbles they played with; the swing in the elm tree and broom stick horse choked life from her. The pain filled her stomach and there was no room for food or for her lungs to fill with air. The air and the food would have been theirs.

12   She hated Chato, not because he let the policeman and doctors put the screaming children in the government car, but because he had taught her to sign her name. Because it was like the old ones always told her about learning their language or any of their ways: it endangered you. She slept alone on the hill until the middle of November when the first snows came. Then she made a bed for herself where the children had slept. She did not lie down beside Chato again until many years later, when he was sick and shivering and only her body could keep him warm. The illness came after the white rancher told Chato he was too old to work for him anymore, and Chato and his old woman should be out of the shack by the next afternoon because the rancher had hired new people to work there. That had satisfied her. To see how

the white man repaid Chato's years of loyalty and work. All of Chato's fine-sounding English talk didn't change things.

It snowed steadily and the luminous light from the snow gradually diminished into the darkness. Somewhere in Cebolleta a dog barked and other village dogs joined with it. Ayah looked in the direction she had come, from the bar where Chato was buying the wine. Sometimes he told her to go on ahead and wait; and then he never came. And when she finally went back looking for him, she would find him passed out at the bottom of the wooden steps at Azzie's Bar. All the wine would be gone and most of the money too, from the pale blue check that came to them once a month in a government envelope. It was then that she would look at his face and his hands, scarred by ropes and the barbed wire of all those years, and she would think, this man is a stranger; for forty years she had smiled at him and cooked his food, but he remained a stranger. She stood up again, with the snow almost to her knees, and she walked back to find Chato. 13

It was hard to walk in the deep snow and she felt the air burn in her lungs. She stopped a short distance from the bar to rest and readjust the blanket. But this time he wasn't waiting for her on the bottom step with his old Stetson hat pulled down and his shoulders hunched up in his long wool overcoat. 14

She was careful not to slip on the wooden steps. When she pushed the door open, warm air and cigarette smoke hit her face. She looked around slowly and deliberately, in every corner, in every dark place that the old man might find to sleep. The bar owner didn't like Indians in there, especially Navajos, but he let Chato come in because he could talk Spanish like he was one of them. The men at the bar stared at her, and the bartender saw that she left the door open wide. Snowflakes were flying inside like moths and melting into a puddle on the oiled wood floor. He motioned to her to close the door, but she did not see him. She held herself straight and walked across the room slowly, searching the room with every step. The snow in her hair melted and she could feel it on her forehead. At the far corner of the room, she saw red flames at the mica window of the old stove door; she looked behind the stove just to make sure. The bar got quiet except for the Spanish polka music playing on the jukebox. She stood by the stove and shook the snow from her blanket and held it near the stove to dry. The wet wool smell reminded her of new-born goats in early March, brought inside to warm near the fire. She felt calm. 15

In past years they would have told her to get out. But her hair was white now and her face was wrinkled. They looked at her like she was a spider crawling slowly across the room. They were afraid; she could feel the fear. She looked at their faces steadily. They reminded her of the first time the white people brought her children back to her that winter. Danny had been shy and hid behind the thin white woman who brought them. And the baby had not known her until Ayah took her into her arms, and then Ella had nuzzled close to her as she had when she was nursing. The blonde woman was nervous and kept looking at a dainty gold watch on her wrist. She sat on the bench near the small window and watched the dark snow clouds gather 16

(continued)

(continued)

around the mountains; she was worrying about the unpaved road. She was frightened by what she saw inside too: the strips of venison drying on a rope across the ceiling and the children jabbering excitedly in a language she did not know. So they stayed for only a few hours. Ayah watched the government car disappear down the road and she knew they were already being weaned from these lava hills and from this sky. The last time they came was in early June, and Ella stared at her the way the men in the bar were now staring. Ayah did not try to pick her up; she smiled at her instead and spoke cheerfully to Danny. When he tried to answer her, he could not seem to remember and he spoke English words with the Navajo. But he gave her a scrap of paper that he had found somewhere and carried in his pocket; it was folded in half, and he shyly looked up at her and said it was a bird. She asked Chato if they were home for good this time. He spoke to the white woman and she shook her head. "How much longer?" he asked, and she said she didn't know; but Chato saw how she stared at the boxcar shack. Ayah turned away then. She did not say good-bye.

17   She felt satisfied that the men in the bar feared her. Maybe it was her face and the way she held her mouth with teeth clenched tight, like there was nothing anyone could do to her now. She walked north down the road, searching for the old man. She did this because she had the blanket, and there would be no place for him except with her and the blanket in the old abode barn near the arroyo. They always slept there when they came to Cebolleta. If the money and the wine were gone, she would be relieved because then they could go home again; back to the old hogan with a dirt roof and rock walls where she herself had been born. And the next day the old man could go back to the few sheep they still had, to follow along behind them, guiding them, into dry sandy arroyos where sparse grass grew. She knew he did not like walking behind old ewes when for so many years he rode big quarter horses and worked with cattle. But she wasn't sorry for him; he should have known all along what would happen.

18   There had not been enough rain for their garden in five years; and that was when Chato finally hitched a ride into the town and brought back brown boxes of rice and sugar and big tin cans of welfare peaches. After that, at the first of the month they went to Cebolleta to ask the postmaster for the check; and then Chato would go to the bar and cash it. They did this as they planted the garden every May, not because anything would survive the summer dust, but because it was time to do this. The journey passed the days that smelled silent and dry like the caves above the canyon with yellow painted buffaloes on their walls.

19   He was walking along the pavement when she found him. He did not stop or turn around when he heard her behind him. She walked beside him and she noticed how slowly he moved now. He smelled strong of woodsmoke and urine. Lately he had been forgetting. Sometimes he called her by his sister's name and she had been gone for a long time. Once she had found him wandering on the road to the white man's ranch, and she asked him why he was going that way; he laughed at her and said, "You know they can't run that ranch without me," and he walked on determined,

limping on the leg that had been crushed many years before. Now he looked at her curiously, as if for the first time, but he kept shuffling along, moving slowly along the side of the highway. His gray hair had grown long and spread out on the shoulders of the long overcoat. He wore the old felt hat pulled down over his ears. His boots were worn out at the toes and he had stuffed pieces of an old red shirt in the holes. The rags made his feet look like little animals up to their ears in snow. She laughed at his feet; the snow muffled the sound of her laugh. He stopped and looked at her again. The wind had quit blowing and the snow was falling straight down; the southeast sky was beginning to clear and Ayah could see a star.

"Let's rest awhile," she said to him. They walked away from the road and up the   20
slope to the giant boulders that had tumbled down from the red sand-rock mesa throughout the centuries of rainstorms and earth tremors. In a place where the boulders shut out the wind, they sat down with their backs against the rock. She offered half of the blanket to him and they sat wrapped together.

The storm passed swiftly. The clouds moved east. They were massive and full,   21
crowding together across the sky. She watched them with the feeling of horses—steely blue-gray horses startled across the sky. The powerful haunches pushed into the distances and the tail hairs streamed white mist behind them. The sky cleared. Ayah saw that there was nothing between her and the stars. The light was crystalline. There was no shimmer, no distortion through earth haze. She breathed the clarity of the night sky; she smelled the purity of the half moon and the stars. He was lying on his side with his knees pulled up near his belly for warmth. His eyes were closed now, and in the light from the stars and the moon, he looked young again.

She could see it descend out of the night sky: an icy stillness from the edge of   22
the thin moon. She recognized the freezing. It came gradually, sinking snowflake by snowflake until the crust was heavy and deep. It had the strength of the stars in Orion, and its journey was endless. Ayah knew that with the wine he would sleep. He would not feel it. She tucked the blanket around him, remembering how it was when Ella had been with her; and she felt the rush so big inside her heart for the babies. And she sang the only song she knew to sing for babies. She could not remember if she had ever sung it to her children, but she knew that her grandmother had sung it and her mother had sung it:

> The earth is your mother,
> she holds you.
> The sky is your father,
> he protects you.
> Sleep,
> sleep.
> Rainbow is your sister,
> she loves you.
> The winds are your brothers,

(continued)

they sing to you.
Sleep,
sleep.
We are together always
We are together always
There never was a time
when this
was not so.

Inquiring into the Story

1. **Explore.** On the left page of your notebook, jot down at least five lines or passages that you believe were key to your understanding of the story. These may include details that seem important, moments that signify turning points, or feelings or ideas suggested by the narrator or another character. On the right page, openly fastwrite about the passages you collected. What do they seem to suggest about possible themes for the story? What do you notice about Ayah, the main character and narrator? What do you consider the significant events that affect all the characters and how do these events change the characters?

2. **Explain.** A recurring detail in the story is the blanket that Ayah received from her son, Jimmie. Trace every mention of the blanket in the story. What accumulated meaning does this detail acquire in the story?

3. **Evaluate.** Some critics have argued that "Lullaby" is a story of healing and recovery. Do you agree or disagree? What evidence in the story would you point to that either supports or contradicts that contention?

4. **Reflect.** When you studied literature in high school, you developed certain routines for writing analytical papers. What were they? Was your experience analyzing Silko's story different from what you're used to when you're asked to interpret literature?

One Student's Response

Noel's Journal

DOUBLE-ENTRY JOURNAL
RESPONSE TO "LULLABY"

"It was worse than if they had died: to lose the children and to know that somewhere, in a place called Colorado, in a place full of sick and dying strangers, her children were without her."

One Student's Response *(continued)*

"She stayed on the hill where they had fled the first time, and she slept rolled up in the blanket Jimmie had sent her."

I think this sets the tone of the whole story. She loses one son to the war and the other two were taken from her. Knowing that one son had died and wouldn't ever come home again. The other two were alive and well but they would not grow up with their mother and were kept from their own culture by the government.

After she lost all her children she finds comfort in the blanket her older son had sent her. She sleeps in the place where she spent the last moments with her other two children.

She carries the blanket with her wherever she goes. This is how she spent her time mourning her loss and memories.

Inquiring into the Details

Why Literary Theory Is Not a Sleep Aid

The discipline of literary studies is interested in theories, or coherent ideas, about how we interpret essays, poems, short stories, drama, and novels. Yawn, you say? I can understand that reaction, even if you're an English major. A mention of theory might seem to be an invitation to nod off.

But here's a way to understand the relevance of theory in any discipline, including literary studies. Good theories help you understand and explain what you see. Here's an example of what I mean. A group of scholars has always been interested in how we tell stories, and one of these scholars, Joseph Campbell, was a mythologist who developed ideas about how most of the stories we tell are variations on the same story that has been told forever: the hero's journey. This journey has identifiable stages, Campbell argued, including this progression: (1) First we see the hero in his or her ordinary world, then (2) the hero is presented with a challenge, (3) he or she resists the challenge, (4) the hero gets encouraged by a wise mentor, (5) and the hero embarks, encountering the first test, and so on until the journey is completed and the hero returns to the ordinary world again, but transformed and possessing something that makes that world better. Think *Star Wars*.

Campbell's theory that stories conform to the outlines of this basic journey can be used to analyze a novel, film, short story, or even personal essay. His ideas provide a framework—better yet, an optic instrument such as a microscope that helps to reveal in a text what you wouldn't ordinarily see.

There are many literary theories that you can turn to when you want to direct your gaze in a certain way at a particular work.

Inquiring into the Details (*continued*)

- **New criticism:** It isn't really new anymore, but still influential. These theories encourage readers to look at a poem or story as an object that can be analyzed independently from the author's intentions or historical contexts.

- **Reader-response criticism:** You can't understand a work independently of a reader's response to it, say reader response theorists. Whatever meaning exists is necessarily a transaction between, say, the short story and the reader's experience of the short story, an experience informed by the reader's personal history and other texts he or she has read.

- **Feminist criticism:** This diverse body of theory argues, among other things, that gender figures prominently in writing and reading literature. A critic might notice, for example, how male authors have historically depicted female characters in their work, or find in often-neglected women writers an alternative view of female characters and even methods of storytelling.

- **New historicism:** We're used to interpreting a poem or story by seeing it in historical context. If you want to understand *Huck Finn*, for instance, consider the history of racial conflict in the American South. New historicism proposes that this way of using history to interpret literature is way too simplistic. New historicists believe that, while history is a useful way to interpret literature, it's only one of many interrelated "discourses" a critic should consider.

If you want to apply a literary theory to your analysis of a work, you don't have to read a score of books about it. You can find excellent summaries of each theory's methods online, including some examples of how to apply them.

▶ Film Criticism

A confession: I'm obsessed with the app "Call of Duty: Nazi Zombies." Or at least I was for about a year. And that's why the James Parker essay "Our Zombies, Ourselves" was so interesting to me. Why are zombies lurching through our minds these days, grasping and groping their way into our cultural imagination? Zombies are featured in video games, films, and popular television shows. What's up with that? The simplistic answer is that zombies are easy to hate and fun to kill. They are no longer human, after all, so it's nearly impossible to step out of bounds morally. Slaughter them with abandon.

Parker suggests our cultural obsession with zombies is more complex than that. They first plodded into a 1968 film, *Night of the Living Dead*, and what surprises Parker is that they took so long to arrive. We *need* zombies, he argues, projecting all of our own anxieties on a creature that is blank enough to provide plenty of room for whatever fears we want to inscribe.

"Our Zombies, Ourselves" analyzes a number of films, especially the *Night of the Living Dead*. Parker is interested in the zombie phenomenon, not only as it

A few of the Nazi zombies who lurch through the computer game "Call of Duty: Black Ops."

is reflected in film, but in other forms as well—books, TV, video games. He asks the inquiry question behind most critical essays: *What does this mean?* In this case, he wonders (as I do) why, now more than never, zombies have captured our imaginations.

Our Zombies, Ourselves

James Parker

The most surprising thing about the modern zombie—indeed, the only surprising thing about the modern zombie—is that he took so long to arrive. His slowness is a proverb, of course: his museumgoer's shuffle, his hospital plod. Plus he's a wobbler: the shortest path between two points is seldom the one he takes. Nonetheless, given all that had been going on, we might reasonably have expected the first modern zombies to start showing up around 1919. Twentieth-century man was already moaning and scratching his head; shambling along with bits falling off him; desensitized, industrialized, hollowed out, metaphysically evacuated....And yet not until 1968, at the dawning of the Age of Aquarius, did the zombie as we know him really make the scene.

1

(continued)

(continued)

2   Look: there he is, out of focus and deep in the shot, in the fifth minute of George A. Romero's *Night of the Living Dead*. He's wandering through a cemetery, wearing a shabby blazer, with the air of a distracted groundskeeper. In the foreground are two soberly dressed young people, Barbara and Johnny. They are visiting their father's grave. Barbara kneels and bows her head, but Johnny's a scoffer. "Hey, c'mon, Barb—church was this morning, huh? Hey, I mean praying's for church, huh?" Sniffs Barbara: "I haven't seen you in church lately." A breeze rises. Dark, frondy tree limbs wave above them like seaweed in the black-and-white afternoon, and the zombie draws near. He has begun to reel and lurch. He grabs Barbara. There's death in his skin tone, but his face is alive with a kind of stricken fixity. He bashes Johnny against a tombstone. Barbara flees in a car, but wrecks it. And now we really see him, framed disastrously in the skewed rear windshield, advancing toward us at an off-kilter zombie trot. No mistaking the message: the world is out of whack, the car is off the road, here comes the zombie.

3   And he's never stopped coming. After fertile decades bumbling in the gore/horror subbasement, he veered toward the mainstream in the early 2000s and currently enjoys a cultural profile unmatched even by his fancy-pants cousin, the vampire. Sure, we've all enjoyed *Twilight, True Blood*, vampire love, the pallor and the pangs, etc.—but it's the zombie, Old Reliable, who's really bringing home the bacon. He's the one who rides the best-seller lists and consumes the pop unconscious, whose titles spatter the humor section of your local bookstore: *Zombie Haiku, The Zen of Zombie, It's Beginning to Look a Lot Like Zombies: A Book of Zombie Christmas Carols*. People, sometimes hundreds of people, go on processional "zombie walks." Video gamers are mowing down fresh multitudes of zombies with a fervor undimmed by habit. And AMC's zombie series, *The Walking Dead*—the DVD of which is released this month—was the surprise cable smash of last year. Are we approaching, have we already reached, a zombie saturation point, or "burnout," as Max Brooks, author of the (very good) 2006 zombie novel *World War Z*, has put it? I say no. The zombie keeps on: it's what he does.

4   His origins, we learn—we who dabble in the recklessly expanding field of zombie studies—are in Caribbean folk nightmare. For the people of Haiti, the *zombi* was one who had died and been buried, only to be malignantly revived and enslaved by a sorcerer, or *bokor*. Look: there's the zombie in 1929, the year William Seabrook published his sensational account of Haitian voodoo lore, *The Magic Island*. He's working in the cane fields, his eyes like "the eyes of a dead man" but his hands "callused, solid, human." And there he is in 1932, in the Halperin Brothers' *White Zombie*—his cinematic debut—trudging with alienated obedience behind his dark master (played by Béla Lugosi). At night he works with other zombies in the sugar mill. The blades of the great thresher groan magnificently, zombifically, as they turn. A zombie falls in. Oh well.

5   So Romero did not invent the zombie. But he cut him loose: the graveyard zombie in *Night of the Living Dead* may be punishing Johnny, in the finest

horror-flick tradition, for being cheeky on hallowed ground, but he himself is no longer a supernatural figure. No demon or magus possesses him, no enchantment holds him. The zombifier seems to be technology: radioactive contamination from an exploded space probe. Zombiedom runs amok, moving virally through the population. The zombie wants live human flesh, and those still in possession of it are advised, via TV and radio, to barricade themselves indoors. Romero was laying down the new canons of zombiehood: the wobbliness of the zombie, the terrible mobility of the virus, the pockets of survival, the squall of information as the grid collapses.

Severed thus from his heritage, sent freewheeling into postmodernity with nothing to say on his own behalf (because he can't talk, because he's a *zombie*), our hero would seem to be in a position of great semiotic vulnerability. And so it has proved: all manner of meanings have been and continue to be plastered onto the zombie. Much can be made of him, because he makes so little of himself. He is the consumer, the mob, the Other, the proletariat, the weight of life, the dead soul. He is too many e-mails in your inbox, a kind of cosmic spam. He is everything rejected and inexpugnable. He comes back, he comes back, feebly but unstoppably, and as he drags you down, a fatal lethargy overtakes you.   6

None of this is to ignore the plentiful variations that have been worked upon Romero's zombie theme since 1968. Recent years, for example, have given us both the Sprinting or Galloping Zombie of Danny Boyle's *28 Days Later* and Zack Snyder's *Dawn of the Dead* remake, and the Comic-Existential Zombie of Edgar Wright's *Shaun of the Dead*. In the Boyle/Snyder model, the zombie is wild-eyed and very fast. The virus, too, has been ferally accelerated: now, scant seconds after having your throat ripped out, you stand up snarling and race off in search of prey. *Shaun of the Dead* is gentler and more profound: here zombiedom seems to germinate through a fog of hangovers, Monday mornings, lapses in conversation. Shaun refuses to *become*; his job (selling televisions) demeans him; his nice girlfriend wants him to give up smoking and stop spending so much time down the pub. He will not, he cannot, and the dead throng the streets. As the future peters out, the present blooms with zombies.   7

But sometimes a zombie is just a zombie. Strike that: a zombie is always just a zombie. The blow-'em-all-away success of *The Walking Dead* is no mystery: the show, and the comic-book series by Robert Kirkman on which it's based, mark a triumphant return to zombie orthodoxy, to the non-galloping zombie and his icons. Once again, and with great gladness, we see shotguns, frantically tuned radios, smoke pillars of apocalypse on the horizon—the full zombie opera. The zombie himself has never looked better, dripping with wounds, full of conviction. With his dangling stethoscope, or his policeman's uniform, or his skateboard, he exhibits the pathos of his ex-personhood. He flaps and sighs. He crookedly advances. He's taking his time. But he'll get there.   8

Inquiring into the Essay

1. **Explore.** You really can't avoid zombies (or vampires, for that matter). They're everywhere we look these days. The question is this: Why? In this essay, James Parker writes that "much can be made of [the zombie] because he makes so little of himself." In your journal, spend some time exploring your thinking about this. Parker has given you some of his ideas. What do you make of them? What is he missing? How would you explain the cultural fascination with these hobbling, slack-jawed, flesh-eating creatures of the night?

2. **Explain.** Try to "say back" what you take to be Parker's thesis in his essay. First, identify the passage in "Our Zombies, Ourselves" that is key to your understanding of the main thing the essay is trying to say. Then use this and any other relevant passages to summarize the key ideas in the essay.

3. **Evaluate.** Is this essay persuasive? Based on your own experiences and observations, along with the exploratory writing you did in response to the first question, what do you find most and least convincing about Parker's argument?

4. **Reflect.** We typically think of the critical essay—if we think about it at all—as a creature of the English class, a form of writing about literature. It is that, to be sure, but as this essay demonstrated, critical analysis can also analyze cultural trends, and pose the same question we ask about literature: What might it mean? Social undercurrents, like zombie love, are always changing. Literature, on the other hand, seems static; after all, Hemingway isn't coming out with another version of *Old Man and the Sea*. Is it true that a published short story or essay has relatively fixed meanings?

Seeing the Form

Young Ladies on the Banks of the Seine by Gustave Coubet

If a photograph can be thought of as a form of nonfiction, then a painting compares well with fiction or poetry. The painting certainly has a strong relationship to the real; after all, the painter sees the world we all live in and expresses that vision in the work. That expression may be realistic, impressionistic, or abstract, but it is firmly rooted in things that can be seen, smelled, heard, and touched. Yet unlike photographers who work with the visual materials presented to them through the viewfinder, the painter can transform these materials through invention. If it works better that the woman's dress is pink rather than blue, then pink it shall be. Similarly, fiction writers' primary obligation is to the story, not reality, and they invent characters and make them do things that contribute tension and meaning to the narrative.

Interpreting a painting, then, such as Gustave Coubet's painting, *Young Ladies on the Banks of the Seine*, is much like interpreting fiction. The painting acts as a text that, like a short story, is a complete invention and whose meaning is implicit

Other Ways of Seeing (*continued*)

Young Ladies on the Banks of the Seine River (1856), Gustave Courbet. Oil on canvas. Petit Palais, Musée Des Beaux-Arts De La Ville De Paris. The Bridgeman Art Library/Getty Images.

rather than explicit. Therefore "reading" Coubet's painting should involve the kind of interpretive moves you might employ in reading any literature.

In analyzing *Young Ladies on the Banks of the Seine* and other paintings, it can be helpful to consider the following basic terms and concepts:

- *Line:* In artistic composition, the line is the direction the viewer's gaze travels when looking at the painting, something that is managed by the placement of forms and their relative size. In a good painting, the viewer's eye is directed to the main focal point of the picture, and away from unimportant elements. Some questions to ask about line include whether the painting succeeds in encouraging your gaze to move smoothly to the main objects of interest, or whether the line is confusing, making you feel as if you're not quite sure where to look. Do things flow visually?

- *Hierarchy:* Do you sense that some visual elements are more important than others? In a well-composed painting, you should. Artists can manage this in a number of ways, including with the size and location of various objects in the

Other Ways of Seeing (*continued*)

painting, and in doing so they are communicating something important about the overall theme of the work. What, for example, might the emphasis on certain objects in the painting imply about its meaning? What is the relationship among these things, and what does that imply?

■ ***Color:*** The arrangement of color in a painting influences its mood. Certain colors are cool—blues, greens, purples, and their many combinations—and these tend to recede in a painting. Other colors—yellows, oranges, and reds—are warm and can be perceived as coming forward. Color is obviously enormously expressive when handled well. How do the colors the artist chose affect the mood of the work? How might that mood contribute to its overall theme or idea?

■ ***Value:*** To create the sense of dimension, artists use light and dark tones. In a black-and-white drawing, these tones are white to black and all the shades of gray in between. In a color painting, value is often managed by using various shades of a color. Without value, a painting looks flat, one-dimensional. With it, the subjects look more realistic. How much emphasis is there on value in the painting? How realistic is the image?

■ ***Composition:*** All of these qualities—line, color, value, hierarchy—and more contribute to a painting's composition. One of the key qualities of composition is balance, and this can be achieved in a number of ways, including arranging visual elements symmetrically or asymmetrically. Or this can be done using something called the "golden mean," an ancient mathematical concept that has historically influenced art and architecture and which represents proportions often seen in nature, including the spiral of a sea shell and the proportions of the human body. What do you notice about the composition of the painting? How is it arranged to influence your feelings, and how does it seem to contribute to the overall theme or idea?

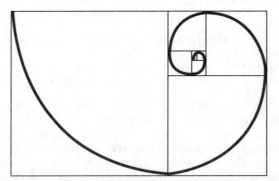

Figure 7.2   The golden mean is a mathematical formula that when applied to a rectangle creates spatial relationships that are particularly pleasing to the eye. This is the so-called golden rectangle. For centuries, artists have exploited this principle, creating proportions in paintings and buildings based on these calculations. Can you see how Coubet's painting is visually organized to adhere to the golden rectangle?

THE WRITING PROCESS

Inquiry Project **Writing a Critical Essay**

Inquiry Question: What might it mean?

Write an essay about a poem, short story, or essay—maybe one of the works in this chapter or something your instructor recommends. Alternatively, do a critical analysis of a visual work of art—a painting, photograph, or film. Whatever the subject, make sure your essay does the following:

- Focuses on an *aspect* of the subject. While you begin with the inquiry question *What does it mean?* your paper should be focused on exploring that, by looking closely at a few things in the work.

- Argues for a particular interpretation of the work, using specifics from it to support your assertion.

- If possible, uses the work of other critics, when relevant, to develop your argument.

Prose+

- Build a web page around your critical essay, embedding video or audio of interviews with the author of the work and links to the work of other critics who comment on it. You might also add images, including those that you think echo the interpretation you're arguing for. Other features might include a bibliography with links to the sources you used, a list of other featured works by the author or artist, a sidebar that highlights an important passage, etc.

- Develop a PowerPoint or Pages presentation for your critical essay, or as a supplement to it. This would be especially effective if you're analyzing a visual work, because you can include close-ups of significant features that are key to your interpretation. But a slide presentation can be effective for conventional literary analysis, too. Consider developing slides that provide background on the work, a statement of your thesis, and then slides of key passages or quotes from criticism that you're using as evidence.

- Using a program such as Microsoft's Photo Story 3 or iMovie, develop a photographic interpretation of a piece of music that you like. Importing the soundtrack and drawing on your own digital photographs or those you find online, create a visual story that reflects your particular interpretation of the music. Add text to some of the images, if relevant.

What Are You Going to Write About?

It's likely that your instructor will ask you to write a critical essay on one or more of the readings in this chapter, or perhaps an assigned reading from another book. But if your assignment is more open-ended, possible subjects are everywhere. Anything that is confusing or ambiguous invites interpretation: a photograph, sculpture, film, cultural trend such as the popularity of reality TV or zombies, etc. The following prompts should help you explore some of these possibilities and consider ways of analyzing an assigned text.

In the conversation between what a text says and what it might be saying, you discover fresh understandings of what you read.

Opening Up

7.3

Use appropriate invention strategies to discover a topic for a critical essay.

Listing Prompts. First, spend some time playing with ideas, without censoring yourself. Lists can be rich sources for triggering topics. Let them grow freely, and when you're ready, use an item as the focus of another list or an episode of fastwriting. Divide your notebook into columns with the following headings

Cultural trends	Great songs	Favorite movies	Favorite books, stories, essays	Memorable pictures, paintings, images

In each column, generate a fast list of things that come to mind. What cultural trends do you find hard to explain, what songs do you find strangely moving, what films or TV shows capture your interest? Are there books you love, paintings or photographs you remember?

If you're writing about a work of literature, try making the following list:

1. Brainstorm a list of questions about the work that you find puzzling.

2. List the names of every important character or person in the story or essay. Choose one or two that seem most important. Under each name, make two new headings: Dreams and Problems. Under Dreams, list the things that character seems to desire most, even if he or she isn't fully aware of it. Under Problems, list everything that seems to be an obstacle to that character's achieving those desires.

3. List details or particulars from the story that seem to say more than they say. In other words, do any details recur? Do any objects have particular significance to one or more characters? Do any descriptions suggest the feelings, dispositions, or values of a particular character?

Fastwriting Prompts. Remember, fastwriting is a great way to stimulate creative thinking. Turn off your critical side and let yourself write "badly."

1. Choose one of the items in a column from your listing prompts to write about. Fastwrite about your experience with that thing. What do you remember? What do you notice? Do you feel something about this? Why?

If you're writing about a work of literature, try these prompts:

2. Write a narrative of thought. Begin with *When I first read this story or essay, I thought . . . And then I thought . . . And then . . . And then . . .*

3. Choose three lines or passages that are key to your current understanding of the themes or ideas behind the story or essay. Write these down on the left page of your notebook. On the opposing right page, fastwrite about each, beginning with *The first thing I notice about this passage is . . . And then . . . And then . . . And then . . .* When the writing stalls, write about the next line or passage until you've written about all three.

4. Use one of the following "seed sentences" as a prompt for fastwriting:

   - What is the relationship between _____ and _____?
   - The most important scene in the story is _____ because _____.
   - The title of the work might be significant because _____.
   - If I was going to divide the poem, story, or essay into parts, the first part would be _____.
   - The narrator in the work seems to want _____.

Visual Prompts. Visual thinking might help you play with ideas about how to analyze the work you're studying. Try these prompts to explore your response to a literary work:

1. Create a cluster using the name of the main character as the core word. Reread the story and then build as many associations as you can from that character. Think about feelings and ideas you associate with that person as well as any particulars you remember from the story.

2. Make a visual map of the story. Begin by placing a brief description of what you believe is the most significant moment in the story at the center of a blank page. This might be a turning point, or the point of highest tension, or perhaps the moment when the main character achieves his or her desires and dreams. Consider that moment the destination of the story. Now map out events or details in the narrative that threaten to lead the protagonist away from that destination, and those that appear to lead the protagonist toward it.

Research Prompts. Critical analysis usually involves working with primary sources: the poem, novel, essay, photograph, or painting. Sometimes, especially if the work isn't a text, you have to observe the object, performance, or behavior. If you're looking for a subject like these for your critical essay, then you need to go out and look. This field work might include

1. Attending a performance (e.g., watching the modern dance, going to see the drama, etc.)

2. Observing a behavior (e.g., observing how people behave in a certain social situation)

3. Going to the museum (e.g., browsing paintings)

4. Seeing the films or shows (e.g., an evening watching zombie films)

On the other hand, if you're looking for a literary text to analyze, you can research your favorite authors' work online, but you can also research top-ten lists of short stories, poems, and essays. There are annual "Best of" collections published every year in your university library.

Inquiring into the Details

Common Literary Devices

Many key concepts provide useful frameworks for analyzing literature. The key is to see the following ideas as an angle for viewing an essay, story, or poem much as you might move around a subject with a camera. Each provides a different way of seeing the same thing. In addition, each becomes a platform from which to pose a question about a text.

- ■ *Plot and significant event:* This is what happens in a story that moves it forward. One way of thinking about plot is to consider this: What are the key moments that propel the story forward? Why do you consider them key? How do they add tension to the story? In an essay, these moments often give rise to the question the writer is exploring. In short stories, there is often a significant event that may happen in or outside of the story, but the entire narrative and its characters act or think in response to that event.

- ■ *Characters:* Imagine a still pond upon which small paper boats float. Someone throws a rock in the pond—big or small—and the ripples extend outward, moving the boats this way and that. Depending on the size of the ripples, some of the boats may list or capsize, sinking slowly. Characters in a short story are like those boats, responding in some way to something that happened, some significant event that is revealed or implied. They move almost imperceptibly, or quite noticeably, or even violently. Is there logic to their response? How exactly are they changed? How do they relate to each other?

- ■ *Setting:* Where a story takes place can matter a lot or a little, but it always matters. Why? Because where a story takes place signals things about characters and who they are. A story set in rural Wyoming suggests a certain austere, ranching culture in which the characters operate. Even if they're not ranchers, they must somehow deal with that culture. Similarly, a story set in Chicago's predominantly black South Side introduces another set of constraints within which characters must operate. In some cases, setting might even become a kind of character.

- ■ *Point of view:* In nonfiction essays, point of view is usually straightforward—we assume the narrator is the author. But in fiction, it's much more complicated; in fact, *how* a story is told—from what perspective—is a crucial aesthetic decision. Stories told from the first-person point of view in the present tense give the story a sense of immediacy—this feels like it's happening *now*—but at the same time limit our understanding of other characters, because we can't get into their heads. So-called omniscient narrators can introduce a feeling of distance from

---

Inquiring into the Details (*continued*)

the action, but they are also gratifyingly godlike because they can see every-thing, hovering above all the action and even entering characters' minds at will. Why might an author have chosen a particular point of view? Is the narrator trust-worthy? What might be his or her biases, and how might they affect the telling?

- ■ ***Theme:*** One way to understand a story or essay is to consider that everything—character, point of view, and setting—all contribute to a central meaning. In a good story, everything is there for a purpose—to say something to the reader about what it means to be human. In essays, this theme may be explicit, because essays both show *and* tell. Short stories, and especially poems, are often short on explanation of theme, operating with more ambiguity. The writer hopes the reader can *infer* certain ideas or feelings by paying close attention to what he or she *shows* the reader. To get at the theme, begin with the simple question *So what?* Why is the author telling this story or sharing this experience? What significance are we supposed to attach to it?

- ■ ***Image:*** Stories and poems ask us to see. When I read them, I imagine that writers take my face in their hands and gently—or sometimes brutally—direct my gaze. What are they insisting that I look at, and how do they want me to see it? Images that recur may also be significant.

Narrowing Down

Now that you've opened up possibilities for review topics, there are choices to make. Which do you want to write about?

What's Promising Material and What Isn't? Try out a possible topic for your critical essay by doing some more-focused writing and by thinking about it.

First, generate some thinking-through-writing.

- ■ **First thoughts?** Interpretation is inspired by this question: *What might it mean?* And that's not a bad question to start with. Spend some time rereading, observing, or studying the work you've tentatively chosen, and if you're using a double-entry journal, collect notes (e.g., key passages, lists of observations, descriptions, etc.) on the left-facing page of your journal. Then, on the right, fastwrite for as long as you can, exploring and speculating about possible interpretations. When the writing stalls, pick up on something in your notes on the left page. This writing should be very open-ended; you don't need to come to conclusions yet.

Now judge what you've generated:

- ■ **Can you refine your question?** Reread your fastwrite. Do you see hints that you might explore about a relationship between two things? For example, what's the relationship between the author's description of the setting in the story and the idea you think is at its heart? Craft a relationship question from your fastwrite, using a template like this:

   What's the relationship between _____ and _____?

  ▪ Drawing on your thinking so far, can you turn the interpretation question (What does it mean?) into an assertion? For example, in the poem "The Bluebird" by Charles Bukowski, the narrator's "secret pact" with the "little" bird represents the bargain that many men in this culture make with themselves to conceal feelings using "toughness."

Considering doing some research to generate ideas on your tentative topic. In addition to searching for relevant material on Google and Google Scholar, search the databases at the university library for published articles or books on the author of your work and criticism of the particular piece you're analyzing. For this research, use specialized databases in the appropriate fields. For example,

  ▪ *Literary works.* Search the *MLA International Bibliography*.

  ▪ *Art.* Check databases such as ARTstor and ARTbibliographies Modern for criticism of contemporary work, or Art and Architecture Complete.

  ▪ *Film.* The AFI Catalog is a definitive database on American films. Many arts and humanities indexes also cover film studies.

Questions About Audience and Purpose. One basic rhetorical question is this: Is your audience familiar with the work you're interpreting? If not, should you provide background so that they share enough knowledge of it to appreciate your analysis? This might include things like

  ▪ *Background on the work.* When was it published or created? How was it received? What was it compared to?

  ▪ *Summary or description.* What is the basic plot? What happens? What does it say? What does it look like?

  ▪ *Background on the author.* Significance in literary or artistic circles? How the thing being analyzed fits into the body of work?

Another key rhetorical consideration is finding ways to interest readers in the work you're analyzing, especially if they're unfamiliar with it. Why should they care about your analysis of Charles Bukowski's poem or your interpretation of the relationship between personality and how people hold a beer? Think about ways in which the thing you're studying is relevant to understanding everyday experience. That's not so hard with your interpretations of barroom behavior. But a poem? Make it interesting. Why is this poem important? How does it speak to how we might live and feel? How does it speak to you?

Writing the Sketch

We'll begin again with an early draft, a sketch that represents an initial attempt to discover what you want to focus on and what you might have to say about the work (or works) you've chosen.

Develop your sketch with the following things in mind:

  ▪ It should have a tentative title.

  ▪ It should be at least 500 to 600 words.

- Write it with the appropriate audience in mind. Are you writing for readers who are familiar with the text?

- Consider writing your sketch as a narrative of thought that tells the story of how you arrived at your current interpretation of the work you're studying. *When I began analyzing _____, I thought _____. And then...And then...And now...*

▶ Student Sketch

When Julie Bird read Leslie Marmon Silko's short story "Lullaby" for the first time, she said "It almost made me cry." In class, we talked a little about some of the traditions in Native American literature, and you can see in her sketch how she tries out several of the ideas we talked about: the importance of the storytelling tradition, the ways in which identity is tied to going home, and the healing power of the natural world. There are all kinds of literary traditions that are lenses through which you can read a story.

But the most important thing is to pay close attention to the text itself. What *exactly* does the story say, and what might it mean? Julie doesn't incorporate many passages from "Lullaby" in her sketch; she's thinking through some ideas about key themes in the story. She underlines several ideas that emerged in this first look. Now she has to return to the story and test the ideas against what the text actually says.

What Is the Role of Nature in "Lullaby"?
Julie Bird

"Lullaby," written by Leslie Marmon Silko, is an intriguing story about the life of a 1 Navajo woman by the name of Ayah and her life. Ayah bared her soul to tell this story, an act of special meaning in a culture that passes on history by oral means. The Navajos often connect their identity to family, home, and nature. When the white man came to take away her children, Ayah, not fully understanding why, grabbed them and ran up the long slope of the mesa, to wait for her husband to come home. While she was waiting, she allowed the sun to relax her and felt as if "she could walk into the sky, stepping through clouds endlessly." The connection of peace to the natural world is key to the essay's theme.

Ayah, using the wool blanket as an instrument, created strong parallels between her 2 mother (the past) and her son Jimmie (her present). This generational timeline establishes her identity by correlating the comfort of the past with the warmth of the present. The wool blanket is the object of that unbroken line. At the end of the story, Ayah is searching for her husband and she is thinking, "She did this because she had the blanket, and there would be no place for him except with her and the blanket in the old abode barn near the arroyo." The blanket is significant to the characters in revealing the importance of family ties to the Navajos.

3   The overall theme of the essay relates to the sorrow and loss Ayah feels at the hands of the white man, and her inability to do anything about it. First, a government man comes to tell her that her son Jimmie was killed at war. Next, more government officials dupe her into signing her name in order to take away her children. To this she states, "Because it was like the old ones always told her about learning their language or any of their ways: it endangered you." When Chato was too old to work, the rancher made them move out of their home, and they had to go to the barn.

4   Through all of the sorrow put upon her, Ayah was able to turn to her identity and connection with her heritage, nature, and roots to find peace and strength to continue on.

Moving from Sketch to Draft

How well does your sketch lead you to an assertion about the meaning of the work or situation you're analyzing? Do you have a clear focus?

Evaluating Your Own Sketch. Among the key concerns in evaluating this early draft of your critical essay is whether you've discovered a workable focus and whether you're beginning to get some clear idea of what you're trying to say. One of the best things you can do at this point is to use your sketch to craft a tentative thesis *or* the question that will be the focus of the next draft.

- **Thesis.** On the back of your sketch, in a sentence or two (but no more), state the main thing you're trying to communicate in answer to the question *What does it mean?*
- **Inquiry question.** Compose a question that reflects what you want to focus on in your interpretation. A relationship? The significance of certain recurring elements? An analysis based on a certain context—when the work was written or a tradition or theory?

Reflecting on What You've Learned. At the beginning of this chapter, I talked about some of the basic elements of critical analysis (see p. 222) and said that a close examination of *evidence* leads to inferences about what the evidence might mean. This leads to an *interpretation* that you think makes sense, and, drawing on the evidence, an *argument* that convinces someone else of the soundness of your interpretation. How well did you incorporate those three elements into your sketch? What needs more development in the next draft? What does this tell you about the act of interpretation? Does the critical essay encourage a kind of thinking that can be distinguished from the thinking encouraged by other forms of writing?

Developing

To develop your sketch into a draft, work on two fronts:

1. Closer analysis of the primary work or phenomenon
2. Research in secondary sources on the context of the thing you're writing about: what other critics say, theories that guide the analysis, relevant background on the work or situation

Analysis. Interpretation is an inductive process. By looking closely at the specifics, you develop ideas about patterns in the work that might be significant. If you're studying a text, for example, then your analysis must be grounded in what exactly you see in the poem, story, or essay. In literary analysis, for example, you might focus on common devices such as setting and characters (see "Inquiring into the Details: Common Literary Devices" on p. 244). What *exactly* is the setting? What do the characters say *exactly* and when? What you look at will depend, of course, on your thesis or inquiry question. This evidence is the foundation of any critical essay, because it helps writers discover the *reasons* that support a particular interpretation.

Research. Any significant work of art—a painting or novel or a cultural artifact such as reality TV or Facebook profile pictures—exists in context. These contexts include:

- **Historical.** When was it created? Is it part of a tradition? In what ways does the work or performance reflect the politics and culture of its time?
- **Theoretical.** What are some critical methods for analyzing the thing (for literary works, for example, see "Inquiring into the Details: Why Literary Theory Is Not a Sleep Aid" on p. 233).
- **Biographical.** Who created the work? What does the author say about it or about his or her aesthetic intentions?
- **Critical.** What do other critics who have studied the work or phenomenon say about it?

To do this research on the context of the thing you're analyzing, you'll rely most heavily on scholarly sources in your university library. For example, here are some academic sources typically used in analyzing a literary work. Search as well for books on your author, work, or topic.

Historical	*Oxford Encyclopedia of American Literature, Cambridge History of English and American Literature, The Literary Encyclopedia*
Theoretical	*MLA International Bibliography, Magill's History of Literary Criticism*
Biographical	*Dictionary of Literary Biography, Biography Index Past and Present, Contemporary Authors*
Critical	*MLA International Bibliography, Book Review Index, Essay & General Literature Index, Magill's Bibliography of Contemporary Literary Criticism*

Drafting

Because a critical essay is an argument, your draft needs to make one. If you're writing a formal critical paper, then your thesis—the interpretation that is at the heart of your argument—should be stated explicitly pretty early in your paper. In a less formal critical essay (see "Our Zombies, Ourselves" earlier in the chapter), the thesis isn't necessarily a fixture of the introduction. You might work your way to it, like the unraveling of a ball of string. The question that is driving your essay, however, should be clear in the beginning (e.g., What does the popularity of zombies in American film say about us?)

Methods of Development. Like most writing, there is no formula for structuring your critical essay, but if you're writing for an audience that is relatively unfamiliar with your subject, you might imagine that your draft needs to answer a series of questions in roughly the following order:

- What do you find particularly interesting in the work or phenomena that inspired your analysis? (Show something specific.)
- What's the question that interests you? (Your thesis that answers that question?)
- Can you summarize or describe what you're analyzing?
- What have other critics or experts said about it? (Maybe some alternative interpretations, different from yours?)
- What's a reason behind your interpretation? What's the evidence that led you to see it?
- What's another reason? And the evidence?
- Can you tell me again what your close analysis or observation helped you to see about the meaning of the work or phenomenon?

What are some of the other ways you might organize your critical essay?

Narrative. An entirely different approach is to use your question as the starting point for a story you tell about how you arrived at an answer. This approach is more essayistic in the sense that it provides the story of *how* you came to know rather than reporting *what* you think. A narrative essay might also involve relevant autobiographical details that influenced your analysis. For example, what feelings or experiences do you *bring* to the reading of a text?

Question to Answer. Because the assignment is designed around a question you're trying to answer about the topic, the question-to-answer design is an obvious choice. Consider spending the first part of your essay highlighting the question you're interested in. The key is to convince readers that yours is a question worth asking, and that the answer might be interesting to discover.

Compare and Contrast. Critical essays often benefit from this method of development. The approach might be to compare and contrast certain elements within the work. In a story there might be several characters, symbols or metaphors, plot developments, and so on—or you might compare the work to others by the same or even different authors. These comparisons have to be relevant to the question you're asking.

Combining Approaches. Frequently, a critical essay uses several or even all of the methods of development mentioned here: question to answer, comparison and contrast, and narrative. Consider how you might put them all to work, especially in certain sections of your draft.

Using Evidence. You need to consider two main kinds of evidence in a critical essay: evidence that comes from so-called *primary* sources—especially the work itself, but also letters or memoirs by the author; and evidence that comes from *secondary* sources, or books, articles, and essays by critics who are also writing about the work or author. Primary sources are generally most important. In more-personal literary responses, however, your personal associations, anecdotes, stories, or feelings may be used as evidence, if they're relevant to the question you're posing.

Workshopping

As you know, a critical essay argues for a particular interpretation of a text or phenomenon. As you prepare to share your draft, you want to look for some of these weak links in your argument; consider asking peer reviewers whether you've addressed them:

- **Insufficient evidence.** Remember that this is a form of writing that works mostly with *primary sources*—the short story, the film(s), the firsthand observations, etc. Most of the information in your essay should be your close examination of the primary sources you're focusing on.

- **Broad focus.** Even lengthy critical essays look only at *certain aspects* of the primary source that most contributed to the writer's interpretation.

- **General interpretation.** After all your analysis, you're not going to write something like "zombies are everywhere in film and are an interesting cultural phenomenon" as your thesis. That might be a setup for your thesis, which must be an interpretation with a much sharper edge: *The rise of the zombie in American film is testimony to the growing cultural nightmare that there are no safe places anymore, especially with the spread of nuclear weapons.*

In addition to these concerns, when you workshop the first draft of your critical essay, you should focus first on what peers make of the purpose and meaning of your essay, both of which guide your revision. The following grid can help you frame these questions for your workshop group.

Questions for Peer Reviewers	
1. Purpose	After reading the draft, can you explain back to me why I think the topic I chose to analyze is significant? Do I convince you that it might be significant to you, too?
2. Meaning	In your own words, how does the essay answer the inquiry question *What does it mean?* What evidence did you find most convincing in support of this interpretation? Least convincing?

Reflecting on the Draft. Take a look at the draft before you and circle the passage you think is the best in the essay so far. Now circle the passage that you think is weakest.

In your notebook, fastwrite for five minutes about both passages. What seems to be working in the better passage? What problems do you notice about the weaker one? Does either one address the question you're writing about? If so, how? If not, how might it? When you compare the two passages, what do you notice about the differences? How might you make the weaker passage more like the stronger one? How might you make the rest of the essay stronger?

Revising

7.4

Apply revision strategies that are effective for the critical essay.

Revision is a continual process—not a last step. You've been revising—"reseeing" your subject—from the first messy fastwriting in your journal. But the things that get your attention vary depending on where you are in the writing process. With your draft in hand, revision becomes your focus through what I'll call "shaping and tightening your draft."

Chapter 10 contains strategies that can help you revise any inquiry project. There are also certain things to think about that are especially useful for shaping a critical essay.

Shaping. When we shape a draft, the focus is on design—the order of information, the chain of reasoning, the coherence of paragraphs and their contribution to the whole composition. In a critical essay, one of the basic units of reasoning is the moments of analysis in your essay, or those places where you actually work with a primary source to tease out its implications.

Here's an example from a critical essay I once wrote on how American Indian writers seem to use memory in their fiction, poetry, and nonfiction. My focus here was on Sherman Alexie's work, and his character Thomas-Builds-the-Fire, who appears in several of the writer's stories.

> I think that the implications of this—that tribal memory and personal memory merge—are profound. Perhaps that's why nobody wants to listen to the stories of Thomas Builds-the-Fire in Spokane/Coeur d'Alène writer Sherman Alexie's recent **Interpretation** works, *Reservation Blues* and *Tonto and the Lone Ranger Fistfight in Heaven.* Thomas, whose stories came to him before he "had the words to speak" (*Reservation* 73), tells stories that many of the Indians on the Spokane reservation refuse to hear, "stealth stories" that work their way into dreams and into "clothes like sand, [that] gave you itches that could not be scratched" (15). I wonder if the antipathy to Thomas's stories is really resistance to the hegemonic power of someone else's story to structure and contain individual experience and memory. Is that **Evidence** why Victor and Junior, two Spokanes who are adrift, unable to find the symmetry between personal past, history, and legend that Momaday discovers in *Rainy Mountain,* "tried to beat those stories out of Thomas, tied him down and taped his mouth shut" (*Reservation* 15).

Notice how the analysis here is *layered.* An interpretation is introduced and then explicated with evidence, which then leads to an elaboration of the initial interpretation and ends with some supporting evidence.

Examine your own paragraphs in a similar way. Take a highlighter and use two different colors, one for interpretation (assertion) and the other for evidence. Look to see if your analysis is layered—working back and forth from your ideas about a work or phenomenon and the evidence from the text or your observations—and if not, revise to encourage that quality in paragraphs or passages of your draft.

Polishing

Shaping focuses on things such as purpose, meaning, and design. No less important is looking more closely at paragraphs, sentences, and words. Are your paragraphs coherent? How do you manage transitions? Are your sentences fluent and concise? Are there any errors in spelling or syntax? Chapter 10 can help you focus on these issues.

Before you finish your draft, work through the following checklist:

✓ Every paragraph is about one thing.

✓ The transitions between paragraphs aren't abrupt.

✓ The length of sentences varies in each paragraph.

✓ Each sentence is concise. There are no unnecessary words or phrases.

✓ You've checked grammar, particularly verb agreement, run-on sentences, unclear pronouns, and misused words (*there/their, where/were,* and so on).

✓ You've run your spellchecker and proofed your paper for misspelled words.

Chapter 10 is a buffet of revision strategies that will help you solve all kinds of revision problems, large and small.

▶ Student Essay

Julie Bird's sketch earlier in this chapter about Leslie Marmon Silko's short story "Lullaby" showed traces of the ideas behind this draft. Julie touches on the question behind her inquiry into the story—how does the character Ayah recover from her many losses?—and finds a tentative answer: Ayah finds peace in nature. Sketches are just that—roughly drawn glimpses into our own thinking about something. When they're most helpful, this "bad" writing can help us discover what we want to say, as it did here for Julie.

But notice how Julie takes the idea that nature is a powerful force in the story and extends and deepens it in the draft. The result is that her thesis is richer and more interesting. How did she do this? By returning to the dialectical process—that motion between creative thinking and critical thinking—and immersing herself in the story itself. Julie also did some research on Silko and Native American literature, testing her assertions. She found not only evidence to support them, but new ways of thinking about what she wants to say.

Nature as Being: Landscape in Silko's "Lullaby"

Julie Bird

1   Leslie Marmon Silko, the author of "Lullaby," is a Native American writer from the Laguna Pueblo culture in New Mexico. Silko's story is about a Navajo woman, Ayah, and how she copes with the loss of her children—one dies in war, several others die in infancy, and two more are taken by the "white doctors" who suspect the children may have been exposed to tuberculosis. How is Ayah, condemned to poverty and surrounded by white indifference or hatred, able to recover from these losses?

2   Reflecting the "interrelatedness of man and nature that permeates Native American literature" (Schweninger 49), it is in the landscape that Ayah finds peace in old age. Arizona's natural environment, such as snow and the slope of the mesa, is an integral character in "Lullaby" that shows the intricate relationship between humans and the natural world.

3   Even the structure of the story echoes these themes. Silko writes her story from the end, to the beginning, to the end in the same cyclical fashion as life in the natural world and on the reservation. The writer portrays this cyclical structure of storytelling beautifully when describing Ayah as an old woman, as she reflects on the birth of her children through to the death of her husband.

4   Trying to find peace in the harmony of the natural world, Ayah turned herself to the memories of a happier past, and the rituals and rhythms of the earth's cycle. When saddened

by thoughts of her dead son Jimmie, lost in some faraway war, Ayah wraps herself in a wool blanket that he had sent to her. This unconscious gesture invariably brings the memory of sitting with her grandma and mother and combing twigs from the freshly washed wool while they weaved it into blankets. Ayah fondly remembers that "the blankets...were soft and woven so tight that rain rolled off them like birds' feathers" (Silko 44). Through Ayah's reference to the feathers, Silko is making the connection to her own beliefs in the natural world. In a sense, Ayah becomes a bird.

When Ayah runs into the foothills of the "juniper trees and black lava" (45) in order to get her children away from the white doctors, she is seeking the place of refuge that is a constant source of comfort. It is her ritual to return to this spot. Ayah comes to the mesa when her son Jimmie dies, when she buries her children who died too soon, when the doctors take her children; in other words, when she is looking for balance. To Ayah, "the sun's warmth relaxed her and took the fear and anger away....It seemed to her that she could walk into the sky, stepping through clouds endlessly" (46).

This harmony that Ayah shares with the natural world is what makes her who she is; it is her identity as a Navajo woman. This is especially obvious at the end of the story when she is sitting with her dying husband, a man crushed by hopelessness and alcoholism. Silko writes that "The light was crystalline....She breathed the clarity of the night sky; she smelled the purity of the half moon and the stars" (51). Silko makes a point that upon the death of her husband, Ayah at last felt a clear ("crystalline") understanding. With the passing of the storm, "steely blue-gray horses startled across the sky" (51), and with the passing away of the last of her family, Ayah was finally free to find her own peace. In old age, Ayah finally achieved her balance with the harmony of nature and was ready for it.

Just hearing the word "snow" evokes images of "freezing" and "icy," but Silko uses snow to project Ayah's feelings of warmth and comfort. Music, like nature, is a very integral part of some Native American cultures, and Silko expresses the correlation between music and the natural world throughout the story. For example, when Ayah is waiting for her husband to return home from a bar, she "sat down with her back against the wide cottonwood tree...and listened to the wind and snow sing a highpitched Yeibechei song" (43).

We learn from Silko that the Yeibechei song is the Navajo Night Chant and is a ceremony of healing. The fact that the snow sings such a song further reinforces the idea that nature is a healing force in the story. When Ayah is watching as the "snow drifted...with the northwest wind hurling it in gusts," and "she smiled at the snow which was trying to cover her little by little" (44), Silko suggests that the snow, like the blanket, is a source of comfort to Ayah. And when Ayah is sitting next to her dying husband, the snow storm clears up and the night is still and clear. This is significant in that it parallels the clearing of Ayah's troubles, the passing of the figurative storm within herself.

At the end, Ayah sings her lullaby: "The earth is your mother,...the sky is your father,...rainbow is your sister,...the winds are your brothers" (51). It is hard to miss the balance of nature with humanity that is a part of the Navajo heritage. But Ayah's lullaby also points to Silko's particular vision of the role of nature. Landscapes aren't something to be looked at as separate from people. As the critic Karen E. Waldron notes, "Silko's poems, essays,

(continued)

(continued)

and novels manifest the relationship between the human being and his or her surroundings as one of *being* rather than viewing" (179) [emphasis added].

10   The most interesting but subtle way in which the story is written deals with Silko's use of color, scent, and smell to make the story come alive and to further reinforce the images of nature as a benign and loving force. When describing the birth of one of Ayah's children, Silko writes, "The morning was already warm ever before dawn and Ayah smelled the bee flowers blooming and the young willow growing at the springs" (44). This passage correlates birth with the smell of spring flowers, very much in the tradition of human harmony with the natural world.

11   Silko, in trying to show Ayah's relationship to the natural world, uses every sense at her disposal to paint a vivid picture to the reader. When reading "Lullaby" you can feel the snow landing gently about you, hear the screech of the hawk as it patiently circles above, and smell the pungent odor of the juniper trees. Silko is also able to make the reader feel the intense pain of loneliness associated with the loss of Ayah's family and culture at the hands of the white man. In the story, Silko weaves the natural world into every nook and cranny of the narrative so the reader is unaware of its existence but can feel its essence as its own entity; in this case it's an entity that is not separate from Ayah but merges with her. Both are "beings"; both share consciousness. And in the end, she finds comfort in that.

Works Cited

Schweninger, Lee. "Writing Nature: Silko and Native Americans as Nature Writers." *Mellis* 18 (1993): 47–60. Print.

Silko, Leslie Marmon. "Lullaby." *Storyteller*. New York: Arcade, 1981. 43–51. Print.

Waldron, Karen E. "The Land as Consciousness." *Such News of the Land: U.S. Women Nature Writers*. Ed. Thomas S. Edwards and Elizabeth A. De Wolfe. Hanover, NH: UP of New England, 2001. 179–190. Print.

Evaluating the Essay

1. Compare Bird's earlier sketch and her draft. What do you notice about her revisions? In particular, do you think the draft is more insightful than the sketch? Why?

2. One of the temptations in writing about Native American literature (or any literature by someone from another or unfamiliar culture) is to make assumptions about what "they" believe or how "they" think. Many of these are based on certain cultural commonplaces that we pick up without thinking much about them. One of these is that Indians have strong ties to nature. Does Bird find support for her assumptions about that? How do you avoid simply accepting such assumptions?

3. When you write about literature, the most important source of information is the text you're writing about—the story, poem, essay, or novel. How well does Bird use evidence from "Lullaby" to convince you that what she says about the story is a reasonable interpretation?

Using What You Have Learned

1. **Apply the methods of critical analysis not only to literature but any-thing whose meanings aren't apparent.** If you're not an English major, why should you learn to write a critical essay? I hope the answer is obvious by now. The act of interpretation is a fundamental part of making sense of the world; it's also an essential academic skill. In the future, you'll be asked to interpret data, field observations, historical narratives, case studies, and many other primary sources. Interpretation is a method of thought you can't practice enough.

2. **Use evidence from primary sources to argue effectively for a convincing interpretation.** The last three chapters—the proposal, the argument, and now the critical essay—are all persuasive forms of writing. In some ways, you build arguments in all three forms in very similar ways. But with a criti-cal essay, you've composed an argument that works with a particular kind of evidence: primary sources. This is a more scholarly approach to argument that builds on the foundations of persuasive writing you've developed in previous chapters.

3. **Use appropriate invention strategies to discover a topic for a critical essay.** Though research has been part of the invention toolbox since the first assignment chapter on the personal essay, it has become increasingly im-portant as we move towards writing on subjects outside our experience and knowledge. Because it relies on close reading and observation, the critical es-say is mostly research. By now it should be apparent that research (reading, interview, observation) *is* an invention strategy—a source of discovery—not just a move to build support for what you already know. This becomes even more obvious if you write a research paper or ethnography in later chapters.

4. **Apply revision strategies that are effective for the critical essay.** Research is, of course, not only an invention strategy but a revision strategy, especially with a form such as the critical essay. When we "do research," particularly on the web, it often seems haphazard—looking here and there unsystematically, hoping to stumble into something usable. In the final two chapters, I hope you see that revising with research is, well, strategic. There are certain *catego-ries* of information that you should look for. For example, in this chapter we talked about this in terms of context: historical, theoretical, biographical, and critical. Various forms of writing—and types of inquiry questions—give you guidance about types of information to research as you draft and revise. Look at your future research-based assignments rhetorically: What are the features of this kind of writing, and are there recognizable categories of information that are typically present?

To be conscious of your process is to get control over it, and to see the *choices* you might make in particular writing or reading situations. Research is a process, too. And you'll find that many of the routines you brought with you to college may not serve you well.

Research Techniques

8

Learning Objectives

In this chapter, you'll learn to

8.1 Identify the "research routines" you've typically used, and practice new ones appropriate to college-level research.

8.2 Refine and improve the effectiveness of search terms.

8.3 Apply research strategies for developing "working knowledge" and "focused knowledge" on your topic.

8.4 Use a method to analyze and evaluate research sources.

8.5 Understand and apply new note-taking strategies that will help you analyze sources *while* you're researching.

Methods of Collecting

This chapter should tell you everything you need to know about finding what you need in the university library and on the web. It is particularly useful for collecting information for research essays, but research is a source of information that can make *any* essay stronger. Every assignment in *The Curious Writer*, therefore, includes suggestions for research as you're searching for a topic and writing your draft. Research also can be an especially useful revision strategy for any essay.

Use this chapter much as you would a toolbox—a handy collection of tips and research tools that you can use for all assignments. Refer to it whenever you discover a topic that raises questions that research can help answer, or whenever it would be helpful to hear what other people say about the things you're thinking about. Below is a quick reference guide for finding information in this chapter on key topics.

Topic	Pages
Crafting effective search terms	260–265
Developing "working knowledge" of a topic	265–267
Developing "focused knowledge" of a topic	267–271
Evaluating sources	271–275

Conducting and using interviews	277–280
Conducting and using surveys	280–284
Note-taking strategies	286–290

Research in the Electronic Age

The digital revolution has profoundly changed the way we do research, and it's mostly a wonderful thing. It's extraordinary, for example, how much information I can access on any topic from right here at my desk. But research in the electronic age has also created some new challenges. For example,

> There's strong evidence that college undergraduates use some pretty standard "research routines" when given a paper assignment, no matter what the assignment says.

- An extraordinary amount of information, while more accessible than ever, is really, really bad, at least for academic research.

- The information that is accessible online is as disorganized as a hoarder's closet.

What this means is (1) that you need to spend more time critically evaluating what you find when searching online, (2) that the quality of the search terms you use will make a big difference in how easy it is to find reliable and relevant information, (3) that the library, which exists in part to *organize* information so it's easier to find, is more important than ever. In this chapter, I'll cover each of these and offer some advice about how to develop your skills.

Research Routines

8.1

Identify the "research routines" you've typically used, and practice new ones appropriate to college-level research.

But first, consider "research style," or ways you typically approach writing a research paper, some of which you might have imported from high school. In your journal or on an online discussion board, answer the following questions about your typical habits when asked to write a research paper.

1. In the past, when you got a research assignment, what's the first thing you did to get started?

2. At what point did you come up with a thesis? How did you decide what your thesis was?

3. What sources did you typically use in your research papers? What were some of the ways that you evaluated sources to help you decide whether to use them in your paper?

4. Did you use the library? How?

There's strong evidence that college undergraduates use some pretty standard "research routines" when given a paper assignment, no matter what the assignment says. One of these, according to a study group, Project Information Literacy, is writing a thesis and making an outline early on in the process. In some cases, this isn't a bad approach. But if your goal is discovery—and that, after all, is the motive behind academic inquiry—then dreaming up a thesis before you've done much research defeats the purpose of doing research in the first place. You might have other routines as well, such as consulting Wikipedia first, waiting until the night before the paper is due before doing any writing, relying exclusively on Google and skimming only the first few sources that appear.

I'm a lousy dancer. I pretty much do the same moves over and over again and try not be self-conscious. Similarly, writers who keep using the same routines never discover new moves that will help them adapt to new demands. In Chapter 1 and Chapter 2, you thought about your writing and reading habits, some of which you may have developed in high school, or simply by accident. To be conscious of your process is to get control over it and seeing the *choices* you might make in particular writing or reading situations. Research is a process, too. And you'll find that many of the routines you brought with you to college may not serve you well. But how could you know what you need to *unlearn* if you don't think about your process? Reflect often on what you're noticing about ways of doing research. You'll then learn more dance moves, whatever the music.

Power Searching Using Google

Say I'm researching why people believe in alien abduction. For better or worse, most of us start with Google. So I type the following in the search window:

I get 5.87 million hits. Okay, that's a lot of stuff to scroll through. If you're like most people, you'll just harvest the first few relevant results on the opening page or two. But that would squander the power of the search engine, ignoring lots of even better potential sources. But how do you find them?

Add a word or two:

That's a little better. Now I've got less than a million results. I might refine the search further by adding some words and putting a few terms in quotation marks. The quotes tell Google that I want documents with that exact phrase. Still, I'd like fewer and better results, from sources I am likely to trust. Here's where some of the more advanced commands can help. Suppose I want to get information from a particular site—say, NASA. What does the federal government's space agency

8.2

Refine and improve the effectiveness of search terms.

have to say about belief in alien abduction? To do this, I'd begin with the operator *site: (website).*

Ninety-seven hits! This more focused search also produced some more reliable sources.

Say I stumbled on a really great article on belief in alien abduction from the website *Psychology Today* and I'd like to see if its website has any related articles on the topic. Or perhaps I'm interested in sources that cite the original article. The operator *related: (URL of site and search terms)* will help you do this:

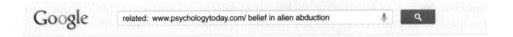

You can also search for particular kinds of documents such as the formats pdf, jpg, doc, etc., by beginning your query with *filetype: (jpg, doc, pdf, etc., and search terms).* To summarize, then, here are some Google search tools you should use:

1. Play with terms, including, perhaps, searching for an exact phrase using quotation marks.
2. Focus your search using some of the following operators:
   a. site:
   b. filetype:
   c. related:

Google Scholar. But perhaps the most useful thing you can do is to try Google Scholar to see if there is any scholarly work published on your topic. You will be amazed at the things that academics research, including belief in alien abduction, and the results you get will produce sources with the highest quality for an academic essay. *To use Google Scholar, the first thing you should do is link with your university library using a setting in Preferences.* Once you do this, the results will allow you to retrieve documents from your campus library without paying for them. To do this, open Google Scholar (scholar.google.com), open "scholar preferences," and scroll down to "library links." Enter the name of your university or college. Click on your school, and then you may have to enter your login credentials. Now you will see links to your own library on your results pages when a document is available (see screenshot on facing page).

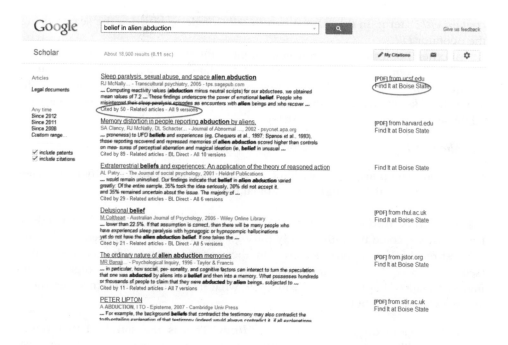

Notice, too, that if you do find a relevant article, you can quickly discover who has cited it (leading you to other potentially useful sources) and "related" work. It's hard to overstate how useful this is for college research.

Power Searching in the Library

Many of us just search electronic card catalogs and library databases using our web-searching routines. And to some extent that will work. But you're going to search far more efficiently if you understand something called "controlled language searches" and "Boolean operators." Library databases often use both, so they're good to know, and they are less complicated than they sound.

Combing Terms Using Boolean Searching. George Boole, an eighteenth-century mathematician, came up with a system for using words like AND, OR, and NOT to help researchers craft logical search queries. Searches still use these words, though it isn't always obvious. Remember that I did a keyword search on *alien abduction* using Google in the previous section? What wasn't obvious is that Google assumes there is an AND between the two terms even if I don't write it; in other words, Google searches for online documents that contain *all* terms whenever I just type a bunch of keywords in the search window. On the other hand, if I had typed *alien OR abduction*, I would be telling Google to find materials that contain *either* term. In that case, I had to *tell* Google to broaden the search using the operator *OR*.

Another Boolean convention you might want to know is *NOT*, to exclude a term (e.g., *alien* AND *abduction* NOT *ufos*). Many databases also allow you to use quotation marks around exact phrases. What you end up with is a way to join a bunch of keywords using the operators to get better results. For example, you might search using the following string:

Alien AND *abduction* AND *stories* NOT *ufos*

When I did that on my university library's websites, I came up with fifty-nine hits—both books and articles—and the great majority were relevant.

Using Controlled Language Searches. Mostly, we search using keywords—terms that we come up with, usually through trial and error, that seem to give us the best results. But in libraries there's another option: controlled language searches (see Figure 8.1). These are the preferred words that librarians use to organize and find information. But how would you know what those authorized terms are? There are two ways to find out:

1. *Library of Congress Subject Headings.* This is the standard that reference librarians use to identify which terms to use to yield the best results on any topic. You can search the *LCSH* online (authorities.loc. gov). Enter in your keywords, and voilà, there's a list of preferred headings you might use to search library databases. I found out that *alien*

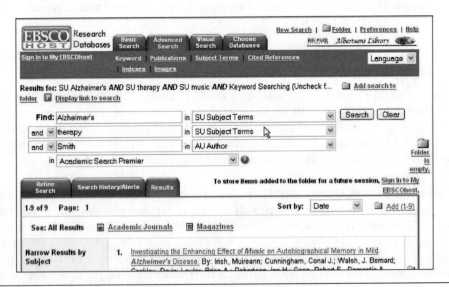

Figure 8.1 Advanced search pages such as EBSCOhost database allow you to exploit Boolean terms using drop-down menus. Further refinements allow the researcher to link terms to different kinds of searches or sources.

abduction was the favored search term, but I also discovered a list of twenty variations, some of which I hadn't thought to use in a database search. For example,

- Alien abduction in literature
- Alien abduction-prevention-case studies
- Alien abduction-psychological aspects

2. *Do a keyword search.* Sometimes you can also find the authorized terms by doing a keyword search on your library database and looking in the results to see if the *LCSH* or other preferred vocabulary is listed in one of the relevant results.

Developing Working Knowledge

Every day we make decisions about how much we need to know about something. Twenty-five years ago, I decided to know enough to tune up my own car, which I did badly. Later, I decided I wasn't interested in keeping up with the changes in electronic ignitions and fuel injection, so now I leave car repair to Davey at State Street Auto. A scholar is someone who, like Davey, has committed his or her professional life to keeping up with the knowledge in his or her field. College professors possess *expert knowledge* of their discipline. In a way, we are all experts on at least one thing: ourselves. Five hundred years ago, the French philosopher Michel de Montaigne argued that it is most important to be a "scholar of the self." Having this expertise can help us in writing insightful personal essays. But if our research projects lead us into unfamiliar territory—and inquiry projects almost always do—then we need to know something about our subjects. But how much?

> **8.3**
>
> Apply research strategies for developing "working knowledge" and "focused knowledge" on your topic.

How much we need to know about a subject is, in part, a personal choice, but a college education does at least two things: It challenges you to develop new knowledge about things that will make you a better citizen and a more productive professional, and it teaches you *how* to better acquire the new knowledge that you might seek by choice. A research project such as the one in this chapter is driven by both goals—you'll be challenged to go beyond superficial knowledge about a meaningful topic, and you'll learn some of the methods for doing that.

You will not end up a scholar on anorexia, college dating, the medical effects of music, or whatever topic you're researching. But you will go way beyond superficial knowledge of your subject; and when you do, it will be like opening a door and entering a crowded room of intelligent strangers, all deep in conversation about your topic. At first you simply listen in before you speak, and that process begins with a *working knowledge*.

All of us know how to develop a working knowledge of something, especially when we need to. For example, I recently developed a working knowledge of podcasting software for a course I was teaching. Now I can knowledgeably talk about how to use Audacity to edit digital recordings for a few minutes without repeating myself. An audio expert would be unimpressed, but someone unfamiliar with the software might find it informative. As a researcher, you've got to know enough about your topic in order to come up with a strong research question, and this begins with two simple questions:

1. What is known about my topic? (Question of fact)
2. What *is* it? (Question of definition)

Exploring the answer to these questions will give you some essential background on your topic, and this will help you develop a more focused and interesting research question.

A Strategy for Developing Working Knowledge

It's hard to beat the Internet as a quick-and-dirty way to develop working knowledge about nearly any topic. But the library can play an important role, too. Combine the two to develop a good working knowledge of your topic, efficiently. There are many ways to do this, but here's a sequence of research steps I recommend (see examples of specific sources in Figure 8.2).

Refine the Research Question. With a working knowledge of your topic, you're now ready to craft a stronger research question that will guide your investigation over time *and* lead to some kind of judgment. It's hard to overstate how

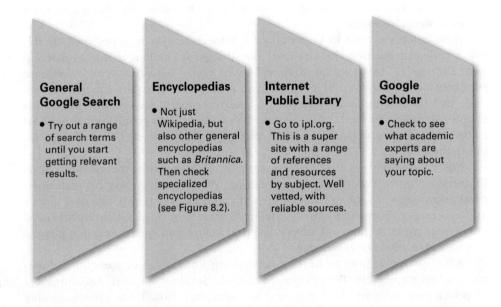

General Google Search

- Try out a range of search terms until you start getting relevant results.

Encyclopedias

- Not just Wikipedia, but also other general encyclopedias such as *Britannica*. Then check specialized encyclopedias (see Figure 8.2).

Internet Public Library

- Go to ipl.org. This is a super site with a range of references and resources by subject. Well vetted, with reliable sources.

Google Scholar

- Check to see what academic experts are saying about your topic.

Source	Examples
General Encyclopedias	Encyclopedia.com, Columbia Encyclopedia, Wikipedia, Oxford Reference, Encyclopedia Britannica
Specialized Encyclopedias	Encyclopedia of Psychology, Encyclopedia of World Art, Encyclopedia of Sociology, Encyclopedia of the Environment, Encyclopedia of Women and Sports, Encyclopedia of African American Culture and History, Encyclopedia of Democracy, Encyclopedia of Science and Technology, Encyclopedia of Children, Adolescents, and the Media
Google (or other search engines)	Google, Mamma, Dogpile
Internet Public Library	ipl.org
Google Scholar	Google Scholar

Figure 8.2   Examples of sources that will help you develop a working knowledge of your topic

important this step is; a good question is the difference between a successful research project and one that flounders.

Now is also a good time to begin building a "working bibliography." (See the "Inquiring into the Details: The Working Bibliography" feature on page 272 for tips on how to do that.)

Developing Focused Knowledge

If working knowledge equips you to sustain a one-minute monologue on your topic, then focused knowledge is enough for you to make a fifteen-minute presentation to your class and to answer most of their questions. Knowing this much doesn't make you an expert, but it does make you far more informed than most people on your topic. Focused knowledge grows from a well-crafted research question, one that isn't too general and allows you to *ignore* information that isn't relevant. With focused knowledge, you should be able to answer some of the following questions about your topic.

- Who are key people who have influenced the published conversation on your topic? (Example: *Among the key advocates for a playoff system in college football was long-time Penn State coach Joe Paterno and even President Barack Obama.*)

- What has already been said about the topic? Up until now, what are the major themes of the conversation? (Example: *Among the arguments against a playoff system is that student athletes will miss too much class. Others add that such a system will lead to the "NFL-ization" of college football, extending the season and compounding the academic problems of student athletes, who already spend as many as forty hours a week on football.)*

■ What is at stake for people? Why is the research question significant? (Example: *Thousands of student athletes in the United States are wedged between two conflicting goals for college football: the public hunger for big-time entertainment and the athletes' desire to complete a degree.)*

A Strategy for Developing Focused Knowledge

To move to this next level of knowing about your topic, launch your research on three fronts:

Library Research. While the web is an intoxicating source of information, academic research still fundamentally depends on library work. Much of this work you can do online. Libraries offer database indexes to magazines, journals, and books that are accessible from your computer at home or at school, and in some cases you can retrieve and print out full-text articles.

But there are still reasons to walk into the university library. Here are six:

1. That's where the books are.
2. Some of the best articles on your topic aren't available as full-text PDFs.
3. Browsing the stacks in your topic's subject area will produce books you won't find any other way.
4. You can read current periodicals not yet online.
5. The reference room has books and other resources that aren't available anywhere else.
6. Reference librarians are irreplaceable.

So you'll want to go to the library—online and on foot—but you won't want to waste your time. The two best ways to avoid this are to have a good research question, one that will allow you to focus your efforts, and to have a handful of good search terms to try. Don't forget to use "controlled language searches," or searches that use the terms librarians have chosen to organize access to materials on every subject (see pp. 263–265). As you recall, you discover these terms in the Library of Congress Subject Headings. Find this online (search for "Library of Congress Authorities") or look for bound copies in the library, which are often called the "big red books" by librarians.

Where should you begin? When you developed working knowledge, you started with more-general sources such as encyclopedias and then shifted to more-specialized sources such as Google Scholar, trying to drill down a little ways into your subject. Now it's time to drill more deeply. For focused knowledge, you can start anywhere—really—especially because you've already got some background knowledge on your research question. The key is to cover a lot of ground.

Searching for Books. Every library has an online index for books (also available at computers in the library, naturally), and using the right search terms, you'll get an instantaneous list of relevant books on your topic and "call numbers" that will help you find them in the stacks. Your results will also tell you if the book is checked out, missing, or unavailable in your college library. If any of these apply to a book you're really hankering for, don't despair. You've got several options:

- *Recall.* Make an online request that the book be returned (usually in a few weeks) by the person who has checked it out.
- *Interlibrary loan.* This is a wonderful, underutilized service, often provided by campus libraries at no charge to students. You can request, usually online, a call-out to a large network of university libraries for the book (or article) you need. It is delivered to you, sometimes within days.
- *Check another library.* If the campus library doesn't have it, check the community library's index online.

The book search form on your university's website, like most search portals, has simple and advanced options. The advanced page is pretty cool because it makes it easy to do a Boolean search on your topic. You can also put "limiters" on the terms, allowing you to control the results for things such as author, title, date, and so on. Learning to use the Advanced Search will really pay off after enduring the initial brief learning curve.

Searching for Periodicals and Newspapers. It's hard to imagine a research question or topic that isn't covered by periodicals. You'll want to check those databases, too. These are organized into four broad categories:

1. General subject databases, or indexes to periodicals across disciplines.
2. Specialized databases, or indexes that are discipline-specific.
3. Genre-specific databases such as Newspaper Source.
4. Government document databases.

Quite often, general subject databases include periodicals that may not be considered scholarly, including magazines such as *Discover, Newsweek*, and *Psychology Today*. These databases are a good place to start. To drill down further, use specialized databases, which are much more likely to produce the most interesting results on your research question because they are written by specialists in the fields of interest. They will also produce articles that can be a chore to understand if you don't know the jargon. That's when your working knowledge on your topic will really pay off. Also consider databases that warehouse certain types of content—plays, government documents, dissertations, and so on. You can see examples of all of these databases in the table on the following page.

Web Research. Web research for inquiry projects should be motivated by the following principles:

1. Maximize coverage.
2. Maximize relevant results.
3. Find stable sources.
4. Find quality sources.

Later in this chapter, I'll elaborate on what I mean by stable, quality sources, but examples would include: web pages and documents with .edu, .gov, or .org domains; those that are routinely updated; and those that might include a bibliography of references that document claims.

On the other hand, depending on your topic, you might seek a range of types of sources. For instance, suppose you're writing about green design and a blog from an architect in Texas has an interesting proposal for using turbines on a highway in Austin, powered by passing cars. The proposal is interesting, and other sites refer to the blogger's idea. While this isn't a conventional academic source, the architect's blog is certainly a relevant and useful one for your essay.

Consider other types of online content as well: images, video, podcasts, discussion boards, and so on. For example, iTunes includes iTunesU, a remarkable collection of lectures, interviews, and video clips on a range of subjects, uploaded from universities around the United States.

The challenge is to find this stuff. Though Google is the dominant player in everyday research, good academic researchers shouldn't limit themselves to a single search service. Google is just the beginning. Try some of the alternative search portals or directories listed here.

Database Type	Examples
Interdisciplinary/general subject databases	Academic Search Premier, Academic One File, JSTOR, ArticleFirst, Project Muse, MasterFILE Premier, WorldCat, Web of Science, ProQuest Central
Discipline-specific databases	ABI/INFORM (business), AnthroSource, America: History and Life, ArtSTOR, Applied Science and Technology, Biography Index, BioOne, Communication and Mass Media, ERIC (education), Health Reference Center, MLA Bibliography (languages and literature), Philosopher's Index, PsycINFO, Sociological Abstracts, Worldwide Political Science Abstracts

Genre-specific databases	National Newspaper Index, Newspaper Source, New York Times Index, Dissertation Abstracts International, Book Review Digest, Literature Criticism Online, Play Index
Government documents	Fed in Print, GPO Monthly Catalog, LexisNexis Government Periodicals Index

Search Type	Examples
General search engines	Google, Ask, Yahoo!, Bing
Metasearch engines	Dogpile, Clusty, SurfWax, Mamma
Subject directories	Yahoo!, About.com, Google, botw.org
Academic search engines or directories	Google Scholar, infomine.ucr.edu, www.academicinfo.net, www.academicindex.net
Search engines for particular content	VideoSurf, Google Books, Google Blogs, Google Images, www.newslink.org, www.internetarchive.org (audio, video, education, etc.), www.usa.org (federal government)

Evaluating Library Sources

One of the huge advantages of finding what you need at the campus library is that nearly everything there was chosen by librarians whose job it is to make good information available to academic researchers. Now that many of the university library's databases are available online, including full-text articles, there really is no excuse for deciding to exclusively use web pages you downloaded from the Internet for your essays.

In general, the more specialized the audience for a publication, the more authoritatively scholars view the publication's content. Academic journals are at the bottom of this inverted pyramid because they represent the latest thinking and knowledge in a discipline, and most of the articles are reviewed by specialists in the field before they are published. At the top of the inverted pyramid are general encyclopedias and general-interest magazines such as *Newsweek* and *Time*. These have broader audiences and feature articles that are written by nonspecialists. They are rarely peer-reviewed. As a rule, then, the lower you draw from the inverted pyramid mentioned above, the more

8.4
Use a method to analyze and evaluate research sources.

authoritative the sources are from an academic point of view. Here are some other guidelines to consider:

- *Choose more-recent sources over older ones.* This is particularly good advice, obviously, if your subject is topical; the social and natural sciences also put much more emphasis on the currency of sources than do humanities disciplines.

- *Look for often-cited authors.* Once you've developed a working knowledge of your topic, you'll start noticing that certain authors seem to be mentioned or cited fairly frequently. These are likely to be the most listened-to authors, and may also be considered the most authoritative on your topic.

- *If possible, use primary sources over secondary sources.* In literary research, primary sources are the original words of writers—their speeches,

Inquiring into the Details

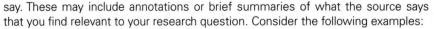

The Working Bibliography

A working bibliography lists sources you've collected that you think will be helpful when you draft your essay. These may include annotations or brief summaries of what the source says that you find relevant to your research question. Consider the following examples:

TOPIC: RELATIONAL AGGRESSION

PRINT SOURCES

Simmons, Rachel. *Odd Girl Out: The Hidden Culture of Aggression in Girls.* New York: Harcourt, 2002.

    Simmons argues that the "secret world of girls' aggression"—the backstabbing, the silent treatment, the bartering of friendship for compliance to a group's "rules"—can be just as bad as the less subtle aggression of boys. Her basic thesis is that girls in American culture are supposed to be "nice" and therefore have no outlet for their anger except for exploiting the one thing they do covet: relationships. Because my essay focuses on the popularity phenomenon in high school—How does it affect girls when they become adults?—Simmons's chapter on parents of these girls seems particularly useful because it shows how the parents' responses are often shaped by their own experiences in school.

WEB SOURCES

"What Is Relational Aggression?" *The Ophelia Project.* 22 Sept. 2003 http://www.opheliaproject.org/issues/issuesRA.shtml.

    The page defines relational aggression by contrasting it with physical aggression. It argues that most research, naturally, has focused on the latter because of need to limit physical injury between children. But girls tend to avoid physical aggression and instead indulge in actions that harm others by disrupting their social relationships, like giving someone the silent treatment. The Ophelia Project is a nonprofit group created in 1997 by parents who wanted to address the problem.

stories, novels, poems, memoirs, letters, interviews, and eyewitness accounts. Secondary sources would be articles that discuss those works. Primary sources in other fields might be original studies or experiments, firsthand newspaper accounts, marketing information, and so on.

Advanced Internet Research Techniques

In a previous section, you saw how to use some advanced search techniques on Google. Don't forget to use this as you probe more deeply for sources on your research question. There are also a few other things you should try, and one of the most productive might be to use multiple search tools.

Go Beyond Google

There are lots of other search portals, and there's evidence that varying your search engines *will* produce unique results. It's worth your time to try them. Here are a few suggestions:

- AltaVista
- Ask
- Bing
- Hotbot
- Lycos
- Yahoo! Search

In addition, there are so-called "metasearch" tools that can search multiple services at one time. Try a few of these:

- Dogpile
- Mamma
- Search.com
- SurfWax
- Yippy

Finally, you might also try out some specialized search tools (sometimes called "vertical" search engines) that focus on particular topics and kinds of content. Google Scholar is one of these. To find more, visit Noodletools and click on "Choose the Best Search."

Evaluating Web Sources

One of the more amusing sites on the web is titled "Feline Reactions to Bearded Men." At first glance, the site appears to be a serious academic study of the physiological responses of cats—heartbeat, respiration, and pupil dilation—to a series of photographs of men with beards. The researchers are listed with their affiliations to respected universities. The article includes an abstract, a methodology, and a results section, as well as a lengthy list of works cited.

The conclusions seem genuine and include the following:

1. Cats do not like men with long beards, especially long dark beards.

2. Cats are indifferent to men with shorter beards.

3. Cats are confused and/or disturbed by men with beards that are incomplete and, to a lesser degree, by men whose beards have missing parts.

The study is a hoax, a fact that is pretty obvious to anyone who critically examines it. For one thing, it was "published" in the *Annals of Improbable Research*, but I can usually fool about a third of my class with the site for five to ten minutes as I discuss the conventions of academic research, some of which are accurately reproduced in the "study."

Everyone knows to be skeptical of what's on the web. But this is even more crucial when using web sources for college writing. Because it's dominated by commercial sites, much of the World Wide Web has limited usefulness to the academic researcher; and although very few online authors are out to fool researchers

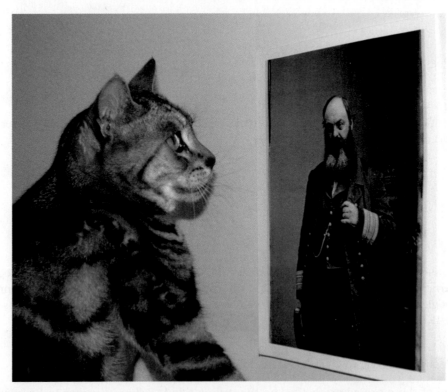

A cat reacts to a picture of a bearded man from the study "Feline Reactions to Bearded Men."

with fake scholarship, many have a persuasive purpose. Despite its "educational" mission, for example, the purpose of the Consumer Freedom website is to promote industry views on laws relating to food and beverages. That doesn't make the information it offers useless, but a careful researcher would be wary of the site's claims and critical of its studies. At the very least, the information provided by Consumer Freedom should be attributed as a proindustry view.

Imagine, as you're researching on the web, that you've been dropped off at night in an unfamiliar neighborhood. You're alert. You're vigilant. And you're careful about whom you ask for directions. You can also be systematic about how you approach evaluating online sources. In general, follow these principles:

- *Favor governmental and educational sources over commercial ones.* These sites are more likely to have unbiased information. How can you tell which are institutional sites when it's not obvious? Sometimes the domain name—the abbreviation *.edu*, *.org*, or *.gov* at the end of an Internet address—provides a strong clue, as does the absence of ads on the site.

- *Favor authored documents over those without authors.* There's a simple reason for this: You can check the credentials of authors if you know who they are. Sometimes sites provide e-mail links so you can write to authors, or you can do a search on the Internet or in the library for other materials they've published.

- *Favor documents that are also available in print over those available only online.* Material that is published in both forms generally undergoes more scrutiny. An obvious example would be newspaper articles, but also some articles from journals and magazines are available electronically and in print.

- *Favor web sources that document their claims over those that don't.* This familiar academic convention is strong evidence that the claims an online author is making are supported and verifiable.

- *Favor web pages that have been recently updated over those that haven't changed in a year or more.* Frequently at the bottom of a web page there is a line indicating when the information was posted to the Internet and/or when it was last updated. Look for it.

An Evaluation Process for Web Sources

1. **Relevance.** Is this web source relevant to my research question?
2. **Authors.** Are there any? If so, can I trust them? Are they recognized experts on the subject? Do they have a bias? Do they say sensible things? If there aren't authors, are there other things about the source that make it credible?
3. **Source.** What's the domain: .edu, .gov, .org.? If it's a commercial site, is the content still useful because of its author, content, or relevance?
4. **Verifiability.** Can you contact the authors? Is there a bibliography of references? Do other credible sites refer to this one?
5. **Stability.** How long has the website been around, and how often is it updated?

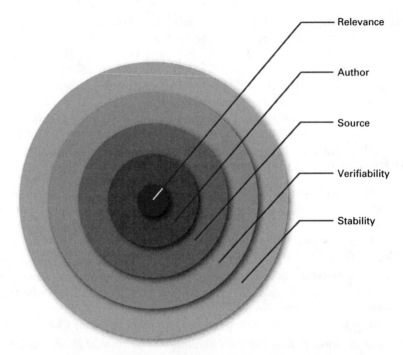

Relevance

Author

Source

Verifiability

Stability

Another way to think about evaluating web sources is to imagine a series of questions you ask yourself, beginning with the relevance of a site or document to your project and then working outward to some judgments about the author, the source, the verifiability of the information, and its stability.

Research with Living Sources: Interviews, Surveys, and Fieldwork

Tethered as we are these days to the electronic world of the web and the increasingly digital university library, it's easy to forget an old-fashioned source for research: a living, breathing human being.

Sometimes the best way to get information about something is to ask someone. Sometimes the best way to see what happens is to go out and look. And sometimes the best way to find out what people think or believe is to invite them to tell you. While we often assume that research means reading, much research also involves interviews, observations, and surveys. Consider whether your research project can benefit from collecting information from these sources.

Interviews

Tethered as we are these days to the electronic world of the web and the increasingly digital university library, it's easy to forget an old-fashioned source for research: a living, breathing human being. People are often the best sources of information

Interviews
- Find a local expert
- Interview people affected by the problem

Field observations
- Photograph, record, and collect
- Observe and describe

Surveys
- Determine attitudes
- Collect comments
- Describe a population

because you can have a real conversation rather than the imagined one simulated by the double-entry notebook. Some kinds of writing, such as the profile, fundamentally depend on interviews; with other genres, such as the personal essay or the research paper, interviews are one of several sources of information. But they can be central to bringing writing to life, because when we put people on the page, abstract ideas or arguments suddenly have a face and a voice. People on the page make ideas matter.

Arranging Interviews. Whom do you interview? Basically, there are two kinds of interviews: (1) the interviewee is the main subject of your piece, as in a profile; (2) the interviewee is a source of information about another subject.

The interviewee as a source of information is the far more common type of interview, and it usually involves finding people who either are experts on the topic you're writing about or have been touched or influenced in some way by it. For example, Tina was writing a research essay on the day-care crisis in her community. Among those affected by this issue were the parents of small children, their day-care teachers, and even the kids themselves; all were good candidates for interviews about the problem. Experts were a little more difficult to think of immediately. The day-care teachers might qualify—after all, they're professionals in the area—but Tina also discovered a faculty member in the College of Health and Social Sciences who specialized in policies related to child care. Interviewing both types of people—experts and those influenced by the issue—gave Tina a much richer perspective on the problem.

How do you find experts in your topic? Here are a few strategies for locating potential interviewees:

- *Check the faculty directory on your campus.* Many universities publish an annual directory of faculty and their research interests, which may be online. In addition, your university's public information office might have a similar list of faculty and areas of expertise.

- *Cull a name from an online discussion group.* Use a specialized search engine such as Google Group's search to search by topic and find someone interesting who might be willing to do an e-mail interview.

- *Ask your friends and instructors.* They might know faculty who have a research interest in your topic or might know someone in the community who is an expert on it.

- *Check the phone book.* The familiar *Yellow Pages* can be a gold mine. For example, want to find a biologist who might have something to say about the effort to bring back migrating salmon? Find the number of the regional office of the U.S. Fish and Wildlife Service in the phone book and ask for the public information officer. He or she may help you find the right expert.

- *Check your sources.* As you begin to collect books, articles, and Internet documents, note their authors and affiliations. I get calls or e-mails from time to time from writers who came across my book on lobsters, posing questions I love to try to answer because no one in Idaho gives a hoot about lobsters. Google searches of authors who are mentioned in your sources may produce e-mail addresses or websites with e-mail links that you might query.

- *Check the* Encyclopedia of Associations. This is another underused book and database in your university's reference room that lists organizations in the United States with interests as varied as promoting tofu and saving salmon.

Conducting the Interview. The kinds of questions you ask fundamentally depend on what type of interview you're conducting. In a profile, your questions will focus on the interview subject. To some extent, this is also true when you interview nonexperts who are *affected* by the topic you're writing about. For example, Tina is certainly interested in what the parents of preschoolers *know* about the day-care crisis in her town, but she's also interested in the feelings and *experiences* of these people. Gathering this kind of information leads to some of the questions you may have used in a profile, but with more focus on the subject's experience with your topic:

- What was your first experience with _____? What has most surprised you about it?

- How does _____ make you feel?

- Tell me about a moment that you consider most typical of your experience with _____.

More often, however, your motive in an interview will be to gather information. Obviously, this will prompt you to ask specific questions about your topic as you try to fill in gaps in your knowledge. But some more general, open-ended questions may also be useful to ask. For example:

- What is the most difficult aspect of your work?

- What do you think is the most significant popular misconception about _____?

- What are the significant current trends in _____?

- If you had to summarize the most important thing you've learned about _____, what would that be?

- What is the most important thing other people should know or understand?
- What do you consider the biggest problem?
- Who has the power to do something about it?
- What is your prediction about the future? Ten years from now, what will this problem look like?

Once you have a list of questions in mind, be prepared to ignore them. Good interviews often take turns that you can't predict, and these journeys may lead you to information and understandings you didn't expect. After all, a good interview is like a good conversation; it may meander, speed up or slow down, and reveal things about your topic and your interview subject that you don't expect. But good interviewers also attempt to control an interview when the turns it's taking aren't useful. You do this through questions, of course, but also with more-subtle tactics. For example, if you stop taking notes, most interview subjects notice, and the astute ones quickly understand that what they're saying has less interest to you. A quick glance at your watch can have the same effect.

E-mail interviews produce a ready-made text with both your questions and the subject's answers. This is pretty wonderful. Live interviews, on the other hand, require more skill. It's usually a good idea to use a tape recorder (with your subject's permission), but never rely exclusively on it, especially as machines can fail and batteries can expire unexpectedly. *Always take notes.* Your notes, if nothing else, will help you know where on the tape you should concentrate later, transcribing direct quotations or gathering information. Note taking during interviews is an acquired skill; the more you do it, the better you get, inventing all sorts of shorthand for commonly occurring words. Practice taking notes while watching the evening news.

Most of all, try to enjoy your interview. After all, you and your interview subject have something important in common—you have an interest in your topic—and this usually produces an immediate bond that transforms an interview into an enjoyable conversation.

Using the Interview in Your Writing. Putting people on the page is one of the best ways to bring writing to life. This is exactly what information from interviews can do—give otherwise abstract questions or problems a voice and a face. One of the most common ways to use interview material is to integrate it into the lead or first paragraph of your essay. By focusing on someone involved in the research question or problem you're exploring, you immediately capture reader interest. For example, here's the beginning of a *Chronicle of Higher Education* essay, "What Makes Teachers Great?"* Quite naturally, the writer chose to begin by profiling someone who happened to be a great teacher, using evidence from the interviews he conducted.

> When Ralph Lynn retired as a professor of history at Baylor University in 1974, dozens of his former students paid him tribute. One student, Ann Richards, who became the governor of Texas in 1991, wrote that Lynn's classes were like "magical

---

*Ken Bain, "What Makes Teachers Great?" *Chronicle of Higher Education* (April 9, 2004): B7-B9.

tours into the great minds and movements of history." Another student, Hal Wingo, the editor of *People* magazine, concluded that Lynn offered the best argument he knew for human cloning. "Nothing would give me more hope for the future," the editor explained, "than to think that Ralph Lynn, in all his wisdom and wit, will be around educating new generations from here to eternity."

This is a strong way to begin an essay, because the larger idea—the qualities that make a great teacher—is then grounded in a name and a face. But information from interviews can be used anywhere in an essay—not just at the beginning—to make an idea come to life.

Information from interviews can also provide strong evidence for a point you're trying to make, especially if your interview subject has expertise on the topic. But interviews can also be a *source* of ideas about what you might want to say in an essay. The essay on great teaching, for instance, offers seven qualities that great teachers embrace in their classrooms—things such as "create a natural critical learning environment" and "help students learn outside of class." All of these claims grew from interviews with sixty professors in a range of disciplines.

The principal advantage of doing interviews is that *you* ask the questions that you're most interested in learning the answers to. Rather than sifting through other sources that may address your research questions briefly or indirectly, interviews generate information that is often relevant to and focused on the information needs of your essay. In other words, interviews are a source of data that can also be a *source* of theories or ideas on your topic. And this is often the best way to use interview material in your essay.

Surveys

The survey is a fixture in American life. We love surveys. What's the best economical laptop? Should the president be reelected? Who is the sexiest man alive? What movie should win Best Picture? Some of these are scientific surveys with carefully crafted questions, statistically significant sample sizes, and carefully chosen target audiences. In your writing class, you likely won't be conducting such formal research. More likely it will be like Mike's—fairly simple, and although not necessarily statistically reliable, your informal survey will likely be more convincing than anecdotal evidence or your personal observation, particularly if it's thoughtfully developed.

Defining a Survey's Goals and Audience. A survey is a useful source of information when you're making some kind of claim regarding "what people think" about something. Mike observed that his friends all seem to hate pennies, and he wanted to generalize from this anecdotal evidence to suggest that most people probably share that view. But do they? And which people are we really talking about? As we discussed this in his writing group, Mike pointed out that his grandfather grew up during the Great Depression and that he has a very different perspective on money than Mike does. "So your grandfather would probably pick up a penny in the parking lot, right?" I asked. "Probably," Mike said.

Quickly, Mike not only had a survey question but began to think about qualifying his claim. Maybe younger adults—Mike's generation—in particular share this attitude about the lowly penny. To confirm this, Mike's survey had both a purpose (to collect information about how people view pennies) and an audience (students on his campus). If he had the time or inclination, Mike could conduct a broader survey of older Americans, but for his purposes the quad survey would be enough.

Types of Survey Questions

1. *Open-ended questions.* Open-ended questions often produce unexpected information, while direct questions are easier to analyze. Open-ended questions are like those on the narrative evaluations students might fill out at the end of the semester, such as "What did you learn in this course?" and "What were the instructor's strengths and weaknesses?"

2. *Direct questions.* Direct questions are the kind used on quizzes and tests, the kind that have a limited number of answers. The simplest, of course, would be a question or statement that people might agree or disagree with: Would you pick up a penny if you saw it lying on the street? Yes? No? You don't know?

How do you decide which types of questions to ask? Here are some things to consider:

- *How much time do you have to analyze the results?* Open-ended questions obviously take more time, while direct questions often involve mere tabulation of responses. The size of your sample is a big factor in this.

- *How good are you at crafting questions?* Direct questions need to be more carefully crafted than open-ended ones because you're offering limited responses. Are the responses appropriate to the question? Have you considered all the alternative ways of responding?

- *Do you want statistical or qualitative information?* Qualitative information—anecdotes, stories, opinions, case studies, observations, individual perspectives—are the stuff of open-ended questions. This can be wonderful information, because it is often surprising and it offers an individual's voice rather than the voiceless results of statistical data. On the other hand, statistical information—percentages, averages, and the like—is easily understood and can be dramatic.

Crafting Survey Questions. To begin, you want to ask questions that your target audience can answer. Don't ask a question about a campus alcohol policy that most students in your survey have never heard of. Second, keep the questions simple and easy to understand. This is crucial because most respondents resist overly long survey questions and won't answer confusing ones. Third, make sure the questions will produce the information you want. This is a particular hazard of open-ended questions. For example, a broad, open-ended question such as "What do you think of the use of animals in the testing of cosmetics?" will probably produce a verbal shrug or an answer of "I don't know." A better question is

Inquiring into the Details

Types of Survey Questions

These are a few of your options when deciding what type of questions to ask in a survey.

1. Limited choice

Do you believe student fees should be used to support campus religious organizations?

____ Yes

____ No

____ I'm not sure

At what point in the writing process do you usually get stuck?

____ Getting started

____ In the middle

____ Finishing

____ I never get stuck

____ Other: _____

2. Scaled response

The Student Film Board should show more foreign films.

____ Strongly agree

____ Agree

____ Neither agree nor disagree

____ Disagree

____ Strongly disagree

3. Ranking

Which of the following do you consider important in designing a classroom to be conducive to learning? Rank them from 1 to 5, with the most important a 1 and the least important a 5.

Comfortable seating	
Natural light from windows	
Carpeting	
Effective soundproofing	
Dimmable lighting	

4. Open-ended

Describe three things you learned in this course.

What steps do you think the university should take to increase attendance at women's soccer games?

more focused: "What do you think about the U.S. Food and Drug Administration's claim that animal testing by cosmetic companies is 'often necessary to provide product safety'?"

Such a question could be an open-ended or direct question, depending on the kind of responses you're seeking. Focusing the question also makes it more likely to generate information that will help you compose your essay on the adequacy of current regulations governing animal testing. Also note that the question doesn't necessarily betray the writer's position on the issue, which is essential—a good survey question isn't biased or "loaded." Imagine how a less neutral question might skew the results: "What do you think of the federal bureaucrats' position that animal testing for cosmetics is 'often necessary to provide product safety'?" An even more subtle bias might be introduced by inserting the term *federal government* rather than *Food and Drug Administration* in the original question. In my part of the world, the Rocky Mountain West, the federal government is generally not viewed favorably, no matter what the issue.

Keep your survey questions to a minimum. It shouldn't take long—no more than a few minutes at most—to complete your survey, unless you're lucky enough to have a captive audience such as a class.

Finally, consider beginning your survey with background questions that establish the identity of each respondent. Typical information you might collect includes the gender and age or, with student-oriented surveys, the class ranking of the respondent. Depending on your topic, you might be interested in particular demographic facts, such as whether someone has children or comes from a particular part of the state. All of these questions can help you sort and analyze your results.

Conducting a Survey

1. **If you can, test it first.** People who design surveys for a living always test them first. Invariably this turns up problems: A survey is too long, a question is poorly worded, the response rate to a particular question is low, and so on. You won't be able to test your draft survey nearly as thoroughly as the experts do, but before you put your faith in an untested survey, ask as many people as you can to try it out and describe their experience answering your questions. Was there any confusion? How long did it take? Is the survey generating relevant information?

2. **Find a way to reach your audience.** Once you're confident in the design of your survey, plan how you'll distribute it. There are several options:

   a. *Distribute in a likely location.* Begin by asking yourself whether your target audience tends to conveniently gather in a particular location. For example, if you're surveying sports fans, then surveying people by the main gate at the football stadium on Saturday might work. If your target audience is first-year college students and your university requires freshman English composition, then surveying one or more of those classes would be a convenient way to reach them. In some situations, you can leave your survey forms in a location that might produce responses from your target audience. For example, a student at my university wanted to survey people about which foothill's hiking trails they liked best, and she left an envelope with the forms and a pencil at several trailheads.

b. *Distribute it online.* Software for designing online surveys is available now, but unless the survey is linked to a website that is visited by the target audience whose opinions you seek, the response rates will most likely be low. Still, it might be possible for you to direct traffic to your online survey by posting a notice on social networks such as Facebook or online discussion groups relevant to the topic. There is free software available on the web to do limited online surveys. The best known is probably Survey Monkey.

Using Survey Results in Your Writing. The best thing about conducting an informal survey is that you're producing original and interesting information about your topic's local relevance. This can be an impressive element of your essay and will certainly make it more interesting.

Because analysis of open-ended questions can be time consuming and complicated, consider the simplest approach: As you go through the surveys, note which responses are worth quoting in your essay because they seem representative. Perhaps the responses are among the most commonly voiced in the entire sample, or they are expressed in significant numbers by a particular group of respondents.

In a more detailed analysis, you might try to nail down more specifically the *patterns* of responses. For example, perhaps you initially can divide the survey results into two categories: people who disagree with the university's general-education requirements and those who agree with it, Group 1 and Group 2. The next step might be to further analyze each of these groups, looking for particular patterns. In particular, pay attention to responses you didn't expect, responses that might enlarge your perspective about what people think about your topic.

Your analysis of the responses to direct questions will usually be pretty simple—probably a breakdown of percentages. In a more sophisticated analysis, you might try to break the sample down, if it's large enough, to certain categories of respondents—men and women, class ranking, respondents with high or low test scores, and so on—and then see if any response patterns correlate to these categories. For example, perhaps a much higher percentage of freshmen than seniors sampled agreed that a good job was the most important reason to go to college.

What might this difference mean? Is it important? How does it influence your thinking about your topic, or how does it affect your argument? Each of these questions involves interpretation of the results, and sample size is the factor that most influences the credibility of this kind of evidence.

Fieldwork: Research on What You See and Hear

In many disciplines, field observations are at the heart of research. Field research is essential. There are a lot of inquiry projects that might benefit from direct observation and description, especially if you're researching something that has a local angle and there might be something relevant to see. Would your essay on farmer's markets, for instance, benefit from listening to and observing people at the Saturday market downtown?

There are two kinds of fieldwork:

1. **Participant observation.** You are involved in the thing you are describing as an active participant.

2. **Direct observation.** You unobtrusively observe the settings or phenomena.

Because you're not doing formal scholarship for this project, whichever method you use as your approach will probably be casual rather than carefully planned and methodologically strict. What you *are* trying to do that is common to all fieldwork is look for patterns in what you see. In particular, you might want to describe what is either *typical* (e.g., a common behavior, complaint, attitude, problem, etc.) or *exceptional* (e.g., significant differences, nonconformance, unusual circumstances, etc.). Remember, too, that you're not limited to making these observations with a notebook and pen alone. You might also digitally record, video, and photograph the things you see for analysis later.

The Ethics of Fieldwork. Because fieldwork often involves research on people, you should always be careful to protect the privacy and wishes of your subjects. For a relatively informal project such as this one—something that isn't likely to be published—there are fewer ethical concerns, but there are some principles that should guide you. The least complicated ethical situation is direct observation in a public setting. In this case, you don't need an invitation from anyone to observe unless you directly approach the people you're observing. Sometimes, though, especially when you're a participant-observer, you'll be actively seeking permission to come watch, record, and interview. How should you handle those situations?

- Make your study subjects aware of the purpose of your project.
- Preserve the anonymity of the people you observe unless they give you permission to use their names.

Note-Taking Strategies. Write down and document in detail what you see and hear. This includes behaviors, descriptions of activities and settings, conversations, maps of movements, etc. This is the raw data you'll analyze for patterns. In addition to looking for things that seem "typical" and "exceptional," consider the following frames for analysis:

- Evidence that confirms, contradicts, or qualifies the theories and claims you've read about in your research.
- What do people do or say during moments of particular significance?
- What "artifacts" seem important? What things do people use?
- *How* do the people you observe talk about themselves or the activity they are participating in?

Using Field Research in Your Writing. The observations and descriptions you gather from the field can be powerful additions to your research project. For example,

- **Give your topic a face.** Use a description of an individual who is affected by the problem you're writing about, as a way to dramatize its impact.

- **Make a scene.** Help your readers *see* what you're writing about.

- **Incorporate images.** Even a written research essay can benefit by pictures, which can be dropped into the text and analyzed.

- **Develop a multimodal essay.** Might your research project be transformed into an audio documentary, or a video podcast? Could you create an online slide show?

Writing in the Middle: Note-Taking Techniques

8.5
Understand and apply new note-taking strategies that will help you analyze sources while you're researching.

Like most students, when I wrote undergraduate research papers I never did any writing until the end—usually late at night with all of my sources fanned out across my desk like cards at a blackjack table. I'm going to propose an alternative that will work much better, and it looks something like this: It's not the night before, but *weeks* before the paper is due, and I'm writing like mad in my notebook *as* I'm reading an article. I'm not exactly writing my paper—I'm using writing to think about what I'm reading, to understand the source, and to *converse* with it.

Throughout *The Curious Writer*, I've promoted what's termed "dialectical thinking"—moving back and forth between suspending judgments and making judgments—and this method is particularly useful when writing about what you read. One way to do this as you research is to use something called the "double-entry journal."

Whatever method you use for "writing in the middle," these things are key:

1. You write as—or immediately after—you read something that's relevant to your project.

2. You use the writing to talk to yourself and *to the source* about what you understand it to be saying, what you find particularly interesting, how you might agree or disagree, what questions the source raises.

3. You carefully jot down bibliographic information so you build your list of references as you research.

I think the double-entry journal makes a great research notebook. You collect passages, ideas, statistics, summaries, and so on from the source on the left facing page, and explore what you make of what you've collected on the right facing page. You can do this in a paper notebook or in a Word document using columns. In the double-entry journal that follows, you can see how this might work.

Double-Entry Journal

In the sample double-entry journal below, notice how the writer collects material in the left column, and then explores in the right, looking left whenever the writing stalls to find traction on something else from the source.

Page	Source Notes	First Thoughts
140	"Carl Sagan suggested that the 'pay dirt' of space alien abduction accounts is not in what they might tell us about alien visitation but in what they might tell us about ourselves."	Really interesting article that summarizes the research, as of 1996, on alien abduction memories. Point seems to be the ways in which these don't necessarily tell us anything about aliens but a lot about ourselves. But what? I think the evidence here suggests that it isn't necessarily some kind of psychiatric problem, but how vulnerable we are to suggestion. The stop sign case, for example. Even when the visual clearly has a yield not a stop sign, the mere suggestion it's a stop sign made people confidently believe it. But maybe the most interesting thing here to me is the dynamic of having a memory of something that is challenged, which is a kind of threat, and as a result we believe even a false memory more strongly. We believe what we want to believe and then actively seek out information that reinforces it, particularly in the face of challenge.
141	"the misinformation effect" Describes "classic experiment" to demonstrate this: a pedestrian accident in which slide shows yield sign but respondents "subtly" told was stop sign. Majority claimed stop sign was there with "high degree of confidence."	
142	"… humans can cook up false memories …" But why aliens? ✓ variety of sources in popular culture of "true" abduction stories ✓ most reported under hypnosis, and this makes it seem more "real" to the abductee because it evokes "strong visual imagery" ✓ when belief is challenged, holder of belief clings to it more strongly ✓ reinforced by other "support groups" of believers	The thing about hypnosis being the source of most abduction reports, and how this might deepen an abductee's belief in it, is also something I need to look into more. (Continued)

Page	Source Notes	First Thoughts
	Clark, Steven E. and Elizabeth F. Loftus. "The Construction of Alien Abduction Memories." *Psychological Inquiry* 7.2 (1996): 140–143. Print.	

Research Log

Another method of note taking that also exploits dialectical thinking is the research log. Rather than using opposing pages, you'll layer your notes and responses, one after another. This is a particularly useful method for those who would prefer to work with a keyboard rather than a pencil. Here's how it works:

1. Begin by taking down the full bibliographic information on the source, something you may already have in your working bibliography.

2. Read the article, book chapter, or web page, marking up your personal copy as you typically do, perhaps underlining key facts or ideas or information relevant to your research question.

3. Your first entry in your notebook or on the computer will be a fast-write, an open-ended response to the reading under the heading What Strikes Me Most. As the title implies, you're dealing with first thoughts here.

4. Next, take notes on the source, jotting down summaries, paraphrases, quotations, and key facts you glean from it. Title this section Source Notes.

5. Finally, follow up with another episode of fastwriting. Title this The Source Reconsidered. This is a *more focused* look at the source; fastwrite about what stands out in the notes you took. Which facts, findings, claims, or arguments shape your thinking now?

One Student's Response

Claude's Research Log

SOURCE

Letawsky, Nicole R., et al. "Factors Influencing the College Selection Process of Student Athletes." *College Student Journal* 37.4 (2003): 604–11. *Academic Search Premier.* EBSCOhost Databases. Albertson's Lib. 5 Apr. 2004.

WHAT STRIKES ME MOST

Really interesting article that studied about 130 student athletes at a large 1-A university. Noted that there have been a lot of research studies on why students choose a particular school but not so much on why student-athletes choose a school. Everyone assumes, of course, that student-athletes go somewhere because they're wined and dined and promised national TV exposure. In other words, it all has to do with the glamour of playing 1-A, particularly the so-called revenue sports like basketball and football. But this study had some surprising findings. They found that the number one reason that student-athletes chose a school was the degree options it offers. In other words, the reasons student-athletes choose a school aren't that much different than the reason regular students choose one. The study also found that the glamour stuff—getting awards, getting on TV, and future professional possibilities—mattered the least to the student-athletes. This study challenges some of the myths about student recruiting, and should be read by recruiters especially. If you want to get a blue-ribbon player at your school, tell him or her about the academic opportunities there.

SOURCE NOTES (CUT AND PASTED FROM ELECTRONIC VERSION)

"This study found that the most important factor for student-athletes was the degree program options offered by the University. Other important factors were the head coach, academic support services, type of community in which the campus is located, and the school's sports traditions. Two of the top three factors were specifically related to the academic rather than athletic environment. This is a key finding and should be understood as recruiting efforts should be broad based, balancing academics and athletics if they are to be effective."

"A somewhat surprising result of the study concerned relatively low ratings associated with factors considered essential to 'Big-Time College Sports.' Television exposure, perceived opportunity to play immediately, and perceived future professional sporting opportunities were among the lowest-ranked factors. Furthermore, the participants rated athletic rewards (a 5-item survey scale containing these and other reward items) consistently lower than both the campus and athletic environment. These results may be due to the fact that respondents were from each of the sports offered by the University. Many of the sports (e.g., swimming, track), although funded and supported similar to the other sports, do not receive the national attention, large crowds, and television exposure."

One Student's Response (*continued*)

THE SOURCE RECONSIDERED

This article did more than anything I've read so far to make me question my thesis that big-time college sports recruiting is way out of control. It's pretty convincing on the point that athletes care about the academic programs when they're choosing a school. But then the second quotation has an interesting part that I just noticed. This study surveyed athletes in all sports, not just the big-time sports like football and basketball at the university where the study was conducted. It seems to me that that would really skew the findings because someone participating in a sport like tennis that doesn't get a lot of attention and doesn't necessarily lead to professional opportunities after school *would* be more interested in academics. They're not dreaming of making a name for themselves, but getting a scholarship to pay for school. Seems like a better study would focus on the big-time sports...

Using What You Have Learned

Let's return briefly to the learning outcomes listed at the beginning of the chapter.

1. **Identify the "research routines" you've typically used, and practice new ones appropriate to college-level research.** Since the beginning of *The Curious Writer*, I've encouraged you to look at the habits you use, often without thinking, to read and write. You have "research routines," too, often learned in high school; while some of these might still serve you well, many may not, particularly in college. This "unlearning" is an essential part of developing your abilities, not just in academic tasks, but also with anything you want to do that is guided by habits you rarely examine.

2. **Refine and improve the effectiveness of search terms.** This is a skill that will not only help make your academic research more efficient, but will aid you with everyday research as well. And the ability to refine search languages will become even more important as information continues to expand on the web and in library databases.

3. **Apply research strategies for developing "working knowledge" and "focused knowledge."** I've tried to encourage you to look at any research project as a developmental process, one in which how much knowledge you have about a topic will determine how effectively you can write about it. If you don't know much, which is often the case in an inquiry-based class, then you need to quickly learn enough to come up with a strong research question. From there, you can mine more deeply into your topic, developing "focused" knowledge with more-advanced research strategies. This a process you can use in nearly any research project.

4. **Use a method to analyze and evaluate research sources**. There are a lot of methods for doing this, and in this chapter you learned just one. But the key is that you actually *use* a method, one that will consistently help you to find credible sources. As we do more and more research online, it's hard to overstate what an essential skill this is.

5. **Understand and apply new note-taking strategies that will help you analyze sources *while* you're researching.** The double-entry journal and research log are two systems for note-taking that I recommend here, but the important thing is that you do some writing *as* you do your research. This is likely a major break with your research routine, but it will make a huge difference in helping you to think about what you're reading and in beginning to build your essay. This is yet another application of the "bad" writing—exploratory, open-ended fastwriting—that you've learned to use in previous assignments.

Will you control the outside sources in your research essay, or will they control you? The appropriate use of sources is really a matter of control. Writers who put research information to work for them see outside sources as serving a clear purpose.

Using and Citing Sources

9

Learning Objectives

In this chapter, you'll learn to

9.1 Use sources effectively and control sources so they don't control you.

9.2 Practice summarizing, paraphrasing, and quoting and apply these to your own work.

9.3 Understand and identify plagiarism to avoid it in your own work.

9.4 Cite sources using MLA and APA documentation styles.

Controlling Information

The first college paper that really meant something to me was an essay on whaling industry practices and their impacts on populations of humpback and sperm whales. Writing from the place of itchy curiosity and strong feelings is a wonderful thing. It will motivate you to read and learn about your topic, and when it comes to writing the draft, you might find that you have little trouble enlisting the voices of your sources to make your point. More often, however, you've chosen a topic because you don't know what you think or feel about it—the inquiry-based approach—or you've been assigned a general topic that reflects the content of a course you're taking. In these cases, writing with sources is like crashing a party of strangers that has been going on for a long time. You shyly listen in, trying to figure out what everyone is talking about, and look for an opening to enter the conversation. Mostly you just feel intimidated, so you hang back feeling foolish.

This kind of writing situation is really a matter of control. Will you control the outside sources in your research essay, or will they control you? Will you enter the conversation and make a contribution to it, or will you let others do all the talking? The easiest way to lose control is simply to turn long stretches of your paper over to a source, usually one with long quotations. I've seen a quotation from a single source run more than a full page in some drafts. Another way to lose control is to do what one of my colleagues calls a "data dump." Fill the truck with a heavy load of information, back it up to the paper, and dump in as much as you can, without analysis, without carefully selecting what is relevant and what isn't, without much thought at all. The writer in this situation sees his or her essay as a hole that must be filled with information.

When you introduce a voice other than your own, make it clear what this new voice adds to the conversation you have going about your topic.

Using Sources

The appropriate use of sources is also a matter of control. Writers who put research information to work for them see outside sources as serving a clear purpose. There are at least five of these purposes:

9.1

Use sources effectively and control sources so they don't control you.

Purpose	Description
Support a claim or idea	The motive we usually imagine for using information in academic writing.
Provide background	What does your audience need to know about your topic to understand why your inquiry question is significant?
Answer a question	Periodically asking relevant questions—and answering them with information from research—creates a structure built on reasoning.
Complicate things	This is the most counterintuitive use of information. Why would you use information that might *not* support your thesis? Because things are *always* complicated, and that's what makes them interesting.

Let's see how this works in an actual passage. In an essay that asks, "Why Did God Make Flies?" writer Richard Conniff argues that the answer might be as a punishment for human arrogance. In the middle of the essay, he draws on research to provide some background for this claim by establishing the long and sometimes unhappy relationship between the housefly and human beings.

The true housefly, *Musca domestica*, does not bite. (You may think this is something to like about it, until you find out what it does instead.) *M. domestica*, a drab fellow of salt-and-pepper complexion, is the world's most widely distributed insect species and probably the most familiar, a status achieved through its pronounced fondness for breeding in pig, horse, and human excrement. In choosing at some point in the immemorial past to concentrate on the wastes around human habitations, *M. domestica* made a major career move. Bernard

Greenberg of the University of Illinois at Chicago has traced human representations of the housefly back to a Mesopotamian cylinder seal from 3000 B.C. But houseflies were probably with us even before we had houses, and they spread with human culture.

Here Conniff demonstrates exquisite control over outside sources, marshalling them in the service of his larger point. But he does this by not simply quoting extensively or going on and on explaining the relevant information, but also by *finding his own way of saying things*. For example, rather than writing that the housefly's fondness for associating with people had significant ecological implications for the insect, Conniff writes that it was "a major career move."

The sections that follow review the techniques of summarizing, paraphrasing, and quoting. You may know these as the three horsemen of note taking. But they should never be thoughtless activities; in fact, they're a great opportunity to exert control over your sources by doing two things:

1. *Taking notes with a particular purpose in mind.* How is the information you're writing about relevant to your purpose in your essay?

2. *Finding your own way of saying things.* By putting other people's words into your own voice, you take possession of the information.

Summarizing

"So basically what you're saying is that we can never win the war on terrorism because it isn't really a war in the conventional sense?"

Imagine that you're in the midst of a conversation with someone about the challenge of defeating terrorism. You've just listened for about a minute to a friend explain in some detail that the battle against terrorism isn't really a battle at all, but a series of surprise attacks that then provoke retaliation, with the two opponents blindly striking out at each other. Your friend adds that the terrorists' tactics are aimed at targets with symbolic rather than military value. Victory for terrorists is not measured in damage inflicted on military forces, but in the terror provoked in the civilian population. You listen to all of this and summarize your friend's larger point: This isn't really war as we've historically understood it.

A summary is usually much shorter than the original. For example, consider the following summary of the earlier extract paragraph about the relationship between houseflies and human beings:

The common housefly is among the "most familiar" insects because it found its long partnership with human beings, one that goes back thousands of years, extremely beneficial.

Can you see how the summary captures the main idea of the longer paragraph? Also note that when the summary refers to identical language in the original—the

9.2

Practice summarizing, paraphrasing, and quoting and apply these to your own work.

phrase "most familiar"—the writer is careful to use quotation marks. Finally, the summary uses original language that breaks with the source, describing the relationship between people and flies as a "long partnership."

Tips for Crafting a Summary

1. If your aim is to summarize an entire work, and if the source isn't a book, read it all once through, marking what seem to be key claims or findings. Academic articles in the social sciences often include abstracts, or ready-made summaries of a study. Books frequently explain their purpose in a preface or introduction. Start there. Then check the concluding chapter.

2. If your aim is to summarize a passage of a longer work, remember to look for the author's most important ideas where he or she is most likely to put them: the first and last sentences of paragraphs or a concluding paragraph.

3. Summary has little to do with your opinion. Save that for the right side of your double-entry journal. Try, as best you can, to capture your understanding of the *source's* meaning or argument.

4. Typically, a summary includes the name(s) of the author(s) or the title of the work, usually attached to a verb that characterizes its nature: so-and-so *argues, finds, explains, speculates, questions*, and so on.

Paraphrasing

Of the three forms of note taking, paraphrasing requires the most attention and the greatest care. Your goal is to craft a restatement, in your own words, of what an original source is saying, in roughly the same length as the original. Paraphrasing usually involves closer work—examining a paragraph or a passage and then finding a way to accurately capture the original's ideas and information but in a fresh and original way. This demands not only faith in our own way of saying things—that's hard enough—but a pretty thorough understanding of what exactly the source is trying to say. You simply can't paraphrase a source you don't understand.

Here's a paraphrase of the earlier extract paragraph on houseflies.

Houseflies, according to Richard Conniff, have had a long partnership with human beings. They are also among "the world's most widely distributed insect species," two factors that explain our familiarity with *Musca domestica*, the housefly's Latin name. This partnership may have been cultivated for thousands of years, or certainly as long as humans—and their animal companions—produced sufficient excrement in which the flies could breed. Ironically, these pests have benefited enormously from their "fondness" for human and animal wastes, and unwittingly we have contributed to their success at our own expense.

A key element of the translation in a paraphrase is trying not to imitate the structure of the original passage. By deliberately setting out to reorganize the information, you'll find writing a paraphrase much easier. And you'll also find it much less likely that you unintentionally plagiarize the material. Notice as well that whenever the paraphrase borrows wording from the original, quotation marks are included.

Tips for Crafting a Paraphrase

1. If a summary is a macroscopic look at a text, a paraphrase is microscopic, usually focusing on a brief passage. Consequently, the plagiarism danger goes from yellow to red (see "Avoiding Plagiarism" on page 300). Make sure to find your own way of saying things, quoting phrases that you borrow from the source.

2. Try the "look away" strategy. Carefully read the passage several times, then set it aside. Compose your paraphrase without looking at the source, trusting that you'll remember what's important. Then check the result against the passage, changing or quoting any borrowed language and refining your prose.

3. Like summary, introduce paraphrased material in your essay by attributing the author or the work.

Quoting

When should you turn to quotation in your essay? There are two main situations:

1. When the source says something in a distinctive way that would be lost by putting it in your own words.

2. When you want to analyze or emphasize a particular passage in the source, and the exact words of the author matter.

For instance, the excerpt from "Why Did God Make Flies?" is eminently quotable because Richard Conniff, its author, writes with such a lively voice. Consider his sentence:

> The true housefly is the world's most widely distributed insect species and probably the most familiar, a status achieved through its pronounced fondness for breeding in pig, horse, and human excrement.

What is it about this that seems quotable? Maybe the way it goes along with fairly straightforward exposition until the second half of the sentence, when suddenly the fly seeks status and feels fondness for you know what.

When you bring someone else's voice into your own writing, it's usually a good idea to introduce the source and provide some justification for making such a move. For instance, you might introduce the preceding quote by saying something like this:

> Richard Conniff, whose popular studies of invertebrate animals have made even leeches lovable, observes that the familiarity of the housefly is no accident. He writes...

It's even more important in academic writing to follow up quoted text with your own commentary. What would you like the reader to notice about what the quotation says? What seems most relevant to your own research question or point? How does the quotation extend an important idea you've been discussing or raise an important question? What does it imply? What do you agree with? What do you disagree with? In other words, when you introduce a voice other than your own, make it clear what this new voice adds to the conversation you have going about your topic.

Tips for Handling Quotations

Integrate quoted material in your essay in the following ways:

1. **Separate it.** There are two ways to do this. Provide an introductory tag that ends in a comma or a colon. *According to Carl Elliott (82), the new drug pushers "are officially known as 'pharmaceutical sales representatives' but everyone calls them 'sales reps.' " Or, Carl Elliott (82) observes that drug salespeople are easy to spot: "Drug reps today are often young, well groomed, and strikingly good looking. Many are women..."*

2. **Embed it.** Integrate quoted material in your own sentence something like this:

   Carl Elliott calls drug reps "the best dressed people in the hospital."

3. **Block it.** Extended quotations (more than 40 words in APA style and more than four lines in MLA) should be indented five spaces in APA style and ten spaces in MLA style in a block. Quotation marks, except those used in the source, are omitted. For instance:

   Carl Elliott, in "The Drug Pushers," highlights the perks doctors have historically received:

   > *Gifts from the drug industry are nothing new, of course. William Helfand, who worked in marketing for Merck for thirty-three years, told me that company representatives were giving doctors books and pamphlets as early as the late nineteenth century. "There is nothing new under the sun," Helfand says, "There is just more of it." The question is: Why is there so much more of it just now? And what changes occurred during the past decade to bring about such a dramatic increase in reps bearing gifts? (86)*

Citing Sources

Of all the rules some of my students believe were invented to torture composition students, requirements that they carefully cite their sources in research papers may cause the most anguish. They rarely question these requirements; they seem like divine and universal law. In fact, these aren't rules but conventions, hardly as old as the Greeks, and historically quite new. For many centuries, writers freely borrowed from others, often without attribution, and the appropriation of someone else's words and ideas was considered quite normal. This is still the view in some non-Western cultures; some students, for example, are quite puzzled in their English as a Second Language classes when they have to cite a source in their research essays.

This convention of explicitly acknowledging the source of an idea, quotation, piece of data, or information with a footnote or parenthetical citation and bibliography arose in the past 150 years. It began when mostly German universities began promoting the idea that the purpose of research was not simply to demonstrate an understanding of what already was known, but to *make a contribution of new knowledge*. Researchers were to look for gaps in existing scholarship—questions that hadn't yet been asked—or to offer extensions of what had already been posed by someone else. Knowledge making became the business of the research writer, and, like gardeners, scholars saw themselves as tending a living thing, a kind of tree that grew larger as new branches were grafted onto existing limbs.

Just as a child clambering up a tree in the park is grateful for the sturdy limbs under his or her feet, research writers acknowledge the limbs they are standing on that have helped them to see a little more of their subjects. That's why they cite their sources. This is an act of gratitude, of course, but it also signals to readers on whose authority the writer's claims, conclusions, or ideas are based. Citation helps readers locate the writer's work on a specific part of the tree of knowledge in a discipline; it gives a useful context of *what has already been said* about a question or a topic.

Student writers cite for exactly the same reasons: not because it's required in most college research writing, but because it makes their research writing more relevant and more convincing to the people who read it.

There are quite a few conventions for citing, and these conventions often vary by discipline. Humanities disciplines such as English often use the Modern Language Association (MLA) conventions, while the social sciences use the American Psychological Association (APA) methods. Both of these documentation styles are detailed later in this chapter. Although there are differences between the two styles, the purpose of each is the same: to acknowledge those from whom you have borrowed ideas and information.

> Citation helps readers locate the writer's work on a specific part of the tree of knowledge in a discipline; it gives a useful context of *what has already been said* about a question or a topic.

Avoiding Plagiarism

Modern authors get testy when someone uses their work without giving them credit. This is where the concept of intellectual property comes from, an idea that emerged with the invention of the printing press and the distribution of multiple copies of an author's work. In its most basic form, plagiarism is stealing someone else's words, ideas, or information. Academic plagiarism, the kind that gets a lot of ink these days, especially with the rise of the Internet, usually refers to more-specific misdeeds. Your university probably has an academic honesty or plagiarism policy posted on the web or in a student handbook. You need to look at it. But it probably includes most or all of the following forms of plagiarism:

> Intentional plagiarism stems from an intellectual laziness and dishonesty that sooner or later are bound to catch up with the person doing it.

1. Handing in someone else's work—a downloaded paper from the Internet or borrowed from a friend—and claiming that it's your own.
2. Using information or ideas that are not common knowledge from any source and failing to acknowledge the source.
3. Handing in the same paper for two different classes.
4. Using the exact language or expressions of a source and not indicating through quotation marks and citation that the language is borrowed.
5. Rewriting a passage from a source using minor substitutions of different words but retaining the same syntax and structure of the original.

Most plagiarism is unintentional. The writer simply didn't know or pay attention to course or university plagiarism policies. Equally common is simple carelessness. How can you avoid this trap? Check out the "Tips for Avoiding Plagiarism" box.

Intentional plagiarism, of course, is a different matter. Many websites offer papers on thousands of topics to anyone willing to pay for them. College instructors, however, have tools for identifying these downloaded papers. The consequences of buying and handing in online papers are often severe, including flunking the course and even expulsion—an academic Hades of sorts. Moreover, even if a person is not caught committing this academic crime, intentional plagiarism stems from an intellectual laziness and dishonesty that sooner or later are bound to catch up with the person doing it. Just don't go there.

9.3
Understand and identify plagiarism to avoid it in your own work.

Tips for Avoiding Plagiarism

- **Don't procrastinate.** Many careless mistakes in citation or proper handling of source material occur in the rush to finish the draft in the wee hours of the morning.

- **Be an active note taker.** Work in the middle of the process to take possession of the material you read, especially exploring your responses to sources *in your own words* and *for your own purposes*.

- **Collect bibliographic information first.** Before you do anything else, take down complete publication information for each source, including the page numbers from which you borrowed material.

- **Mark quoted material clearly.** Whenever you quote a source directly, make sure that it's obvious in your notes.

- **Be vigilant whenever you cut and paste.** The great usefulness of cutting and pasting passages in electronic documents is also the downfall of many research writers. Is the copied material directly borrowed, and if so, is it properly cited?

Exercise 9.1

The Accidental Plagiarist

Most plagiarism problems are accidental. The writer simply isn't aware that he or she has stumbled into the problem. Here's a low-stakes exercise that can test your understanding of how to avoid the simplest—and most common—types of accidental plagiarism. Get this wrong and the grammar police won't accost you in the middle of the night, throw you against the wall, and make you spell difficult words. You'll just learn something.

Using the words and ideas of others in your own writing is essential in most research essays and papers. Doing this without plagiarizing isn't exactly like walking through a minefield, but you do have to step carefully. For example, Beth is exploring the question "What might explain the high rate of divorce in the early years of marriage?" She's interested in divorce because she just went through one. In her research, Beth encounters Diane Ackerman's book, *The Natural History of Love*, and finds the following paragraph:

"Philandering," we call it, "fooling around," "hanky-panky," "skirt chasing," "man chasing," or something equally picturesque. Monogamy and adultery are both hall-marks of being human. Anthropologist Helen Fisher proposes a chemical basis for adultery, what she calls "The Four-Year Itch." Studying the United Nations survey of marriage and divorce around the world, she noticed that divorce usually occurs early in marriage, during the couple's first reproductive and parenting years. Also, that this peak time for divorce coincides with the period in which infatuation normally ends, and a couple has to decide if they're going to call it quits or stay together as companions. Some couples do stay together and have other children, but even more don't. "The human animal," she concludes, "seems built to court, to fall in love, and to marry one person at a time; then, at the height of our reproductive years, often with a single child, we divorce them; then, a few years after, we remarry once again."

Beth thought this was pretty interesting stuff, and in her draft she summarized the paragraph in the following way:

> According to Diane Ackerman, a hallmark of being human is "monogamy and adultery," and she cites the period right after infatuation subsides—about four years for most couples—as the time when they call it quits.

STEP ONE: In small groups, analyze Beth's summary. Does Beth plagiarize the original passage, and if so, do you have ideas about how she could fix it? Revise the summary on a piece of newsprint and post it on the wall.

STEP TWO: Discuss the proposed revisions. How well do they address any plagiarism problems you see in Beth's summary?

STEP THREE: Now compare the following paraphrases of the same Ackerman passage. Which has plagiarism problems and which seems okay?

PARAPHRASE 1

Divorce may have a "chemical basis," something that may kick in after four years of marriage and ironically when partners are reaching their highest potential for having children. Researcher Helen Fisher calls it "The Four-Year Itch," the time that often signals a shift from infatuation into a more sober assessment of the relationship's future: Are they going to stay together or "call it quits"? Most end up deciding to end the relationship.

PARAPHRASE 2

When infatuation fades and couples are faced with the future of their relationship, biochemistry may help them decide. According to researcher Helen Fisher, "divorce usually occurs early in marriage, during the couple's first reproductive and parenting years" (Ackerman 165). She suggests that this is often about four years into the relationship, and argues that humans may be designed to behave this way because the pattern seems so entrenched (Ackerman 166).

STEP FOUR: In class, discuss which paraphrase seems acceptable and which does not. Note that the problems are pretty subtle.

STEP FIVE: Now practice your own *summary* of the following passage, applying what you've learned so far in the exercise about ways to avoid plagiarism when using the words and ideas of other people. This passage in Ackerman's book follows the passage you worked with earlier.

> Our chemistry makes it easy to follow that plan, and painful to avoid it. After the seductive fireworks of first attraction, which may last a few weeks or a few years, the body gets bored with easy ecstasy. The nerves no longer quiver with excitement. Nothing new has been happening for ages, why bother to rouse oneself? Love is exhausting. Then the attachment chemicals roll in their thick cozy carpets of marital serenity. Might as well relax and enjoy the calm and security some feel. Separated even for a short while, the partners crave the cradle of the other's embrace. Is it a chemical craving? Possibly so, a hunger for the soothing endorphins that flow when they're together. It is a deep, sweet river, just right for dangling one's feet in while the world waits.

MLA Documentation Guidelines

The professional organization in charge of academic writing in literature and languages, the Modern Language Association (MLA), uses one of two methods of citing sources that you should be familiar with. The second, the American Psychological Association (APA) system, is described in the next section. Your English class will most likely use the MLA system.

9.4
Cite sources using MLA and APA documentation styles.

The guidelines presented in this section are based on the seventh edition of the *MLA Handbook for Writers of Research Papers* (2009).

You must cite a source in your paper in the following situations:

1. Whenever you quote from an original source.

2. Whenever you borrow ideas from an original source, even when you express them in your own words by paraphrasing or summarizing.

3. Whenever you borrow factual information from a source that is not common knowledge (see "Inquiring into the Details: The Common Knowledge Exception").

Inquiring into the Details

The Common Knowledge Exception

The business about common knowledge causes much confusion. Just what does this term mean? Basically, *common knowledge* means facts that are widely known and about which there is no controversy.

Sometimes, it's really obvious whether something is common knowledge. The fact that the Super Bowl occurs in late January and pits the winning teams from the American and National Football Conferences against each other is common knowledge. The fact that former president Ronald Reagan was once an actor and starred in a movie with a chimpanzee is common knowledge, too. And the fact that most Americans get most of their news from television is also common knowledge, although this information is getting close to leaving the domain of common knowledge.

But what about a writer's assertion that most dreaming occurs during rapid eye movement (REM) sleep? This is an idea about which all sources seem to agree. Does that make it common knowledge?

It's useful to ask next, *How common to whom? Experts in the topic at hand or the rest of us?* As a rule, consider the knowledge of your readers. What information will not be familiar to most of your readers or may even surprise them? Which ideas might even raise skepticism? In this case, the fact about REM sleep and dreaming goes slightly beyond the knowledge of most readers, so to be safe, it should be cited. Use common sense, but when in doubt, cite.

Citing Sources

The foundation of the MLA method of citing sources *in your paper* is putting the last name of the author and the page number of the source in parentheses as closely as possible to the borrowed material. For example,

> Researchers believe that there is an "infatuation chemical" that may account
>
> for that almost desperate attraction we feel when we're near someone special
>
> (Ackerman 164).

The parenthetical citation tells a reader two things: the source of the information (for example, the author's name) and where in the work to find the borrowed idea or material. A really interested reader—perhaps an infatuated one—who wanted to follow up on this would then refer to the Works Cited at the back of the paper. This would list the work by the author's last name and all the pertinent information about the source:

> Ackerman, Diane. *A Natural History of Love*. New York: Vintage, 1994. Print.

Here's another example of parenthetical author/page citation from another research paper. Note the differences from the previous example:

> "One thing is clear," writes Thomas Mallon, "plagiarism didn't become a truly
>
> sore point with writers until they thought of writing as their trade.... Suddenly
>
> his capital and identity were at stake" (3–4).

The first thing you may have noticed is that the author's last name—Mallon—was omitted from the parenthetical citation. It didn't need to be included, because it had already been mentioned in the text. *If you mention the author's name in the text of your paper, then you only need to parenthetically cite the relevant page number(s).* This citation also tells us that the quoted passage comes from two pages rather than one.

Where to Put Citations. Place the citation as close as you can to the borrowed material, trying to avoid breaking the flow of the sentences, if possible. To avoid confusion about what's borrowed and what's not—particularly in passages longer than a sentence—mention the name of the original author *in your paper*. Note that in the next example the writer simply cites the source at the end of the paragraph, not naming the source in the text. Doing so makes it hard for the reader to figure out whether Blager is the source of the information in the entire paragraph or just part of it:

> Though children who have been sexually abused seem to be disadvantaged in many areas, including the inability to forge lasting relationships, low self-esteem, and crippling shame, they seem advantaged in other areas. Sexually abused children seem to be more socially mature than other children of their same age group. It's a distinctly mixed blessing (Blager 994).

In the following example, notice how the ambiguity about what's borrowed and what's not is resolved by careful placement of the author's name and parenthetical citation in the text:

> Though children who have been sexually abused seem to be disadvantaged in many areas, including the inability to forge lasting relationships, low self-esteem, and crippling shame, they seem advantaged in other areas. According to Blager, sexually abused children seem to be more socially mature than other children of their same age group (994). It's a distinctly mixed blessing.

In this latter version, it's clear that Blager is the source for one sentence in the paragraph, and the writer is responsible for the rest. Generally, use an authority's last name, rather than a formal title or first name, when mentioning him or her in your text. Also note that the citation is placed *inside* the period of the sentence (or last sentence) that it documents. That's almost always the case, except at the end of a blocked quotation, where the parenthetical reference is placed after the period of the last sentence.

Inquiring into the Details

Citations That Go with the Flow

There's no getting around it—parenthetical citations can be like stones on the sidewalk. Readers stride through a sentence in your essay and then have to step around the citation at the end before they resume their walk. Yet citations are important in academic writing because they help readers know whom you read or heard that shaped your thinking.

Inquiring into the Details (*continued*)

However, you can minimize citations that trip up readers and make your essay more readable by doing the following:

- Avoid lengthy parenthetical citations by mentioning the name of the author in your essay. That way, you usually have to include only a page number in the citation.
- Try to place citations where readers are likely to pause anyway—for example, the end of the sentence or right before a comma.
- Remember that you *don't* need a citation when you're citing common knowledge or referring to an entire work by an author.
- If you're borrowing from only one source in a paragraph of your essay and all of the borrowed material comes from a single page of that source, don't bother repeating the citation over and over again with each new bit of information. Just put the citation at the end of the paragraph.

The citation can also be placed near the author's name, rather than at the end of the sentence, if it doesn't unnecessarily break the flow of the sentence. For example:

Blager (994) observes that sexually abused children tend to be more socially

mature than other children of their same age group.

When You Mention the Author's Name. It's generally good practice in research writing to identify who said what. The familiar convention of using attribution tags such as "According to Fletcher,..." or "Fletcher argues that..." and so on helps readers attach a name to a voice, or an individual to certain claims or findings. When you mention the author of a source, you can drop his or her name from the parenthetical citation and just list the page number. For example,

Robert Harris believes that there is "widespread uncertainty" among students

about what constitutes plagiarism (2).

You may also list the page number directly after the author's name.

Robert Harris (2) believes that there is "widespread uncertainty" among students

about what constitutes plagiarism.

When There Is No Author. Occasionally, you may encounter a source in which the author is anonymous—where the article doesn't have a byline or for some reason the author hasn't been identified. This isn't unusual with pamphlets, editorials, government documents, some newspaper articles, online sources, and short filler articles in magazines. If you can't parenthetically name the author, what do you cite?

Most often, cite the title (or an abbreviated version, if the title is long) and the page number. If you choose to abbreviate the title, begin with the word under which it is alphabetized in the Works Cited. For example:

According to the Undergraduate Catalog, "the athletic program is an integral

part of the university and its total educational purpose" (7).

Here is how this publication would be listed at the back of the paper:

Works Cited

Undergraduate Catalog, Boise State University 2012–2013.

Boise, ID: BSU, 2012. Print.

For clarity, it's helpful to mention the original source of the borrowed material in the text of your paper. When there is no author's name, refer to the publication (or institution) you're citing or make a more general reference to the source. For example:

An article in *Cuisine* magazine argues that the best way to kill a lobster is to

plunge a knife between its eyes ("How to Kill" 56).

or

According to one government report, with the current minimum size limit, most

lobsters end up on dinner plates before they've had a chance to reproduce ("Size

at Sexual Maturity" 3–4).

Works by the Same Author. Suppose you end up using several books or articles by the same author. Obviously, a parenthetical citation that merely lists the author's name and page number won't do, because it won't be clear *which* of several works the citation refers to. In this case, include the author's name, an abbreviated title (if the original is too long), and the page number. For example:

One essayist who suffers from multiple sclerosis writes that "there is a subtle

taxonomy of crippleness" (Mairs, *Carnal Acts* 69).

The Works Cited list would show multiple works by one author as follows:

Works Cited

Mairs, Nancy. *Carnal Acts*. Boston: Beacon, 1996. Print.

- - -. *Voice Lessons*. Boston: Beacon, 1994. Print.

It's obvious from the parenthetical citation which of the two Mairs books is the source of the information. Note that in the parenthetical reference, no punctuation separates the title and the page number, but a comma follows the author's name. If Mairs had been mentioned in the text of the paper, her name could have been dropped from the citation.

Also notice that the three hyphens used in the second bibliographic entry are meant to signal that the author's name in this source is the same as in the preceding entry.

When One Source Quotes Another. Whenever you can, cite the original source for material you use. For example, if an article on television violence quotes the author of a book and you want to use the quote, try to hunt down the book. That way, you'll be certain of the accuracy of the quote and you may find some more usable information.

Sometimes, however, finding the original source is not possible. In those cases, use the term *qtd. in* to signal that you've quoted or paraphrased a quotation from a book or article that you found elsewhere. In the following example, the citation signals that Bacon's quote was culled from an article by Guibroy, not Bacon's original work:

> Francis Bacon also weighed in on the dangers of imitation, observing that "it
>
> is hardly possible at once to admire an author and to go beyond him" (qtd. in
>
> Guibroy 113).

Personal Interviews. If you mention the name of your interview subject in your text, no parenthetical citation is necessary. On the other hand, if you don't mention the subject's name, cite it in parentheses after the quote:

> Instead, the recognizable environment gave something to kids they could
>
> relate to. "And it had a lot more real quality to it than, say, *Mister Rogers...,*"
>
> says one educator. "Kids say the reason they don't like *Mister Rogers* is that it's
>
> unbelievable" (Diamonti).

Regardless of whether you mention your subject's name, you should include a reference to the interview in the Works Cited. In this case, the reference would look like this:

Works Cited

Diamonti, Nancy. Personal interview. 5 Nov. 1999.

Several Sources in a Single Citation. Suppose two sources both contributed the same information in a paragraph of your essay. Or perhaps even more common is when you're summarizing the findings of several authors on a certain topic—a fairly common move when you're trying to establish a context for your own research question. You cite multiple authors in a single citation in the usual fashion, using author name and page number, but separating each with a semicolon. For example,

> A whole range of studies have looked closely at the intellectual development of
>
> college students, finding that they generally assume "stages" or "perspectives"
>
> that differ from subject to subject (Perry 122; Belenky et al. 12).

If you can, however, avoid long citations, because they can be cumbersome for readers.

Sample Parenthetical References for Other Sources. MLA format is pretty simple, and we've already covered some of the basic variations. You should also know five additional variations, as follow:

AN ENTIRE WORK

If you mention the author's name in the text, no citation is necessary. The work should, however, be listed in the Works Cited.

> Leon Edel's *Henry James* is considered by many to be a model biography.

A VOLUME OF A MULTIVOLUME WORK

If you're working with one volume of a multivolume work, it's a good idea to mention which volume in the parenthetical reference. The following citation attributes the passage to volume 2, page 3, of a work by Baym and three or more other authors. The volume number always precedes the colon, which is followed by the page number:

> By the turn of the century, three authors dominated American literature: Mark
>
> Twain, Henry James, and William Dean Howells (Baym et al. 2: 3).

SEVERAL SOURCES FOR A SINGLE PASSAGE

Occasionally, a number of sources may contribute to a single passage. List them all in one parenthetical reference, separated by semicolons:

> American soccer may never achieve the popularity it enjoys in the rest of the
>
> world, an unfortunate fact that is integrally related to the nature of the game
>
> itself (Gardner 12; "Selling Soccer" 30).[1]

---

[1] Jason Pulsifer, University of New Hampshire, 1991. Used with permission

A LITERARY WORK

Because so many literary works, particularly classics, have been reprinted in so many editions, it's useful to give readers more information about where a passage can be found in one of these editions. List the page number and then the chapter number (and any other relevant information, such as the section or volume), separated by a semicolon. Use arabic rather than roman numerals, unless your teacher instructs you otherwise:

> Izaak Walton warns that "no direction can be given to make a man of a dull
>
> capacity able to make a Flie well" (130; ch. 5).

When citing classic poems or plays, instead of page numbers, cite line numbers and other appropriate divisions (book, section, act, scene, part, etc.). Separate the information with periods. For example, (*Othello* 2.3.286) indicates act 2, scene 3, line 286 of Shakespeare's work.

AN ONLINE SOURCE

Online sources frequently don't have page numbers. So how can you cite them parenthetically in your essay? Most of the time, you won't include page numbers, particularly when you're citing web pages.

Rarely, digital documents include paragraph numbers. If so, use the abbreviation *par.* or *pars.*, followed by the paragraph number or numbers you're borrowing material from. For example:

> In most psychotherapeutic approaches, the personality of the therapist can have
>
> a big impact on the outcome of the therapy ("Psychotherapy," par. 1).

Sometimes the material has an internal structure, such as sections, parts, chapters, or volumes. If so, use the abbreviation *sec., pt., ch.,* or *vol.* (respectively), followed by the appropriate number.

In many cases, a parenthetical citation can be avoided entirely by simply naming the source in the text of your essay. A curious reader will then find the full citation to the article on the Works Cited page at the back of your paper. For example:

> According to Charles Petit, the worldwide effort to determine whether frogs are
>
> disappearing will take somewhere between three and five years.

Finally, if you don't want to mention the source in text, parenthetically cite the author's last name (if any) or article title:

> The worldwide effort to determine whether frogs are disappearing will take
>
> somewhere between three and five years (Petit).

Format

The Layout. A certain fussiness is associated with the look of academic papers. The reason for it is quite simple—academic disciplines generally aim for consistency in format so that readers of scholarship know exactly where to look to find what they want to know. It's a matter of efficiency. How closely you must follow the MLA's requirements for the layout of your essay is up to your instructor, but it's really not that complicated. A lot of what you need to know is featured in Figure 9.1.

Printing. Compose your paper on white, $8^1/_2$" × 11" printer paper. Make sure the printer has sufficient ink or toner.

Margins and Spacing. The old high school trick is to use big margins. That way, you can meet your page length requirements with less material. Don't try that trick with this paper. Leave half-inch margins at the top and one-inch margins at the bottom and sides of your pages. Indent the first line of each paragraph five spaces, and blocked quotes ten spaces. Double-space all of the text, including blocked quotes and Works Cited.

Title Page. Your paper doesn't need a separate title page. Begin with the first page of text. One inch below the top of the page, type your name, your instructor's name, the course number, and the date (see the following). Below that, type the title, centered on the page. Begin the text of the paper below the title.

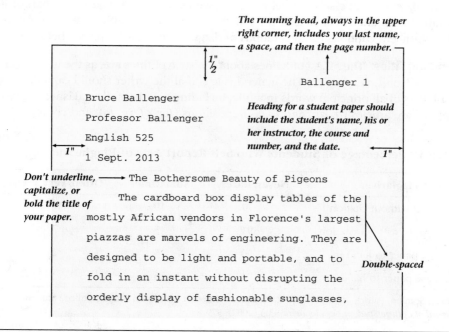

Figure 9.1 The basic look of an MLA-style paper

Julie Bird

Professor Ballenger

English 102

1 June 2013

Nature as Being: Landscape in Silko's "Lullaby"

Leslie Marmon Silko, the author of "Lullaby," is a Native American writer from the Laguna Pueblo culture...

Note that every line is double-spaced. The title is not underlined (unless it includes the name of a book or some other work that should be underlined) or boldfaced.

Pagination. Make sure that every page, including the first one, is numbered. That's especially important with long papers. Type your last name and the page number in the upper right corner, flush with the right margin: Ballenger 3. Don't use the abbreviation *p.* or a hyphen between your name and the number.

Placement of Tables, Charts, and Illustrations. With MLA format, papers do not have appendixes. Tables, charts, and illustrations are placed in the body of the paper, close to the text that refers to them. Number illustrations consecutively (Table 1 or Figure 3), and indicate sources below them (see Figure 9.2). If you use a chart or illustration from another text, give the full citation. Place any table caption above the table, flush left. Captions for illustrations or diagrams are usually placed below them.

Handling Titles. The MLA guidelines about the style of titles are, as the most recent *Handbook* observes, "strict." The general rule is that the writer should capitalize the first letters of all principal words in a title, including any that follow dashes. The exceptions are articles (*a, an,* and *the*), prepositions (*for, of, in, to*), and coordinating

Table 1   Percentage of Students Who Self-Report Acts of Plagiarism

Acts of Plagiarism	Never/Rarely	Sometimes	Often/Very Freq.
Copy text without citation	71	19	10
Copy paper without citation	91	5	3
Request paper to hand in	90	5	2
Purchase paper to hand in	91	6	3

Source: Scanlon, Patrick M., and David R. Neumann. "Internet Plagiarism Among College Students." *Journal of College Student Development* 43.3 (2002): 379.

Figure 9.2   Example of format for a table

conjunctions (*and, or, but, for*). These exceptions apply *only if the words appear in the middle of a title*; capitalize them if they appear at the beginning or end.

The rules for underlining a title or putting it in quotation marks are as follows:

1. *Italicize the Title* if it is a book, play, pamphlet, film, magazine, TV program, CD, audiocassette, newspaper, or work of art.

2. "Put the Title in Quotes" if it is an article in a newspaper, magazine, or encyclopedia; a short story; a poem; an episode of a TV program; a song; a lecture; or a chapter or essay in a book.

Here are some examples:

The Curious Researcher (Book)

English Online: The Student's Guide to the Internet (CD-ROM)

"Once More to the Lake" (Essay)

Historic Boise: An Introduction into the Architecture of Boise, Idaho (Book)

"Psychotherapy" (Encyclopedia article)

Idaho Statesman (Newspaper)

"One Percent Initiative Panned" (Newspaper article)

Under the most recent guidelines (the *MLA Handbook, Seventh Edition)*, the underlining of titles is out and the use of italics is in. Now, for instance, your Works Cited page would list the book title <u>Bombproof Your Horse</u> as *Bombproof Your Horse*. (And yes, that's horse not house.)

Language and Style

Names. Though it may seem as if you're on familiar terms with some of the authors you cite by the end of your research project, it's not a good idea to call them by their first names. Typically, initially give the full names of people you cite, and then only their last names if you mention them again in your essay.

Ellipsis Dots. Those are the three (always three unless you're omitting material that comes at the end of a sentence, where they join a period) dots that indicate you've left out a word, phrase, or even whole section of a quoted passage. It's often wise to do this because you want to emphasize only certain parts of a quotation rather than burden your reader with unnecessary information, but be careful to preserve the basic intention and idea of the author's original statement. The ellipsis dots can come at the beginning of a quotation, in the middle, or at the end, depending where it is you've omitted material. For example,

"After the publication of a controversial picture that shows, for example, either

dead or grieving victims..., readers, in telephone calls and in letters to the

editor, often attack the photographer for being tasteless...."

Quotations. Quotations that run more than four lines long should be blocked, or indented ten spaces from the left margin. The quotation should be double-spaced and quotation marks should be omitted. In an exception from the usual convention, the parenthetical citation is placed *outside* the period at the end of the quotation. A colon is a customary way to introduce a blocked quotation. For example,

> Chris Sherman and Gary Price, in *The Invisible Web*, contend that much of the Internet, possibly most, is beyond the reach of researchers who use conventional search engines:
>
>> The problem is that vast expanses of the Web are completely invisible to general-purpose search engines like AltaVista, HotBot, and Google. Even worse, this "Invisible Web" is in all likelihood growing significantly faster than the visible Web that you're familiar with. It's not that search engines and Web directories are "stupid" or even badly engineered. Rather, they simply can't "see" millions of high quality resources that are available exclusively on the Invisible Web. So what is this Invisible Web and why aren't search engines doing anything about it to make it visible? (xxi)

Preparing the Works Cited Page

The Works Cited page ends the paper. Several other lists of sources may also appear at the end of a research paper, though these are much less common in college research essays. An Annotated List of Works Cited not only lists the sources used in the paper, but also includes a brief description of each. A Works Consulted list includes sources that may or may not have been cited in the paper but shaped your thinking. A Content Notes page, keyed to superscript numbers in the text of the paper, lists short commentaries or asides that are significant but not central enough to the discussion to be included in the text of the paper.

The Works Cited page is the workhorse of most college papers. The other source lists are used less often. Works Cited is essentially an alphabetical listing of all the sources you quoted, paraphrased, or summarized in your paper. If you have used MLA format for citing sources, your paper has numerous parenthetical references to authors and page numbers. The Works Cited page provides complete information on each source cited in the text for the reader who wants to know. (In APA format, this page is called References and is only slightly different in how items are listed.)

If you've been careful about collecting complete bibliographic information—author, title, editor, edition, volume, place, publisher, date, page numbers—then preparing your Works Cited page will be easy. If you've recorded that information on notecards, all you have to do is put them in alphabetical order and then transcribe them into your paper. If you've been careless about collecting that information, you may need to take a hike back to the library.

Format

Alphabetizing the List. Works Cited follows the text of your paper on a separate page. After you've assembled complete information about each source you've cited, put the sources in alphabetical order by the last name of the author. If the work has multiple authors, use the last name of the first listed. If the source has no author, then alphabetize it by the first key word of the title. If you're citing more than one source by a single author, you don't need to repeat the name for each source; simply place three hyphens followed by a period (- - -.) for the author's name in subsequent listings.

Indenting and Spacing. Type the first line of each entry flush left, and indent subsequent lines of that entry (if any) five spaces. Double-space between each line and each entry. For example:

Works Cited

Bianchi, William. "Education by Radio: America's Schools of the Air." *TechTrends: Linking Research & Practice to Improve Learning* 52.2 (2008): 36–44. Print.

Campbell, Gardener. "There's Something in the Air: Podcasting and Education." *EDUCAUSE Review,* vol. 40, no. 6 (November/December 2005): 32–47. Print.

Checho, Colleen. "The Effects of Podcasting on Learning and Motivation: A Mixed Method Study of At-Risk High School Students." Diss. University of Nevada, Reno. Ann Arbor, UMI, 2007. Print.

Davis, Anne, and Ewa McGrail. "'Proof-Revising' With Podcasting: Keeping Readers in Mind as Students Listen to and Rethink Their Writing." *The Reading Teacher* 62.6 (2009): 522–29. Print.

Grisham, Dana L., and Thomas Devere Wolsey. "Writing Instruction for Teacher Candidates: Strengthening a Weak Curricular Area." *Literacy Research and Instruction* 50.4 (2011): 348–64. Print.

Klaus, Carl H. *The Made-Up Self: Impersonation in the Personal Essay.* Iowa City: University of Iowa Press, 2010. Print.

"What Is Educational Podcasting?" *Educate.* Russell Educational Consultancy and Productions. No date. Web. 7 July 2012.

Citing Books. You usually need three pieces of information to cite a book: the name of the author or authors, the title, and the publication information. If you're citing an e-book, however, some additional information may be required. See below.

CITING A BOOK IN PRINT	CITING AN E-BOOK
1. Author(s)	1. Author(s)
2. *Title*	2. *Title*
3. Edition and/or volume (if relevant)	3. Edition and/or volume (if relevant)
4. Where published, by whom, and date	4. If also in print, where published, by whom, and date; in any case, sponsoring organization, date of electronic publication
5. Medium: Print	5. Medium: Web
	6. Date of access
SAMPLE CITATION: BOOK IN PRINT	**SAMPLE CITATION: E-BOOK (WEB ONLY)**
Donald, David H. *Lincoln.* New York: Simon, 1995. Print.	Lincoln, Abraham. *The Writings of Abraham Lincoln.* B & R Samisdat Express. 2009. Web. 28 Jan. 2011.

Title. Titles of books are italicized, with the first letters of all principal words capitalized, including those in any subtitles. Titles that are not italicized are usually those of pieces found within larger works, such as poems and short stories in anthologies. These titles are set off by quotation marks. Titles of religious works (the Bible, the Qur'an, etc.) are neither underlined nor enclosed within quotation marks. (See the guidelines in the earlier "Handling Titles" section.)

Edition. If a book doesn't indicate an edition number, then it's probably a first edition, a fact you don't need to cite. Look on the title page. Signal an edition like this: *2nd ed., 3rd ed.,* and so on.

Publication Place, Publisher, and Date. Look on the title page to find out who published the book. Publishers' names are usually shortened in the Works Cited list: for example, *St. Martin's Press Inc.* is shortened to *St. Martin's.*

It's sometimes confusing to know what to cite about the publication place, because several cities are often listed on the title page. Cite the first.

The date a book is published is usually indicated on the copyright page. If several dates or several printings by the same publisher are listed, cite the original publication date. However, if the book is a revised edition, give the date of that edition. One final variation: If you're citing a book that's a reprint of an original edition, give both dates. For example:

Stegner, Wallace. *Recapitulation*. 1979. Lincoln: U of Nebraska P, 1986. Print.

This book was first published in 1979 and then republished in 1986 by the University of Nebraska Press.

Page Numbers. You don't usually list page numbers of a book. The parenthetical reference in your paper specifies that. But if you use only part of a book—an introduction or an essay—list the appropriate page numbers following the publication date. Use periods to set off the page numbers. If the author or editor of the entire work is also the author of the introduction or essay you're citing, list her by last name only the second time you cite her. For example:

Lee, L. L., and Merrill Lewis. Preface. *Women, Women Writers, and the West*. Ed.

Lee and Lewis. Troy, MI: Whitston, 1980. v–ix. Print.

Publication Medium. A recent update to the MLA's guidelines now requires that you include the type of source. In most cases, a book citation will end with the word "Print." An online book would end with "Web."

Sample Book Citations
A BOOK BY ONE AUTHOR

Keen, Sam. *Fire in the Belly*. New York: Bantam, 1991. Print.

In-Text Citation: (Keen 101)

A BOOK BY TWO AUTHORS

Ballenger, Bruce, and Barry Lane. *Discovering the Writer Within*. Cincinnati:

Writer's Digest, 1996. Print.

In-Text Citation: (Ballenger and Lane 14)

A BOOK WITH MORE THAN THREE AUTHORS
If a book has more than three authors, list the first and substitute the term *et al.* for the others.

Belenky, Mary Field, et al. *Women's Ways of Knowing*. New York: Basic Books,

1973. Print.

In-Text Citation: (Belenky et al. 21–30)

SEVERAL BOOKS BY THE SAME AUTHOR

Baldwin, James. *Going to Meet the Man*. New York: Dell-Doubleday, 1948. Print.

- - -. *Tell Me How Long the Train's Been Gone*. New York: Dell-Doubleday, 1968.

Print.

In-Text Citation: (Baldwin, *Going* 34)

A COLLECTION OR ANTHOLOGY

Crane, R. S., ed. *Critics and Criticism: Ancient and Modern*. Chicago: U of Chicago

P, 1952. Print.

In-Text Citation: (Crane xx)

A WORK IN A COLLECTION OR ANTHOLOGY

The title of a work that is part of a collection but was originally published as a book should be italicized. Otherwise, the title of a work in a collection should be enclosed in quotation marks.

Bahktin, Mikhail. *Marxism and the Philosophy of Language*. *The Rhetorical*

Tradition. Ed. Patricia Bizzell and Bruce Herzberg. New York: St. Martin's,

1990. 928–44. Print.

In-Text Citation: (Bahktin 929–31)

Jones, Robert F. "Welcome to Muskie Country." *The Ultimate Fishing Book*. Ed. Lee

Eisenberg and DeCourcy Taylor. Boston: Houghton, 1981. 122–34. Print.

In-Text Citation: (Jones 131)

AN INTRODUCTION, PREFACE, FOREWORD, OR PROLOGUE

Scott, Jerie Cobb. Foreword. *Writing Groups: History, Theory, and Implications*. By

Ann Ruggles Gere. Carbondale: Southern Illinois UP, 1987. ix–xi. Print.

In-Text Citation : (Scott ix–xi)

Rich, Adrienne. Introduction. *On Lies, Secrets, and Silence*. By Rich. New York:

Norton, 1979. 9–18. Print.

In-Text Citation: (Rich 12)

A BOOK WITH NO AUTHOR

American Heritage Dictionary. 3rd ed. Boston: Houghton, 1994. Print.

In-Text Citation: (*American Heritage Dictionary* 444)

AN ENCYCLOPEDIA

> "Passenger Pigeon." *Encyclopedia Britannica Online.* Encyclopedia Britannica,
>
> Inc., 2012. Web. 26 June 2012.
>
> *In-Text Citation:* ("Passenger Pigeon")
>
> "City of Chicago." *Encyclopaedia Britannica.* 1999 ed. Print.
>
> *In-Text Citation:* ("City of Chicago" 397)

A BOOK WITH AN INSTITUTIONAL AUTHOR

> Hospital Corporation of America. *Employee Benefits Handbook.* Nashville: HCA,
>
> 1990. Print.
>
> *In-Text Citation:* (Hospital Corporation of America 5–7)

A BOOK WITH MULTIPLE VOLUMES

Include the number of volumes in the work between the title and publication information.

> Baym, Nina, et al., eds. *The Norton Anthology of American Literature.* 5th ed. 2
>
> vols. New York: Norton, 1998. Print.
>
> *In-Text Citation:* (Baym et al. 2: 3)

If you use one volume of a multivolume work, indicate which one, along with the page numbers, followed by the total number of volumes in the work.

> Anderson, Sherwood. "Mother." *The Norton Anthology of American Literature.* Ed. Nina
>
> Baym et al. 5th ed. Vol. 2. New York: Norton, 1998. 1115–31. 2 vols. Print.
>
> *In-Text Citation:* (Anderson 1115)

A BOOK THAT IS NOT A FIRST EDITION

Check the title page to determine whether the book is *not* a first edition (2nd, 3rd, 4th, etc.); if no edition number is mentioned, assume it's the first. Put the edition number right after the title.

> Ballenger, Bruce. *The Curious Researcher.* 7th ed. Boston: Longman, 2011. Print.
>
> *In-Text Citation:* (Ballenger 194)

Citing the edition is necessary only for books that are *not* first editions. This includes revised editions (*Rev. ed.*) and abridged editions (*Abr. ed.*).

A BOOK PUBLISHED BEFORE 1900

For a book this old, it's usually unnecessary to list the publisher.

Hitchcock, Edward. *Religion of Geology*. Glasgow, 1851. Print.

In-Text Citation: (Hitchcock 48)

A TRANSLATION

Montaigne, Michel de. *Essays.* Trans. J. M. Cohen. Middlesex, England: Penguin,

1958. Print.

In-Text Citation: (Montaigne 638)

GOVERNMENT DOCUMENTS

Because of the enormous variety of government documents, citing them properly can be a challenge. Because most government documents do not name authors, begin an entry for such a source with the level of government (U.S. Government, State of Illinois, etc.)—unless it is obvious from the title—followed by the sponsoring agency, the title of the work, and the publication information. Look on the title page to determine the publisher. If it's a federal document, then the *Government Printing Office* (abbreviated *GPO*) is usually the publisher.

United States. Bureau of the Census. *Statistical Abstract of the United States.*

Washington: GPO, 2005. Print.

In-Text Citation: (United States, Bureau of the Census 79–83)

A BOOK THAT WAS REPUBLISHED

A fairly common occurrence, particularly in literary study, is to find a book that was republished, sometimes many years after the original publication date. In addition, some books first appear in hardcover, and then are republished in paperback. To cite, put the original date of publication immediately after the book's title, and then include the more current publication date, as usual, at the end of the citation. Do it like so:

Didion, Joan. *Slouching Towards Bethlehem*. 1968. New York: Farrar, 1992. Print.

In-Text Citation: (Didion 31)

Badke, William. *Research Strategies: Finding Your Way through the Information

Fog.* Lincoln, NE: Writers Club P, 2000. Web. 12 July 2009.

In-Text Citation: (Badke)

Citing Periodicals. These days, you're more likely to find an article through a library database or on the web than in a print journal or magazine. Citation of each type of source is quite similar, with the differences listed in the following table.

PRINT ARTICLE	ARTICLE FROM A DATABASE OF THE WEB
1. Author(s)	1. Author(s)
2. "Article Title"	2. "Article Title"
3. *Periodical Title*	3. *Periodical Title*
4. Volume and issue	4. Volume and issue
5. Date published	5. Date published
6. Page numbers	6. Page numbers, if any (usually present in versions also in print)
7. Medium: Print	7. *Website, Database* or Sponsor
	8. Medium: Web
	9. Date of access
SAMPLE CITATION: PRINT ARTICLE	**SAMPLE CITATION: DATABASE ARTICLE**
Newcomb, Matthew. "Sustainability as a Design Principle for Composition." *College Composition and Communication* 63.4 (2012): 593–614. Print.	Pereira, Tony. "The Transition to a Sustainable Society: A New Social Contract." *Environment, Development and Sustainability* 14.2 (2012): 273–281. *Crossref.* Web. 26 June 2012.

Format. Citations for magazines, journals, newspapers, and the like aren't much different from citing books. MLA's 2009 update, however, introduced some significant changes in how you handle online periodicals (see the table).

Author's Name. List the author(s) as you would for a book citation.

Article Title. Unlike book titles, article titles are usually enclosed in quotation marks.

Periodical Title. Italicize periodical titles, dropping introductory articles (*Aegis*, not *The Aegis*). If you're citing a newspaper your readers may not be familiar with, include in the title—enclosed in brackets but not italicized—the city in which it was published. For example:

Barber, Rocky. "DEQ Responds to Concerns About Weiser Feedlot." *Idaho*

   Statesman [Boise] 23 Apr. 2004: B1. Print.

Volume and Issue Numbers. Most scholarly journals have both. The latest MLA guidelines require that you include both in your citation. These will appear as weird decimals after the journal title. For example, the sixth volume and third issue of the journal *Diseases of the Dairy Cow* would be 6.3. Popular periodicals frequently don't have issue numbers, and you're not required to use them.

Name of Website, Database, or Sponsor. If the name of the site is different from the title of the piece you're citing, include that name in italics. In addition, if the the website's name is different from the organization that hosts it include the sponsor's name as well. The name of the site's sponsor isn't always obvious. Try looking at the bottom of the page or click on the "About Us" link if there is one. If the publisher is unclear include *n.p.* (for "no publisher") in your citation. If you do include a publisher's name, don't italicize it. Finally, if your source is from a library database, identify it (e.g. *ProQuest, JSTOR, Google Scholar,* etc.).

Date. When citing popular periodicals, include the day, month, and year of the issue you're citing—in that order—following the periodical name. Academic journals are a little different. Because the volume number indicates when the journal was published within a given year, just indicate that year. Put it in parentheses following the volume number and before the page numbers (see examples in "A Journal Article" section on following page).

Page Numbers. Include the page numbers of the article at the end of the citation, followed by a period. Just list the pages of the entire article, omitting abbreviations such as *p.* or *pp.* It's common for articles in newspapers and popular magazines *not* to run on consecutive pages. In that case, indicate the page on which the article begins, followed by a "+" (*12+*).

Newspaper pagination can be peculiar. Some papers wed the section (usually a letter) with the page number (*A4*); other papers simply begin numbering anew in each section. Most, however, paginate continuously. See the sample citations for newspapers that follow, for how to deal with these peculiarities.

Online sources, which often have no pagination at all, present special problems. For guidance on how to handle them, see the "Citing Online and Other Sources" section.

Publication Medium. Indicate the form in which you found the periodical, usually either "Print" or "Web."

Date of Access. If you did find the journal or magazine online, end your citation with the date you first accessed it.

Sample Periodical Citations
A MAGAZINE ARTICLE

> Elliot, Carl. "The New Drug Pushers." *Atlantic Monthly* Apr. 2006: 82–93. Print.
>
> *In-Text Citation:* (Elliot 92)
>
> Williams, Patricia J. "Unimagined Communities." *Nation* 3 May 2004: 14. Print.
>
> *In-Text Citation:* (Williams 14)

Citations for magazines that you find online should also include the publication medium ("Web") and the date you accessed the material. For example,

Kaufman, Ken. "Stopover Country." *Audubon Magazine* May–June 2009. Web. 1

July 2009.

In-Text Citation: (Kaufman)

Notice that both the website's name and its publisher are included in the online article below.

Schoen, John W. "Jobless Consumers Will Hold Up Recovery." *Msnbc.com.*

Microsoft, 2 July 2009. Web. 3 July 2009.

In-Text Citation: (Schoen)

A JOURNAL ARTICLE

There's a good chance that you found a journal article using your library's online database. If so, include the database name, italicized, in your citation. Remember to also include the volume and issue number whenever you cite any journal.

Here's an article from a library database.

Niservich, P. M. "Training Tips for Vegetarian Athletes." *IDEA Fitness Journal* 6.4

(2009). *Physical Education Index.* Web. 2 July 2009.

In-Text Citation: (Niservich)

Here is sample citation for an article in print:

Allen, Rebecca E., and J. M. Oliver. "The Effects of Child Maltreatment on

Language Development." *Child Abuse and Neglect* 6.1 (1982): 299–305. Print.

In-Text Citation: (Allen and Oliver 299–300)

A NEWSPAPER ARTICLE

Some newspapers have several editions (morning edition, late edition, national edition), and each may feature different articles. If an edition is listed on the masthead, include it in the citation.

Mendels, Pamela. "Internet Access Spreads to More Classrooms." *New York Times*

1 Dec. 1999, morning ed.: C1+. Print.

In-Text Citation: (Mendels C1)

Some papers begin numbering pages anew in each section. In that case, include the section number if it's not part of pagination.

Brooks, James. "Lobsters on the Brink." *Portland Press* 29 Nov. 2005, sec. 2: 4.

Print.

In-Text Citation: (Brooks 4)

The decline of print newspapers means you are more likely to find an article online. Because these often lack page numbers, you can omit them; but don't forget to include the website's name, publisher (if different), and the date you accessed the article.

Wald, Matthew. "Court Backs EPA on Emissions Rulings." *New York Times*. New

York Times, 26 June 2012. Web. 26 July 2012.

In-Text Citation: (Wald)

AN ARTICLE WITH NO AUTHOR

"The Understanding." *New Yorker* 2 Dec. 1991: 34–35. Print.

In-Text Citation: ("Understanding" 35)

AN EDITORIAL

"Downward Mobility." Editorial. *New York Times* 27 Aug. 2006: 31. Print.

In-Text Citation: ("Downward" 31)

AN OPINION PIECE

Vanden Heuvel, Katrina. "Women Who Don't Have Anything Close to 'It All.'"

Washingtonpost.com. The Washington Post, 26 June 2012. Web. 4 July

2012.

In-Text Citation: (Vanden Heuvel)

A LETTER TO THE EDITOR

Boulay, Harvey. Letter. *Boston Globe* 30 Aug. 2006: 14. Print.

In-Text Citation: (Boulay 14)

A letter to the editor you find online would be cited like this:

Willett, Catherine. "Go Ahead and Test but Spare the Animals." *NYTimes.com*.

New York Times, 2 July 2009. Web. 2 July 2009.

In-Text Citation: (Willett)

A REVIEW

Page, Barbara. Rev. of *Allegories of Cinema: American Film in the Sixties*, by David

E. James. *College English* 54 (1992): 945–54. Print.

In-Text Citation: (Page 945–46)

AN ABSTRACT

> Edwards, Rob. "Air-Raid Warning." *New Scientist* 14 Aug. 1999: 48–49. Abstract.
>
> *MasterFILE Premier.* Web. 1 May 2002.

In-Text Citation: (Edwards)

The following citation is from another useful source of abstracts, the *Dissertation Abstracts International.* In this case, the citation is from the print version of the index.

> McDonald, James C. "Imitation of Models in the History of Rhetoric: Classical,
>
> Belletristic, and Current-Traditional." U of Texas, Austin. *DAI* 48 (1988):
>
> 2613A. Print.

In-Text Citation: (McDonald 2613A)

Citing Online and Other Sources

AN INTERVIEW

If you conducted the interview yourself, list your subject's name first, indicate what kind of interview it was (telephone, e-mail, or personal interview), and provide the date.

> Kelley, Karen. Personal interview. 1 Sept. 2012.

In-Text Citation: (Kelley)

Or avoid parenthetical reference altogether by mentioning the subject's name in the text: According to Lonny Hall,…

If you're citing an interview done by someone else (perhaps from a book or article) and the title does not indicate that it was an interview, you should, after the subject's name, include *Interview.* Always begin the citation with the subject's name.

> Stegner, Wallace. Interview. *Conversations with Wallace Stegner.* By Richard
>
> Eutlain and Wallace Stegner. Salt Lake: U of Utah P, 1990. Print.

In-Text Citation: (Stegner 22)

If there are other works by Stegner on the Works Cited page:

(Stegner, *Conversations* 22)

As radio and TV interview programs are increasingly archived on the web, these can be a great source of material for a research essay. In the following example, the interview was on a transcript I ordered from the Fresh Air website. Note that the national network, National Public Radio, *and* the local affiliate that produced the program, WHYY, are included in the citation along with the airdate.

> Mairs, Nancy. Interview by Terry Gross. *Fresh Air.* Radio. NPR. WHYY,
>
> Philadelphia. 7 June 1993.

In-Text Citation: (Mairs)

The following citation is for an interview published on the web. The second date listed is the date of access.

Messner, Tammy Faye Bakker. Interview. *The Well Rounded Interview.* Well

Rounded Entertainment. Aug. 2000. 14 July 2002. Web.

In-Text Citation: (Messner)

SURVEYS, QUESTIONNAIRES, AND CASE STUDIES

If you conducted the survey or case study, list it under your name and give it an appropriate title.

Ball, Helen. "Internet Survey." Boise State U, 2012.

In-Text Citation: (Ball)

RECORDINGS

Generally, list a recording by the name of the performer and italicize the title. Also include the recording company, catalog number, and year. (If you don't know the year, use the abbreviation *n.d.*)

Orff, Carl. *Carmina Burana.* Cond. Seiji Ozawa. Boston Symphony. RCA, 6533–2-RG,

n.d. CD.

In-Text Citation: (Orff)

TELEVISION AND RADIO PROGRAMS

List the title of the program (italicized), the station, and the broadcast date. If the episode has a title, list that first in quotation marks. You may also want to include the name of the narrator or producer after the title.

"Congress Takes Student Loans, Highway Bill to the Wire." *All Things Considered.*

Natl. Public Radio, Washington, DC, 26 June 2012. Radio.

In-Text Citation: ("Congress Takes Student Loans")

ONLINE AUDIO OR VIDEO

Sarah Palin 20/20 Interview with Charlie Gibson, Part 2/4. YouTube. YouTube,

12 Sept. 2008. Web. 3 July 2009.

In-Text Citation: (*Sarah Palin 20/20 Interview*)

"Bad Bank." *This American Life.* Prod. Ira Glass. *NPR.* Chicago Public Radio,

27 Feb. 2009. Web. 3 July 2009.

In-Text Citation: ("Bad Bank")

ONLINE IMAGES

"Passenger Pigeon." Online image. 26 June 2012. *Sarroffillustration.com*.

2 July 2012.

In-Text Citation: ("Passenger Pigeon")

BLOG

O'Brien, Terence. "EPA May Have Suppressed Global Warming Study." *Switched*.

AOL News, 2 July 2009. Web. 3 July 2009.

In-Text Citation: (O'Brien)

PODCAST

Kermode, Mark. "Drag Me to Hell." *5 Live*. BBC Radio, 12 May 2009. Web.

3 July 2009.

In-Text Citation: (Kermode)

WIKI

"Emily Dickinson." *Wikipedia*. Wikipedia Foundation, 2009. Web. 3 July 2009.

In-Text Citation: ("Emily Dickinson")

FILMS, VIDEOTAPES, AND DVD

Begin with the title (italicized), followed by the director, the distributor, and the year. You may also include names of writers, performers, or producers. End with the date and any other specifics about the characteristics of the film or video-tape that may be relevant (length and size).

Saving Private Ryan. Dir. Steven Spielberg. Perf. Tom Hanks, Tom Sizemore, and

Matt Damon. Paramount, 1998. DVD.

In-Text Citation: (*Saving*)

You can also list a video or film by the name of a contributor you'd like to emphasize.

Capra, Frank, dir. *It's a Wonderful Life*. Perf. Jimmy Stewart and Donna Reed. RKO

Pictures, 1946. Film.

In-Text Citation: (Capra)

ARTWORK

List each work by artist. Then cite the title of the work (italicized) and where it's located (institution and city). If you've reproduced the work from a published source, include that information as well.

Homer, Winslow. *Casting for a Rise*. Hirschl and Adler Galleries, New York. *Ultimate*

Fishing Book. Ed. Lee Eisenberg and DeCourcy Taylor. Boston: Houghton,

1981. Print.

In-Text Citation: (Homer 113)

LECTURES AND SPEECHES

List each by the name of the speaker, followed by the title of the address (if any) in quotation marks, the name of the sponsoring organization, the location, and the date. Only indicate what kind of address it was (Lecture, Speech, etc.) when no title is given.

Naynaha, Siskanna. "Emily Dickinson's Last Poems." Sigma Tau Delta, Boise, ID.

15 Nov. 1999. Lecture.

Avoid the need for parenthetical citation by mentioning the speaker's name in your text.

PAMPHLETS

Cite a pamphlet as you would a book.

New Challenges for Wilderness Conservationists. Washington, DC: Wilderness

Society, 2006. Print.

In-Text Citation: (*New Challenges*)

A Sample Paper in MLA Style. Most of the student essays in *The Curious Writer* use MLA style. For a fully documented research paper, see Gordon Seirup's essay, "College Dating."

▶ Student Essay

Like some of the best research, Gordon Seirup's essay "College Dating" grows from his own experience with his topic—as a student at a large western university. Building on his own observations, interviews with peers, and reading, Seirup goes on to describe five distinct patterns in college dating. One of the basics of any research project is to do exactly that: *Look for patterns in the data and attempt to describe them*. Seirup's writing here is accessible, interesting, and informative—not the usual qualities we expect in a conventional research paper. He also does a great job varying his sources: drawing from web pages, interviews, and academic articles. Goron Seirup's essay is cited using MLA guidelines.

Gordon E. Seirup

Professor Ballenger

English 101

6 October 2006

College Dating

First there was the passing notes, hand holding, and name-calling of middle school. Then you survived your first heartbreak when your high school sweetheart decided it would be best to "just be friends." Now swept away in college life you hardly take the time to step back and ask yourself, "What am I doing here? Whose bed did I just wake up in, and how the hell did I get here?!" If you have not yet taken the time to ponder what it is you plan to do with the so-called best four years of your life, besides studying and eating dorm food, perhaps it is about time you did. What do you want to be accomplishing in these prime dating years? More importantly, is that what you are accomplishing? In short, my purpose is to discuss the question: "What role should dating play in college students' lives?"

If you assume that most college students have thought how their dating decisions today might affect them tomorrow, think again. The students I spoke with informally here on the Colorado State University campus all hesitated when asked to simply "define dating." Once done struggling through that answer, they were asked, "What is the purpose of dating in college?" These students' answers ranged from "getting laid!" to "discover more about yourself through others" to "find the person you want to marry" to "I have no clue." Are the college masses blissfully unaware of exactly what it is they are doing when they pursue relationships?

First, what is dating? For my purposes, dating is defined as seeing someone socially in a one-on-one setting. Other terms used within the following pages are "hooking up" and "courtship," defined as noncommittal sexual acts and nonse-rial exclusive dating with the intention of marriage, respectively. What I mean by "nonserial" dating is that when you choose to date someone, you intend to marry that person. While this may not work out, and might lead you to enter this process again, you sincerely choose each person you date as a potential spouse. While you may court more than one person, it isn't your intention to do so.

4   I have defined five major approaches to college dating based on their common purpose, values, and motivations, in addition to their general line of reasoning: Casual Dating, Exclusive Dating, Courting, Cannot Date, and Hooking Up.

5   Casual dating was popular during the American 1950s, although Beth Bailey notes that "between 1890 and 1925, dating—in practice and in name—had gradu-ally, almost imperceptibly, become a universal custom in America" (19). The emer-gence of public dating rituals coincided with the emergence of mass media, espe-cially TV and magazines that made dating a feature of the typical American romance (Bailey 9). Casual dating was modeled on popular TV shows, and analyzed in mostly women's magazines—where to go, how much to spend, when to allow a first kiss. A major motive for dating was, according to Bailey, public competition to spend the most, choose the best partner, and so on.

6   However, dating these days is much less ritualized. Rather than focusing on public display, these days casual daters value meeting new people, discovering and/ or reinventing who you are as a person, and enjoying yourself. The original scenario for casual dating typically went something like this: Guy meets Girl, decides he would like to see her socially, and asks her to join him at the diner for hamburgers and a shared milkshake. If this date goes well, they may see each other again. After about three dates there is a good chance Guy would be graced with a goodnight kiss.

These dates did not imply exclusivity or any concrete commitment at all. 7
While social enjoyment is the driving force behind the Casual Dating approach,
there are two other important aspects: meeting new people and discovering yourself. By the simple act of participating in these dates, each party naturally learns
more about himself and herself through their interaction. "Dating one-on-one
gives you a chance to become comfortable with new people," says Julie Baugher,
Georgetown University's premier relationship columnist (Baugher, "'Rules'").

The key to developing sufficient attachment for a couple to want to date 8
multiple times is that elusive quality called "chemistry." One study that attempted to
pin down exactly what college students mean by chemistry suggested that it involves
similarity of interests and backgrounds, as well as "reciprocity," or the feeling that
both partners are giving something to each other (Peretti and Abplanalp 5).

But chemistry isn't necessarily a scarce phenomenon, and it's possible to find 9
it with more than one person. According to Lee Ann Hamilton, a health educator
at the University of Arizona, "College is the time to re-invent yourself and try new
things; many people don't want to be tied down" (qtd. in Hill). It is very important
to keep in mind that not being "tied down," as Ms. Hamilton put it, is a fundamental aspect of the Casual Dating approach.

Columnist Julie Baugher has laid out some guidelines helpful to circumvent- 10
ing our typical defensive maneuvers when it comes to dating. (It may be useful
to remember these next time you are asked out for a date.) "Don't think about
whether you want to Date him with an uppercase 'D' (meaning exclusive dating).
Don't conclude that he isn't 'Your type.' Don't assume this is the beginning of a
long-term relationship that you're not ready for" (Baugher, "Dating"). Approaching
it casually, couples may date as many people as there are nights available in the
week, so long as all parties involved know the arrangement.

Seirup 4

11   Similar to the Casual Dating approach is the Exclusive Dating approach. Both parties value dating as an activity for social enjoyment, as well as self-education. Exclusive dating may be thought of as the "next step" from casual dating, and indeed commonly tends to grow out of casual dating. When exclusively dating, you are not only learning more about yourself, but also consciously aware of what you are learning about your partner. Which characteristics can you see yourself living with for the rest of your life? Which make you want to run away and never date again? "Through several short-term relationships, students can find personalities with which they are most compatible," claims Matt West, a writer at the University of Virginia. "Relationships at this age allow you to explore what you like and don't like in a partner," agrees Mary Anne Knapp, a clinical social worker. Through a series of exclusive relationships, one forms a model of the ideal spouse (qtd. in Pleiss).

12   However, here is the crucial detail for this approach: This flirtation with long-term commitment is solely a mental exercise. Marriage is not a goal of the exclusive dating approach. Exclusively dating college students are aware of their proximity to marriage; however, they are not going to let that detail dominate their lives. The goal is gaining knowledge. This distinction is memorably worded by Jennifer Graham, a senior staff writer at Stanford University: "I think I'm going to put marriage on the backburner and, at least for the time being, refrain from appraising my peers' credentials for parenthood. There's no need to sap all the joy from life." Don't misinterpret Graham as saying she wishes to ignore completely her peers' credentials for parenthood; rather the issue is at which stage in the dating process qualifications for marriage become important. When making the choice of whether or not to date someone, these marriage-related thoughts are minimally important. However, while in a relationship, it would

be wise to consider these credentials to learn what you are looking for when you are shopping for a spouse.

Expert testimony supports the Exclusive Dating approach. Clinical social worker Mary Anne Knapp says these exclusive relationships are healthy and "serve more of a purpose than just having a permanent date every Friday night," since "having a supportive partner, someone who knows you and is on your side, is good for a positive outlook on life" (qtd. in Pleiss 1).

13

The premise of the Courting approach is that dating should play no role in the lives of college students. Believers in courtship argue for a return to the practice of courtship rather than dating, and hold marriage absolutely paramount. Furthermore, proponents argue that this courtship should take place after college. In general, students who advocate the Courting approach share strong religious backgrounds, and actively use their faith to both justify their opinion and denounce others'. In fact, the approach is as much their adamant opposition to dating as it is their support of courtship, saying casual dating is "a bankrupt convention...a training ground for divorce [and]...a cheap imitation of the love and intimacy of a real marriage" (Jensen). Furthermore, they believe that the practice of casual dating is futile: "If the couple never intends to get married in the first place, then breaking up is a foregone conclusion, and their relationship is doomed" (Jensen).

14

Advocates of this approach value the unique bonds that are formed between husband and wife as well as purity upon entering marriage. Courtship "is the only way to date with true love, respect and honesty because it is rooted in a desire to take the relationship to its complete and glorious fulfillment" (Jensen). Those seeking courtship seek others who seek the same; assuming that if you have kept pure in pursuit of marriage, you should expect the same of your spouse

15

to-be—though today the selection of potential partners may be slim. "It's hard enough to meet somebody who doesn't have a past relationship that is like a skeleton in her closet," says Matt Sweet, finance major at the University of Virginia (qtd. in Jensen). According to those who take the Courting approach, if more college students adopted their strategy, this wouldn't be a problem.

16   Believers in courtship share both a wholehearted commitment to a relationship that will lead to marriage and the best possible education while in college. Value is placed on the concept of college students being just that—students. During college they have neither the time nor energy to responsibly court a spouse. Therefore, it is best for people to engage in courtship only after graduation and they are settled into their careers.

17   Proponents of the Cannot Date approach also believe that dating should play no role in the lives of college students. They don't oppose dating, but these students have tried to date, or at least wanted to, but deemed it to be impossible. Like the Courting approach, these students value their standing as students and hold education as a very high priority. This approach is aptly described by a student at the University of Arizona: "While pursuing a double major, interning, working, maintaining a social life and attending school full time," Danielle Demizjian, a business economics and finance senior, finds "exclusive dating too much of a commitment" (qtd. in Hill). This is a common complaint among college students. Despite their desire to date, exclusively or casually, there just does not seem to be the time, though time alone is not the only issue. For those students advanced in their time management skills, the emotional burden may be too great. Jaime Dutton, a sophomore at Johns Hopkins University, says, "It's hard enough to have fun here with all the work you have to do, [and] there's no reason

to have the extra drama in your life" (qtd. in Saxe). Nicole Kucewitz, a writer for the *Rocky Mountain Collegian*, agrees: "Relationships take time and patience, and in college, both of these can be very limited."

Finally, there is the Hooking Up approach. This last group has an alternate social structure to replace traditional dating. Their philosophy is this: At the college level, formal dating is unnecessary. For social activities, in contrast with the one-on-one date, groups are ideal. As for sexual needs, noncommittal hooking up is not only acceptable, it's preferred. Common values amongst this group include enjoying yourself socially with friends, casually fulfilling sexual needs, and avoiding commitment. This "new age" form of dating is the solution that has flourished as a result of the gripes of the Cannot Date approach.

18

Many of the students who Hook Up see the dating arena as split into two distinct groups: "People are either single or practically married" (Burney). Hooking Up is the solution for those people who wish to largely retain their single status while still satisfying their social and sexual needs, and avoiding the "marriage-type" exclusive relationship. Dan, a student at Duke University, puts it this way: "In the real world, there is an expectation that after the third date, you might get a hookup. At Duke, there is the expectation that after the third hookup, you might get a date" (qtd. in Beckett). So perhaps once college students reach the "real world" this approach will fade away, but it remains wildly popular on campus.

19

One reason for its popularity is that Hooking Up avoids potential complications of exclusive dating or even casual dating. With this approach, future hookup partners spend time in groups and get to know each other in a friendlier context first, avoiding the awkward chesslike strategies common to the predate period. Or even simpler, the story goes like this: "Now all a guy in a decent

20

fraternity has to do to hookup on a Saturday night is to sit on the couch long enough at a party. It's slow at first, but eventually a girl will plop herself down beside him, they'll sit there drinking, he'll make a joke, she'll laugh, their eyes will meet, sparks will fly, and the mission is accomplished. And you want me to tell this guy to call a girl, spend $100 on dinner and hope for a goodnight kiss" (qtd. in Beckett)? This trend is perpetuated by "the beds [being] short walks from the parties. This increases the likelihood of the drunken hookup, while simultaneously decreasing the frequency of actual dates," according to Tom Burney, a columnist and student at Duke University (qtd. in Beckett).

21   With this tendency to go from partying to hooking up, a critic may be quick to draw the conclusion that sex is the driving force behind this approach. On the contrary, students' motives are often to get to know potential partners as friends (at least superficially) first. David Brunkow, computer science major at Colorado State University, attests to this: "Most of the people I've been with were already my friends...It's so much easier that way. You already know they're a good person and that they're not going to screw you over. Also, if things don't work out, you don't lose your friend" (qtd. in Borra).

22   Research seems to confirm Brunkow's contention. According to Paul and Hayes, the best hookups were more likely to be prefaced by hanging out, flirting, mutual attraction, and talking. The worst hookups often resulted from a friend's instigation (Paul and Hayes 648).

23   Of the five categories I've offered to describe college dating, Hooking Up is both the most common and the most controversial. In a recent study, three quarters of students interviewed reported that they had hooked up at least once and at least a third said this involved sex with a stranger or a new acquaintance

Seirup 9

(Paul, McManus, and Hayes 84). Students who choose Hooking Up may not believe that there are other, socially sanctioned choices, as this paper suggests. Do participants think Hooking Up is a good thing? One would assume so since it's so popular these days. But there is some evidence that the practice is driven by "pluralistic ignorance" or the mistaken assumption that their discomfort with the behavior is unique. This is particularly true of women (Lambert, Kahn, and Apple 132), a situation which could lead to abuses.

While no one approach is clearly ideal for all students, there seems to be one to suit everyone, despite a wide range of personal beliefs. Casual Dating, Exclusive Dating, Courting, Cannot Date, and Hooking Up represent distinct alternatives to college students, difficult choices that add to the complexities—both academic and non-academic—that college students find themselves caught up in every day. But it's crucial that students at least be aware that there are choices to make.

24

Works Cited

Bailey, Beth. "The Worth of a Date." *From Front Porch to Back Seat: Courtship in Twentieth-Century America*. 1998. Baltimore: Johns Hopkins University Press. Print.

Baugher, Julia. "Dating with a Lower Case 'd.'" *Hoya* 4 Oct. 2002. Web. 8 Oct. 2003.

Baugher, Julia. "'Rules' Teach Ladies Tricks to Winning Love." *Hoya* 15 Nov. 2002. Web. 7 Oct. 2003.

Beckett, Whitney. "What Lies Between the Hookup and Marriage?" *Chronicle* 5 Sept. 2003. Web. 13 Oct. 2003.

Borra, Jessup. "The 'He-Said-She-Said' on Dating." *Rocky Mountain Collegian* 17 Oct. 2002. Web. 19 Oct. 2003.

Burney, T. "Dating Sea Nuggets." *Chronicle* 26 Mar. 2003. Web. 13 Oct. 2003.

Seirup 10

Graham, Jennifer. "Graduation Time: Cap and Gown or Wedding Gown?" *Stanford Daily* 17 July 2003. Web. 13 Oct. 2003.

Hill, Tessa. "UA students Have Lost That Lovin' Feeling." *Arizona Daily Wildcat* 30 Jan. 2003. Web. 8 Oct. 2003.

Jensen, Mark. "A Return to Courtship." *Cavalier Daily* 26 Apr. 2002. Web. 19 Oct. 2003.

Kucewicz, Nicole. "Ins and Outs of the College Dating Game: Fun or Forever?" *Rocky Mountain Collegian* 15 Aug. 2001. Web. 19 Oct. 2003.

Lambert, Tracy, Arnold Kahn, and Kevin Apple. "Pluralistic Ignorance and Hooking Up." *Journal of Sex Research* 40.2 (2003): 129–33. Print.

Paul, Elizabeth, Brian McManus, and Allison Hayes. "Hookups: Characteristics and Correlates of College Students' Spontaneous and Anonymous Sexual Experiences." *Journal of Sex Research* 37.1 (2000): 76–88. Print.

Paul, Elizabeth, and Kristen Hayes. "The Casualties of Casual Sex: A Qualitative Exploration of the Phenomenology of College Student Hookups." *Journal of Social and Personal Relationships* 19 (2002): 639–61. Print.

Peretti, Peter, and Richard Abplanalp, Jr. "Chemistry in the College Dating Process: Structure and Function." *Social Behavior and Personality* 32.2 (2004): 147–54. Print.

Pleiss, Carissa. "Couples Can Offer Support, Comfort." *Collegian* 11 Feb. 2003. Web. 17 Oct. 2003.

Saxe, Lindsay. "Books before Relationships?" *Johns Hopkins News–Letter* 28 Mar. 2003. Web. 8 Oct. 2003.

West, Matt. "Steering clear of marriage until after college." *Cavalier Daily* 26 Apr. 2001. Web. 19 Oct. 2005.

Evaluating the Essay

1. I've been saying all along that in a research essay you try to *do* something with the information you've collected that leads, ultimately, to some kind of judgment: What's true? What's important? What's the relationship? We usually look for a thesis as an explicit statement of that judgment. One of the interesting things about "College Dating," though, is that the thesis isn't that obvious. Is this a problem? Does the essay make judgments in other ways?

2. Seirup presents "five major approaches" to college dating. Do these make sense to you? Is there another category he's missing?

3. Was this an interesting piece of writing? Why or why not?

MLA VERSUS APA: SOME BASIC DIFFERENCES

MLA Approach	APA Approach
(Author page #)—Example:	**(Author, year)—Example:**
According to Ackerman, there is an infatuation chemical (164).	According to Ackerman (1994), there is an infatuation chemical.
Usually no title page.	Usually title page and abstract. An abstract is a short summary of the paper's content, always less than 120 words in APA style.
Pagination uses writer's last name and page number. For example:	Pagination uses running head and page number. A "running head" is the paper's abbreviated title. For example:
Smith 5	EXPORTING JOBS 5
Figures and tables included within the paper.	Figures and tables included in section at the end of the paper.
Bibliography called Works Cited page.	Bibliography called References page.

APA Documentation Guidelines

The American Psychological Association's (APA) citation conventions are the other dominant approach to acknowledging sources. If you're headed for courses in the social sciences, then this is the system you'll use. It's no harder than the MLA; in fact, the two systems are quite similar. Both use parenthetical citations. Both organize the bibliography (or References page) in very similar ways. But there are a few significant differences, some of which are summarized in the accompanying table. Detailed descriptions of the APA system then follow.

How the Essay Should Look

Page Format. Papers should be double-spaced, with at least one-inch margins on all sides. Number all pages consecutively, beginning with the title page; put the page number in the upper right corner. Above or five spaces to the left of the page number, place an abbreviated title of the paper on every page, in case pages get separated. As a rule, the first line of all paragraphs of text should be indented five to seven spaces.

Title Page. Unlike a paper in MLA style, an APA-style paper has a separate title page, containing the following information: the title of the paper, the author, and the author's affiliation (e.g., what university she is from). Each line of information should be centered and double-spaced. (See Figure 9.3.) At the top of the title page, flush left and in uppercase letters, you may also include a *running head*, or an abbreviation of the title (fifty characters or less, including spaces). A page header, which uses the first two or three words of the title followed by the page number, begins on the second page. This is different from the running head, which tends to be longer and appears only on the title page.

Abstract. Although it's not always required, many APA-style papers include a short abstract (no longer than 120 words) following the title page. (See Figure 9.4.) An abstract is essentially a short summary of the paper's contents. This is a key feature, because it's usually the first thing a reader encounters. The abstract should

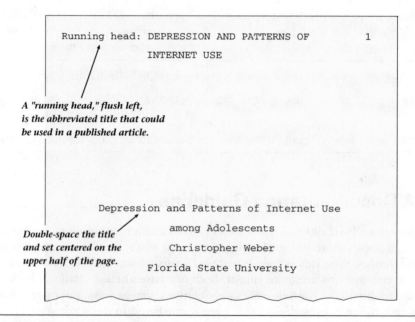

Figure 9.3 Title page in APA style

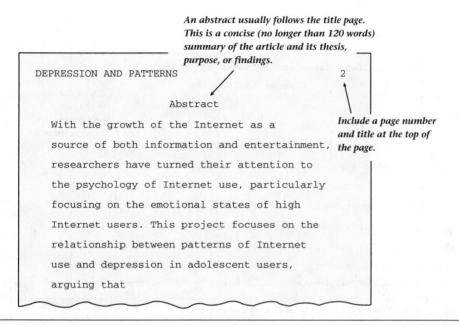

An abstract usually follows the title page. This is a concise (no longer than 120 words) summary of the article and its thesis, purpose, or findings.

DEPRESSION AND PATTERNS   2

Abstract

With the growth of the Internet as a

source of both information and entertainment,

researchers have turned their attention to

the psychology of Internet use, particularly

focusing on the emotional states of high

Internet users. This project focuses on the

relationship between patterns of Internet

use and depression in adolescent users,

arguing that

Include a page number and title at the top of the page.

Figure 9.4   The abstract page

include statements about what problem or question the paper examines and what approach it follows; the abstract should also cite the thesis and significant findings. Type *Abstract* at the top of the page. Type the abstract text in a single block, without indenting.

Body of the Paper. The body of the paper begins with the centered title, followed by a double space and then the text. A page header (usually an abbreviated title and "3" if the paper has a title page and abstract) should appear in the upper right corner. (See Figure 9.5.)

You may find that you want to use headings within your paper. If your paper is fairly formal, some headings might be prescribed, such as *Introduction, Method, Results,* and *Discussion.* Or create your own heads to clarify the organization of your paper.

If you use headings, the APA recommends a hierarchy like this:

Centered, Boldface, Uppercase and Lowercase

Flush Left, Boldface, Upper- and Lowercase Heading

    Indented, boldface, lowercase except first letter of first word

    Indented, boldface, italicized, lowercase except first letter of first word

    Indented, italicized, lowercase except first letter of first word

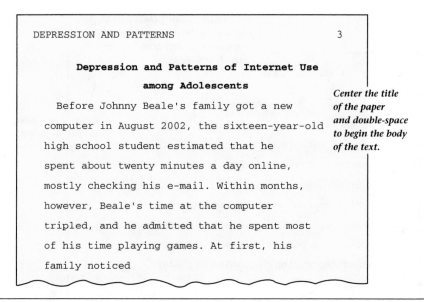

Figure 9.5 The body of the paper in APA style

Papers rarely use all five levels of headings; two or three is probably most common, particularly in student papers. When you use multiple levels, always use them consecutively. In other words, a level 1 heading would always be followed by a level 2 heading (if there is one).

For example,

The Intelligence of Crows

Current Understandings of Crow Intelligence

References Page. All sources cited in the body of the paper are listed alphabetically by author (or title, if anonymous) on the page titled *References*. See Figure 9.6. This list should begin a new page. Each entry is double-spaced; begin each entry flush left, and indent subsequent lines five to seven spaces. Explanation of how to cite various sources in the references follows in the "Preparing the References List" section.

Appendix. This is a seldom-used feature of an APA-style paper, although you might find it helpful for presenting specific or tangential material that isn't central to the discussion in the body of your paper: a detailed description of a device described in the paper, a copy of a blank survey, or the like. Each item should begin on a separate page and be labeled *Appendix*, followed by *A*, *B*, and so on, consecutively, if there is more than one item.

Notes. Several kinds of notes might be included in a paper. The most common is *content notes*, or brief commentaries by the writer keyed to superscript numbers

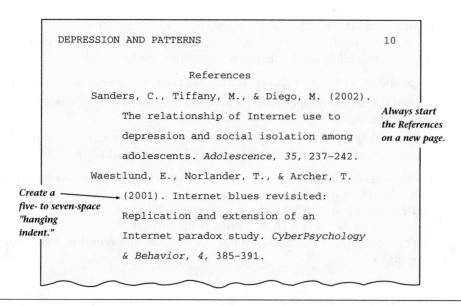

DEPRESSION AND PATTERNS   10

References

Sanders, C., Tiffany, M., & Diego, M. (2002).

The relationship of Internet use to

depression and social isolation among

adolescents. *Adolescence, 35,* 237–242.

Waestlund, E., Norlander, T., & Archer, T.

(2001). Internet blues revisited:

Replication and extension of an

Internet paradox study. *CyberPsychology*

& Behavior, 4, 385–391.

Always start the References on a new page.

Create a five- to seven-space "hanging indent."

Figure 9.6   The References page

in the body of the text. These notes are useful for discussion of key points that are relevant but might be distracting if explored in the text of your paper. Present all notes, numbered consecutively, on a page titled *Endnotes*. Each note should be double-spaced. Begin each note with the appropriate superscript number, keyed to the text. Indent each first line five to seven spaces; consecutive lines run the full page measure.

Tables and Figures. The final section of an APA-style paper features tables and figures mentioned in the text. Tables should all be double-spaced. Type a table number at the top of the page, flush left. Number tables Table 1, Table 2, and so on, corresponding to the order in which they are mentioned in the text. A table may also include a title. Each table should begin on a separate page.

Figures (illustrations, graphs, charts, photographs, drawings) are handled similarly to tables. Each should be titled *Figure* and numbered consecutively. Captions may be included, but all should be typed on a separate page, clearly labeled *Figure Captions*, and listed in order. For example:

Figure Captions

Figure 1. A photograph taken in the 1930s by Dorothea Lange.

Figure 2. Edward Weston took a series of green pepper photographs like this one. This is titled "No. 35."

Language and Style. The APA is comfortable with the italics and bold functions of modern word processors, and underlining is a thing of the past. The guidelines for *italicizing* call for its use when writing the following:

- The title of books, periodicals, and publications that appear on microfilm.
- When using new or specialized terms, but only the first time you use them (e.g., "the authors' *paradox study* of Internet users...").
- When citing a phrase, letter, or word as an example (e.g., "the second *a* in *separate* can be remembered by remembering the word *rat*").

The APA calls for quotation marks around the title of an article or book chapter when mentioned in your essay.

Been nagged all your life by the question of whether to spell out numbers or use numerals in APA style? Here, finally, is the answer: Numbers less than 10 that aren't precise measurements should be spelled out, and numbers 10 or more should be digits.

Citing Sources in Your Essay

When the Author Is Mentioned in the Text. The author/date system is pretty uncomplicated. If you mention the name of the author in text, simply place the year his work was published in parentheses immediately after his name. For example:

Herrick (1999) argued that college testing was biased against minorities.

When the Author Isn't Mentioned in the Text. If you don't mention the author's name in the text, then include that information parenthetically. For example:

A New Hampshire political scientist (Sundberg, 2012) recently studied the state's

presidential primary.

Note that the author's name and the year of her work are separated by a comma.

When to Cite Page Numbers. If the information you're citing came from specific pages, chapters, or sections of a source, that information may also be included in the parenthetical citation. Including page numbers is essential when quoting a source. For example:

The first stage of language acquisition is called "caretaker speech" (Moskowitz,

1985, pp. 50–51), in which children model their parents' language.

The same passage might also be cited this way if the author's name is mentioned in the text:

Moskowitz (1985) observed that the first stage of language acquisition is called

"caretaker speech" (pp. 50–51), in which children model their parents' language.

A Single Work by Two or More Authors. When a work has two authors, always mention them both whenever you cite their work in your paper. For example:

Allen and Oliver (1998) observed many cases of child abuse and concluded that

maltreatment inhibited language development.

If a source has more than two authors but fewer than six, mention them all the first time you refer to their work. However, any subsequent references can include the surname of the first author followed by the abbreviation *et al*. When citing works with six or more authors, *always* use the first author's surname and *et al*.

A Work with No Author. When a work has no author, cite an abbreviated title and the year. Place article or chapter titles in quotation marks, and *italicize* book titles. For example:

The editorial ("Sinking," 2012) concluded that the EPA was mired in bureaucratic

muck.

Two or More Works by the Same Author. Works by the same author are usually distinguished by the date; works are rarely published the same year. But if they are, distinguish among works by adding an *a* or *b* immediately following the year in the parenthetical citation. The reference list will also have these suffixes. For example:

Douglas's studies (1986a) on the mating habits of lobsters revealed that the

females are dominant. He also found that the female lobsters have the uncanny

ability to smell a loser (1986b).

This citation alerts readers that the information came from two studies by Douglas, both published in 1986.

An Institutional Author. When citing a corporation or agency as a source, simply list the year of the study in parentheses if you mention the institution in the text:

The Environmental Protection Agency (2012) issued an alarming report on ozone

pollution.

If you don't mention the institutional source in the text, spell it out in its entirety, along with the year. In subsequent parenthetical citations, you can abbreviate the name as long as the abbreviation will be understandable. For example:

A study (Environmental Protection Agency [EPA], 2012) predicted dire conse-

quences from continued ozone depletion.

And later:

Continued ozone depletion may result in widespread skin cancers (EPA, 2012).

Multiple Works in the Same Parentheses. Occasionally, you'll want to cite several works at once that speak to a topic you're writing about in your essay. Probably the most common instance is when you refer to the findings of several relevant studies, something that is a good idea as you try to establish a context for what has already been said about your research topic. For example,

A number of researchers have explored the connection between Internet use

and depression (Sanders, Field, & Diego, 2000; Waestlund, Norlander, & Archer,

2001).

When listing multiple authors within the same parentheses, order them as they appear in the references. Semicolons separate each entry.

Interviews, E-Mail, and Letters. Interviews and other personal communications are not listed in the references at the back of the paper, because they are not *recoverable data*, but they are parenthetically cited in the text. Provide the initials and surname of the subject (if not mentioned in the text), the nature of the communication, and the complete date, if possible.

Nancy Diamonti (personal communication, November 12, 2012) disagrees with

the critics of *Sesame Street*.

In a recent e-mail, Michelle Payne (personal communication, January 4, 2012)

complained that...

New Editions of Old Works. For reprints of older works, include both the year of the original publication and that of the reprint edition (or the translation).

Pragmatism as a philosophy sought connection between scientific study and real

people's lives (James, 1906/1978).

A Website. When referring to an *entire* website (see the following example), cite the address parenthetically in your essay. As for e-mail, it isn't necessary to include a citation for an entire website in your references list. However, you will cite online documents that contribute information to your paper (see the "Citing Online and Other Sources" section).

One of the best sites for searching the so-called Invisible Web is the Librarians

Index to the Internet (http://www.lii.org).

Preparing the References List

All parenthetical citations in the body of the paper correspond to a complete listing of sources on the References page. The format for this section was described earlier (see the "References Page" section).

Order of Sources. List the references alphabetically by author or by the first key word of the title if there is no author. The only complication may be if you have several articles or books by the same author. If the sources weren't published in the same year, list them in chronological order, the earliest first. If the sources were published in the *same* year, include a lowercase letter to distinguish them. For example:

> Lane, B. (1991a). Verbal medicine...
>
> Lane, B. (1991b). Writing...

While the alphabetical principle—listing authors according to the alphabetical placement of their last names—works in most cases, there are a few variations you should be aware of.

- If you have several entries by the same author, list them by year of publication, beginning with the earliest.
- Because scholars and writers often collaborate, you may have several references in which an author is listed with several *different* collaborators. List these alphabetically using the second author's last name. For example,

> Brown, M., & Nelson, A. (2002)
>
> Brown, M., & Payne, M. (1999)

Order of Information. A reference to a periodical or book in APA style includes this information, in order: author, date of publication, article title, periodical title, and publication information.

Electronic sources include some additional information. If you're harvesting your books and articles online or from a library database, you need to cite in a way that makes it clear how readers can find the book or document. That seems simple, right? It isn't always. Typically, you include the URL for an online document in your citation, even if it's long and ugly. But URLs can change, and they are vulnerable to transcription mistakes. To solve this problem, the APA created something called the Digital Object Identifier (see description on p. 349). This is a number that is a permanent link to the document. But not all documents have them, and if not, use their URLs.

One other bit of information you usually include in a citation for an electronic document is the retrieval date, or exactly when you accessed the work online. This can be omitted, however, when the document you're citing is "archival." An archival copy is a final version, and it's usually the version that appeared in print.

Author. List up to eight authors using last name, comma, and then initials. Invert all authors' names. Use commas to separate authors' names and add an ampersand (&) before the last author's name. When citing more than eight authors, list the first six, then add ellipses ("…") and add the last name. When citing an edited book, list the editor(s) in place of the author(s), and add the abbreviation Ed. or Eds. in parentheses following the initials. End the list of names with a period.

Date. List the year the work was published, along with the date if it's a magazine or newspaper (see the following "Sample References" section), in parentheses, immediately after the last author's name. Add a period after the closing parenthesis.

Article or Book Title. APA style departs from MLA here, at least with respect to periodicals. In APA style, only the first word of the article title is capitalized and appears without italics or quotation marks. Book titles are italicized; capitalize only the first word of the title and any subtitle. End all titles with periods.

Periodical Title and Publication Information. Italicize the complete periodical title; type it using both uppercase and lowercase letters. Add the volume number (if any), also italicized. Separate the title and volume number with a comma (e.g., *Journal of Mass Communication, 10,* 138–150). If each issue of the periodical starts with page 1, then also include the issue number in parentheses immediately after the volume number (see examples following). End the entry with the page numbers of the article. Use the abbreviation *p.* or *pp.* if you are citing a newspaper. Other APA-style abbreviations include the following:

chap.	p. (pp.)
Ed./Eds. (Editor/Editors), ed. (edition)	Vol.
Rev. ed.	No.
2nd ed.	Pt.
Trans.	Suppl.

For books, list the city and state or country of publication (use postal abbreviations) and the name of the publisher; separate the city and publisher with a colon. End the citation with a period. The following cities do not require state or country abbreviations:

Baltimore	Amsterdam
Boston	Jerusalem
Chicago	London
Los Angeles	Milan
New York	Moscow
Philadelphia	Paris
San Francisco	Rome
	Stockholm
	Tokyo
	Vienna

Remember that the first line of each citation should begin flush left, and all subsequent lines should be indented five to seven spaces. Double-space all entries.

Retrieval Date. If you're citing an electronic document, you often indicate when you accessed the book or article. This is important because online documents can change, and the retrieval date gives readers a "snapshot" of what version you were looking at when you did your research. Retrieval dates can be omitted when you're citing a permanent or "archival" version of the work.

DOI or URL. These are more ingredients for your alphabet soup. So readers can locate the electronic documents you're citing, you need to tell them where you found them. You frequently do this by including the URL. But more and more documents in the social sciences include something called the Digital Object Identifier (DOI), a permanent link to the work. The DOI is often listed on the article's first page. It may also be hidden under the "Article" button that appears with the work on certain library databases.

Here's a summary of the similarities and differences in APA style when citing print and electronic journals and magazines:

Print Periodical	Electronic Periodical
• Author(s)	• Author(s)
• (Date)	• (Date)
• Article title	• Article title
• Periodical title	• Periodical title
• Issue and volume number	• Issue and volume number
• Page numbers	• Page numbers
	• Retrieval date (unless archival)
	• DOI (if available) or URL (if DOI unavailable)

Sample References: Articles

A JOURNAL ARTICLE

When citing an online article, include information about how readers can find it. Use the DOI, if available. For example,

Mori, K., Ujiie, T., Smith, A., & Howlin P. (2009). Parental stress associated with

caring for children with Asperger's syndrome. *Pediatrics International, 51*(3),

364–370. doi:10.1111/j.1442-200X-2008.0278.x

In-Text Citation: (Mori, Smith, & Howlin, 2009); (Mori et al., 2009) in subsequent citations. If authors are quoted, include page numbers.

If there is no DOI, include the document's URL.

Wing, L. (1981). Asperger's syndrome: A clinical account. *Psychological Medicine,*

    11(1), 115–129. Retrieved from http://search.ebscohost.com/login

    .aspx?direct=true&db=psyh&AN=1981-30537-001&site=ehost-live

In-Text Citation: (Wing, 1981)

Cite a print journal article like this:

Blager, F. B. (1979). The effect of intervention on the speech and language of

    children. *Child Abuse and Neglect, 5,* 91–96.

In-Text Citation: (Blager, 1979)

If the author is mentioned in the text, just parenthetically cite the year:

Blager (1979) stated that...

If the author is quoted, include the page number(s):

(Blager, 1979, p. 92)

A MAGAZINE ARTICLE

Maya, P. (1981, December). The civilizing of Genie. *Psychology Today,* 28–34.

In-Text Citation: (Maya, 1981)

Maya (1981) observed that...

When citing a magazine article from a database, include the URL. Many databases include a "permanent link" to the article on the citation page. Use that if available. Notice also that the database name is no longer included.

Horowitz, A. (July, 2008). My dog is smarter than your dog. *Discover Magazine*

    219(9), 71. Retrieved from http://search.ebscohost.com.libproxy.boisestate

    .edu/login.aspx?direct=true&db=aph&AN=32580478&site=ehost-live

In-Text Citation: (Horowitz, 2008). If quoting, include page numbers (Horowitz, 2008, p. 71)

AN ARTICLE ON A WEBSITE

This article has no author, so the citation begins with the title.

Enhancing male body image. (2006). *Nationaleatingdisorders.org.* Retrieved July 9,

    2009, from http://www.nationaleatingdisorders.org/

In-Text Citation: ("Enhancing," 2006)

If quoting, include the page number(s): (Maya, 1981, p. 28)

A NEWSPAPER ARTICLE

Honan, W. (2004, January 24). The war affects Broadway. *New York Times*, pp. C15–16.

In-Text Citation: (Honan, 2004)

Honan (2004) argued that . . .

Honan (2004) said that "Broadway is a battleground" (p. C15).

If there is no author, a common situation with newspaper articles, alphabetize using the first "significant word" in the article title. The parenthetical citation would use an abbreviation of the title in quotation marks, then the year.

There's a good chance that you'll find newspaper articles online. Here's how you cite them:

Jennings, D. (2009, July 7). With cancer, you can't hurry recovery. *The New York*

Times. Retrieved from http://www.nytimes.com

In-Text Citation: (Jennings, 2009)

Sample References: Books

A BOOK

Lukas, A. J. (1986). *Common ground: A turbulent decade in the lives of three*

American families. New York: Random House.

In-Text Citation: (Lukas, 1986)

According to Lukas (1986), . . .

If quoting, include the page number(s).

AN ONLINE BOOK

If you're citing an entire book you found online, include the URL. Sometimes, however, the Internet address may not lead to the work itself, but rather information on how to find it. In that case, use the phrase "Available from" rather than "Retrieved from." For example,

Suzuki, D. T. (1914). *A brief history of early Chinese philosophy*. Available from

http://www.archive.org/details/briefhistoryofea00suzuuoft

In-Text Citation: (Suzuki, 1914)

When citing a chapter from an online book, include a bit more information, including the name of the database (if any) from which you retrieved it.

Hollin, C. R. (2002). Criminal psychology. In Hollin, C. R., *Oxford handbook*

of criminology (pp. 144–174). Retrieved from Academic Research Premier

database.

In-Text Citation: (Hollin, 2002)

A SOURCE MENTIONED BY ANOTHER SOURCE

Frequently you'll read an article that mentions another article you haven't read. Whenever possible, track down that original article and read it in its entirety. But when that's not possible, you need to make it clear that you know of the article and its findings or arguments indirectly. The APA convention for this is to use the expression *as cited in* parenthetically, followed by the author and date of the indirect source. For example, suppose you want to use some information from Eric Weiser's piece that you read about in Charlotte Jones's book. In your essay, you would write something like:

Weiser argues (as cited in Jones, 2002) that...

A BOOK OR ARTICLE WITH MORE THAN ONE AUTHOR

Rosenbaum, A., & O'Leary, D. (1978). Children: The unintended victims of marital

violence. *American Journal of Orthopsychiatry, 4,* 692–699.

In-Text Citation: (Rosenbaum & O'Leary, 1978)

Rosenbaum and O'Leary (1978) believed that...

If quoting, include the page number(s).

A BOOK OR ARTICLE WITH AN UNKNOWN AUTHOR

The politics of war. (2004, June 1). *New York Times*, p. 36.

In-Text Citation: ("Politics," 2004)

Or mention the source in the text:

In "The Politics of War" (2004), an editorialist compared Iraq to...

If quoting, provide page number(s) as well.

The Chicago manual of style (14th ed.). (1993). Chicago: University of Chicago

Press.

In-Text Citation: (*Chicago Manual of Style*, 1993)

According to the *Chicago Manual of Style* (1993),...

If quoting, include the page number(s).

A BOOK WITH AN INSTITUTIONAL AUTHOR

American Red Cross. (1999). *Advanced first aid and emergency care.* New York:

Doubleday.

In-Text Citation: (American Red Cross, 1999)

The book *Advanced First Aid and Emergency Care* (American Red Cross, 1999)

stated that...

If quoting, include the page number(s).

A BOOK WITH AN EDITOR

Crane, R. S. (Ed.). (1952). *Critics and criticism*. Chicago: University of Chicago Press.

In-Text Citation: (Crane, 1952)

In his preface, Crane (1952) observed that...

If quoting, include the page number(s).

A SELECTION IN A BOOK WITH AN EDITOR

McKeon, R. (1952). Rhetoric in the Middle Ages. In R. S. Crane (Ed.), *Critics and criticism* (pp. 260–289). Chicago: University of Chicago Press.

In-Text Citation: (McKeon, 1952)

McKeon (1952) argued that...

If quoting, include the page number(s).

A REPUBLISHED WORK

James, W. (1978). *Pragmatism*. Cambridge, MA: Harvard University Press. (Original work published 1907).

In-Text Citation: (James, 1907/1978)

According to William James (1907/1978), ...

If quoting, include the page number(s).

AN ABSTRACT

The growth of online databases for articles has increased the availability of full-text versions and abstracts of articles. Although the full article is almost always best, sometimes an abstract alone contains some useful information. If the abstract was retrieved from a database or some other secondary source, include information about it. Aside from the name of the source, this information might involve the date, if different from the year of publication of the original article, an abstract number, or a page number. In the following example, the abstract was retrieved from an online database, Biological Abstracts.

Garcia, R. G. (2002). Evolutionary speed of species invasions. *Evolution, 56,* 661–668. Abstract retrieved from Biological Abstracts.

In-Text Citation: (Garcia, 2002), or Garcia (2002) argues that...

A BOOK REVIEW

> Dentan, R. K. (1989). A new look at the brain [Review of the book *The dreaming brain*]. *Psychiatric Journal, 13,* 51.

> *In-Text Citation:* (Dentan, 1989)

> Dentan (1989) argued that...

If quoting, include the page number(s).

An online book review would include the same information below, but with the review's URL and the phrase ("Retrieved from...").

ONLINE ENCYCLOPEDIA

> Turner, B. S. (2007). Body and society. In G. Ritzer (Ed.), *Blackwell encyclopedia of sociology*. Retrieved July 7, 2009, from http://blackwellreference.com

> *In-Text Citation:* (Turner, 2007)

Because they are collaboratively written, Wikipedia articles have no single author. Usually, therefore, the citation will begin with the article title. For example,

> Ticks (n.d.). Retrieved July 9, 2009 from Wikipedia: http://en.wikipedia.org /wiki/Ticks

> *In-Text Citation:* ("Ticks," n.d.)

Sample References: Other

A GOVERNMENT DOCUMENT

> U.S. Bureau of the Census. (2004). *Statistical abstract of the United States* (126th ed.). Washington, DC: U.S. Government Printing Office.

> *In-Text Citation:* (U.S. Bureau of the Census, 2004)

> According to the U.S. Census Bureau (2004),...

> If quoting, include the page number(s).

A LETTER TO THE EDITOR

> Hill, A. C. (2006, February 19). A flawed history of blacks in Boston [Letter to the editor]. *The Boston Globe*, p. 22.

> *In-Text Citation:* (Hill, 2006)

> Hill (2006) complained that...

> If quoting, include page number(s).

A PUBLISHED INTERVIEW

Personal interviews are not cited in the References section of an APA-style paper, unlike published interviews. Here is a citation for a published interview:

Cotton, P. (2004, April). [Interview with Jake Tule, psychic]. *Chronicles*

Magazine, 24–28.

In-Text Citation: (Cotton, 2004)

Cotton (2004) noted that...

If quoting, include the page number(s).

A FILM OR VIDEOTAPE

Hitchcock, A. (Producer & Director). (1954). *Rear window* [Motion Picture].

Los Angeles: MGM.

In-Text Citation: (Hitchcock, 1954)

In *Rear Window*, Hitchcock (1954)...

PODCAST, VIDEO, AND AUDIO

Shier, J. (Producer and Director). (2005). Saving the grizzly: One hair at a

time. *Terra: The nature of our world*. Podcast retrieved from http://www

.lifeonterra.com/episode.php?id=1

In-Text Citation: (Shier, 2005)

Uhry, A. (2009, July 6). Private education in America. *The Economist*. Podcast

retrieved from http://podcast.com/episode/40782102/5356/

In-Text Citation: (Uhry, 2009)

A TELEVISION PROGRAM

Burns, K. (Executive Producer). (1996). *The west* [Television broadcast]. New

York and Washington, DC: Public Broadcasting Service.

In-Text Citation: (Burns, 1996)

In Ken Burns's (1996) film,...

For an episode of a television series, use the scriptwriter as the author, and provide the director's name after the scriptwriter. List the producer's name after the episode.

Hopley, J. (Writer/Director), & Shannon, J. (Writer/Director). (2006). Buffalo

burrito/Parkerina [Television series episode]. In J. Lenz (Producer),

Mr. Meaty. New York: Nickelodeon.

In-Text Citation: (Hopley & Shannon, 2006)

Fans were appalled by the second episode, when Hopley and Shannon (2006)...

A MUSICAL RECORDING

Wolf, K. (1986). Muddy roads [Recorded by E. Clapton]. *On gold in California*

[CD]. Santa Monica, CA: Rhino Records. (1990).

In-Text Citation: (Wolf, 1986, track 5)

In Wolf's (1986) song,...

A COMPUTER PROGRAM

OmniPage Pro 14 (Version 14) [Computer software]. (2003). Peabody, MA:

Scansoft.

In-Text Citation: (OmniPage Pro, Version 14, 2003)

Scansoft's new software, OmniPage Pro, (2003) is reputed...

DISCUSSION LISTS

Discussion lists abound on the Internet. They range from groups of flirtatious teenagers to those with a serious academic purpose. Although virtually all of these discussion lists are based on e-mail, they do vary a bit. The most useful lists for academic research tend to be e-mail discussion lists. Newsgroups, or Usenet groups, are extremely popular among more-general Internet users. Various search engines can help you find these discussion groups on your topic. You can join or monitor the current discussion or, in some cases, search the archives for contributions that interest you. Google is a great search tool for newsgroups and includes an archive for many of them. *If there are no archives, don't include the citation in your references, because the information isn't recoverable.* However, you may still cite these in your essay as personal communications.

The method of citation varies slightly if it's a newsgroup, an online forum, or an electronic mailing list. For example, a newsgroup posting would be cited like this:

Hord, J. (2002, July 11). Why do pigeons lift one wing up in the air? [Msg 5].

Message archived at rec.pets.birds.pigeons

In-Text Citation: (Hord, 2002), or Hord asks (2002)...

Note that the citation includes the subject line of the message as the title and the message number of the "thread" (the particular discussion topic). The prefix for this newsgroup is *rec*, which indicates the list is hobby oriented.

Electronic mailing lists would be cited this way:

Cook, D. (2002, July 19). Grammar and the teaching of writing. Message posted

to the CompTalk electronic mailing list, archived at http://listserv.comptalk

.boisestate.edu

In-Text Citation: (Cook, 2002), or According to Cook (2002)...

E-MAIL

E-mail is not cited in the list of references. But you should cite e-mail in the text of your essay. It should look like this:

In-Text Citation: Michelle Payne (personal communication, January 4, 2012) argued that responding to personal writing...

BLOG

Notice in the example that the blogger uses a screen name.

Rizaro. (7 July, 2009). Anxiety and suicide. Message posted to *HelptoHealth.co.cc*

A Sample Paper in APA Style. To see a documented student research paper in APA style, go to Kersti Harter's ethnographic essay "Beyond 'Gaydar.'"

▶ Student Essay

The term *gaydar* entered the American lexicon in the past decade or two, though few thought the idea that gay men and women can intuitively distinguish gay from straight was much more than urban legend. Recent research, however, seems to confirm that there just might be something to it. The ethnographic essay that follows asks whether gay men use means other than intuition to make judgments about the sexual orientation of strangers.

This study of four Boise gays is a fascinating look at gay culture. But it's a limited one, too. Like all qualitative research, "Beyond Gaydar" hopes to find useful insight into the many by looking at the few. This project, like most ethnographies conducted in a composition class, is based on only several weeks of fieldwork, rather than the years that most ethnographies require. Still, the essay offers a useful glimpse at the world of young gay men, and it seems to amplify some of the published research. Kersti Harter's essay is cited using APA guidelines.

Running head: BEYOND GAYDAR   1

Kersti Harter

Beyond "Gaydar": How Gay Males Identify Other Gay Males

A Study with Four Boise, Idaho Men

Introduction

1

While people who do not fit into the codified norms of behavior in contemporary urban life are often marginalized by the mainstream, this very fact often serves to empower and reinforce the behavior of its members in marginalized groups. This is the case within gay male culture in United States urban society. Because gay males remain heavily stigmatized, they have formed a large "outside" group with subtle yet unmistakably designated patterns and categories of behavior, action, clothing, and taste. These patterns and behaviors may not be identifiable to the larger society, but they are well-known among gay men. One of these social rituals is the patterns through which gay men attempt to identify other gay males. I had very little prior knowledge that this pattern existed, but through interviews and observations of several gay men in Boise, Idaho, aged 18–25, I discovered how some gay males identify others who are gay.

I was able to model this pattern and the categories of behavior that exist within it.

Background

2

Several studies suggest that so-called "gaydar," the use of intuition to determine the sexual orientation of someone without asking the person outright whether he or she is gay, might have a basis in fact. A recent study (Lawson, 2005) demonstrated that when provided with "neck-up" photographs of strangers who weren't wearing jewelry or makeup, homosexuals were better than heterosexuals in making the correct identification of the stranger's sexual orientation, making

BEYOND GAYDAR   2

this judgment in 2 seconds or less (p. 30). Martins et al. (2005) also reported that "gay men were found to be particularly good at detecting the scent of other gay men" (p. 694). In addition, another study argued that "eye gaze," with distinct variations, is "crucial to forces that either trigger or reinforce one gay's perception of another gay's identity during social encounters" (Nicholas, 2004).

Identifying Other Gay Males: Place

There are, however, other methods of gay identification used by male   3
homosexuals that don't rely on "gaydar" or intuition. One such method, depicted in Figure 1, relies on contextual cues or markers. The number one identifier among the four contextual cues is place: if he's in the gay bar, he's likely gay. But

Figure 1.   The sequence of judgments used by gay men to identify other gay men

this does not mean for sure that any man in a gay club is gay. Julian recounted a story in which he accidentally "hit on" a straight male who was in a gay club:

> It was at a gay club, so I'm not entirely at fault. This guy was just sitting there, kind of like, I don't know, just sitting there at the bar, looking kind of, well, sitting there sulking I guess. And I thought he was pretty good looking, so I thought I'd go talk to him, I wasn't going to pick him up or anything. And so I went up and was talking to him, and he would answer me in one-syllable replies. And I just walked off and I found out that he was actually the bouncer that worked there and he had the night off.

4   Julian's story suggests that "gaydar" isn't always reliable. Sexual orientation signaling is based on more than intuition. It also means that place is not the only identifier of gay males, although it is often accurate. So what happens when the identifier of place fails to confirm sexual orientation?

Action

5   Then we must move onto appearance. I use "appearance" here because my participants claimed that movement as well as personal style played into identifying whether a man is gay. I have subdivided appearance into action, or movements and other behaviors, and clothing, which I discuss below. During my group interview, both Aaron and Steven claimed that movement is the more important part of appearance in determining a man's orientation:

> Me: Does clothing or movement clue you in more to whether or not a person is gay? Aaron: Movement...You can tell by the way a person gesticulates, by how they walk. I can tell how I walk...I'm like God, everyone knows I'm a homo [laughs]! Like I like it, but yeah, it's definitely how they move.

6   It seems that certain movements are ingrained qualities that help gay males identify other gay males. So, in Figure 1, I've identified the next step

BEYOND GAYDAR   4

my subjects might use to identify another gay male as "Action." Some of these
movements are evident even to straight observers, and occasionally the actions have to do with associations with other gay men. For example, another
participant, Jeff, pointed out, "Well, if they are with a guy, then yeah, they're
gay."

If action is not enough to identify the man's orientation, an observer   7
might move on to more subtle parts of clothing style or even personal tastes.
But this would probably not happen in such a situation, and actions are likely
telling enough.

Clothing and Personal Style

There are times, however, when gay men are in places less exclusively   8
gay, or in places not defined as gay at all. Then one must skip to the latter steps,
identifying the less obvious markers of sexual orientation such as personal style.

When I began my research, I sat with my friend Steven in a popular downtown   9
Boise coffee shop, The Flying M. While being widely known as the "gay" coffee
shop, it is not exclusively so. Wednesday, according to Steven, has become known
to some in the gay community as "Gay Night." This Wednesday was the first time
that I met his friend Aaron, who later helped me in the group interview. I would ask
Steven, "Is that guy over there gay?" and so on, and he would answer yes, because
the man was simply at this coffee shop on Gay Night, or because he acted a certain
way, or dressed a certain way.

When he would identify them as gay because of the way they looked, David   10
would often cite things like button-down Abercrombie and Fitch shirts or spiky hair.
There was a definite gay look that he was able to identify. Steven was able to identify gay males, even though we were in a setting that was not necessarily exclusively gay. Clothing, though it is used less than place and action, still can provide

clues about sexual orientation. There are also categories of gay male dress style that the men that I interviewed identified.

Stylistic Stereotypes Among Gay Males

11   To outsiders, clothing and personal style would be one of the easiest identifiers of gay males. But it is actually, according to my subjects, a less obvious marker than place or action. Personal style also comes in many shapes and forms in the gay community. It's as if there is a set of emic values (distinctions that members of a group recognize that may not be apparent to outsiders) that are stereotypical of the gay male. This is an instance where the pattern of behavior in the group is broken down into diverse categories.

12   For example, Green and Ashmore, in "Taking and Developing Pictures in the Head: Assessing the Physical Stereotypes of Eight Gender Types" (1998), asked college students to picture various stereotypes in their heads and describe what they saw. They asked them to picture both "nerd" and "homosexual," and they found that:

> Perceivers have similar pictures of the homosexual and the nerd in their heads. Both were frequently described as being slender and of average height, wearing glasses, and wearing the "uniform" of the male college student (e.g., button-down shirt, pants or jeans, sneakers or casual shoes). (p. 1627)

13   Though these college students pictured "the nerd" and "the homosexual" together, the men I talked with identified a picture of the homosexual that was quite different from the one these college students identified. The men also emphasized that there were many different types of gay male style, not just one. They all identified several emic stereotypes, and disagreed with the "nerd" and "homosexual" being lumped together in similar stylistic categories.

BEYOND GAYDAR   6

When I mentioned this article to Julian, he explained to me why people might   14
lump the "nerd" with the "homosexual":

> In Europe they used to associate Jews and homosexuals, they were kind of
> lumped together. And so maybe whoever's on the outside is kind of labeled
> together...I don't think that's a look that gay guys go for as far as trying
> to look like that...there's sort of that geek chic that a lot of people do,
> pretty much if you see that you know they're straight.

According to Julian, though the outside sees homosexuals and nerds having   15
similar styles because of their roles as the "outsiders," homosexuals have a different
view of their styles, one that is much more rich and varied.

In the essay "Gay Masculinity in the Gay Disco," Cheseboro and Klenk (1981)   16
identify several categories of symbol-using in the gay disco. Though written more
than twenty-five years ago, it gives insight into some incipient analyses of stylistic categories that gay men employ. Cheseboro and Klenk describe "The Virility
Component":

> One concept asserted in the gay disco is an exaggerated, if not flagrant,
> form of masculinity in appearance...an extreme case of this composite image
> includes an explicitly displayed, muscularly developed body, a flannel shirt,
> a leather vest, denim or leather pants, construction or cowboy boots. (p. 95)

Though perhaps less in vogue now, the hyper-masculine male look is still a   17
symbolic type that some gay males employ. At first, I described these men as "bears,"
a more masculine type of gay male, but Julian corrected me and said that perhaps I
was referring to something more like a butch. Julian thought that perhaps butch gay
males care about their appearance and attempt to look masculine while bears don't
really care about their appearance at all, and are more like the general straight male.

18   Julian's uncertainty about what exactly the hyper-masculine gay man would be called perhaps reflects current fashion. With the rise of more males in high fashion, the advent of television programs such as *Queer Eye for the Straight Guy*, and the heterosexual adaptation of the homosexual stereotype, or the "metrosexual," it seems that the bear style has fallen out of favor. It seems that now, instead of taking its fashion cues from the heterosexual world, homosexuals are creating styles that are being used by the world of high fashion and by straight people, who dress more in the mainstream. Julian expressed this concern:

> Me and some of my friends were talking and we were mad because we feel that straight people are stealing our stuff, like have you noticed the guys wearing pink shirts? Yeah, I just don't think they have a right to do that. Like my friends and I were joking that we might go up to one of these guys and be like, "You better have put that in the laundry with something red," you know like it was white before.

19   There is a feeling of resentment within the gay community that symbols are being appropriated by the larger population. In *Gays, Lesbians, and Consumer Behavior* (1996), Wardlow explains the cause of this resentment:

> When the symbolism of the community becomes framed as the basis for a target market from an "outside" perspective, the styles become divorced of the meanings they once held...and the style takes on new or more vague meanings. Based on the perspectives expressed in our interviews, the issue is not so much that meaning has become diluted or that a symbol has been stolen, as it is that manufacturers are selling the product as "cool" or "hip" without reference to its meaning. (pp. 99–100)

BEYOND GAYDAR   8

The manufacturing world is taking symbols highly popularized in the gay com-   20
munity and making them available for the mainstream, for example, the pink shirts
that Julian cited which are becoming increasingly popular with heterosexual males.

Appealing to both a homosexual and a heterosexual (or perhaps metrosexual)   21
audience is a good strategy for a clothing manufacturer; it can target two highly
valuable markets at once. Based on my research, it's obvious that no other company
does this better than Abercrombie and Fitch, as every interviewee cited the popular
clothing company and its ubiquity among gay males. This leads me to the associated stereotypes of "flamer" and "Abercrombie bitch." Both of these types would
wear Abercrombie and Fitch clothing, but the flamer would not wear it exclusively.
These two types would perhaps, if we could put all the different gay styles on a
spectrum, fall closer to femininity than butch or bear would.

What happens when place, action, and personal style all fail to disclose a   22
man's sexual orientation, or when one of these categories is missing or fragmen-
tary? Then clues can be found in personal taste, or habitus.

Subtle Clues in Personal Taste

Among the gay men I interviewed, I found that there is a distinct musi-   23
cal taste that gay males recognize is characteristically gay. I focused on musical taste because my interviewees discussed it the most when I brought up gay
preferences in things other than clothing. During the group interview, I asked
them to comment on gay musical taste. Jeff mentioned that "they all listened to
techno" and expressed his exasperation over it. They cited Barbara Streisand as
gay music. Steven stressed that, "You can't be gay and not have Cher."

So how could musical taste signal sexual orientation? It's difficult to imagine   24
such a situation when place, action, and personal style would fail to show sexual

orientation. Personal taste might be a more cultivated part of the gay habitus, one which would be formed later after the other qualifications were met, and therefore would not be present without the other gay qualities. In other words, musical taste cannot be seen as only a signal to other gay men of a man's orientation. For example, a man who contradicted the other gay qualities regarding place, action, and personal style would probably not be viewed by the others as gay, if he simply expressed an affection for alternative music.

Conclusions

25   In interviewing four gay males in Boise, Idaho, over a period of a month, I saw some general patterns emerge. I discovered that the most importance in discovering sexual orientation was placed on the actual location where a man was seen. Behaviors and movements were also highly important, though being in a gay location might outweigh any straight symbolism that a certain man would possess, e.g., Julian's experience of assuming a man in a gay bar was gay, when in reality he was straight. Clothing can also be a signal to other males of sexual orientation, but it is not as telling as place and action. Personal tastes in things like music are less of a signal of sexual orientation and more of a cultivated gay taste.

26   In concluding my research, I also should point out that these things I have observed have merely scratched the surface of gay male identification. I do not even attempt to explain verbal behavior and its relation to nonverbal clues. I did not consider hearsay among the gay community or when gay males have simply identified themselves verbally. I do not assume that these are the only ways that gay males identify each other or that they are the most commonly used. I also do not want to trivialize intuition or conclude that there is absolutely nothing to "gaydar."

BEYOND GAYDAR   10

References

Cheseboro, J. W., and Klenk, K. L. (1981). Gay masculinity and the gay disco. In J. W. Cheseboro (Ed.), *Gayspeak: Gay male and lesbian communication* (pp. 87–103). New York: Pilgrim Press.

Green, R. J., and Ashmore, R. D. (1998). Taking and developing pictures in the head: Assessing the physical stereotypes of eight gender types. *Journal of Applied Social Psychology, 28*(17), 1609–1636.

Lawson, W. (November–December 2005). Gay men really do find it easier to spot other gays. *Psychology Today,* 30.

Martins, Y., Crabtree, C. R., Runyan, Vainius, A. A., and Wysocki, C. J. (2005). Preference for human body odors is influenced by gender and sexual orientation. *Psychological Science, 16*, 694–701.

Nicholas, C. L. (2004). Gaydar: Eye-gaze as identity recognition among gay men and lesbians. *Sexuality and Culture, 8* (Winter), 60–86.

Wardlow, D. L. (1996). *Gays, lesbians, and consumer behavior: Theory, practice, and research issues in marketing.* New York: Harrington Park Press.

(All references to "Julian," Steven, Jeff, or Aaron come from either participant observation or interviews collected between November 3, 2004, and November 29, 2004.)

Evaluating the Essay

1. As its author admits, "Beyond Gaydar" is based on a month of interviews and observations and therefore "only scratches the surface" of how gay men identify other gay men. If you were going to redesign the study in ways to make its findings more authoritative, what would you suggest?

2. Your own feelings about homosexuality may have strongly affected your reading of this research. Part of becoming a sophisticated reader is developing an awareness of how your own biases and predispositions influence your understandings of and reactions to what you read. Reflect on this. Can you identify particular ideas in the essay that you resisted or didn't evaluate critically because of how you felt?

3. What are the ethical issues the student author of this essay needed to address?

Using What You Have Learned

1. **Use sources effectively and control sources so they don't control you.** In college you'll be writing about subjects you know little about. As a novice researcher in these domains, this is a juggling act. You need to understand what you read, evaluate its relevance, assess its credibility, and then deploy it in your own work. That's a lot. This is one reason why it's so tempting to throw up your hands and simply "dump" information into your writing without thinking much about it. Now you have some tools to avoid this, and one of the most important is writing *while* you collect and read information. Assert control over information before you start a draft and you'll find the draft much easier to write.

2. **Practice summary, paraphrase, and quotation and apply these to your own work.** The Citation Project published a study recently that reviewed the research routines of college students writing research papers. One of their findings was that students almost never summarize their sources. What they do is something called "patchwriting," in which students essentially reproduce what they read, changing some words and maybe some grammatical structures. Patchwriting may not be plagiarism, but it doesn't involve much critical understanding of the source. Of the three—summary, paraphrasing, and quotation—summary may be the most academically useful because it requires a reader to understand and think about a source. When you can, always use summary as you're reading—and after you've read—something you want to use in your writing.

3. **Understand and identify plagiarism to avoid it in your own work.** It's no secret that plagiarism is a huge problem on college campuses. What is less well-known is that the vast majority of it is *unintentional*. If you ever

have any questions about what constitutes plagiarism, return to this chapter and reread the definition on page 300. And if you ever have questions, don't hesitate to ask your instructor.

4. **Cite sources using MLA and APA documentation styles.** Citation can be mind-numbing. I find it so. But remember that it's not just about following rules but telling a story. When you cite an author, you are signaling where the ideas came from that changed the way you think. When you get these authors in conversation with each other, you are creating a scene that's probably never been staged before between these particular authors. And the best part? It's *your* story.

Revision is work. But it's also an opportunity for surprise. The trick is to see what you have written in ways you haven't seen it before.

Revision Strategies 10

Learning Objectives

In this chapter, you'll learn to

10.1 Understand the meaning—and value—of revision and apply it to your own work when appropriate

10.2 Recognize five types of revision and apply most relevant strategies to a particular draft

Why Revise?

One draft and done. That was Shauna's motto about revision, and when she said it nearly everyone in the class nodded. "I know I should revise but usually I write papers at the last minute so I don't really have the time," she added.

Surprisingly, one of the least discussed topics in writing classes is *time*. Perhaps no other factor influences a writer's success than having the time to do the work, and the academic culture doesn't provide a lot of time to write. You may have multiple writing assignments at the same time in different classes with deadlines that may land on the same day. Getting a single draft done on the due date seems like a major accomplishment, much less a revision. And in some classes (though not this one), it isn't even clear that instructors expect students to revise their work before they hand it in. Why do it?

Before I make a pitch for revision, let's be clear on a few things. Revision isn't a virtue, nor is it always a necessary step in the writing process, and it also doesn't always occur at the end of the process. Revision is also more than "fixing" things. In Figure 10.1, you can see that "proofreading" and "editing," while very important parts of rewriting, may not involve revision. They are things that help burnish the surface of prose and make it easier to see the subject underneath it.

Revision involves "re-seeing." You started with a certain idea about what you were writing about and you realize, no, that's not it at all. Or perhaps when you began writing you had one inquiry question, but the draft tells you there's another, better question lurking there. "Deep revision" might lead you to start all over, or shift subjects entirely, or even switch

> The motive for revision is like a photographer's inclination to take more than one shot—both writer and photographer know not to trust their first look at something.

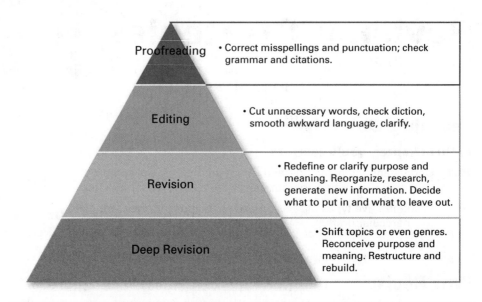

Figure 10.1   Four levels of rewriting

genres. Sometimes revision helps you to re-see not just the subject but the draft itself: It's apparent that the beginning is all wrong, or that there is essential information missing, or that the strongest part of the paper is something you can build on in the next draft.

One of the most powerful analogies for revision comes from photography, a word from Greek that means "light writing." Typically, most of us take only one picture of a subject, even in the digital age when it's cheap and easy to shoot multiple images. In other words: one draft and done. But what would happen if you took ten pictures of the same subject—say, an old wagon in a field—varying angle, distance, and time of day? Your first shot would likely be the most obvious image, the one everyone takes of the wagon. But by the fourth or fifth image, you're have to strain a bit to get the shot. Maybe you lie on the ground and shoot upwards, or you try a close-up of the wooden wheel in the evening when the light is thick. The more shots you take, the more likely it is that you will start seeing your subject in a way that you hadn't initially seen it. The wagon becomes infinitely more interesting. That's the payoff for re-seeing, for what we call *revision* when we talk about writing. The motive for revision is like a photographer's inclination to take more than one shot—both writer and photographer know not to trust their first look at something. They also know that the longer they look, the more likely it is that they will see something interesting.

Why revise? Not because it's necessary, or it's good for you, or someone expects you to. Revise because there's more to learn and think about. Revise because you really care about what you're saying and you want to say it well. Revise because it yields the unexpected—new insights, new perspectives, new ways of seeing.

Divorcing the Draft

Sometimes I ask my students to generalize about how they approach the writing process for most papers by asking them to divide a continuum into three parts corresponding to how much time, roughly, they devote to pre-writing, drafting, and rewriting. Then I play "writing doctor" and diagnose their problems, particularly resistance to revision. Figure 10.2 depicts a typical example for most of my first-year writing students.

Revision, as the name implies, is a *re-seeing* of the paper's topic and the writer's initial approach to it in the draft.

The writing process shown in Figure 10.2 obviously invests lots of time in the drafting stage and very little time in prewriting or rewriting. For most of my students, this means toiling over the first draft, starting and then starting over, carefully hammering every word into place. For students who use this process, strong resistance to revision is a typical symptom. It's easy to imagine why. If you invest all that time in the first draft, trying to make it as good as you can, you'll be either too exhausted to consider a revision, delusional about the paper's quality, or, most likely, so invested in the draft's approach to the topic that revision seems impossible or a waste of time.

There also is another pattern among resistant revisers. Students who tend to spend a relatively long time on the prewriting stage also struggle with revision. My theory is that some of these writers resist revision as a final stage in the process because *they have already practiced some revision at the beginning of the process*. We often talk about revision as occurring only after you've written a draft, which of course is a quite sensible idea. But the process of revision is an effort to *re-see* a subject, to circle it with questions, to view it from fresh angles; and many of the open-ended writing methods we've discussed in *The Curious Writer* certainly involve revision. Fastwriting, clustering, listing, and similar invention techniques all invite the writer to re-see. Armed with these discoveries, some writers may be able to write fairly strong first drafts.

What is essential, however, whether you revise at the beginning of the writing process or, as most writers do, after you craft the draft, is achieving some separation from what you initially thought, what you initially said, and how you said it. To revise well, writers must divorce the draft.

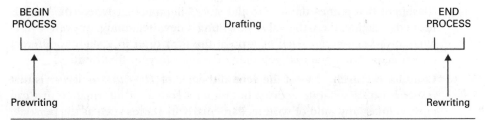

Figure 10.2 How some writers who resist revision typically divide their time among the three elements of the writing process: prewriting, drafting, and rewriting. The most time is devoted to writing the first draft, but not much time is given to prewriting and rewriting.

Strategies for Divorcing the Draft

10.1

Understand the meaning—and value—of revision and apply it to your own work when appropriate

You can do some things to make separation from your work easier, and spending less time on the first draft and more time on the revision process is one of them. But aside from writing fast drafts, what are other strategies for re-seeing a draft that already has a hold on you?

1. **Take some time.** Absolutely the best remedy for revision resistance is set-ting the draft aside for a week or more. Professional writers, in fact, may set a piece aside for several years and then return to it with a fresh, more criti-cal perspective. Students simply don't have that luxury. But if you can take a week or a month—or even a day—the wait is almost always worth it.

2. **Attack the draft physically.** A cut-and-paste revision that reduces a draft to pieces is often enormously helpful, because you're no longer confronted with the familiar full draft, a version that may have cast a spell on you. By dismem-bering the draft, you can examine the smaller fragments more critically. How does each piece relate to the whole? Might there be alternative structures? What about gaps in information? (See Revision Strategy 10.18 later in this chapter for a useful cut-and-paste exercise.)

3. **Put it away.** Years ago I wrote a magazine article about alcoholism. It was about twenty-five pages long and it wasn't very good. I read and reread that draft, completely puzzled about how to rewrite it. One morning, I woke up and vowed I would read the draft just once more, then put it away in a drawer and start all over again, trusting that I would remember what was important. The result was much shorter and much better. In fact, I think it's the best essay I've ever written. Getting a troublesome draft out of sight—literally—may be the best way to find new ways to see it.

4. **Ask readers to respond.** Bringing other people's eyes and minds to your work allows you to see your drafts through perspectives other than your own. Other people have a completely different relationship with your writing than you do. They will see what you don't. They easily achieve the critical distance that you are trying to cultivate when you revise.

5. **Write different leads.** The nonfiction writer John McPhee once talked about beginnings as the hardest thing to write. He described a lead as a "flashlight that shines down into the story," illuminating where the draft is headed. Imagine, then, the value of writing a new beginning, or even several alternative beginnings; each may point the next draft in a slightly different direction, perhaps one that you didn't consider in your first draft.

6. **Conduct research.** One of the central themes of *The Curious Writer* is that research isn't a separate activity, but rather a source of information that can enrich almost any kind of writing. Particularly in genres such as the personal essay, in which the writer's voice, perspective, and experience dominate the draft, listening to the voices and knowledge of others about a topic can deepen and shift the writer's thinking and perspectives.

7. **Read aloud.** I always ask students in workshop groups to read their drafts aloud to each other. I do this for several reasons, but the most important is the effect that *hearing* a draft has on a writer's relationship to it. In a sense, we often hear a draft in our heads as we compose it or reread it, but when we read the words aloud, the draft comes alive as something separate from the writer. As the writer listens to herself—or listens to someone else read her prose—she may cringe at an awkward sentence, suddenly notice a leap in logic, or recognize the need for an example. Try reading the work aloud to yourself, and the same thing may happen.

8. **Write in your journal.** One of the strategies you can use to divorce the draft is to return to your notebook and fastwrite to yourself about what you might do to improve the piece. You can do this by asking yourself questions about the draft and then—through writing—attempting to answer them. The method can help you see a new idea that may become key to the structure of your next draft. Too often we see the journal exclusively as a prewriting tool, but it can be useful throughout the writing process, particularly when you need to think to yourself about ways to solve a problem in revision.

Later in this chapter, we'll build on some of these basic strategies, with specific revision methods that may work with particular kinds of writing and with drafts that have particular problems. All of these methods encourage a separation between the writer and his or her draft, or rely on that critical distance to be effective.

Five Categories of Revision

The following kinds of writers are typically ones who most need to revise:

1. Writers of fast drafts
2. Writers who compose short drafts
3. Writers who indulge in creative, but not critical, thinking
4. Writers who rarely go past their initial way of seeing things
5. Writers who have a hard time imagining a reader other than themselves
6. Writers who rely on limited sources of information
7. Writers who still aren't sure what they're trying to say
8. Writers who haven't found their own way of saying what they want to say
9. Writers who haven't delivered on their promises
10. Writers who think their draft is "perfect"

10.2

Recognize five types of revision and apply most relevant strategies to a particular draft

These are the usual suspects for revision, but there are many more. In general, if you think there's more to think about, more to learn, more to say, and better ways to say it, then revision is the route to surprise and discovery. Most writers agree that rewriting is a good idea, but where should they start?

Problems in drafts vary enormously. But the diagnosis tends to involve concerns in five general areas: purpose, meaning, information, structure, and clarity and style. Here are some typical reader responses to drafts with each kind of problem:

1. **Problems with Purpose**
   - "I don't know why the writer is writing this paper."
   - "The beginning of the essay seems to be about one thing, and the rest of it is about several others."
   - "I think there are about three different topics in the draft. Which one do you want to write about?"
   - "So what?"

2. **Problems with Meaning**
   - "I can't tell what the writer is trying to say in the draft."
   - "There doesn't seem to be a point behind all of this."
   - "I think there's a main idea, but there isn't much information on it."
   - "I thought the thesis was saying something pretty obvious."

3. **Problems with Information**
   - "Parts of the draft seemed really pretty vague or general."
   - "I couldn't really *see* what you were talking about."
   - "It seemed like you needed some more facts to back up your point."
   - "It needs more detail."

4. **Problems with Structure**
   - "I couldn't quite follow your thinking in the last few pages."
   - "I was confused about when this happened."
   - "I understood your point, but I couldn't figure out what this part had to do with it."
   - "The draft doesn't really flow very well."

5. **Problems with Clarity and Style**
   - "This seems a little choppy."
   - "You need to explain this better. I couldn't quite follow what you were saying in this paragraph."
   - "This sentence seems really awkward to me."
   - "This doesn't have a strong voice."

Problems with Purpose

A draft that answers the *So what?* question is a draft with a purpose. Often enough, however, writers' intentions aren't all that clear to readers, so they don't have a strong reason to keep reading.

It's a little like riding a tandem bike. The writer sits up front and steers while the reader occupies the seat behind, obligated to pedal but with no control over where the bike goes. As soon as the reader senses that the writer isn't steering anywhere in particular, then the reader will get off the bike. Why do all that pedaling if the bike seems to be going nowhere?

Frequently, when you begin writing about something, you don't have any idea where you're headed; that's exactly *why* you're writing about the subject in the first place. When we write such discovery drafts, revision often begins by looking for clues about your purpose. What you learn then becomes a key organizing principle for the next draft, for trying to clarify this purpose for your readers. The first question, therefore, is one writers must answer for themselves: "Why am I writing this?" Of course, if it's an assignment, it may be hard to get past the easy answer—"Because I have to"—but if the work is going to be any good, there must be a better answer than that. Whether your topic is open or assigned, you have to find your own reason to write about it, and what you discover becomes an answer to your bike partner's nagging question, yelled into the wind from the seat behind you: "If I'm going to pedal this hard, you better let me know where we're going."

In general, writers' motives behind writing often involve more than one of these following four purposes.

1. **To explore.** One way to handle complicated questions is to approach the answers in an open-ended way; the writer writes to discover what he thinks or how he feels and then reports to the reader on these discoveries.

2. **To explain.** Much of the writing we encounter in daily life is meant simply to provide us with information: This is how the coffeemaker works, or this is the best way to prepare for a trip to New Zealand. Expository writing frequently explains and describes.

3. **To evaluate.** In a sense, all writing is evaluative, because it involves making judgments. For instance, when you explain how to plan a New Zealand vacation, you're making judgments about where to go. But when the explicit purpose is to present a judgment about something, the writer encourages readers to see the world the way the writer does. He or she may want the reader to think or behave a certain way: It makes sense to abolish pennies because they're more trouble than they're worth, or you should vote for the bond issue because it's the best way to save the foothills.

4. **To reflect.** Less frequently, we write to stand back from what we're writing about and consider *how* we're thinking about the subject, the methods we're using to write about it, and what we might learn from this writing situation that might apply to others.

Revision Strategy 10.1: The Motive Statement

It may help to begin a revision by attempting to determine your *primary motive* for the next draft. Do you want to explore your topic, explain something to your readers, offer a persuasive judgment, or step back and reflect on what you're saying or how you're saying it? The genre of writing has a great deal to do with this (see the following table). If you're writing a personal essay, your purpose is likely to be exploratory. If you're writing a review, a proposal, a critical essay, or an argument essay, it's likely that your primary motive is to evaluate. One way, then, to get some basic guidance for the next draft is to carefully craft the second half of the following sentence: *My primary motive in writing this paper is to explore/ evaluate/explain/reflect about* _____

GENRE	PRIMARY MOTIVE
Personal essay	Explore
Profile	Explore or explain
Review	Evaluate
Proposal	Evaluate
Argument	Evaluate
Critical essay	Evaluate
Ethnographic essay	Explore or evaluate
Research essay	Explore or evaluate
Reflective essay	Reflect

Of course, any one essay may involve all four motives, but for the purpose of this exercise, choose your *main* purpose in writing the essay. Composing the second half of the sentence above may not be so easy, because it challenges you to limit your subject. For instance, the following is far too ambitious for, say, a five-page essay: *My main motive in writing this paper is to evaluate the steps taken to deal with terrorism and judge whether they're adequate.* That's simply too big a subject for a brief persuasive paper. This is more reasonable: *My main motive in writing this paper is to evaluate passenger screening procedures in Europe and decide whether they're better than those in the United States.*

Because largely exploratory pieces often are motivated by questions, a writer of a personal essay might compose the following sentence: *My main motive in writing this essay is to explore why I felt relieved when my father died.*

After you craft your motive sentence, put it on a piece of paper or an index card and post it where you can see it as you revise the draft. Periodically ask yourself, *What does this paragraph or this section of the draft have to do with my main motive?* The answer will help you decide what to cut and what needs more development in the next draft. Remember, the essay should be organized around this motive from beginning to end.

Revision Strategy 10.2: What Do You Want to Know About What You Learned?

Because inquiry-based writing is usually driven by questions rather than answers, one way to discover your purpose in a sketch or draft is to generate a list of questions it raises for you. Of course, you hope that one of them might be behind your

One Student's Response

Julia's Draft

What do I understand about this topic now that I didn't understand before I started writing about it?

    After writing this essay, I understand more clearly that there's a relationship between a girl's eating disorders and how her father treats her as a child.

LIST OF QUESTIONS

- Why the father and not the mother?
- What is it about father/daughter relationships that make them so vulnerable to feminine body images?
- Is the father's influence on a girl's body image greater at certain ages or stages in her life?
- How can a father be more informed about his impact on a daughter's body image?

purpose in the next draft. Try the following steps with a draft that needs a stronger sense of purpose.

1. Choose a draft or sketch you'd like to revise, and reread it.

2. On the back of the manuscript, craft an answer to the following question: *What do I understand about this topic now that I didn't understand before I started writing about it?*

3. Next, if you can, build a list of questions—perhaps new ones—that this topic still raises for you. Make this list as long as you can, and don't censor yourself (see "One Student's Response" above).

4. Choose one or more of the questions as a prompt for a fastwrite. Follow your writing to see where it leads and what it might suggest about new directions for the revision.

5. If you can't think of any questions, or find you didn't learn much from writing about the topic (step 2), you may have several options. One is to abandon the draft altogether. Is it possible that this topic simply doesn't interest you anymore? If abandoning the draft isn't possible, then you need to find a new angle. Try Revision Strategy 10.3.

Revision Strategy 10.3: Finding the Focusing Question

The best topics, and the most difficult to write about, are those that raise questions for you. In a sketch or first draft, you may not know what these questions are. But if your subsequent drafts are going to be purposeful and focused, then discovering the main question behind your essay is essential. This is particularly important in essays that are research based, because the drafts are longer and you're often trying to manage a lot of information. This revision strategy works best when it's a class activity.

1. Begin by simply putting your essay topic on the top of a large piece of paper such as newsprint or butcher paper. If yours is a research topic—say, Alzheimer's disease—jot that down. Post your paper on the classroom wall.

2. Spend a few minutes writing a few sentences explaining why you chose to write about this topic in the first place.

3. Make a quick list of everything you *already know* (if anything) about your topic—for instance, surprising facts or statistics, the extent of the problem, important people or institutions involved, key schools of thought, common misconceptions, familiar clichés that apply to the topic, observations you've made, important trends, and typical perspectives. Spend about five minutes on this.

4. Now spend fifteen or twenty minutes brainstorming a list of questions about your topic that you'd love to learn the answers to. Make this list as long as possible.

5. As you look around the room, you'll see a gallery of topics and questions on the walls. You can help each other. Circulate around the room and do two things: Add a question that you're interested in about a particular topic, and check the question (yours or someone else's) that seems most interesting.

When you return to your own newsprint or butcher paper, it should be covered with questions. How will you decide which of them might provide the best focus for the next draft? What you're going to see are mostly factual questions. Generally, there are two kinds of questions: factual questions and questions that attempt to *do* something with information. When we know little about a topic, it's natural to begin with fact or definition questions: What is known about this? What *is* it? Look at your list and identify which factual questions you might want to pursue. Ultimately, though, for a research essay you'll need to use what you're learning about your topic and frame a *doing* question, a question that will purposefully *use* the information you've gathered. These include the following:

- What should be done about this? (policy question)
- What is the value of this? (value question)
- What might this mean? (interpretation question)
- What is the relationship? (relationship question)
- Might this be true? (hypothesis question)

If you can, try to draft a question about your topic that might fit into one of these doing question categories. Because relationship questions are particularly powerful guides to research, the next exercise looks more closely at how your topic might use cause-effect or comparison-contrast to analyze your topic.

Revision Strategy 10.4: What's the Relationship?

One of the more common purposes for all kinds of essays is to explore a relationship between two or more things. We see this in research all the time. What's the relationship between AIDS and IV drug use in China? What's the relationship between gender and styles of collaboration in the workplace? What's the social class relationship between Huck and Tom in *The Adventures of Huckleberry Finn*?

One way, then, to clarify your purpose in revision is to try to identify the relationship that may be at the heart of your inquiry. Relationships between things can be described in a couple different ways.

- *Cause and effect*. What is the relationship between my father's comments about my looks and my eating disorder when I was a teenager? What is the relationship between the second Iraqi war and destabilization in Saudi Arabia? What is the relationship between the decline of the Brazilian rain forest and the extinction of the native eagles? What is the relationship between my moving to Idaho and the failure of my relationship with Kevin?

- *Compare and contrast*. How is jealousy distinguished from envy? How might writing instruction in high school be distinguished from writing instruction in college? What are the differences and similarities between my experiences at the Rolling Stones concert last month and my experiences at the Stones concert fifteen years ago?

Review your sketch or draft to determine whether what you're really trying to write about is the relationship between two (or more) things. In your journal, try to state this relationship in sentences similar to those listed here. With this knowledge, return to the draft and revise from beginning to end with this purpose in mind. What do you need to add to the next draft to both clarify and develop the relationship you're focusing on? What should you cut that is irrelevant to that focus?

Problems with Meaning

Fundamentally, most of us write something in an attempt to say something to someone else. The note my wife, Karen, left for me yesterday said it in a sentence: "Bruce—could you pick up some virgin olive oil and a loaf of bread?" I had no trouble deciphering the meaning of this note. But it isn't always that easy. Certain poems, for example, may be incredibly ambiguous texts, and readers may puzzle over them for hours, coming up with a range of plausible interpretations of meaning. (See Figure 10.3.)

Where Does Meaning Come From?

Depending on the writing situation, you may know what you want to say from the start or you may *discover* what you think as you write and research. Inquiry-based projects usually emphasize discovery, while more-conventional argument

Figure 10.3 Depending on the genre, writers say it straight or tell it slant. In short stories, for example, the writers' ideas may be ambiguous, inviting interpretation. Nonfiction genres—the kind you will most often write in college and beyond—usually avoid ambiguity. Writers say what they mean as clearly and as persuasively as they can.

papers may rely on arriving at a thesis earlier in the process. It's something like the difference between sledding with a saucer or a flexible flyer. The saucer is likely to veer off course, and you might find yourself somewhere unexpected, yet interesting.

Terms to Describe Dominant Meaning

- Thesis
- Main point
- Theme
- Controlling idea
- Central claim or assertion

No matter what you think about a topic when you start writing—even when you begin with a thesis to which you're committed—you can still change your mind. You *should* change your mind if the evidence you've gathered leads you away from your original idea. Unfortunately, writers of thesis-driven papers and other deductive forms are far more resistant to any change in their thinking. In some writing situations—say, essay exams—this isn't a problem. But it's often important in academic writing, including arguments, to always be open to new insight.

Ideas about what we want to say on a writing topic grow from the following:

1. **Thesis.** This is a term most of us know from school writing, and it's most often associated with types of writing that work deductively from a main idea. Here's a sample thesis:

   The U.S. Securities and Exchange Commission is incapable of regulating an increasingly complex banking system.

2. **Theory.** We have strong hunches about how things work all the time, but we're not certain we're right. We test our theories and report on the accuracy of our hunches. Here's an example of a theory:

   Certain people just "don't have a head" for math.

3. **Question.** In a question-driven process, the emphasis is on discovery, and you might work more inductively. You see or experience something that makes you wonder. Here's a question that led a writer to ideas about girls, advertising, and sexuality.

   Why does my ten-year-old want to dress like a hooker?

The revision strategies that follow assume either that you've got a tentative thesis and want to refine it or that you're still working on discovering what you want to say.

Methods for Discovering Your Thesis

Use the following strategies if you're not quite sure whether you know what you're trying to say in a sketch or draft. How can you discover clues about your main point or meaning in what you've already written?

Revision Strategy 10.5: Find the "Instructive Line"

It may seem odd to think of reading your own drafts for clues about what you mean. After all, your writing is a product of your own mind. But often a draft can reveal to us what we didn't know we knew—an idea that surfaces unexpectedly, a question that we keep asking, or a moment in a narrative that seems surprisingly significant. Part of the challenge is to recognize these clues to your own meanings and understand what they suggest about the revision.

This isn't always easy, which is one reason it's often so helpful to share your writing with other readers; they may see the clues that we miss. However, this revision strategy depends on reading your own drafts more systematically for clues about what your point might be. What do you say in this draft that might suggest what you really want to say in the next one?

1. **Find the "instructive line."** Every draft is made up of many sentences. But which of these is *the most important sentence or passage*? What do I mean by *important*? Which line or passage points to a larger idea, theme, or feeling that seems to rise above much of the draft and illuminates the

significance or relevance of many other lines and passages? The writer Donald Murray calls this the "instructive line," the sentence that seems to point upward toward the meaning of what you've set down. Underline the instructive line or passage in your draft. It may be subtle, only hinting at larger ideas or feelings, or quite explicitly stated. In a narrative essay, the instructive line might be a moment of stepping back to reflect: "As I look back on this now, I understand that..." In a review or persuasive essay, it might be an assertion of some kind: "American moviegoers are seduced by the 'twist' at the end of a film, and learn to expect it."

2. **Follow the thread of meaning.** If the instructive line is a ball of string, tightly packed with coils of meaning that aren't readily apparent, then to get any guidance for revision you need to try to unravel it. At the top of a journal page, write the line or passage you selected in your draft as most important. Use it as a prompt for five minutes of exploratory writing, perhaps beginning with the following seed sentence: *I think/feel this is true because... and also because... and also... and also...*

3. **Compose a thesis.** Reread your fastwriting in the preceding step and, keeping your original passage in mind, craft a single sentence that best captures the most important idea or feeling you'd like to bring into the next draft. For example, *Because of the expectation, encouraged by Hollywood, that every good movie has a surprise ending, American moviegoers often find even superior foreign films a disappointment.*

4. **Post it.** Put this thesis on the wall above your computer, or use a Post-it note and place the thesis on your computer screen. Revise with the thesis in mind, from beginning to end. Add information that will *illustrate, extend, exemplify, complicate, clarify, support, show, provide background,* or *prove* the thesis. Cut information from the draft that does none of these things.

Revision Strategy 10.6: Looping Toward a Thesis

I've argued throughout *The Curious Writer* for a dialectical approach to writing: moving back and forth between creative and critical modes of thinking, from your observations of and your ideas about, from generating and judging, from specifics and generalities. This is how writers can make meaning. The approach can also be used as a revision strategy, this time in a technique called *loop writing*. When you loop write, you move back and forth dialectically between both modes of thought—opening things up and then trying to pin them down. I imagine that this looks like an hourglass. (See Revision Strategy 10.7 for a variation on loop writing.)

1. Reread the draft quickly, and then turn it upside down on your desk. You won't look at it again but will trust that you'll remember what's important.

2. **Narrative of thought.** Begin a three-minute fastwrite on the draft, in which you tell yourself the story of your thinking about the essay. When you first

started writing it, what did you think you were writing about, and then what, and then…? Try to focus on your ideas about what you were trying to say and how it evolved.

3. **Summary.** Sum up what you said in your fastwrite by answering the following question in a sentence: *What seems to be the most important thing I've finally come to understand about my topic?*

4. **Examples.** Begin another three-minute fastwrite. Focus on scenes, situations, case studies, moments, people, conversations, observations, and so on that stand out for you as you think about the draft. Think especially of specifics that come to mind that led to the understanding of your topic that you stated in the preceding step. Some of this information may be in the draft, but some may *not* yet be in the draft.

5. **Summary.** Finish by restating the main point you want to make in the next draft. Begin the revision by thinking about a lead or introduction that dramatizes this point. Consider a suggestive scene, case study, finding, profile, description, comparison, anecdote, conversation, situation, or observation that points the essay toward your main idea. For example, if your point is that your university's program to help second-language learners is inadequate, you could begin the next draft by telling the story of Maria, an immigrant from Guatemala who was a victim of poor placement in a composition course that she was virtually guaranteed to fail. Follow this lead into the draft, always keeping your main point or thesis in mind.

Revision Strategy 10.7: Reclaiming Your Topic

When you do a lot of research on your topic, you may reach a point when you feel awash in information. It's easy at such moments to feel as if you're losing control of your topic—besieged by the voices of experts, a torrent of statistics and facts, and competing perspectives. Your success in writing the paper depends on making it your own again, gaining control over the information for your own purposes, in the service of your own questions or arguments. This revision strategy, a variation of Revision Strategy 10.6, should help you gain control of the material you collected for a research-based inquiry project.

1. Spend ten or fifteen minutes reviewing all of the notes you've taken and skimming key articles or passages from books. Glance at your most important sources. If you have a rough draft, reread it. Let your head swim with information.

2. Now clear your desk of everything but your journal. Remove all your notes and materials. If you have a rough draft, put it in the drawer.

3. Now fastwrite about your topic for seven full minutes. Tell the story of how your thinking about the topic has evolved. When you began, what did you

think? What were your initial assumptions or preconceptions? Then what happened, and what happened after that? Keep your pen moving.

4. Skip a few lines in your notebook, and write *Moments, Stories, People, and Scenes*. Now fastwrite for another seven minutes, this time focusing more on specific case studies, situations, people, experiences, observations, facts, and so on that stand out in your mind from the research you've done so far, or perhaps from your own experience with the topic.

5. Skip a few more lines. For another seven minutes, write a dialogue between you and someone else about your topic. Choose someone who you think is typical of the audience you're writing for. If it helps, think of someone specific—an instructor, a fellow student, a friend. Don't plan the dialogue. Just begin with the question most commonly asked about your topic, and take the conversation from there, writing both parts of the dialogue.

6. Finally, skip a few more lines and write this two-word question in your notebook: *So what?* Now spend a few minutes trying to summarize the most important thing you think your readers should understand about your topic, based on what you've learned so far. Distill this into a sentence or two.

As you work your way to the last step, you're reviewing what you've learned about your topic without being tyrannized by the many voices, perspectives, and facts in the research you've collected. The final step, step 6, leads you toward a thesis statement. In the revision, keep this in mind as you reopen your notes, reread your sources, and check on facts. Remember in the rewrite to put all of this information in the service of this main idea—as examples or illustrations, necessary background, evidence or support, counterexamples, and ways of qualifying or extending your main point.

Revision Strategy 10.8: Believing and Doubting

In persuasive writing such as the argument, review, proposal, or research paper, we often feel that a thesis involves picking sides—"the play was good" or "the play was bad," "the novel was boring" or "the novel was fun to read." Instead of *either/or*, consider *both/and*. This might bring you to a more truthful, more sophisticated understanding of your subject, which rarely is either all bad or all good. One way to do this is to play Peter Elbow's doubting game and believing game.

1. Set aside ten to twelve minutes for two episodes of fastwriting in your journal or on the computer. First, spend a full five minutes playing the "believing game" (see the following prompts), exploring the merits of your subject even if (and especially if) you don't think it has any. Then switch to the "doubting game." Write fast for another five minutes using a skeptical mind.

THE BELIEVING GAME	**THE DOUBTING GAME**
Give the author, performer, text, or performance the benefit of the doubt. Suspend criticism.	Adopt a critical stance. Look for holes, weaknesses, omissions, problems.

1. What seems true or truthful about what is said, shown, or argued?
2. How does it confirm your own experiences or observations of the same things?
3. What did you like or agree with?

4. Where is it strongest, most compelling, most persuasive?
5. How does it satisfy your criteria for being good, useful, convincing, or moving?

1. What seems unbelievable or untrue?
2. What does it fail to consider or consider inadequately?
3. Where is the evidence missing or insufficient, or where do the elements not work together effectively?
4. How does it fail to meet your criteria for good in this category of thing?
5. Where is it the least compelling or persuasive? Why?

2. From this work in your notebook, try to construct a sentence—a thesis—that is more than a simple statement of the worth or worthlessness of the thing you're evaluating, but an expression of *both* its strengths and weaknesses: *Although _____ succeeds (or fails) in _____, it mostly _____.* For example: *Although reality television presents viewers with an often interesting glimpse into how ordinary people handle their fifteen minutes of celebrity, it mostly exaggerates life by creating drama where there often is none.*

Methods for Refining Your Thesis

You may emerge from writing a draft with a pretty clear sense of what you want to say in the next one. But does this idea seem a little obvious or perhaps too general? Does it fail to adequately express what you really feel and think? Use one or more of the following revision strategies to refine a thesis, theme, or controlling idea.

Revision Strategy 10.9: Questions as Knives

Imagine that your initial feeling, thesis, or main point is like an onion. Ideas, like onions, have layers, and to get closer to their hearts you need to cut through the most obvious outer layers to reveal what is less obvious, probably more specific, and almost certainly more interesting. Questions are to ideas as knives are to onions: They help you slice past your initial impressions. The most important question—the sharpest knife in the drawer—is simply *Why? Why* was the Orwell essay interesting? *Why* do you hate foreign films? *Why* should the university do more for second-language speakers? *Why* did you feel a sense of loss when the old cornfield was paved over for the mall?

Why may be the sharpest knife in the drawer, but there are other *W* questions with keen blades, too, including *What?, Where?, When?,* and *Who?* The result is a much more specific, more interesting controlling idea for the next draft.

1. Subject your tentative thesis to the same kind of narrowing. Write your theme, thesis, or main point as a single sentence in your notebook.

2. Slice it with questions and restate it each time.

3. Continue this until your point is appropriately sliced; that is, when you feel that you've gone beyond the obvious and stated what you think or feel in a more specific and interesting way.

As before, rewrite the next draft with this new thesis in mind, reorganizing the essay around it from beginning to end. Add new information that supports the idea, provides the necessary background, offers opposing views, or extends it. Cut information that no longer seems relevant to the thesis.

Revision Strategy 10.10: Qualifying Your Claim

In your research you discovered that, while 90 percent of Americans think that their fellow citizens are too "fat," only 39 percent would describe themselves that way. This evidence leads you to make the following claim: *Although Americans agree that obesity is a national problem, their response is typical: It's somebody else's problem—an attitude that will cripple efforts to promote healthier lifestyles.* This seems like a logical assertion if the evidence is reliable. But if you're going to try to build an argument around it, a claim should be rigorously examined. Toulmin's approach to analyzing arguments provides a method for doing this.

1. Toulmin observes that sometimes a claim should be *qualified* to be more accurate and persuasive. The initial question is simple: *Is what you're asserting always or universally true?* Essentially, you're being challenged to examine your certainty about what you're saying. This might lead you to add words or phrases to it that acknowledge your sense of certainty: *sometimes, always, mostly, in this case, based on available evidence,* and so on. In this case, the claim is already qualified by specifying that it is limited to Americans, but it is also based on evidence from a single source. The claim, therefore, might be qualified to say this: *Although one survey suggests that Americans agree that obesity is a national problem, their response is typical: It's somebody else's problem—an attitude that will cripple efforts to promote healthier lifestyles.*

2. Imagining how your claim might be rebutted is another way to strengthen it. How might someone take issue with your thesis? What might be the exceptions to what you're saying is true? For example, might someone object to the assertion that Americans "typically" respond by putting their heads in the sand when personally confronted with problems? You must decide, then, whether this clever aside in your claim is something you're prepared to support. If not, cut it.

Problems with Information

Writers who've spent enough time generating or collecting information about their topics can work from abundance rather than scarcity. This is an enormous advantage, because the ability to throw stuff away means you can be selective about what you use, and the result is a more focused draft. But as we revise, our purpose and point might shift, and we may find ourselves in the unhappy position of working from scarcity again. Most of our research, observation, or fastwriting was relevant to the triggering subject in the initial sketch or draft, not to the generated subject we decide is the better direction for the next draft. In some cases, this might require that you research the new topic or return to the generating activities of listing, fastwriting, clustering, and so on that will help provide information for the next draft.

More often, however, writers don't have to begin from scratch in revision. Frequently, a shift in the focus or refining a thesis in a first draft just means emphasizing different information or perhaps filling in gaps in later drafts. The strategies that follow will help you solve this problem.

Revision Strategy 10.11: Explode a Moment

The success of personal essays that rely on narratives frequently depends on how well the writer renders an important scene, situation, moment, or description. When you're telling a story from experience, not all parts of the story are equally important. As always, emphasis in a narrative depends on the writer's purpose in the essay. For example, Matt's essay on the irony of the slow poisoning of Butte, Montana, his hometown, by a copper mine that once gave the city life would emphasize those parts of the story that best highlight that irony. Or a description of the agonizing death of the snow geese that unwittingly landed on the acid pond—their white beauty set against the deadly dark water—might be an important scene in Matt's next draft; it nicely portrays life and death, beauty and ugliness in much the same way the town and the mine might be contrasted. Matt should "explode that moment" because it's an important part of the story he's trying to tell about his Montana hometown.

If you're trying to revise a draft that relies on narratives, this revision strategy will help you first identify moments, scenes, or descriptions that might be important in the next draft, and then develop these as more-important parts of your story.

1. Choose a draft that involves a story or stories.

2. Make a list in your journal of the moments (for example, scenes, situations, and turning points) that stand out in the narrative.

3. Circle one that you think is most important to your purpose in the essay. It could be the situation that is most telling, a dramatic turning point, the moment of a key discovery that is central to what you're trying to say, or a scene that illustrates the dilemma or raises the question you're exploring in the draft.

4. Name that moment at the top of a blank journal page (for example, *the snow geese on the acid pond*).

5. Now put yourself back into that moment and fastwrite about it for seven full minutes. Make sure that you write with as much detail as possible, *drawing on all your senses*. Write in the present tense if it helps.

6. Use this same method with other moments in the narrative that might deserve more emphasis in the next draft. Remember that real time means little in writing. An experience that took seven seconds can easily take up three pages of writing if it's detailed enough. Rewrite and incorporate the best of the new information in the next draft.

Revision Strategy 10.12: Beyond Examples

When we add information to a draft, we normally think of adding examples. If you're writing a research essay on living with a sibling who suffers from Down syndrome, you might mention that your brother typically tries to avoid certain cognitive challenges. Members of your workshop group wonder, "Well, what kind of challenges?" In revision, you add an example or two from your own experience, to clarify what you mean. This is, of course, a helpful strategy; examples of what you mean by an assertion are a kind of evidence that helps readers more fully understand your work. But also consider other types of information it might be helpful to add to the next draft. Use the following list to review your draft for additions you might not have thought of for revision.

- **Presenting counterarguments.** Typically, persuasive essays include information that represents an opposing view. Say you're arguing that beyond "avoidance" behaviors, there really aren't personality traits that can be attributed to most people with Down syndrome. You include a summary of a study that says otherwise. Why? Because it provides readers with a better understanding of the debate, and enhances the writer's ethos because you appear fair.

- **Providing background.** When you drop in on a conversation between two friends, you initially may be clueless about the subject. Naturally, you ask questions: "Who are you guys talking about? When did this happen? What did she say?" Answers to these questions provide a context that allows you to understand what is being said and to participate in the conversation. Such background information is often essential in written communication, too. In a personal essay, readers may want to know when and where the event occurred or the relationship between the narrator and a character. In a critical essay, it might be necessary to provide background on the short story because readers may not have read it. In a research essay, it's often useful to provide background information about what has already been said on the topic and the research question.

- **Establishing significance.** Let's say you're writing about the problem of obesity in America, something that most of us are generally aware of these days. But the significance of the problem really strikes home when you add information from research suggesting that 30 percent of American adults are overweight, up from 23 percent just six years ago. It is even more important to establish the significance of a problem about which there is little awareness or consensus. For example, most people don't know that America's national park system is crumbling and in disrepair. Your essay on the problem needs to provide readers with information that establishes the significance of the problem. In a profile, readers need to have a reason to be interested in someone—perhaps your profile subject represents a particular group of people of interest or concern.

- **Giving it a face.** One of the best ways to make an otherwise abstract issue or problem come to life is to show what it means to an individual person. We can't fully appreciate the social impact of deforestation in Brazil without being introduced to someone such as Chico Mendes, a forest defender who was murdered for his activism. Obesity might be an abstract problem until we meet Carl, a 500-pound 22-year-old who is "suffocating in his own fat." Add case studies, anecdotes, profiles, and descriptions that put people on the page, to make your essay more interesting and persuasive.

- **Defining it.** If you're writing about a subject your readers know little about, you'll likely use concepts or terms that readers will want you to define. What exactly do you mean, for example, when you say that the Internet is vulnerable to cyberterror? What exactly is cyberterror anyway? In your personal essay on your troubled relationship with your mother, what do you mean when you call her a narcissist? Frequently, your workshop group will alert you to things in the draft that need defining, but also go through your own draft and ask yourself, *Will my readers know what I mean?*

Revision Strategy 10.13: Research

Too often, research is ignored as a revision strategy. We may do research for the first draft of a paper or essay but never return to the library or search the web to fill in gaps, answer new questions, or refine the focus of a rewrite. That's crazy, particularly because well-researched information can strengthen a draft of any kind. That has been one of the themes of *The Curious Writer* since the beginning of the book: Research is not a separate activity reserved only for the research paper, but a rich source of information for any type of writing. Try some of these strategies:

1. For quick facts, visit refdesk.com. This enormously useful website is the fastest way to find out the exact height of the Great Wall of China or the number of young women suffering from eating disorders in America today.

2. Return to the *Library of Congress Subject Headings*, the reference mentioned in Chapter 8 that will help you pinpoint the language you should use to search library databases on your topic. Particularly if the focus of your next draft is shifting, you'll need some fresh information to fill in the gaps. The *LCSH* will help you find more of it, more quickly.

3. To maximize web coverage, launch a search on at least three different search engines (for example, Google, Bing, and Yahoo!), but this time search using terms or phrases from your draft that will lead you to more-specific information that will fill gaps in the draft.

4. Interview someone relevant to your topic. (See Chapter 8.)

5. To ferret out some new sources on your topic, search library databases under author rather than keyword. Focus on authors that you know have something to say on your topic.

6. Return to any of the steps in Chapter 8 that involve developing deeper knowledge about your topic.

Revision Strategy 10.14: Backing Up Your Assumptions

Targeted research is particularly important when you're making an argument. In addition to providing evidence that is relevant to your thesis, frequently an argument rests on the assumptions behind that assertion. Stephen Toulmin calls these assumptions *warrants*. A warrant bridges the evidence with a related claim by revealing the assumptions on which it rests. A warrant essentially answers this question: What do you have to believe is true to believe a claim? For example, suppose your claim is the following: *Reading a lot makes people better writers*. And here's the evidence supporting the claim: *English majors read a lot and they are also strong writers*. What do you need to assume is true to believe this assertion? Lots. One particularly key warrant is that what's true of English majors is true of all "people." Warrants are often implicit, so it can be really helpful to tease them out into the open and see if they're sound.

1. Write your claim on the top of a journal page, and then list the assumptions or warrants on which it seems to rest. For example, the claim about obesity includes an assumption that most Americans equate the words *obesity* and *fat*. Also, there's an assumption that public attitudes—particularly the view that there is a problem but it isn't my problem—hinder progress on public policy.

2. Which of the warrants behind your claim would be stronger if there were "backing" or evidence to support them? This will give you new direction for research. It might strengthen the argument on the obesity problem, for example, to draw on evidence from the civil rights struggle. Is there any evidence that attitudes toward personal responsibility for racism lagged behind acknowledgment of racial inequality as a national problem? Was progress finally made when this gap narrowed?

Problems with Structure

When it's working, the structure of a piece of writing is nearly invisible. Readers don't notice how the writer is guiding them from one piece of information to the next. When structure is a problem, the writer asks readers to walk out on a shaky bridge and trust that it will help them get to the other side, but the walkers can think of little else but the shakiness of the bridge. Some professional writers, such as John McPhee, obsess about structure, and for good reason; when you're working with a tremendous amount of information, as McPhee often does in his research-based essays, it helps to have a clear idea about how you'll use it.

It's helpful to distinguish two basic structures for writing. One typically organizes the information of experience, and one organizes our thinking so that it's clear and convincing. Typically, we use narrative, and especially chronology, to organize our experiences, though how we handle time can vary considerably. Writing that presents information based on the writer's reasoning—perhaps making an argument or reporting on an experiment—is logically structured. The most common example is the thesis-example, or thesis-proof, paper. Much formal academic writing relies on logical structures that use deduction or induction.

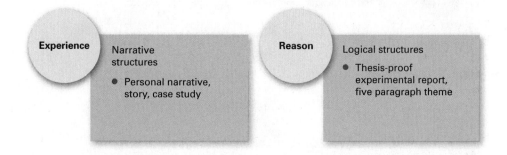

And yet some kinds of writing, such as the researched essay or ethnography, may *combine* both patterns, showing how the writer reasoned through to the meaning of an experience, observation, reading, and so on. These essays tell a "narrative of thought."

Formal Academic Structures

In some academic writing, the structure is prescribed. Scientific papers often have sections—Introduction, Methodology, Results, Discussion—but within those sections writers must organize their material. Certain writing assignments may also require you to organize your information in a certain way. The most common of these is the thesis/support structure. In such essays, you typically establish your thesis in the first paragraph, spend the body of the paper assembling evidence that supports the thesis, and conclude the essay with a summary that restates the thesis in light of what's been said.

Thesis/support is a persuasive form, so it lends itself to arguments, critical essays, reviews, proposals, and similar pieces. In fact, you may have already structured your draft using this approach. If so, the following revision strategy may help you tighten and clarify the draft.

Beginning

- Establishes purpose (answers So what? question)
- Introduces question, dilemma, problem, theory, thesis, claim (sometimes dramatically)
- Helps readers understand—and feel—what's at stake for them

Middle

- Tests theory, claim, thesis against the evidence
- Develops reasons, with evidence, for writer's thesis or claim
- Tells story of writer's inquiry into question, problem, or dilemma

End

- Proposes answer, even if tentative, for writer's key question
- Revisits thesis or claim, extending, qualifying, contradicting, or reconfirming initial idea
- Raises new questions, poses new problems, or offers new understanding of what is at stake for readers

Revision Strategy 10.15: Beginnings, Middles, Ends, and the Work They Do

Stories, we are often told, always have a beginning, middle, and end. This may be the most fundamental structure of all, and it doesn't just apply to narratives. The illustration below explains what a beginning, middle, and end might contribute to making nearly any piece of writing coherent and convincing. Apply some of these ideas to your draft.

1. Divide into three parts a draft you'd like to revise—beginning, middle, and end—by drawing lines on the paper to distinguish each section. Where you decide to divide the draft is entirely up to you; there's no formula to this. But you may change your mind as you go along.

2. Now use the illustration below to analyze your beginning, middle, and end. Does each section do at least *one* of the listed tasks? If not, revise that section so that it does. This may involve adding a sentence or two—or possibly a couple of paragraphs—of new information, perhaps moving some from elsewhere in the draft.

3. Generally speaking, the middle of an essay does the most work, and so proportionally it should have the most information. For example, many essays look like this:

If you find, for example, that your beginning takes three pages of a five-page essay, then you might want to cut away at the first few pages and concentrate on developing the body of your essay.

Revision Strategy 10.16: Reorganizing Around Thesis and Support

Because the thesis/support structure is fairly common, it's useful to master. Most drafts, even if they weren't initially organized in that form, can be revised into a thesis/support essay (personal essays would be an exception). The order of information in such an essay generally follows this design:

■ **Lead paragraph:** This paragraph introduces the topic and explicitly states the thesis, usually as the last sentence in the paragraph. For example, a thesis/support paper on the deterioration of America's national parks system might begin this way:

> Yellowstone National Park, which shares territory with Idaho, Montana, and Wyoming, is the nation's oldest park and, to some, its most revered. Established on March 1, 1872, the park features the Old Faithful geyser, which spouts reliably every 76 minutes on average. What isn't nearly as reliable these days is whether school groups will get to see it. Last year 60% of them were turned away because the park simply didn't have the staff. <u>This essay will argue that poor funding of our national parks system is a disgrace that threatens to undermine the Park Service's mission to preserve the areas "as cumulative expressions of a single national heritage" ("Famous Quotes").</u>

The thesis (underlined) is the final sentence in the paragraph, for emphasis.

- **Body:** Each succeeding paragraph until the final one attempts to prove or develop the thesis. Often, each paragraph is devoted to a single *reason* why the thesis is true, frequently stated as the topic sentence of the paragraph. Specific information then explains, clarifies, and supports the reason. For example, here's a typical paragraph from the body of the national parks essay:

> <u>One aspect of the important national heritage at risk because of poor funding for national parks is the pride many Americans feel about these national treasures.</u> *Newsweek* writer Arthur Frommer says the national park system is among the "crowning glories of our democracy." He adds, "Not to have seen them is to have missed something unique and precious in American life" (12). To see the crumbling roads in Glacier National Park, or the incursion of development in Great Smoky Mountains National Park, or the slow strangulation of the Everglades is not just an ecological issue; it's a sorry statement about a democratic nation's commitment to some of the places that define its identity.

The underlined sentence is the topic sentence of the paragraph and is an assertion that supports and develops the thesis in the lead of the essay. The rest of the paragraph offers supporting evidence of the assertion, in this case a quotation from a *Newsweek* writer who recently visited several parks.

- **Concluding paragraph:** This paragraph reminds the reader of the central argument, not simply by restating the original thesis from the first paragraph, but also by reemphasizing some of the most important points. This may lead to an elaboration or restatement of the thesis. One common technique is to find a way at the end of the essay to return to the beginning. Here's the concluding paragraph from the essay on national park funding:

> We would never risk our national heritage by allowing the White House to deteriorate or the Liberty Bell to rust away. <u>As the National Park Service's own mission states, the parks are also "expressions" of our "single national heritage," one this paper contends is about preserving not only trees, animals, and habitats, but also our national identity.</u> The Old Faithful geyser reminds Americans of their constancy and their enduring spirit. What will it say about us if vandals finally end the regular eruptions of the geyser because Americans didn't support a park ranger to guard it? What will we call Old Faithful then? Old Faithless?

Note that the underlined sentence returns to the original thesis but doesn't simply repeat it word for word. Instead, it amplifies the original thesis, adding a definition of "national heritage" to include national identity. It returns to the opening paragraph by finding a new way to discuss Old Faithful. Revise your draft to conform to this structure, beginning with a strong opening paragraph that explicitly states your thesis and concluding with an ending that somehow returns to the beginning without simply repeating what you've already said.

Revision Strategy 10.17: Multiple Leads

A single element that may affect a draft more than any other is the beginning. There are many ways into the material, and of course you want to choose a beginning or lead that a reader might find interesting. You also want to choose a beginning that makes some kind of promise, providing readers with a sense of where you intend to take them. But a lead also has less-obvious effects on both readers and writers. How you begin often establishes the voice of the essay; signals the writer's emotional relationship to the material, the writer's ethos; and might suggest the form the essay will take.

This is, of course, why beginnings are so hard to write. But the critical importance of where and how we begin also suggests that examining alternative leads can give writers more choices and more control over their essays. To borrow John McPhee's metaphor, if a lead is a "flashlight that shines down into the story," then pointing that flashlight in four different directions might reveal four different ways of following the same subject. This can be a powerful revision strategy.

1. Choose a draft that has a weak opening, doesn't have a strong sense of purpose, or needs to be reorganized.

2. Compose four *different* openings to the *same* draft. One way to generate ideas for this is to cluster your topic and write leads from four different branches. Also consider varying the type of lead you write.

3. Bring a typed copy of these four leads (or five if you want to include the original lead from the first draft) to class and share them with a small group. First, simply ask your classmates to choose the beginning they like best.

4. Choose the lead *you* prefer. It may or may not be the one your classmates chose. Find a partner who was not in your small group and ask him or her the following questions after sharing the lead you chose:

   ▪ Based on this lead, what do you predict that this paper is about?

   ▪ Can you guess the question, problem, or idea I'm writing about in the rest of the essay?

   ▪ Do you have a sense of what my thesis might be?

   ▪ What is the ethos of this beginning? In other words, how do I come across to you as a narrator or author of the essay?

If the predictions were fairly accurate using the lead you preferred, this might be a good alternative opening to the next draft. Follow it in a fastwrite in your notebook to see where it leads you. Go ahead and use the other leads elsewhere in the revision, if you like.

If your reader's predictions were off, the lead may not be the best choice for the revision. However, should you consider this new direction an appealing alternative for the next draft? Or should you choose another lead that better reflects your current intentions rather than strike off in new directions? Either way, follow a new lead to see where it goes.

Revision Strategy 10.18: The Frankenstein Draft

One way to divorce a draft that has you in its clutches is to dismember it; that is, cut it into pieces and play with the parts, looking for new arrangements of information or new gaps to fill. Writing teacher Peter Elbow's cut-and-paste revision can be a useful method, particularly for drafts that don't rely on narrative structures (although sometimes playing with alternatives, particularly if the draft is strictly chronological, can be helpful). Research essays and other pieces that attempt to corral lots of information seem to benefit the most from this strategy.

1. Choose a draft that needs help with organization. Make a one-sided copy.

2. Cut apart the copy, paragraph by paragraph. (You may cut it into smaller pieces later.) Once you have completely disassembled the draft, shuffle the

paragraphs to get them wildly out of order so the original draft is just a memory.

3.   Now go through the shuffled stack and find the *core paragraph*. This is the paragraph the essay really couldn't do without because it helps answer the *So what?* question. It might be the paragraph that contains your thesis or establishes your focusing question. It should be the paragraph that explains, implicitly or explicitly, what you're trying to say in the draft. Set this aside.

4.   With the core paragraph directly in front of you, work your way through the remaining stack of paragraphs and make two new stacks: one of paragraphs that don't seem relevant to your core (such as unnecessary digressions or information) and those that do (they support the main idea, explain or define a key concept, illustrate or exemplify something important, or provide necessary background).

5.   Put your reject pile aside for the moment. You may decide to salvage some of those paragraphs later. But for now focus on your relevant pile, including the core paragraph. Now play with order. Try new leads, ends, and middles. Consider trying some new methods of development as a way to organize your next draft (see the "Methods of Development" box). As you spread the paragraphs out before you and consider new arrangements, don't worry about the lack of transitions; you can add those later. Also look for gaps, places where more information might be needed. Consider some of the information in the reject pile as well. Should you splice in *parts* of paragraphs that you initially discarded?

6.   As a structure begins to emerge, begin taping together the fragments of paper. Also splice in scraps in appropriate places and note what you might add in the next draft that is currently missing.

Methods of Development

- Narrative
- Problem to solution
- Cause to effect, or effect to cause
- Question to answer
- Known to unknown, or unknown to known
- Simple to complex
- General to specific, or specific to general
- Comparison and contrast
- Combinations of any of these

Now you've created a Frankenstein draft. But hopefully this ugly mess of paper and tape and scribbled notes holds much more promise than the monster did. On the other hand, if you end up with pretty much the original organization, perhaps your first approach wasn't so bad after all. You may at least find places where more information is needed.

Problems with Clarity and Style

One thing should be made clear immediately: Problems of clarity and style need not have anything to do with grammatical correctness. You can have a sentence that follows all the rules and still lumbers, sputters, and dies like a Volkswagen bug towing a heavy trailer up a steep hill. Take this sentence, for instance:

> Once upon a point in time, a small person named Little Red Riding Hood initiated plans for the preparation, delivery, and transportation of foodstuffs to her grandmother, a senior citizen residing at a place of residence in a wooded area of indeterminate dimension.

Strong writing at the sentence and paragraph levels always begins with clarity.

This beastly sentence opens Russell Baker's essay "Little Red Riding Hood Revisited," a satire about the gassiness of contemporary writing. It's grammatically correct, of course, but it's also pretentious, unnecessarily wordy, and would be annoying to read if it wasn't pretty amusing. This section of the chapter focuses on revision strategies that improve the clarity of your writing and will help you consider the effects you want to create through word choice and arrangement.

Maybe because we often think that work with paragraphs, sentences, and words always involves problems of correctness, it may be hard to believe at first that writers can actually manage readers' responses and feelings by using different words or rearranging the parts of a sentence or paragraph. Once you begin to play around with style, however, you will discover that it's much more than cosmetic. In fact, style in writing is a lot like music in movies. Chris Douridas, a Hollywood music supervisor who picked music for *Shrek* and *American Beauty*, said recently that he sees "music as an integral ingredient to the pie. I see it as helping to flavor the pie and not as whipped cream on top." Certainly people don't pick a movie for its music, but we know that the music is central to our experience of a film. Similarly, *how* you say things in a piece of writing powerfully shapes the reader's experience of *what* you say.

But style is a secondary concern. Strong writing at the sentence and paragraph levels always begins with clarity. Do you say what you mean as directly and economically as you can? This can be a real problem, particularly with academic writing, in which it's easy to get the impression that a longer word is always better than a shorter word and that the absence of anything interesting to say can be remedied by sounding smart. Nothing could be further from the truth.

Solving Problems of Clarity

Begin by revising your draft with one or more revision strategies that will make your writing more direct and clear.

Revision Strategy 10.19: The Three Most Important Sentences

Writers, like car dealers, organize their lots to take advantage of where customers are most likely to look and what they're most likely to remember. In many essays and papers, there are three places to park important information and to craft your very best sentences. These are,

- the very first sentence
- the last line of the first paragraph
- the very last line of the essay

The First Sentence. Obviously, there are many other important places in a piece of writing—and longer essays, especially, have more and different locations for your strongest sentences. But in an informal piece of modest length, the first sentence not only should engage the reader, it should, through strong language and voice, introduce the writer as well. For example, here's the first line of Richard Conniff's researched essay "Why Did God Make Flies?": "Though I've been killing them for years now, I have never tested the folklore that, with a little cream and sugar, flies taste very much like black raspberries." In more formal writing, the first line is much less about introducing a persona than introducing the subject. Here's the first line of an academic piece I'm reading at the moment: "Much of the international debate about the relationship between research and teaching is characterized by difference." This raises an obvious question—"What is this difference?"—and this is exactly what the author proposes to explore.

The Last Line of the First Paragraph. The so-called "lead" (or "lede" in journalism speak) of an essay or article does three things: It establishes the purpose of the work, raises interesting questions, and creates a register or tone. A lead paragraph in a shorter essay is just that—the first paragraph—while a lead in a longer work may run for paragraphs, even pages. Whatever the length, the last sentence of the lead launches the work and gets it going in a particular direction. In conventional thesis-proof essays, then, this might be the sentence where you state your main claim. In inquiry-based forms such as the essay, this might be where you post the key question you're exploring or illuminate the aspect of the problem you want to look at.

The Last Line of the Essay. If it's good, this is the sentence readers are most likely to remember.

Try this revision strategy:

1. Highlight or underline each of the three key sentences in your draft.

2. Ask yourself these questions about the first line and, depending on your answers, revise the sentence:

   - Is the language lively?

   - Does it immediately raise questions the reader might want to learn the answers to?

   - Will they want to read the second sentence, and why?

3. Analyze the last sentence of your "lead" paragraph for ideas about revision. Ask yourself this:

   - Is the sentence well crafted?

   - Does it hint at or explicitly state your motive for asking readers to follow along with you in the paragraphs and pages that follow?

4. Finally, scrutinize your last sentence:

   - Is this one of the best-written sentences in the piece?

   - Does it add something?

Revision Strategy 10.20: Untangling Paragraphs

One of the things I admire most in my friends David and Margaret is that they both have individual integrity—a deep understanding of who they are and who they want to be—and yet they remain just as profoundly connected to the people close to them. They manage to exude both individuality and connection. I hope my friends will forgive the comparison, but good paragraphs have the same qualities: Alone they have their own identities, yet they are also strongly hitched to the paragraphs that precede and that follow them. This connection happens quite naturally when you're telling a story, but in expository writing the relationship between paragraphs is more related to content than time.

The following passage is the first three paragraphs from Paul de Palma's essay on computers, with the clever title "http://www.when_is_enough_enough?.com." Notice the integrity of each paragraph—each is a kind of mini-essay—as well as the way each one is linked to the paragraph that precedes it.

A paragraph should be unified, focusing on a single topic, idea, or thing. It's like a mini-essay in that sense.

In the misty past, before Bill Gates joined the company of the world's richest men, before the mass-marketed personal computer, before the metaphor of an information superhighway had been worn down to a cliché, I heard Roger Schank interviewed on National Public Radio. Then a computer science professor at Yale, Schank was already well known in artificial intelligence circles. Because those circles did not include me, a new programmer at Sperry Univac,

I hadn't heard of him. Though I've forgotten details of the conversation, I have never forgotten Schank's insistence that most people do not need to own computers.

That view, of course, has not prevailed. Either we own a personal computer and fret about upgrades, or we are scheming to own one and fret about the technical marvel yet to come that will render our purchase obsolete. Well, there are worse ways to spend money, I suppose. For all I know, even Schank owns a personal computer. They're fiendishly clever machines, after all, and they've helped keep the wolf from my door for a long time.

It is not the personal computer itself that I object to. What reasonable person would voluntarily go back to a typewriter? The mischief is not in the computer itself, but in the ideology that surrounds it. If we hope to employ computers for tasks more interesting than word processing, we must devote some attention to how they are actually being used, and beyond that, to the remarkable grip that the idol of computing continues to exert.

> Note how the first sentence in the new paragraph links with the last sentence in the preceding one. As before, the first sentence links with the last sentence in the previous paragraph.
>
> The final sentence is the most important one in a paragraph. Craft it carefully.

Well-crafted paragraphs such as these create a fluent progression, all linked together like train cars; they make readers feel confident that this train is going somewhere. This might be information that clarifies, extends, proves, explains, or even contradicts. Do the paragraphs in your draft work well on their own and together?

1. Check the length of every paragraph in your draft. Are any too long, going on and on for a full page or more? Can you create smaller paragraphs by breaking out separate ideas, topics, discussions, or claims?

2. Now examine each paragraph in your draft for integrity. Is it relatively focused and unified? Should it be broken down further into two or more paragraphs because it covers too much territory?

3. Instruction about the so-called "topic sentence" might lead writers to believe that the first sentence in a paragraph is the most important sentence. Actually, I think it's typically the last sentence in a paragraph that carries the most freight. In particular, how strong is the final sentence in each paragraph? Does it prepare readers to move into the next paragraph? In general, each paragraph adds some kind of new information to the old information in the paragraphs preceding it. This new material may clarify, explain, prove, elaborate on, contrast, summarize, contradict, or alter time. Sometimes you should signal the nature of this addition using transition words and phrases (see the "Inquiring into the Details: Transition Flags" box). Are there any awkward transitions? Should you smooth them using transition flags?

Revision Strategy 10.21: Cutting Clutter

"Once upon a point in time—at coordinates as yet too sensitive to disclose—a small person named Little Red Riding Hood initiated an operation involving the preparation, transportation, and delivery of foodstuffs to her grandmother, a senior citizen residing in a forest of indeterminate dimension."

Russell Baker's overinflated version of "Little Red Riding Hood," excerpted above, suffered from what writer and professor William Zinsser called "clutter." This disease afflicts much writing, particularly in academic settings. Clutter, simply put, is saying in three or four words what you might say in two, or choosing a longer word when a shorter one will do just as well. It grows from the assumption that simplicity means simplemindedness. This is misguided. Simplicity is a great virtue in writing. It's respectful of the readers, for one thing, who are mostly interested in understanding what you mean without unnecessary detours or obstacles.

In case Russell Baker's tongue-and-cheek example of cluttered writing isn't convincing because it's an invention, here's a brief passage from a memo I received from a fellow faculty member some years ago. I won't make you endure more than a sentence.

> While those of us in the administration are supporting general excellence and consideration of the long-range future of the University, and while the Faculty Senate and Caucus are dealing with more immediate problems, the Executive Committee feels that an ongoing dialogue concerning the particular concerns of faculty is needed to maintain the quality of personal and educational life necessary for continued educational improvement.

That's a 63-word sentence, and while there is nothing inherently wrong with long sentences, I'm pretty sure that at least half of the words are unnecessary. For the fun of it, see if you can cut at least thirty words from the sentence without

Inquiring into the Details

Transition Flags

One way to connect paragraphs is to signal to a reader with words what the relationship is between them.

- **Clarifying:** *for example, furthermore, specifically, also, to illustrate, similarly*
- **Proving:** *in fact, for example, indeed*
- **Time:** *first…second…finally, subsequently, following, now, recently*
- **Cause or effect:** *therefore, consequently, so, accordingly*
- **Contrast or contradiction:** *on the other hand, in contrast, however, on the contrary, despite, in comparison*
- **Summarizing:** *finally, in the end, in conclusion, summing up, to conclude*

compromising the writer's intent. Look for ways to say the same things in fewer words, and look for shorter words that might replace longer ones. What kinds of choices did you make to improve the clarity of the sentence?

Now shift your attention to one of your own drafts and see if you can be as ruthless with your own clutter as you were with the memo writer's.

1. One of the most common kinds of clutter is stock phrases, things we mindlessly say because we've simply gotten in the habit of saying them. *Due to the fact that…* is the one that drives me most crazy. Why not the simpler word *Because*? The following table lists some of the most common stock phrases used in student writing. Read your draft from beginning to end, and when you see one of these, cut it down to size.

STOCK PHRASE	SIMPLER VERSION
Due to the fact that…	Because
At the present time…	Now
Until such time as…	Until
I am of the opinion that…	I think
In the event of…	When
This is an appropriate occasion to…	It's time
Proceed with the implementation of…	Begin
Referred to as…	Called
Totally lacked the ability to…	Couldn't
A number of…	Many
In the event of…	If
There is a need for…	Must

2. Another thing to consider is choosing a shorter, simpler word rather than a longer, more complicated word. For example, why not say *many* rather than *numerous*, or *ease* rather than *facilitate*, or *do* rather than *implement*, or *found* rather than *identified*? Go through your draft and look for opportunities such as these to use simpler, more direct words.

3. In his book *Style: Ten Lessons in Clarity and Grace*, Joseph Williams cleverly calls the habit of using meaningless words "verbal tics." These are words, he writes, that "we use almost as unconsciously as we clear our throats." My favorite verbal tic is the phrase *in fact*, which I park at the front of a sentence when I feel like I'm about to clarify something. Mostly I can do without it. In fact, most of us have verbal tics, and we should learn to recognize them. Williams mentions a few common ones, including *kind of, actually, basically, generally, given, various*, and *certain*. For example, *It's generally assumed that certain students have various reasons for being apolitical these days*. A better version would be *Students have reasons for being apolitical these days*.

Go through your draft and search for words and phrases that you use out of habit, and cut them if they don't add meaning.

Revision Strategy 10.22: The Actor and the Action Next Door

I live in a relatively urban neighborhood, and so I can hear Kate play her music across the street and Gray powering up his chainsaw to cut wooden pallets next door. I have mixed feelings about this. Kate and I have different taste in music and Gray runs the saw at dusk. But I am never confused about who is doing what. That's less obvious in the following passage:

> A conflict that was greeted at first with much ambivalence by the American public, the war in Iraq, which caused a tentativeness that some experts call the "Vietnam syndrome," sparked protests among Vietnam veterans.

The subject, or actor, of the sentence (*the war in Iraq*) and the action (*sparked protests*) are separated by a few city blocks. In addition, the subject is buried behind a long introductory clause. As a result, it's a bit hard to remember who is doing what. Putting actor and action next door to each other makes the writing livelier, and bringing the subject up front helps clarify who is doing what.

> The war in Iraq sparked protests among Vietnam veterans even though the conflict was initially greeted with public ambivalence. Some experts call this tentativeness the "Vietnam syndrome."

Review your draft to determine whether the subjects in your sentences are buried or are in the same neighborhood as the verbs that modify them. If they're too far away, rewrite to bring the actors up front in your sentences and to close the distance between actors and actions.

Improving Style

These revision strategies will improve the style of your writing. In the same way that a John Williams score can make movies such as *Indiana Jones and the Temple of Doom* and *Star Wars* more memorable and moving, style in writing can add to readers' experiences of a text. These are often calculated moves. Writers adopt a style because it serves a purpose, perhaps encouraging a certain feeling that makes a story more powerful, enhancing the writer's ethos to make an essay more convincing, or simply giving certain information particular emphasis. For example, here's the beginning of an article about Douglas Berry, a Marine drill sergeant.

> He is seething, he is rabid, he is wound up tight as a golf ball, with more adrenalin surging through his hypothalamus than a cornered slum rat, he is everything these Marine recruits with their heads shaved to dirty nubs have ever feared or ever hoped a drill sergeant might be.

The style of this opening is calculated to have an obvious effect—the reader is pelted with words, one after another, in a breathless sentence that almost simulates the experience of having Sgt. Douglas Berry in your face. There's no magic to this. It is all about using words that evoke action and feeling, usually verbs or words based on or derived from verbs.

Revision Strategy 10.23: Actors and Actions

As you know, verbs make things happen in writing, and how much energy prose possesses depends on verb power. Academic writing sometimes lacks strong verbs, relying instead on old, passive standbys such as *it was concluded by the study* or *it is believed*. Not only are the verbs weak, but the actors—the people or things engaged in the action—are often missing completely from the sentences. *Who* or *what* did the study? *Who* believes?

This is called *passive voice*, and while it's not grammatically incorrect, it can suck the air out of a room. While reasons exist for using passive voice (sometimes, for instance, the writer wants the reader to focus on the action, not the actor), you should avoid it in your own writing. One of the easiest ways to locate passive voice in your drafts is to conduct a *to be* search. Most forms of the verb *to be* usually signal passive voice. For example,

> It is well known that medieval eating habits were unsavory by contemporary health standards. Cups were shared, forks were never used, and the same knives used to clean under fingernails or to gut a chicken were used to cut and eat meat.

What is missing, of course, are the actors. To revise into active voice, you simply need to add the actors, whenever possible:

> Medieval diners had unsavory eating habits by contemporary health standards. They shared cups with friends, they never used forks, and they used their knives, the same ones they used to clean under their fingernails or gut a chicken, to cut and eat their meat.

1. Conduct a *to be* search of your own draft. Whenever you find passive construction, try to put the actor into the sentence.

2. Eliminating passive voice is only one strategy for giving your writing more energy. Try to use lively verbs as well. Can you replace weak verbs with stronger ones? How about *discovered* instead of *found*, or *seized* instead of *took*, *shattered* instead of *broke*. Review every sentence in the draft and, when appropriate, revise with a stronger verb.

Revision Strategy 10.24: Smoothing the Choppiness

Consider the following sentences, each labeled with the number of syllables:

> When the sun finally rose the next day I felt young again.(15) It was a strange feeling because I wasn't young anymore.(15) I was fifty years old and felt like it.(10) It was the smell of the lake at dawn that thrust me back into adolescence.(19) I remembered the hiss of the waves.(9) They erased my footprints in the sand.(9)

This really isn't awful; it could pass as a bad Hemingway imitation. But do you notice the monotony of the writing—the steady, almost unvarying beat that threatens to dull your mind if it goes on much longer? The cause of the plodding rhythm is the unvarying length of the pauses. The last two sentences in the passage each have nine syllables, and the first two sentences are nearly identical in length as well (fifteen syllables each).

Now notice how this choppiness disappears by varying the lengths of the pauses through combining sentences, inserting other punctuation, and dropping a few unnecessary words.

When the sun finally rose the next day I felt young again,(15) and it was a strange feeling because I wasn't young.(13) I was fifty years old.(6) It was the smell of the lake at dawn that thrust me back into adolescence and remembering the hiss of the waves as they erased my footprints in the sand.(39)

The revision is much more fluent, and the reason is simple: The writer varies the pauses and the number of syllables within each of them—15, 13, 6, 39.

1. Choose a draft of your own that doesn't seem to flow or seems choppy in places.

2. Mark the pauses in the problem areas. Put slash marks next to periods, commas, semicolons, dashes, and so on—any punctuation that prompts a reader to pause briefly.

3. If intervals between seem similar in length, revise to vary them, combining sentences, adding punctuation, dropping unnecessary words, or varying long and short words.

Revision Strategy 10.25: Fresh Ways to Say Things

It goes without saying that a tried-and-true method of getting to the heart of revision problems is to just do or die. Do you know what I mean? Of course you don't, because the opening sentence is laden with clichés and figures of speech that manage to obscure meaning.

Removing clichés and shopworn expressions from your writing will make it sound more as if you are writing from your own voice rather than someone else's.

1. Reread your draft and circle clichés and hand-me-down expressions. If you're not sure whether a phrase qualifies for either category, share your circled items with a partner and discuss them. Have you heard these things before?

2. Cut clichés and overused expressions and rewrite your sentences, finding your own way to say things. In your own words, what do you really mean by "do or die" or "striking while the iron is hot" or becoming a "true believer"?

Using What You Have Learned

Take a few moments to reflect on what you have learned in this chapter and how you can apply it.

1. **Understand the meaning—and value—of revision and apply it to your own work when appropriate.** Even if an instructor doesn't explicitly require a revision for a writing assignment, you now have experience with what a difference it can make in the quality of your work.

2. **Recognize five types of revision and apply most-relevant strategies to a particular draft.** As you continue to develop as a writer, you'll become a more critical reader of your own work, and this judgment gets easier. Learn to recognize your weaknesses—maybe you're not great at organizing drafts or you're wordy—and find strategies that help you address those problems.

Credits

Text

Page 261. GOOGLE is a trademark of Google Inc.

Page 264. Courtesy of EBSCO.

Photo

Page 2. Radius/SuperStock

Page 9. Stanca Sanda/Alamy

Page 38. Stockbyte/Getty Images

Page 39 (l). Andrija Markovic/Can Stock Photo

Page 39 (m). Gillmar/Shutterstock

Page 39 (r). Andrija Markovic/Can Stock Photo

Page 49. Bruce Ballenger

Page 56. Image Courtesy of The Advertising Archives

Page 68. Bruce Ballenger

Page 74. Originally published in the *Unexpected World of Nature # 3* (Thirteen/WNET, 2008). Copyright © 2008 Josh Neufeld

Page 76. "Mable" Laura Zazulak

Page 102. Paramount Pictures/Everett Collection

Page 107 (bl). Dorothea Lange/Library of Congress, Prints & Photographs Division, FSA/OWI Collection, [LC-USF34-9095]

Page 107 (ml). Dorothea Lange/Library of Congress, Prints & Photographs Division, FSA/OWI Collection, [LC-USF34-9097-C]

Page 107 (tl). Dorothea Lange/Library of Congress, Prints & Photographs Division, FSA/OWI Collection, [LC-USZ62-58355]

Page 107 (mr). Dorothea Lange/Library of Congress, Prints & Photographs Division, FSA/OWI Collection, [LC-DIG-fsa-8b29516]

Page 107 (tr). Dorothea Lange/Library of Congress, Prints & Photographs Division, FSA/OWI Collection, [LC-USF34-9093-C]

Page 109. Amazon Kindle Fire Review from CNET. Reprinted by permission of The YGS Group on behalf of CNET.

Page 111. Everett Collection

Page 114. Rosie Greenway/Getty Images

Page 134. Paramount Pictures/Everett Collection

Page 134. Chris Pizzello/AP Images

Page 136. James Nesterwitz/Alamy

Page 143. Alexandra Muresan, www.ixycreativity.ro

Page 150 (l). Benjamin Damm

Page 150 (r). Benjamin Damm

Page 151 (bl). Benjamin Damm

Page 151 (br). Benjamin Damm

Page 151 (tl). Benjamin Damm

Page 151 (tr). Benjamin Damm

Page 157. Library of Congress, Prints & Photographs Division, FSA/OWI Collection, [LC-USF34-014113-D]

Page 170. Don Ryan/AP Images

Page 176. Photo B.D.V./Corbis

Page 185. Joe Heller/PoliticalCartoons.com

Page 187. AP Images

Page 218. Richard Megna/Fundamental Photographs, NYC

Page 224. Illustration by Monika Umba, www.umbastudio.com

Page 235. Sveinung Svendsen/IFC Films/Everett Collection

Page 239. *Young Ladies on the Banks of the Seine River* (1856), Gustave Courbet. Oil on canvas. Petit Palais, Musée Des Beaux-Arts De La Ville De Paris. The Bridgeman Art Library/Getty Images

Page 258. Moschen/Shutterstock

Page 274. Robert Bull

Page 277 (l). Brian Jackson/Fotolia

Page 277 (m). Tim/Fotolia

Page 277 (r). Xuejun li/Fotolia

Page 292. Andy Sotiriou/Photodisc/Getty Images

Page 370. Stockbyte/Getty Images.

Page 394 (b). Rafael Ben-Ari/Fotolia

Page 394 (m). DelMonaco/Shutterstock

Page 394 (t). Steven Russell Smith Photos/Shutterstock

Inquiring into the Details icon. Frederick Bass/Getty Images

One Student's Response icon. Purestock/Getty Images

Writing Beyond the Classroom icon. Fuse/Getty Images

Index

A

Abstracts
  APA style for, 340–341, 353–354
  MLA style for, 325
Academic discourse
  features of, 65–66
  from outside in, 62–63
Academic reading
  purposes of, 40–43, 45
  scenarios for, 46–47
Academic writing. *See also* Writing
  argument and, 183–184
  critical essays and, 221
  personal essay and, 71–72
  proposals and, 140–141
  reviews and, 106
Ackerman, Diane, *The Natural History of Love,* 301
Ad hominem, 181
Amazon Kindle Fire, 109
American Psychological Association (APA) style, 299. *See also* APA documentation style
Anthology citations, 318
APA documentation style. *See also* Source citations
  abstract in, 340–341
  authors in, 344–346
  body of paper in, 341–343
  books in, 348, 351–354
  e-mail in, 346
  explanation of, 339
  format for, 340
  interviews in, 346
  language and style in, 344
  letters in, 346
  multiple works in same parentheses in, 346
  online sources in, 351–352
  periodicals in, 348–351
  references in, 314, 347–357
  source citations in, 344–346
  student essay in, 358–367
  tables and figures in, 343
  title page in, 340
Appeal to authority, 181

Appeal to popularity, 181
Appleman, Jenna
  "Avoidable Accidents: How to Make Reality TV Safer," 166–168
  "Loving and Hating Reality TV," 158–159
Argument
  academic writing and, 183–184
  analysis of, 178, 180, 210–211
  audience for, 177, 178, 199, 204
  claims in, 174–175
  credibility, emotion, and logic in, 177–178
  development of, 199–201, 204–206
  drafts for, 203–204, 206–207
  editorial cartoons as, 185
  evaluation of, 180–182
  evidence in, 175–176, 208
  example of student, 212–216
  examples of, 186–193
  explanation of, 172–174
  features of, 184
  interviews for, 201
  motives for writing, 182
  nature of, 171–172, 216–217
  peer review of, 208–209
  public, 183
  reasons in, 175
  research for, 200–202, 204–206
  revision of, 209–212
  sketch writing for, 201–203
  student sketch for, 202–203
  as therapy, 178–179
  topics for, 195–199
  writing process for, 194
Aristotle, 177, 182
Art criticism, 238–240
Artwork citations, 327–328
Audience
  for argument, 177, 178, 199, 204
  for critical essays, 246
  neutral, 177, 207
  for personal essays, 89
  for proposals, 155–156
  for reviews, 121
  survey, 281, 283–284

Authors
  APA style for, 344–346
  MLA style for, 306–308
"Avoidable Accidents: How to Make Reality TV Safer" (Appleman), 166–168

B

Baker, Russell, 404
Ballenger, Bruce, "The Importance of Writing Badly," 58–60
Begging the question, 182
Beliefs
  about reading, 43–45
  about writing, 5, 8
  unlearning unhelpful, 7–8
Believing, as reading perspective, 48
Berthoff, Ann E., 8
"Beyond Gaydar" (Harter), 358–367
Bibliographies, working, 272
Bird, Julie
  "Nature as Being: Landscape in Silko's 'Lullaby,'" 254–256
  "What Is the Role of Nature in 'Lullaby'?," 247–248
Bissinger, Buzz, "Why College Football Should Be Banned," 144–146
Blogs, 183, 327
"The Bluebird" (Bukowski), 223–224
Books
  APA style for, 348, 351–354
  library searches for, 269
  in MLA style, 316–320
  online, 351–352
Boole, George, 263
Boolean searches, 263–264
Brainstorming, tips for, 11
Bukowski, Charles, "The Bluebird," 223–224
Burns, Laura
  "How to Not Feel Good and Feel Good About It," 133–134
  "Recipe for a Great Film: Unlikeable People, Poor Choices, and a Little Redemption," 126

C

Campbell, Joseph, 233
Case studies
  function of, 140
  MLA style for, 326
Catalist (web site), 205
Cause-and-effect relationship, 207
Characters, 244
Charts. *See* Tables/charts/illustrations
Choppy writing, 407
"A Christmas Story" (Ebert),
  110–113
Chronicle of Higher Education, 41,
  42, 279–280
Cicero, 182
Citations. *See* Source citations
Claim questions, 31
Claims, 174–175
Clarity, revision goals to improve,
  400–406
Clichés, 408
Clustering
  examples of, 198
  explanation of, 25, 197
Cofer, Judith Ortiz, "One More
  Lesson," 78–81
"College Dating" (Seirup), 329–338
Color, in artwork, 240
Common knowledge exception, 303
Comparison and contrast
  in critical essays, 250–251
  in reviews, 129
Composition, artwork, 240
Computer programs, 356
Connecting, as reading perspective, 48
Conniff, Richard, "Why God Created
  Flies," 294–295, 298
Conversing, as invention strategy, 25
"CO$_2$ Paper Pie Chart" (Muresan), 143
Courbet, Gustave, *Young Ladies
  on the Banks of the Seine,*
  238–239
Creative thinking, 26–27
Credibility, in argument, 177
Critical essays
  about film, 234–238
  about literature, 219–220
  about paintings, 238–240
  academic writing and, 221
  drafts for, 248–251
  evaluation of, 257
  examples of, 225–233
  features of, 222

  literary devices for, 244–245
  motives for writing, 220–221
  peer review of, 251–252
  research for, 249
  revision of, 252–254
  sketch writing for, 246–247
  student, 254–256
  student sketches for, 247–248
  topics for, 242–244
  writing process for, 241, 257
Critical thinking, 27

D

Databases
  citing periodicals from, 320–325
  library-based, 269–271
De Palma, Paul, 402–403
Development
  of argument, 199–201, 204–206
  of critical essays, 245–246, 249
  of personal essays, 94–95
  of proposals, 160–161
  of reviews, 127–129
Dialectical thinking, writing process
  and, 26
Digital Object Identifier (DOI),
  349, 350
Direct questions, 281, 283
Discourse communities, 62
Discussion lists, 356–357
Documentation styles. *See* APA
  documentation style; MLA
  documentation style
Double-entry journals
  with critical reading, 57–60
  explanation of, 55
  as research tool, 286–288
  techniques for, 57
  with visual text, 55–56
Doubting, as reading perspective, 48
Drafts. *See also* Revision; Revision
  goals; Revision strategies
  for argument, 203–204,
  206–207
  checklist for, 99
  for critical essays, 248–251
  for personal essays, 92–96
  for proposals, 159–160,
  162–163
  for reviews, 126–130
  taking fresh look at, 373–375
DVD citations, 327

E

"Earning a Sense of Place"
  (Stewart), 92
Ebert, Roger, "A Christmas Story,"
  110–113
EBSCOhost database, 264
Editorial cartoons, 185
Editorials, 324
Either/or fallacy, 181–182
Elbow, Peter, 398
Ellipsis dots, 313
E-mail, citations for, 346
E-mail interviews, 277, 279
Emotion, in argument, 177
Encyclopedia of Associations, 278
Encyclopedias. *See also specific
  encyclopedias*
  APA style for, 354
  MLA style for, 319
Essai, 70–71
Ethical issues
  plagiarism as, 191–193,
  300–301
  related to field research, 285
Ethnography, 48–49
Ethos, 177, 178
Evaluation. *See also* Reviews
  as academic reading question,
  41, 43
  of critical essays, 256
  elements of, 103–104
  of personal essays, 93–94,
  100–101
  refining criteria for better,
  123–124
"Every Morning for Five Years"
  (Zazulak), 75–76
Evidence
  in argument, 175–176, 208
  in personal essays, 96
  in proposals, 163
  in reviews, 104, 123–124, 130
Expert knowledge, 265
Explanation, as academic reading
  question, 41–43
Exploration, as academic reading
  question, 41, 42

F

False analogy, 181
False cause, 181

Fastwriting
    for argument, 196–197
    for critical essays, 242–243
    explanation of, 25
    for personal essays, 86, 94, 119
    for proposals, 153–154
    for reviews, 119, 122
    rules for, 5–6
Feminist criticism, 234
Field research
    ethical issues related to, 285
    explanation of, 284–285
    integrating information from, 286
    note-taking strategies for, 285
Film criticism. *See also* Critical essays
    example of, 235–237
    nature of, 234–235
Films
    APA style for, 355
    MLA style for, 327
Focused knowledge
    explanation of, 267–268
    research strategies to develop,
        268–271

G

Genres, 13, 14
Golden mean, 240
Google, 261–263, 270
Google Groups, 205, 277
Google Scholar, 262–263
Gornick, Vivian, 84
Government documents, 320, 354
"Grand Theft Auto Takes on
    New York" (Schiesel),
    115–117
"Green Dining" proposal, 147–149

H

Habits of mind, 8–9
Harter, Kersti, "Beyond Gaydar,"
    358–367
Hasty generalization, 180
Hemingway, Ernest, 219
Hierarchy, in artwork, 239–240
"How to Not Feel Good and Feel
    Good About It" (Burns),
    133–134
Hunting and gathering, as reading
    perspective, 48
Hypothesis questions, 31

I

Illustrations. *See* Tables/charts/
    illustrations
Images
    Internet as source for, 205–206
    as literary device, 245
    MLA style for, 327
"The Importance of Writing Badly"
    (Ballenger), 58–60
Inquiry-based approach
    beliefs about writing, 5
    discovery emphasis in, 381–382
    habits of mind, 8–9
    motives for writing and, 4,
        104–105, 378–379
    process of, 32–33
    questioning and, 30–32
    reading and, 39–67
    writing and, 3–37
Internet. *See also* Web sites
    evaluating sources on, 273–276
    Google searches on, 261–263
    as research tool, 205, 261–263,
        270, 273
    search engines, 261–263, 271, 273
    as source for images, 205–206
Interpretation questions, 31
Interpreting, as reading perspec-
    tive, 48
Interviews
    APA style for, 346, 355
    for argument, 201, 205
    arranging for, 277–278
    e-mail, 277, 279
    integrating information from,
        279–280
    method to conduct, 278–279
    MLA style for, 308, 325–326
    for proposals, 161
    as research tool, 277
    for reviews, 123, 128
Invention strategies, 25
"Is Humiliation an Ethically
    Appropriate Response to
    Plagiarism?" (Young), 191–193

J

Jensen, Robin, 176
Journals (periodicals), APA style for,
    348–349
Journal writing
    double-entry, 55–60, 286–288

    guidelines for, 7
    prompts for, 6
Judgment
    evaluation and, 104
    process of making, 27
    suspension of, 10, 27

K

Keyword searches, 264–265
Kindle Fire (Amazon), 109
Knowledge
    expert, 265
    focused, 267–271
    of genre, 46
    of subject, 46
    working, 265–267

L

Lange, Dorothea, *Migrant Mother,*
    106, 107
Language
    APA style for, 344
    MLA style for, 313–314
Language use, for personal essays, 73
Lead paragraphs, 395–398, 401–402
Learning goals
    for reading process, 39, 67
    for writing process, 3, 37
Lectures, 328
Letters to the editor, 183, 324,
    354–355
Library of Congress Subject Headings
    (LCSH), 264–265, 268
Library research
    book searches and, 269
    evaluation of, 271–272
    overview of, 268
    periodical and newspaper
        searches and, 269–271
    power searches and, 263–265
    preparing for sketches using, 205
    source evaluation and, 271–272
Limited choice questions, 282
Line, in artwork, 239
Listing, 25
Listing prompts
    for argument, 195–196
    for critical essays, 242
    for personal essays, 85
    for proposals, 153
    for reviews, 119

Literary devices, 244–245
Literary theory, 233–234
Literature, 219–220. *See also*
    Critical essays
Logic
    in argument, 177, 178
    Rogerian, 210
    Toulminian, 210
Logical fallacies
    explanation of, 180
    list of common, 180–182
    looking out for, 210
"Loving and Hating Reality TV"
    (Appleman), 158–159
"Lullaby" (Silko), 225–232

M

Magazines. *See* Periodicals/
    newspapers
Mapping. *See* Clustering
Marlin, Seth, "Smoke of Empire,"
    99–100
McCloud, Scott, 185
Meaning problems, 376, 381–388
Metacognitive thinking, 16n
Migrant Mother (Lange), 106, 107
MLA documentation style. *See also*
    Source citations
    authors' names and, 306–308
    books in, 316–320
    citation location in, 304–306
    explanation of, 303
    format for, 311–313
    guidelines for use of, 304–306
    language and style in, 313–314
    multiple sources in single citation
        in, 308–309
    online sources in, 310, 325–328
    parenthetical references for other
        sources in, 309–310
    periodicals in, 320–325
    personal interviews in, 308
    quotations in, 308, 314
    student essay in, 328–339
    tables/charts/illustrations in, 312
    title pages in, 311–312
    titles in, 312–313
    when there is no author, 306–307
    Works Cited page in, 304, 314–328
*The MLA Handbook for Writers
    of Research Papers,* 7th
    ed. (Modern Language
    Association), 303

Modern Language Association (MLA)
    style, 299. *See also* MLA docu-
    mentation style
Montaigne, Michel de, 70
Moss, Kate, 176
Motives
    for revision, 377–378
    for writing, 4
    for writing argument, 182
    for writing critical essays, 220–221
    for writing personal essays,
        70–71, 73
    for writing proposals, 140
    for writing reviews, 104–106
Multivolume works, MLA style
    for, 309
Muresan, Alexandra, "CO_2 Paper
    Pie Chart," 143
Musical recordings, 356

N

Names, MLA style for, 313
Narrative
    in argument, 207
    in critical essays, 250
    in personal essays, 95–96
    in reviews, 129
    revision of, 97–98
The Natural History of Love
    (Ackerman), 301
"Nature as Being: Landscape in
    Silko's 'Lullaby'" (Bird),
    254–256
New criticism, 234
New historicism, 234
Newspapers. *See* Periodicals/
    newspapers
Note taking
    double-entry, 286–288
    for fieldwork, 285
    methods for, 286–290
    research log method of, 288–290

O

Observation, 25
"One More Lesson" (Cofer), 78–81
Online reviews, 109
Online source documentation, 310,
    325–328, 351–352
Op-ed essays, 183
Open-ended questions, 278,
    281–283

"Our Zombies, Ourselves" (Parker),
    235–237
Overused expressions, 408

P

Pamphlets, 328
Paragraphs
    in body, 396
    concluding, 397
    lead, 395–398, 401–402
    method to connect, 404
    well-crafted, 402–403
Paraphrases, 296–297
Parenthetical citations, 304, 308–310
Parker, James, "Our Zombies,
    Ourselves," 235–237
Passive voice, 407
Pathos, 177, 178
Peer review
    of argument, 208–209
    of critical essays, 251–252
    of personal essays, 96–97
    of proposals, 163–164
    questions for, 96–97, 130, 163,
        209, 252
    of reviews, 130–131
Periodicals/newspapers
    APA style for, 348–351
    library searches for, 269–271
    MLA style for, 320–325
Personal essays
    academic writing and, 71–72
    audience for, 89
    development of, 88–89, 94–96
    drafts for, 92–96
    evaluation of, 93–94, 100–101
    examples of, 75–81
    features of, 73
    methods for trying out, 89–90
    motives for writing, 70–71
    nature of, 69–70
    peer review of, 96–97
    prompts for writing, 85–88
    questions for, 73, 89–90
    revision of, 97–98
    sketch writing for, 91
    by student, 98–100
    topics for, 73, 84–85, 88–89
    writing process for, 82–83
Personal experiences, 69–70
Photo essays, 183
Plagiarism
    "accidental," 301–302

explanation of, 191–193
tips to avoid, 300–301
Plato, 182
Pleasure seeking, 48
Plot, 244
Podcasts, 327, 355
Point of view, 244–245
Policy questions, 31
Portfolios, 18
Post hoc, 181
PowerPoint
    argument in, 183
    proposals in, 147–149
"PowerPoint Is Evil" (Tufte),
    186–190
Primary research, 130
Prior knowledge
    argument and, 206
    influence of, 62
Problem-based learning, 140
Problems
    in argument, 207
    of consequence, 138
    of manageable scale, 139
    proposals to solve, 137–138
Project Information Literacy, 261
Prompts
    fastwriting, 86, 119, 153–154,
        196–197, 242–243
    listing, 85, 119, 153, 195–196, 242
    research, 88, 120, 154, 197,
        243–244
    visual, 86–87, 119–120, 154,
        197, 243
Proposals
    academic writing and, 140–141
    audience for, 155–156
    development of, 160–161
    drafts for, 159–160, 162–163
    evidence in, 163
    examples of, 144–149
    features of, 142–143
    generating material for,
        156–157
    motives for writing, 140
    narrowing focus for, 155–156
    nature of, 137–138, 169
    PowerPoint, 147–149
    problem exploration in,
        138–139
    research, 141
    revision of, 164–166
    sketch writing for, 157, 160
    by student, 166–168

student sketch for, 158–159
topics for, 153–155
writing process for, 152
Public argument, 183
Purpose
    of argument, 199
    for critical essays, 246
    of personal essays, 88–89, 94
    of proposals, 155
    for reading, 46
    of reviews, 121
    revision goals to fix problems
        related to, 376–381

Q

Questionnaires, 326
Questions
    for academic reading, 41
    for argument, 207
    for critical essays, 250
    direct, 281, 283
    to drive writing process, 30–31, 37
    focusing, 379–380
    for interviews, 278–279
    as inventive strategy, 25
    as leads, 9
    open-ended, 278, 281–283
    for personal essays, 73, 89–90
    research, 266–267
    for review writing, 130
    "so what," 29–30, 156, 376
    survey, 281–283
    types of, 30–31
Quotations
    explanation of, 297
    source citations for, 297–298,
        308, 314

R

Radio programs, MLA style for, 326
Ranking questions, 282
Reader-response criticism, 234
Readers. *See* Audience
Reading. *See also* Academic reading
    beliefs about, 43–45
    frames for, 46
    purposes of, 40–43, 45
    rhetorical choices and, 45–49
    scenarios for, 46–47
    shifting your perspective as
        strategy for, 48
    visual text, 54
    to write, 50–58

*Reading Images: The Grammar of
    Visual Design* (Kress & van
    Leeuwen), 54
Reality TV shows, 63–66
Reasons, in argument, 175
"Recipe for a Great Film: Unlikeable
    People, Poor Choices, and a
    Little Redemption" (Burns), 126
Recordings, MLA style for, 326
Recursive process, 25
Re-experience, for reviews, 128
References (APA style). *See also*
    APA documentation style
    authors in, 348
    books in, 351–354
    dates in, 348
    discussion lists in, 356–357
    DOI or URL in, 349
    example of, 367
    explanation of, 314, 347
    journals in, 349–351
    miscellaneous examples of,
        354–356
    order of information in, 347–349
    order of sources in, 347
    periodicals in, 348–349
    retrieval dates in, 349
Reflection
    as academic reading question,
        41, 43
    in personal essay writing, 90, 94
    as reading perspective, 48
Relationship questions
    explanation of, 30
    for revision, 381
Research
    for argument essays, 200–202,
        204–206
    for critical essays, 249
    field, 284–286
    as invention strategy, 25
    for personal essays, 98
    primary, 130
    for proposals, 160–161
Research logs
    example of, 289–290
    explanation of, 288
Research prompts
    for argument, 197
    for critical essays, 243–244
    for personal essays, 88
    for proposals, 154
    for reviews, 120
Research proposals, 141

Research techniques
    common habits and, 260–261
    electronic, 260–265
    fieldwork as, 284–286
    focused knowledge and, 267–271
    Google searches as, 261–263
    Internet-based, 273–276
    interviews as, 276–280
    library, 263–265, 268–273
    note taking as, 286–290
    overview of, 259–260
    source evaluation and, 273–276
    surveys as, 280–284
    working knowledge and, 265–267
Resistance, as reading perspective, 48
Reviews. See also Evaluation
    academic writing and, 106
    audience for, 121
    criteria for, 123–125
    development of, 121–123,
        127–129
    drafts of, 126–127, 129–130
    elements of, 103–104, 135
    evaluating material for, 120–121
    evidence in, 104, 123–124, 130
    examples of, 110–117
    features of, 108–109
    motives for writing, 104–106
    online, 109
    peer review of, 130–131
    revision of, 131–133
    sketch writing for, 125, 127
    by student, 133–134
    student sketch for, 125–126
    topics for, 119–120
    writing process and, 118
Revision. See also Drafts
    of argument, 209–212
    categories of, 375–376
    of critical essays, 252–254
    function of, 371–372, 374–375
    levels of, 372
    of personal essays, 97–98
    of proposals, 164–166
    resistance to, 373
    of reviews, 131–133
Revision goals. See also Drafts
    to fix clarity problems, 376,
        400–406
    to fix information problems,
        376, 389–392
    to fix meaning problems, 376,
        381–388
    to fix purpose problems, 376–381

    to fix structure problems, 376,
        393–400
    to fix style problems, 400, 406–408
Revision strategies. See also Drafts
    backing up assumptions as, 392
    believing and doubting games as,
        386–387
    cut-and-paste, 398–400
    cutting clutter as, 404–405
    to discover purpose, 378–379
    exploding a moment as, 389–390
    finding focusing question as,
        379–380
    finding fresh ways to say things
        as, 408
    finding instructive line as, 383–384
    finding relationship as, 381
    going beyond examples as,
        390–391
    looping toward thesis as, 384–385
    most important sentences in,
        401–402
    motive statement as, 377–378
    multiple leads as, 397–398
    qualifying your claim as, 388
    questions as knives as, 387–388
    reclaiming topic as, 385–386
    reorganizing around thesis and
        support as, 395–397
    role of actor and action in,
        406, 407
    smoothing and choppiness as,
        407–408
    untangling paragraphs as, 402–403
    use of beginnings, middles, and
        ends as, 395
    use of research as, 391–392
Rhetorical choices
    reading situations and, 45–49
    writing situations and, 13–16
Rhetorical knowledge, 14, 37
Rhetorical triangle, 210
Rogerian logic, 210
Rogers, Carl, 178–179

S

San Francisco Bicycle Coalition
    (SFBC), 150–151
Scaled response questions, 282
Schiesel, Seth, "Grand Theft Auto
    Takes on New York," 115–117
Search engines, 271, 273. See also
    Google

Seirup, Gordon, "College Dating,"
    329–338
Self-evaluation survey, 19–22
Self-perception, 46
Setting, 244
Silko, Leslie Marmon, "Lullaby,"
    225–232
Sketch writing
    for argument, 201–203
    for critical essays, 246–247
    for personal essays, 91–94
    for proposals, 157, 160
    for reviews, 125, 127
Slippery slope, 181
"Smoke of Empire" (Marlin),
    99–100
"Social Networking Social Good?"
    (Thompson), 212–216
Source citations
    APA style for, 339–368 (See also
        APA documentation style)
    common knowledge and, 303
    function of, 299
    MLA style for, 303–339 (See also
        MLA documentation style)
    plagiarism and, 300–302
Sources
    control of, 293–295
    paraphrases and, 296–297
    purpose of, 294
    quotations and, 297–298
    summaries and, 295–296
"So what?" question
    function of, 29–30, 376
    for proposals, 156
Speeches, 328
Spirit of inquiry, 4
Stewart, Amanda, "Earning a Sense
    of Place," 92
Stock phrases, 405
Straw man, 181
Structure, revision to fix problems
    related to, 376, 393–400
Student essays
    "Avoidable Accidents: How
        to Make Reality TV Safer"
        (Appleman), 166–168
    "Beyond Gaydar" (Harter),
        358–367
    "College Dating" (Seirup),
        329–338
    "How to Not Feel Good and
        Feel Good About It" (Burns),
        133–134

"Nature as Being: Landscape in Silko's 'Lullaby'" (Bird), 254–256

"Smoke of Empire" (Marlin), 99–100

"Social Networking Social Good?" (Thompson), 212–216

Student sketches
  "Earning a Sense of Place" (Stewart), 92
  "Loving and Hating Reality TV" (Appleman), 158–159
  "Recipe for a Great Film: Unlikeable People, Poor Choices, and a Little Redemption" (Burns), 126
  "Twitter a Profound Thought?" (Thompson), 202–203
  "What Is the Role of Nature in 'Lullaby'?" (Bird), 247–248

Style: Ten Lessons in Clarity and Grace (Williams), 405

Style revision, 400, 406–408

Subjects. *See* Topics

Summaries, 295–296

Surprise element, 11–13

Surveys
  function of, 280–281
  integrating information from, 284
  method to conduct, 283–284
  MLA style for, 326
  questions for, 281–283

T

Tables/charts/illustrations
  APA style for, 343
  MLA style for, 312

Television programs
  APA style for, 355–356
  MLA style for, 326
  reality, 63–66

Theme, 245

Thesis
  looping toward, 384–385
  reorganizing around, 395–397

Thinking
  creative, 26–29
  critical, 27–29
  metacognitive, 16n
  writing process and, 24, 26, 37

"This I Believe" (NPR), 83–84

Thompson, Florence, 106

Thompson, Rebecca
  "Social Networking Social Good?," 212–216
  "Twitter a Profound Thought?," 202–203

Title pages
  APA style for, 340
  MLA style for, 311–312

to be, 407

Topics
  for critical essays, 242–244
  focus on, 121–122
  for personal essays, 73, 84–85, 88–89
  for proposals, 153–155
  for reviews, 119–120

Toulmin, Stephen, 210

Toulminian logic, 210–211

Translations, 320

Tufte, Edward, "PowerPoint Is Evil," 186–190

"Twitter a Profound Thought?" (Thompson), 202–203

U

Unlearning, 7–8

Updating, as reading perspective, 48

URLs, 349, 350

V

Value, in artwork, 240

Value questions, 30

Verbs, 407

Video games, 113–117

Videotapes, 327, 355

Visual prompts
  for argument, 197
  for critical essays, 243
  for personal essays, 86–87
  for proposals, 154
  for reviews, 119–120

Visual texts
  double-entry journal writing with, 55–57
  guidelines for reading, 54

Voice, 407

W

Web sites. *See also* Internet
  APA style for, 346, 350
  design of, 162

evaluation of, 273–276

gathering information from, 122–123

MLA style for, 322

"What Is the Role of Nature in 'Lullaby'?" (Bird), 247–248

White, E. B., 96

"Why College Football Should Be Banned" (Bissinger), 144–146

"Why God Created Flies" (Conniff), 294–295, 298

Wikis, 327

Williams, Joseph, 405

Working bibliographies, 272

Working knowledge
  research techniques and, 265–266
  strategy to develop, 266–367

Works Cited (MLA style). *See also* MLA documentation style
  alphabetization in, 315
  books in, 316–320
  examples of, 315, 337–338
  explanation of, 304, 314–315
  indenting and spacing in, 315
  online and miscellaneous sources in, 325–328

Workshopping
  for argument, 208–209
  for critical essays, 251–252
  for personal essays, 96–97
  for proposals, 163–164
  for reviews, 130–131

World Wide Web. *See* Internet

Writing. *See also* Academic writing; Reading, to write
  beliefs about, 5, 8
  choppy, 407
  cluttered, 404–405
  control of information and, 293–294
  importance of producing bad, 58–60, 88
  to learn, 13
  motives for, 4
  rhetorical choices and, 13–16
  willingness to produce bad, 10–11
  as you read, 54–57

Writing process
  for argument, 195
  for critical essays, 241
  first reflection on your, 16–17

Writing process (*Continued*)
   goals for, 3, 37
   memoirs and, 44
   nature of, 23–24
   for personal essays, 82–83
   problem solving in, 22, 23
   for proposals, 152
   as recursive and flexible, 24
   reflections on, 17–18
   role of questions in, 30–31
   thinking and, 24, 26–30, 37

Writing situations
   explanation of, 13
   rhetorical choices and, 13–16

Y

Yahoo Groups, 205
Yellow Pages, 278
Young, Loye, "Is Humiliation an
   Ethically Appropriate Response
   to Plagiarism?," 191–193

*Young Ladies on the Banks
   of the Seine* (Courbet),
   238–239
YouTube, 183

Z

Zazulak, Laura, "Every Morning
   for Five Years," 75–76
Zinsser, William, 404